The
Psychology
of Human
Learning

The Psychology of Human Learning

MICHAEL J. A. HOWE
University of Exeter

HARPER & ROW, PUBLISHERS

NEW YORK

Cambridge
Hagerstown
Philadelphia
San Francisco

1817

London
Mexico City
Sao Paolo
Sydney

Sponsoring Editor: George A. Middendorf
Project Editor: Pamela Landau
Senior Production Manager: Kewal K. Sharma
Compositor: Bi-Comp, Inc.
Printer and Binder: The Maple Press Company
Art Studio: Vantage Art, Inc.

The Psychology of Human Learning

Library of Congress Cataloging in Publication Data

Howe, Michael J. A.   1940-
   The psychology of human learning.

   Bibliography: p.
   Includes indexes.
   1. Learning, Psychology of. 2. Child development.
3. Child psychology. 4. Language acquisition.
I. Title.
LB1051.H7929   370.15′2   79-21557
ISBN 0-06-042938-0

TO SYLVIA, NICHOLAS, AND LUCY

Contents

Preface

My aim in this book is to tell undergraduate readers what is known about the forms and functions of learning in human life. I have taken a fairly broad approach and discuss some aspects of perceptual learning, learned movements, and the acquisition of social habits and skills, in addition to the language-based forms of learning that are unique to humans. Experimental investigations of learning are often conducted, by necessity, in the artificial circumstances of the laboratory, but I have aimed to write about the contributions of research to our understanding of the functions of learning in people's lives, rather than simply reviewing the results of experiments. Learning has a number of functions for the individual, and they cannot be ignored if experimental research is to contribute to an understanding of the nature of human beings.

I have not attempted to be comprehensive, and I have paid little attention to methodological issues in research into human learning, except when these directly influence interpretation of the findings. Much research into human learning is theoretical in the broad sense that it attempts to make learning phenomena explicable, but most of the explanatory views that are discussed in these pages are views that also try to account for aspects of human development, memory, adaptation, and information-processing, rather than simply being theories about learning processes. The absence of the latter kind of theory among the influences on recent research reflects the necessity to examine learning in the broad contexts of human life.

The book is roughly divided into four parts. The first four chapters provide a background and a base for the rest of the book by introducing some of the concepts, the methods, and the terminology of experimental research into learning, indicating how psychologists have arrived at their current state of knowledge, and describing some of the broad functions and characteristics of human learning. Chapters 5, 6, and 7 are mainly about the ways in which people *learn to do* various things. Aspects of social learning are described, and a brief discussion considers the acquisition of perceptual and motor abilities. Chapters 8 to 11 concern the ways in which we *learn about* various matters, including the ways we acquire and remember knowledge and intellectual skills. In the final chapters, I examine some of the possible reasons for the fact that people differ so much in what they learn and consider how individuals can be helped to learn effectively.

I would like to thank my colleagues at the Exeter University Department of Psychology for many instances of generous help. I am especially grateful to Stephen Lea, Leslie Reid, and Gordon Stanley, who read and commented upon chapters of the manuscript, and to the publishers' reviewers. I am also grateful to the staff at Harper & Row for their help and encouragement. My thanks also to Angela Boobyer, Yvonne Pretty, Geraldine Setter, Ann Smith, and Sheila Westcott, who were responsible for the typing.

MICHAEL J. A. HOWE

The Psychology of Human Learning

CHAPTER

Learning in the Human Species

OVERVIEW

Chapter 1 describes some of the broad functions of learning in human life, and considers ways in which learning is especially significant for our own species. There are important differences in the ways in which learning contributes to the capabilities of humans and other animals. The chapter discusses the learned capacities of humans for manipulating objects and making tools, through which they gain control over important aspects of their world. We consider some of the many ways in which learning helps to insure the survival and well-being of humanity.

THE IMPORTANCE OF LEARNING

Fifty years ago, Edward L. Thorndike, a pioneer in the use of experimental methods to investigate learning, produced a short book called *Human Learning.* On the first page he noted that in learning resides humanity's power to change, possibly the most impressive of all human gifts.

Change, and the ability to change, are at the heart of all the varied meanings and definitions that have been applied to the term "learning." An organism that can change its characteristics and alter its activities has a huge advantage over forms of matter that cannot, the latter being tightly bound to the physical environment surrounding them. The power to change frees an organism from being fixed in place and function. In a simple organism the scope of such freedom may simply be to permit the individual to move around physically, with whatever advantages that provides.

The sharpest contrast to the inanimate, unchanging, inorganic world is found in human beings. They have a degree of liberty that extends well beyond the possibility of physical movement, a capacity shared by crude mechanical systems. Human freedom of action stretches to include a mental life that can sustain itself with a considerable degree of autonomy. Through an ability to learn, human beings have inherited a strong measure of independence to choose, to explore and to make important decisions about their own life. Such independence goes far beyond anything conceivable in the other species that inhabit the earth.

The power to change is evident in all manifestations of learning. As the Greek thinker Heraclitus pointed out 2500 years ago, constant change, or "continuous flux," is a basic property of the world. Life, growth, entropy, death, and decay combine to preserve a continuous world order. Many, but not all, of humanity's forms of change depend on learning. Those modifications to which learning contributes are mainly ones that help individuals adapt to the circumstances of their life and to acquire skills and habitual patterns of action that aid in dealing with the environment. The information they acquire about the natural world makes it possible for humans to gain the materials necessary to sustain life and to avoid sources of danger. In brief, learning enables human beings to make adaptive modifications that allow the species to survive and prosper.

Research into human learning normally involves measurement of particular instances of learning under carefully controlled conditions. Experimental research will be emphasized throughout this book, but the present chapter concentrates on some broad issues concerning the functions of learning in human life. A concern with detailed evidence is necessary when describing research into learning. However, it is also important to be aware of the wider framework of human life in which learning takes place. A broadly based interest in the nature of acquired abilities and in the results of experience provides the justification for undertaking experimental research into human learning.

We humans are utterly dependent upon what we can learn. Edward Thorndike, among others, drew attention to the fact that learned changes in human minds have produced human civilization. Homes and machines, language and art, customs and laws, science, religion, and all the achievements of human culture depend upon the ability to learn. The continuing use and maintenance of all these also require the modifiability that learning makes possible. To illustrate the dependence of civilized people upon what they learn, Thorndike tried to imagine the outcome of a state of affairs in which their ability to learn was reduced by half. He predicted that in such an event most of human civilization would be unusable by the next generation, and that civilization would soon vanish altogether.

The ubiquity of human learning and our taking it for granted can restrict awareness of how much we rely upon learning. The relatively smooth transmission of culture from one generation to the next creates an illusion that the knowledge, skills, social and motor habits that are shared by most individuals in a modern society are easily acquired by each of us through some process of absorption or simple unfolding. Yet this is indeed an illusion. Even basic abilities that are gained so early in life that we cannot remember having learned them—walking, running, picking up an object, for instance—are only mastered after considerable learning has taken place. Acquiring a human language necessitates many instances of learning every day over a period of years, notwithstanding the possibility that humans possess an innate language acquisition device. Alberta Siegel illustrated civilization's dependence upon learning in her statement that "every generation is only twenty years removed from barbarism." She remarked that we spend around twenty years on the task of civilizing our offspring. Only as a result of such lengthy training do "those savages," as she calls them, "gradually acquire their society's language, culture, and its systems of values, morality and customs" (Siegel, 1971, p. 613).

The research methods developed by natural scientists have been applied to the investigation of learning in order to further our understanding of the changes that learning induces. The potential value of increased knowledge about the manner in which we learn has long been apparent to professionals involved in education and training. It is also apparent to those who have become aware of the need to help themselves or their family acquire abilities that are necessary for social living, or for furthering a career or for any of the numerous activities, interests, and accomplishments that enable people to have a full and satisfying existence.

Modern living forces us to continue learning throughout our lives. Attention has been paid to the special pressures on learning ability that are imposed by the rapid changes in the contemporary world, but the experience of change in society is not exclusive to recent generations. The early Victorians, for instance, were as obsessed with the problems of cultural change as we are today. Their concern was justified, particularly since they had not been given the opportunity to come to accept fast-changing alterations in the structure of life as being the norm rather than the exception. The increasing rapidity of cultural change experienced by modern generations accentuates the problems of individual adaptation. People today need to have considerable sophistication to cope with the many complexities of everyday life. As developed countries approach yesterday's goal of universal literacy, more and more learned capacities are necessary. Well into adulthood, people today have to face the possibility of changing jobs and acquiring the new skills that are needed to make good use of a pattern of life in which time for leisure is substantially increased. Increasingly complex communications also necessitate the individual being increasingly well-informed in order to make effective choices as a consumer. Complex societies produce highly complicated legislation, and there is frequent transmission of information between the individual and those centralized agencies responsible for taxation, health, social services, insurance, and the registration of property and facilities. To deal with all of these a person today must possess an armory of knowledge and skills, and be prepared to undertake considerably more new learning than was necessary in the past. Although human learning abilities are highly developed, it is not certain that our capacity to learn will always continue to meet the demands that may be placed upon it.

People these days are less fatalistic than previous generations, and where improvements are seen to be necessary, attempts to bring them about are likely to proceed with minimal hesitation. In the 1960s there was a marked increase in both the number and the variety of large-scale efforts to meet practical problems involving learning. Educational programs aimed at promoting learning have proliferated, with varying degrees of success. Their goals have included the provision of educational enrichment to help individuals who have been handicapped by an impoverished early environment, and finding ways to help children who are classified as being mentally retarded. Professionals who are engaged in these aspects of education are eager to make use of whatever hard knowledge can be gained from scientific inquiry into the nature of learning. Thus practical necessities, in addition to the less immediate goal of scientific understanding, have led to a sustained demand for research into human learning.

HUMAN AND ANIMAL LEARNING

As we begin to examine some of the properties of learning in man, it is useful to make some comparisons between human learning and the kinds of learning that are encountered in other species. There are differences between humans and all other living species, both in the forms learning takes and in the functions it performs for the individual; yet there are strong arguments against our ignoring research into animal learning. One reason for maintaining an interest in animal learning is that, although large interspecies differences can be observed, there is no lack of similarities and continuities. Humans share with all other creatures the need to adapt to the physical environment. Knowing how different animals adapt themselves to their circumstances and how learning contribute to adaptation, gives us a necessary perspective from which we can observe how human activities contribute to the development and survival of humans as biological organisms.

A second reason for our paying some attention to animal learning lies in the historical background and development of scientific research into learning. With some exceptions, the most notable being the German psychologist Hermann Ebbinghaus, those scientists who first began to undertake such research used sub-primate animals as their experimental subjects. They did so for practical reasons. The ease and convenience of running experiments on lower animals, such as the white Norwegian rat, was one important consideration. The apparent simplicity of learning processes in lower mammals offered another advantage to pioneering experimental psychologists.

The first investigators were considerably more optimistic than are contemporary researchers concerning the likelihood of animal research making a direct contribution to the understanding of human learning. Nowadays we are fully aware of the magnitude of species differences, and of the possible errors that may occur when we apply to human learning extrapolations made from whatever has been discovered in research on other animals. Many contemporary psychologists who study animal learning believe that the applicability of their research to the understanding of human learning is a matter for the long run, not for the immediate future. But most of the early researchers, including Thorndike, Watson, and Pavlov, firmly believed that research on learning in animals would soon make an immediate practical contribution to our knowledge about learning in human beings.

Animal research has undoubtedly made some important contributions to the psychology of human learning, and a few psychologists continue to believe that many findings of research into animal learning are directly applicable to humans. Quite apart from the issue of applicability, the fact that early investigators worked with subhuman species, exerted and continues to exert crucial influences on research. The methods and techniques devised by early researchers have strongly influenced the subsequent course of experimental research into human learning. The kinds of problems they studied, the forms of learning observed, the theories advanced, and the descriptive language used, all continue to influence contemporary investigations. Even today, studies of human learning betray traces of an earlier animal research tradition.

LIMITATIONS OF UNLEARNED BEHAVIOR

In general, learning plays a larger role in the survival of higher species than of simple organisms, and the higher species display more ability to make complex and highly organized changes as a result of learning. Virtually all complex human abilities depend upon learning, but we should not assume that this dependence is necessarily paralleled in other species. Many insects that are relatively simple in structure display some highly complicated and coordinated activities, which are largely controlled by inborn, or wired-in, mechanisms that are genetically transmitted. The functioning of such organisms is much less dependent upon learning than are activities of comparable complexity in humans or other higher mammalian species.

Insects provide numerous examples of such wired-in patterns of behavior. For instance, Thorpe (1974) describes a sequence of actions by the female hunting wasp. At one stage the insect makes a burrow in sandy soil, and afterwards flies off to find and sting its prey. The prey is paralysed by the sting, but it is not killed. The wasp next returns with its prey to the burrow, not flying on this occasion, since the weight of the prey necessitates it being dragged along the ground. The wasp appears to have little difficulty in finding the nest again, despite the fact that the outward journey was by air and despite the closure of the burrow at the time the wasp left it. What happens later depends on the particular variety of wasp. One kind of wasp lays her eggs beside her prey, a paralyzed cricket, seals the burrow and flies away, never returning to it. The cricket, preserved intact, provides food for the young wasp grubs when they hatch some months later.

We are justifiably impressed by such descriptions of insects able to carry through lengthy behavioral sequences of highly organized activities, and the insect world provides numerous examples of sequentially patterned routines. In the past, observations of complicated patterns of behavior led naturalists to believe that insect species must possess considerable intelligence. The spectre of a world dominated by giant insects has often provided a theme for science fiction stories and comic strips. As it happens, complex behavior that can be observed in insects and other lower species is controlled to some extent by mechanisms that are built into the organism and do not have to be acquired through learning. This behavior, then, is subject to a basic limitation from which learned activities are free. Behavior controlled by built-in mechanisms, although often complex, highly organized, and impressive in many respects, is much less flexible than learned behavior. It is more stereotyped in form and it cannot easily be modified to meet changing circumstances. In fact, the difference is one of degree and not an absolute one, since sequences of animal activities that rely primarily upon unlearned mechanisms characteristically contain some learned elements, and, conversely, reflexes and processes that are not learned often play a role in the acquisition of primarily learned abilities. For instance, in the hunting wasp mentioned above, a good deal of learning must occur for the wasp to acquire the knowledge about the local landscape necessary for locating the burrow. Moreover, species that depend largely upon mechanisms that are not learned do have some other capacities to facilitate adaptation. Learning is not the only adaptive device possessed by living species.

A simple experiment illustrates the relatively rigid, stereotyped character of unlearned behavior of one variety of wasp. During the normal sequence of events, the paralyzed prey is dragged to the side of the burrow and left there for a moment while the wasp enters. It appears to ascertain that all is in order before taking in the prey. The experimental procedure of one naturalist was to move the paralyzed creature a few inches away from the burrow after the wasp had entered it. On emerging, the wasp's response was to drag its prey back to the side of the burrow and then reenter, alone. If the prey was moved away once again the wasp would repeat this sub-sequence of activities. In fact, it repeated the activity each time the interruption of the normal sequence occurred. Apparently, the wasp is unable to make the necessary adaptive changes when it meets new circumstances or altered situations. The wasp cannot vary its pattern of responses in the manner that would usually be possible if the responses were acquired through learning.

An individual animal that possesses considerable ability to learn has a better chance of surviving until adulthood than one that does not. This is particularly so if it has to exist in a widely and unpredictably varying environment. However, in a species which depends upon learning and maturation during a lengthy period of development, individuals may be protected from predators and other threats. In the case of some species that produce offspring in very large numbers, the failure of a large proportion of individuals to reach maturity does not threaten survival of the species or the gene pool through which life is transmitted. For these species, there are advantages to be gained from using largely inborn mechanisms to control and organize behavior, especially if the individual organisms are small in size. In very small organisms, sheer size limits the complexity of the nervous system and may preclude learning as a primary means of controlling behavior. The amount of brain capacity that is required to control activities of a given degree of organization by means of built-in mechanisms may be considerably less than the amount that is necessary for the acquisition and maintenance of learned behaviors of equivalent complexity.

Among humans, since the number of offspring that any woman can produce is sharply limited, survival of the species depends upon a large proportion of individuals surviving until maturity. For this reason, among others, an otherwise humanlike species whose activities were controlled by inborn mechanisms would not survive for long. Very few individuals would reach maturity if they lacked the ability to alter and vary their actions to meet the frequently changing environmental demands that higher species experience.

LEARNING IN HUMANS AND OTHER SPECIES: SOME DIFFERENCES

Human learning is different in certain respects from learning in other animals, even those species in which learned capacities are most highly developed. Some differences are readily noticed. The sheer complexity of human mental processing is unparalleled, and it contributes to our reasoning and thinking abilities. Man has a unique ability to communicate symbolically, using languages that are fundamentally different from any means of communication possessed by other species, although it has recently been demonstrated that chimpanzees are capable of learning the rudiments of a human language.

A less obvious difference, but one which is nevertheless crucial, can be observed by comparing learned movements. Differences in motor skills can make as large a contribution to setting humans apart from other species, as do differences in specifically intellectual skills. Konrad Lorenz has remarked that in lower animals the ability to acquire new sequences of movements is extremely limited. In the highest mammals, new patterns of movements can be learned, but the range and flexibility of the actions are very restricted in comparison to the learned motor abilities found in humans. Many of the feats at which we marvel when we watch circus animals, balancing objects, controlling balls, would not appear at all impressive if they were performed by members of our own species. Our admiration of the circus performances of bears and seals is not unrelated to the fact that the animals are less well equipped than humans are to learn abilities involving sequences of precise and coordinated movements.

Learning in lower animals more often affects receptive rather than motor capabilities. It may contribute to the ability to detect appropriate environmental cues, and discover the circumstances in which particular actions are appropriate. Learning may enable an animal to locate objects more successfully, to aim at prey more accurately, and to time movements more precisely, but the actual form of the activities, once initiated, may depend more upon built-in mechanisms than upon learning. Abilities for acquiring entirely new organized movements through learning are most highly developed in the higher mammals, especially the primates.

In contrast with learned movements, receptive learning, based on what is perceived, leads to some quite remarkable feats of behavior in lower animals. In numerous instances learning contributes to achievements in animals that humans cannot match. Some instances of perceptual learning are particularly impressive. To return for a moment to the example of the hunting wasp, we recall that after making its burrow the wasp *flies* away to find and sting its prey, and having done so it *drags* the paralyzed creature back *along the ground,* returning to the burrow with no apparent difficulty. How is this achieved? Objects close to the burrow may be used as cues to help the wasp find it again, but to acquire this knowledge about its surroundings the wasp must do some very rapid learning about the characteristics of the vicinity. The wasp's speedily gained knowledge of the landscape in the region of the burrow is sufficiently detailed and stable for its success to be unaffected by the removal of some of the objects that are close to the burrow entrance.

Abilities for learning about details of their physical environments are highly developed in many species of insects, birds and fishes. The acts of navigation performed by certain birds and fishes are particularly striking. Such species probably have sensory-orienting equipment (that humans do not possess) for detecting magnetic forces or for estimating the sun's direction, but most forms of animal navigation also depend to a marked extent on the ability to acquire perceptual knowledge about the physical characteristics of a region. Particularly remarkable are the homing flights by shearwaters of over three thousand miles after being released from captivity. Equally impressive is a species of fish (described by Thorpe, 1974), which inhabits tropical tidal pools. At low tide the fish can reach its destination by jumping from one pool to another along a lengthy series of pools. While the fish is swimming, it cannot see the next pool in the chain. In order to navigate successfully, it must remember detailed information about the complex pattern taken by the series of pools. Otherwise the fish would be fatally stranded on dry land as a result of an inappropriately directed leap. Perceptual learning may take place at high tide, when the fish swim over the rocks. It is possible that they learn the locations of the depressions and the essential features and layout of the sequence of pools in the area of the home base.

Observations of bees provide further illustrations of some striking capabilities of lower species for acquiring, through organized perceptual learning, accurate information about the landscape of the home environment. Thorpe (1974) states that if a beehive is moved to a new site, the bees that are absent from the hive when it is being moved return to the original location and are unlikely to find the newly moved hive at all. Yet, if the hive is moved at a time when all the bees are inside, it is observed that when the bees leave the hive for the purpose of undertaking their normal foraging activities, they hesitate and spend some time hovering near the hive, flying around it, before they depart. The bees appear to be surveying the new sights and learning the landmarks by which they will be able to find the hive again on their return.

These instances of animal learning suggest that while abilities to learn in nonhuman species may be very different in form and function from learning in man, animal learning is not in a straightforward sense always simpler than human learning. There are large differences in the functions learning performs for different species, in the way it contributes to an animal's existence, and in the nature of the activities that are modified by experience. The view that the primary difference between humans and other animals is that man learns more extensively and more efficiently is an oversimplification. Humans are demonstrably superior to other species at those kinds of learning that involve making major modifications to repertoires of movements, but many animal species are able to undertake feats of perceptual learning that, from a human point of view, are very impressive indeed.

When techniques or data from animal learning research are employed with the expectancy that they will throw some light upon human learning processes, it is essential to keep in mind the magnitude and variety of interspecies differences. As we noted, early developments in empirical research on learning in animals have influenced the kinds of problems studied in research into human learning and the investigative methods that have been employed.

Investigations that have been subject to this influence may not prove to be accurately directed at solving those problems of human learning that future generations may perceive to be the key ones. For instance, research into *classical conditioning* has increased our understanding of some acquired involuntary actions, such as ones that are involved in digestion and in sphincter control. Classical conditioning research has also helped us to understand emotional responses and the ways in which fears and phobias are acquired. Yet the research findings have not turned out to be very widely applicable to the understanding of voluntary behavior in humans. Ivan Pavlov, who initiated research into conditioning, believed that it would have great applicability to learning in humans. It now appears, however, that the kinds of changes studied in experiments on classical conditioning play a fairly restricted role in human learning.

Conversely, direct investigations of human learning, tend to emphasize the acquisition of skills that are largely unique to the human species. Psychologists who have studied human learning have been especially interested in language and verbal behavior, partly because the linguistic and skills of human beings enable them to do things of which other species are incapable. Psychologists have paid little attention to human distinctiveness in other forms of learned behavior, and have tended to neglect important species differences in learning. The motor dexterity that underlies the manipulative skills humans need for making tools and building the physical human environment, and the ability possessed by some animals to retain perceptual information about the physical environment, provide two instances of specialized learned activities underlying the distinct patterns of abilities achieved by different species.

THE EMERGENCE OF THE HUMAN LEARNER

How did it come about that humans became "special" and apart from other species in the advanced· development of abilities in which learning plays a major role? Attempts to answer this question are inevitably speculative, if only because the species that provided the links between man and other animals are now extinct. The evidence of available fossil remains provides no real substitute, unless we add a great deal of conjecture. The sheer number of factors that must have contributed to the evolution of modern man precludes any simple cause-and-effect analysis. At best, we can isolate some of the important influences on the nature of humans as a species that is specialized in, expert at, and highly dependent upon the ability to learn. We shall consider some pertinent lines of thought, while bearing in mind that these are speculative and that we may get a distorted impression if one part of a chain containing many links is considered apart from the numerous other interlinked factors. There is fairly strong support for some speculations. For instance, the evolution of the hand, which is essential for manipulating and throwing objects, and for fashioning implements and building, was caused in part by the necessity for the ancestors of humans to move between the branches of trees. The necessary skills are regularly employed by modern apes inhabiting environments similar to those in which the early predecessors of humans probably lived.

An account advanced by J. S. Bruner (1965) emphasizes bipedalism and tool-using in the evolution of humans as members of a species that modify themselves and their world by learning and by reasoning intelligently. Bruner has suggested that the evolution of the large brain in humans occurred gradually, as a sequel to his extensive use of primitive implements or tools. In support of this view, there is firm evidence that bipedal locomotion evolved before large human brains, and it is probable that the evolution of the large human brain was also preceded by tool-using and hunting activities (Washburn, 1978).

Those individuals who were successful at using tools would have had a better chance of surviving to maturity and producing offspring than individuals who depended largely upon brute strength. Natural selection, based on more frequent survival and breeding among the more capable users of tools and artifacts, may have led to species changes in the direction of larger brains and smaller jaws. Bruner argues that it is only when objects regularly have to function as tools that a large brain is of real value. As the human species evolved, each succeeding generation did not have to reinvent the tools that had been developed, but each individual needed to acquire the skills necessary for using tools effectively.

Bruner draws attention to two further possible developments in human evolution. First, in a species becoming increasingly prone to stand on its rear limbs, as is necessary if the hands are to be free for manipulating weapons and implements, natural selection might well favor those individuals with heavy and strong pelvic structures. The latter are necessary to meet the physical strains resulting from regular and sustained bipedal standing and movement. One way to strengthen the pelvic structures is to reduce the size of the birth canal. Such an evolutionary development produces an obstetrical paradox, since an increasingly large brain had to emerge through an increasingly small birth canal. The resolution of this paradox, according to Bruner, was the human newborn in its present form. Extreme immaturity and relatively small size at birth, coupled with the need for a long period of postnatal development that involves extensive physiological maturation and extended nurturance by the mother, combine to overcome the difficulties such a paradox presents. Although this account of evolutionary processes that affect human learning is a speculative one, it gives us a glimpse of a way in which, over many generations, a number of events might combine to lead to the evolution of humans as a species in which intelligence and ability to learn are developed to a very high level.

USING TOOLS AND IMPLEMENTS

Using natural objects as implements and making tools have undoubtedly been important for the emergence of humanity. It is difficult to decide whether tool-using is a cause or a result of the evolution of *homo sapiens* as a special variety of primate. The view that using tools and implements has played a causative role receives support from archaeological evidence, since objects used as tools have been found alongside skeletal evidence of man's predecessors.

Did we become human because of using tools, or did we use tools because we were becoming human? This question presents some of the difficulties encountered with the old problem of deciding whether chicken or egg came first, but some helpful evidence is available. To use tools regularly and systematically it is necessary to have manipulative abilities in advance of those possessed by sub-primate mammals. Humans do have the ability to exert close and precise physical control over natural objects. Such control depends upon coordinated movements of fingers and especially the thumb, and the proportion of the human brain alloted to such activities is far from negligible. There is evidence that the extinct primate species *ramapithecus*, a possible forerunner of man which lived around 30 million years ago, regularly killed small animals (to provide food) with blunt stone implements. It would appear that ramapithecines were extensive tool-users. But it is tool-making rather than tool-using that really sets modern man apart from other existing species. Many animals make regular or sporadic use of sticks or stones as implements, and modern primates undoubtedly possess simple tool-using abilities.

Although it is not easy to specify a particular line of demarcation, the transition from using objects as implements to systematically manufacturing tools is an important one. As humans evolved, increasingly large modifications were made to available natural objects. For example, a flint may be used in its existing state, or a slight chip may be made in it to increase its effectiveness, or more extensive reshaping may be undertaken. All three of these stages can be found in the vicinity of remains of the primate *australopithecus*, which existed around three million years ago and may have been a direct ancestor of man. One finds traces of implements that have been deliberately fashioned from pebbles, so it appears very probable that *australopithecus* had tool-making abilities that are not observed in any existing primate group other than humans. No modern primates consistently and regularly fashion tools by the systematic modification of natural objects.

Their tool-making habits gave the *australopithecus* an essentially human quality. Yet in size and appearance, indicated by features such as the shape of the head and brain size (somewhat smaller than that of a present-day gorilla), *australopithecus* was more similar to a modern chimpanzee than to humans as we know them today. So, to return to the question of whether human beings or tool-making came first, it seems to be at least equally accurate to say that we became human as a result of making and using tools as it is to state the reverse.

It is difficult to discover how and why the abilities of humans to manipulate objects and make implements evolved, but the human hand is an important part of the equation. The fact that primates can grasp objects, an ability that partly resulted from life in trees, gives them an "unspecific" capacity to control their movements that facilitates exploration and the manipulation of objects in the vicinity. The behavior of an animal that is engaged in exploratory activities or certain other behaviors, such as the "play" observed in dolphins, is not under the strict control of either built-in mechanisms or environmental forces. The animal displays some degree of independence and freedom from rigid biological constraints. We might also ask why some animals explore and demonstrate curiosity. One possible reason is that opportunities to practice activities and gain experience in conditions of security may help the individual to survive. Also, it is possible that an animal which pays attention to novel or unusual aspects of its environment may thereby gain for itself a measure of protection from unexpected events. Exploratory activities, learning to manipulate objects, and manifesting curiosity may all have survival value for the individual animal.

Exploratory behaviors are not unknown in sub-primate species. For instance, when ravens are not hungry, they sometimes use actions normally used in feeding for exploring new objects. Cats and other domestic animals also engage in exploratory acts. Both the habit of exploration and the possession of hands appear to be crucial for the superiority of humans to other mammals. Hands serve as finely shaped instruments for precisely manipulating and controlling physical objects. This permits detailed examination of objects, resulting in acquisition of knowledge about the objects' characteristics and their possible uses.

RETAINING INFORMATION IN MEMORY

Introducing the notion of knowledge serves to remind us of another characteristic of humans that is important for human learning, the ability to remember large amounts of information. The world we humans experience is only partly situated in the external environment. Many of the ideas, thoughts, and memories that guide our actions are produced by mental activities that are largely independent of external control. Even when people do respond to environmental events, the contents of their minds help interpret the events and play a part in determining the form of responses. We might ask how it comes about that people acquire their own "internal world," the store of retrievable knowledge and skills that forms their inner life. A serious attempt to answer this question must consider linguistic abilities and the symbolic functions that human languages employ. However, neglecting linguistic factors for the moment, we can cast some light on the matter by drawing attention not to the capacities of humans but to one of their limitations.

It is important to realize that humans have a very limited capacity to deal with entirely new information from the outside world. We simply cannot process large quantities of new information in a short time. There has been much controversy among psychologists over the tenability of a "single-channel" account of attention, according to which we can only attend to one thing at a time (Reason, 1977). Even if the single-channel account is incorrect, it is certain that the ability of humans to receive simultaneous information from more than one input is highly restricted.

People do cope, despite the constant barrage of data arriving via the sensory receptors. They are able to manage because humans have acquired ways of using their mental capacities to help them deal with incoming information from the environment (Kay, 1977). We are able to use what we already know in order to anticipate new events. Through discerning regularities in perceived events, we can improve the accuracy of predictions. Using the knowledge we possess helps us to estimate which of the varied kinds of incoming data are likely to be significant. Because humans possess a store of quickly retrievable knowledge within their own brain, they are able to act not merely as passive *receivers* of information from the outside world, but as active *users* of that information. Rather than regarding the relationship of humans to their environment as one whereby they *respond* to *stimuli*, it is more accurate to see them as *making use of the information* that the world makes available. They select from the array of data that reach their sensory organs only those items that they can effectively use. As a result, they are able to deal with a volume of input data far exceeding their capacity to receive or to process. It is conceivable that if the forerunners of humans had possessed larger attentional capacities, and if they had been able to receive simultaneously a variety of signals from a range of sources, there might have been less impetus in human evolution toward the development of the processing capacities of the modern human brain.

ANALYTIC PROCEDURES IN THE STUDY OF LEARNING

Three general characteristics of human learning deserve notice. First, learning can be regarded as a biological device that functions to protect the human individual and to extend his capacities. Second, learning is neither independent of nor entirely separate from a number of other human abilities. It is misleading to consider instances of learning as if they operated entirely in isolation. Third, learning is cumulative. What an individual learns at any time is influenced by his previous learning, developmental and learning processes being closely intertwined.

It was previously noted that learned modifications are not random changes. Most instances of learning take the form of adaptive changes, by means of which individuals improve their effectiveness at meeting the various requirements for human existence. For human and near-human species, it is especially important to be able to adjust to changes in the environment. For individuals, acquiring abilities that improve their chances of being able to adapt to new features of their surroundings has undoubted survival value. Hence, the human propensities to explore, to manipulate, and to manifest interest or curiosity in what is novel have considerable utility.

A human being is a relatively small animal, weak, slow of movement, and with rather poor sensitivity in some receptors including smell and hearing. Humans depend upon their especially effective adaptive powers in order to survive in competition with stronger and faster animals. Humans survive because they learn quickly and easily. By using objects as implements, humans increase their physical power. Increased control over the physical environment makes it easier to meet essential human needs.

Learning does not take place in complete isolation from other activities; it influences and is affected by a number of important functions. We might visualize a person as comprising a large number of systems and subsystems working in close cooperation with each other. Each part reviews inputs of data that are necessary for it to function. When investigators study the various human functions—for instance, learning, memory, perception and attention—they are following a procedure of analytical science. As a rule, it makes sense to begin the scientific investigation of something that is large and complicated by examining component parts that are easier to understand than the complete system. The knowledge thus obtained can be used as one attempts the more difficult task of trying to understand the entire system in all its complexity.

On the whole, analytical procedures have worked well in the physical sciences. But an analytical approach is effective only under certain conditions, one being that the separate parts that are identified and examined on their own do actually correspond to parts that have a clear and relatively distinct function in the total system being studied. This is a reason why early psychological investigation of mental concepts such as the "will" foundered. The difficulty lies in the fact that the functions implied by the term "will" do not correspond to a distinct mental subsystem. In the case of concepts such as "learning" and "perception," an analytical approach is more likely to be profitable. One can specify the functions denoted by such terms with reasonable certainty that the underlying brain activities are, in some respects, distinct and separable.

Analytical approaches are appropriate when the operation of each part of a system is relatively independent of the state of the other parts. A mechanical clock constitutes such a system. In a clock, if the mainspring breaks, all that is necessary for repairing the system is to replace the spring. The breakage will not have seriously affected the other components. Something approaching this degree of independence between the elements contributing to complex systems is encountered in many of the phenomena explored in Newtonian physics. However, in the study of biological systems, and particularly in investigations of humans, it is unusual to encounter such a degree of independence between the various processes that are involved. Typically, the operation of each of the various parts that contribute to a biological system is heavily influenced by the operation of the other parts. Under such circumstances the power of straightforward scientific procedures is inevitably restricted. For practical reasons, it is often essential to undertake separate examination of the smaller units that make up larger mechanisms and systems, but it is far from certain that knowing about such units will guarantee a complete understanding of their combined operation.

The acquisition of human skills depends upon each of a number of functions that are additional to learning in the narrow sense of forming new bonds. Perception is one of the functions that influences what a person learns. Learning based upon vision is obviously not possible for a blind man. In contrast, an organism that is equipped with special sensory capacities can make use of them to acquire knowledge and to behave adaptively. Bees, for example, possess sensory receptors that are sensitive to changes in ultraviolet rays. For bees, such waves provide a useful source of information. Most animals, including humans, are unable to receive and act upon signals of this form since they do not possess the necessary sensory mechanisms.

Another factor is attention, which determines how many of the signals and events to which a person is sensitive are actually processed. As we have mentioned, man's attention span is strictly limited. Therefore, considerable selectivity in attention is necessary, and it matters a good deal which potential signals happen to be selected by the individual learner. Yet another function that affects human learning is memory. Much of the information we act upon is internal, stored, information. It follows that the effective environment for the individual is partly determined by what the person can remember.

CUMULATIVE ASPECTS OF HUMAN LEARNING AND DEVELOPMENT

The fact that learning is influenced by the contents of memory demonstrates the importance for future learning of abilities that have already been learned. The potential to learn is undoubtedly limited by a number of relatively fixed human characteristics, such as the sensory equipment necessary for receiving inputs and the physical form that limitations to a person's capacities for action. However, characteristics that individuals have acquired themselves, largely through learning, also exert an influence. As has been remarked, the kind of person each of us is, the individual we have become, is partly determined by what we have learned. Since people are changed by what they learn, their new learning on an occasion in the future may be noticeably different from their learning on an occasion in the past that ostensibly provided a similar experience. To give a concrete example, if I read a chapter from a textbook of advanced physics today, what I would learn from it, if anything, would be very different from what I might learn if I were first to take a course in basic physics. The difference in what I learn on the two hypothetical occasions can be explained only by reference to acquired differences in myself, the learner.

The cumulative nature of human learning provides a kind of snowballing effect, by which one thing leads to another. The greater the structure of knowledge people have about a particular topic, the more easily they can assimilate new ideas and new items of information that are related to it. Similar cumulative factors influence the growth of learned motor and social abilities.

In psychology, it is customary to use the word "development" when one is considering human change over long periods of time. In such instances the cumulative form of such change is readily apparent. The word "learning" more often refers to relatively rapid changes, in which the impact on the individual of a specific event or sequence of events is observed. On the whole, the convention of calling rapidly apparent changes, "learning," and modifications that take place over long periods of time, "development," is a useful one for practical purposes. Furthermore, it is often the case that long-term changes in human abilities do not solely involve learning, but also reflect the influence of additional factors such as physiological maturation. This is especially likely in young learners. However, when a distinction is made between the terms "learning" and "development" in describing changes, certain misunderstandings can arise. The long-term and cumulative effects of learning upon the individual may be neglected through being meshed with a range of phenomena said to manifest development.

In circumstances where both learning and additional factors contribute to long-term changes, the precise role of learning and the way in which it combines with other influences often receive scant attention. In most areas of learned achievement, the manner in which separate instances of learning combine to influence the individual over a lengthy period of time is understood very imperfectly. Such ignorance might be of less concern if learning usually took place in isolation from other influences upon human actions and capacities, but that does not appear to be the case. There is no harm in stating that long-term changes are developmental ones, so long as it is appreciated that saying something has developed does not in itself explain how or why the observed changes have taken place. The observed human changes to which it is usual to apply the term "development" include alterations in the individual that are clearly induced through learning. When we study human learning we cannot regard such developmental changes as being entirely outside our area of concern.

It has been emphasized by Piaget that by no means all the changes that occur in the developing child's achievements take the form of simple additions to the individual's capabilities following experiences involving the environment. Individuals certainly do respond to environmental events, but the relationship between child and environment is more accurately described as one comprised of sequences of give-and-take. The learner undertakes active operations which utilize in schemes of actions the intellectual structures he already possesses. According to Piaget's account, the child's development is strongly influenced by the joint operation of two forms of adaptive behavior, *accommodation,* in which the child adjusts his actions to meet external needs, and *assimilation,* in which objects or events are incorporated into the child's intellectual structures. Many instances of learning may be regarded as contributing to accommodation or assimilation, particularly the former.

The findings of experimental research into specific instances of learning and the results of developmental research into those kinds of change that follow lengthy periods of experience ought to be complementary. In practice, matters are sometimes hindered by differences between the two research traditions in the ways in which the relationship between individuals and their world is conceived. When researchers follow alternative traditions, it is not uncommon to find that even when two research studies provide data on closely related aspects of learned change, the data from the two sources do not readily combine to make a joint contribution to scientific knowledge.

AN ILLUSTRATION OF LEARNING IN HUMAN LIFE

In the previous section, three related aspects of human learning were discussed: adaptive functions for biological survival, dependence upon other capacities, and the cumulative forms of some learned acquisitions. At this point, a concrete illustration may help to indicate some of the ways in which these attributes can be influential in real life. The following description demonstrates the role of experience in enabling the individual to acquire valuable abilities. It shows that at each stage in a lengthy sequence of progressive changes the performance of individuals is influenced both by the biological equipment they bring to the tasks confronting them and by the capacities they have acquired as a result of previous learning. In particular, the example demonstrates that one can make a little contribution to knowledge about the manner in which individuals are affected by what they learn unless attention is paid to the characteristics of the person in whom learning takes place.

Humans explore, manipulate objects, and use and make tools. Basic to these skills is the ability to reach out to objects and pick them up. Most children are able to do this by around the age of six months. This may appear to be a very simple feat, but in fact it depends upon the coordination of a number of different sub-skills. In order to pick up a toy brick the infant has to be able, first, to attend visually to the target and, second, to move an arm and hand in a coordinated manner. Third, and this is more difficult, the infant must integrate visual attending and arm movements so that the movement of the hand towards the object is precisely controlled by what is seen. Fourth, the infant has to undertake a complex pattern of coordinated movements involving the finger and thumb in order to pick up the object once the hand has reached it. Each of these four essential sub-skills necessitates the infant possessing simpler and more basic skills that have to be acquired first.

How do human infants gain the ability to pick up objects? They possess no built-in skills that are sufficient for the task, although rudimentary visual attending abilities in the newborn and crude motor reflexes involving arm movements do form a starting point from which learning may commence. The analysis is complicated by the fact that learning is not the only factor contributing to the new abilities that the baby acquires. Certain processes of physiological maturation that occur in the months following birth are equally crucial.

The origins of reaching skills that are visually directed can be seen in the reflexes of very young infants. As infants begin to interact with the surrounding environment them in the months following birth, some of their initial reflexes are modified or diminish, and learned actions that are controlled by them begin to emerge. Actions become more highly organized and more precise, and activities that are initially separate become coordinated with each other. Observations made by B. L. White (1971) show that by around one month of age the infant can maintain his direction of gaze for some time and is able to track a moving object with the head and eyes in a series of jerky fixations. However, visual attention is restricted by the infant's fixed focal distance, preventing focusing on objects that are very close to the face. By two months the direction of gaze becomes increasingly variable, and the eyes sometimes converge and fixate upon the infant's own hand. He can now focus on close objects and track moving objects to anticipate their motion. By the end of the third month rapid head rotations are observed. These facilitate shifts in the direction of gaze, and the infant's hand receives a good deal of visual attention. At this stage the infant may swipe at an object, but he does not yet grasp it. Soon afterwards he can be seen to glance repeatedly from an object to the approaching hand and back again. The alternation of glances appears to indicate the beginnings of the coordination between eye and hand that is necessary for successful visually directed reaching. By around the fourth month the infant watches his hands and joins them, and the activity of alternately glancing between his hands and an object that is approached by them occurs more frequently. Soon afterwards the hand-regarding behavior begins to decrease, and objects that are encountered by the infants' hands are crudely grasped. At around five months of age the hand opens in anticipation of contact as it approaches an object.

This brief account conveys something of the variety and complexity of the different changes that take place as the infant gains more experience. Learning is undoubtedly involved, but a research strategy restricted to the investigation of particular short-term learned changes would not bring us very far toward an understanding of the acquisition of all the skills underlying visually directed reaching and picking up objects. It is equally essential to know about the timing and sequence of instances of learning, the manner in which abilities become coordinated, and the cumulative changes that occur when learning takes place on a large number of occasions over a lengthy period. The appropriate coordinations and integration of the component activities can only occur if the underlying abilities become available at appropriate times. It is also essential that certain nonlearned changes take place, associated with physiological maturation of the nervous system.

Although such complex arrays of interacting and interdependent capabilities may be essential for the acquisition of important skills, many investigators have preferred to confine their experimental research to circumstances where the roles and outcomes of learning are more clearly circumscribed. In fact, most psychological studies into human learning, and the majority of the experimental investigations to be described in the present book, have considered instances where the effects of learning on performance are relatively precise and readily discernible. Most often, researchers have chosen to investigate learning that can be observed over much shorter time scales than is necessary for the acquisition of all a complex skill like visually directed reaching.

However, there have been some attempts to investigate the ways in which particular instances of learning contribute within a complex array of sequentially related changes such as those just described. A series of experiments by B. L. White and his colleagues provides one interesting attempt of a kind that may become increasingly common in the future. White wanted to know whether it was possible to accelerate infants' progress in visually directed reaching capabilities. These skills are basic to many human abilities that involve using objects as implements. Clearly, it would be useful to find out if one can help infants acquire them earlier in life than is usual.

The first attempts were influenced by White's observation that the ability to sustain visual attention is an important underlying skill. Accordingly, he prepared some distinctive patterned visual stimuli, and he found that these effectively increased visual attention. Infants who were regularly exposed to the visual stimuli made longer fixations than infants in a control group. Paradoxically, however, those children who received this form of visual enrichment took longer than the infants in the control group to achieve a criterion standard of performance at visually directed reaching. Thus the eventual outcome of providing the visual stimuli was a negative one.

Why did the experimental intervention fail to achieve the desired end result, despite the demonstrable improvement that took place in visual attending? One possibility that occurred to White, with hindsight, was that the enriching visual stimuli might have been provided at an inappropriate stage in the infants' progress toward acquiring reaching skills. Achieving a compound skill is not just a matter of collecting the necessary components and combining them to produce the required outcome. One must also take into account the sequence in which sub-skills emerge. If one is to provide stimuli that really will enrich learning, it may be important not only to insure that particular kinds of stimulation are made available but also to present them at the most appropriate stage. We habitually reason in this manner in the case of those advanced intellectual abilities that depend upon the cumulative acquisition of numerous prior skills. For instance, it is widely appreciated that many concepts in advanced mathematics cannot be learned at all unless the student already understands elementary mathematical concepts. It is quite possible that appropriate sequencing of the various component skills is equally necessary in the case of some basic abilities that babies acquire early in life.

With these considerations in mind, White designed a further experiment. When he reviewed the observational evidence concerning the various stages through which infants pass as they learn to reach out to small objects and pick them up, White's attention was drawn to the fact that most infants spend a good deal of time simply looking at their hands, particularly around the third month of life. Since this activity is so common, it is not unreasonable to suggest that it has a real function for infants. If that is the case, an activity which decreases the infants' opportunities for watching their hands might retard the children in some respect. In this instance, it is conceivable that one effect of the attractive visual stimuli which White showed to the infants was to decrease the amount of time they spend in looking at their hands, depriving them of an experience that was important.

The next step was to find a way of giving increased visual attention without simultaneously restricting the infants' opportunity to look at their hands. White's solution was to supply the infants with brightly colored patterned mittens. These produced increased attending, but directed it toward the hands rather than away from them. The main result of the experiment was that infants in the condition receiving the mittens not only increased their visual attending but also made accelerated progress toward visually directed reaching.

This brief account of research by B. L. White illustrates the potential value of those investigations of human learning that take into account the background of broad, long-term changes that form the context for specific learned acquisitions. It is not typical of current research into learning, but it suggests one way in which learning specialists may be able to make practical contributions to human psychology. The above account emphasizes the fact that

practical programs designed to improve learning by giving interventions that provide "enrichment" are only likely to be effective if
they are based upon detailed knowledge about the children such
programs are intended to help. It is especially important to know
about the extent to which individuals already possess knowledge
and skills that can serve as a foundation for new learning.

SUMMARY

1. Learning is crucial to the power of humans to change their activities
   and their circumstances, and this ability is vital for human survival.
2. Man can pass on what he has learned to other individuals, forming
   cultures which amplify human achievements.
3. There are both similarities and major differences between animal and
   human learning. The traditions of research into animal learning have
   influenced the study of human learning.
4. Some species can undertake complex sequences of activities that are
   largely independent of learning, but unlearned activities are often inflexible and cannot be as easily adapted to meet the demands of a
   changing environment as can learned behaviors.
5. Some nonhuman species are very good at forms of perceptual learning
   that enable them to navigate and to acquire essential knowledge about
   the regions they inhabit.
6. Humans and other primates are generally more successful than lower
   species at instances of learning that involve making controlled movements and coordinations. As a result, humans can manipulate objects
   and are able to use and make tools. This ability is a vital factor in
   gaining control over the resources that enable humans to survive. Acquiring the ability to use objects as tools and implements may have
   contributed to the evolution of *Homo sapiens* as a special variety of
   primate.
7. Man engages in play and exploratory activities that demonstrate a high
   degree of autonomy and freedom from control by inborn mechanisms or
   environmental forces.
8. Humans can retain large amounts of information in memory, and this
   ability contributes to human independence.
9. Learned adaptations, which contribute to human survival and well-
   being, are closely related to and dependent upon other human
   capacities.
10. Learning is cumulative, with skills acquired early in life forming a
    basis for further learned achievements. Learning and developmental
    processes are closely linked.
11. Research shows that the acquisition of human skills may depend upon
    the coordination of a number of simpler learned abilities that have
    been previously acquired at appropriate times.

Suggestions for Further Reading

Eisenberg, L. (1972) "The *human* nature of human nature." *Science*, 176 (No. 4031):123–128.

Thorpe, W. H. (1974) *Animal Nature and Human Nature.* London: Methuen.

Washburn, S. L. (1978) "Human behavior and the behavior of other animals." *American Psychologist*, 33:405–418.

White, B. L. (1971) *Human Infants: Experience and Psychological Development.* Englewood Cliffs, New Jersey: Prentice-Hall.

CHAPTER **2**

The Scientific
Investigation
of Human Learning

OVERVIEW

In the present chapter we examine how scholars have made attempts to understand the processes of human learning. We consider some early efforts by philosophers to describe laws of learning, and the first attempts to study learning empirically, as part of a science of psychology. Within the present century there have been many changes in the study of human learning. An earlier emphasis on the need to restrict scientific accounts to phenomena that can be directly observed has given way to increased readiness to theorize about the nature of the various mental processes that underlie learning.

BEGINNING TO STUDY LEARNING

Civilized people have always been interested in learning, with the achievements of the erudite and the learned arousing wonder and awe, and sometimes fear. Yet only recently have scientists begun to investigate learning in a rigorous manner. The present chapter will trace some of the ways in which active inquiry into human learning has developed until the present. The aim is not to provide a complete history of research into learning, but to give the reader useful background knowledge. It will then be possible to perceive modern research developments as being more readily understandable and as less arbitrary in the choice of areas of concern and methods of investigation than they might appear to be. Knowledge of the developments that have led up to present-day research contributes the necessary perspective.

A Slow Start

Several factors contributed to the delay in applying the principles and methods of empirical sciences to the study of human learning as part of an experimental science of psychology. One brake on progress was the belief in simple dualistic conceptions of human psychology, whereby minds as well as souls were regarded as being independent entities entirely outside the control of the mechanisms governing bodily processes. Dualistic viewpoints have sometimes been accompanied by the acceptance of a strongly nativist position, in which human knowledge is seen as being largely innate. Plato's view that a major function of learning is to draw out knowledge possessed by the soul in previous existences (Warren, 1921, p. 24) is echoed to some extent by a number of more recent philosophers.

This outlook does not encourage its adherents to pay close attention to the function of experience in the acquisition of human abilities.

Modified forms of such a nativist position are by no means entirely untenable, and dualistic beliefs have not prevented some philosophers, including Descartes, from making major contributions to psychology. Descartes regarded the human mind as being partly rational and open to experience and partly controlled by automatic mechanisms (Boring, 1950, p. 159). His statement that knowledge that cannot be completely accounted for by the data of experience, a view later to be developed in the complex nativist philosophy of Kant, is shared by some modern writers. In this century Arnold Gesell, who wrote extensively on infancy and childhood, regarded the process of human development as being essentially the unfolding of innate predispositions. More recently, Noam Chomsky has suggested that the acquisition and use of language are only possible because we possess some innate device for acquiring language.

Many contemporary researchers studying child learning and development, while unwilling to accept the necessity for innate brain mechanisms that have functions so specialized as those implied by Chomsky, agree that firm evidence exists for some kinds of organization being present at birth in higher parts of the brain. Instances cited as evidence include the temporally integrated patterns of crying and sucking that can be observed in newborns. Furthermore, innate differences in perceptual thresholds and activity level have a large influence from the earliest months of life. But no modern psychologist would deny that the achievements of the human species are, in the main, the outcomes of experience. If one accepts this, the potential value of investigating human learning processes is apparent.

Metaphors and Analogies

Darwin's evolutionary theory demonstrated major continuities between humans and other species and thereby provided knowledge that makes belief in cruder forms of dualism hard to sustain. Progress in the biological sciences has contributed to our understanding of learning, through providing models, analogies, and metaphors that have helped psychologists to conceptualize possible forms of the mechanisms underlying human functions.

Nineteenth-century progress in biology led to advances in the use of experimental methods for investigating living organisms. Psychologists such as Ebbinghaus were to draw upon these methods for research into human learning. Extensive knowledge about biological functions—growth, development, adaptation, habituation and inhibition—became available. The scientific findings provide a rich source of possible analogies which may help us to understand the nature of learning.

The attempt to understand or explain physical phenomena is made easier if an investigator's everyday world provides concrete exemplars that suggest possible mechanisms to account for the workings of the objects of study. For example, research into human memory has profited from an infusion of ideas produced by computer developments involving artificial memories and artificial intelligence systems. In designing computer systems it became apparent that any device which use large amounts of information must include careful provision for input and output of information from large stores. Knowing about the requirements of artificial information-processing systems has helped experimental psychologists to become aware of some of the requirements of a human memory.

In the past, efforts to investigate learning processes were hindered by the absence of obvious parallels in everyday experience, parallels that would have helped to conceptualize acquisition processes. Very few of the phenomena explored in Newtonian physics provide much assistance in the understanding of human learning. When descriptions of biological phenomena were made available, it became easier to imagine possible mechanisms for psychological functioning. It is noteworthy that the eminent developmental psychologist Jean Piaget commenced his research career with an extensive knowledge of biological science. Piaget's immense contribution is not unrelated to his readiness to suggest a variety of parallels between changes observed in biological systems and psychological developments in human behavior. Yet the biological sciences are clearly not the sole source of valuable analogies. Apart from the computer developments previously mentioned, advances in disciplines such as communications theory, information theory, cybernetics, and systems theory have all provided useful ideas. Biology itself has sometimes gained from metaphors arising within economics, as in the notion of "survival of the fittest," and economic metaphors, for instance, the concept of "response competition," also have a place in psychology.

THE CONCEPT OF ASSOCIATION

Immediately upon deciding to investigate learning we encounter a number of questions about how to begin. What does learning achieve? What does it involve, and what forms does it take? What kinds of phenomena have to occur in order for it to be said that learning has taken place? Are there any kinds of changes or any other phenomena that are found in all of the different circumstances in which learning is said to have occurred? Scholars who encountered problems like these have found that the concept of *association* provides a useful starting-point.

The ability to detect and form connections between events provides a living being with a way of beginning to make sense out of the world of sensation and experience. Imagine individuals who find themselves in a strange and unfamiliar universe. They perceive a variety of signals—sounds, sights, and other stimuli—but the input is apparently random, and for them the sensory inputs have, no particular order, organization or coherence. How might such individuals begin to impose order in the mass of stimulation? In such circumstances an organism will profit by being able to detect and store information about any regularities, similarities, and patterns in events, and by perceiving which phenomena tend to occur together or in regular sequences. It would be especially valuable to be able to predict which events are likely to go together on future occasions and, in effect, to know the consequences of particular happenings, either those in the environment or acts initiated by the individual. If individuals can discern those events that are paired in time or place and can retain this knowledge, they thereby impose some degree of regularity and order upon the world they experience. Instead of events appearing to be entirely random and arbitrary, they are seen to take a more organized and patterned form, becoming predictable and ultimately meaningful to the perceivers.

The ability to detect associations or connections provides a key for imposing order, and associative abilities enable a person to learn about regularities in experienced phenomena. As it happens, principles of association have received emphasis in most attempts to explain mental processes. The majority of scholars who have investigated learning have expressed interest in the form associations take and the manner in which they are acquired.

Early Associationist Views of Learning

The view that associative principles have an important role in human mental processes was advanced by Aristotle and many subsequent thinkers. Thomas Hobbes speculated on the function of associative factors in learning. For him and his successors in the British Empiricist philosophical tradition, the contents of the mind were regarded as being determined largely by experience, involving what Locke called "the association of ideas." A number of associative principles were advanced, in the form of statements about circumstances which are believed to lead to connections being formed between thoughts. These philosophers worked out laws of association and they attempted to apply them to conscious thought. Knowledge was viewed as a complex of experiences joined through association, the latter providing a fundamental mechanism of mental activity. Thus, early in the eighteenth century David Hume suggested that ideas become connected to each other for any of three reasons: resemblance (or similarity), contiguity in time or place (that is, items occurring together), and cause-and-effect. Hume later eliminated causality from his list of basic learning principles, and he suggested that it was the outcome of repeated experiences of contiguity. He attributed the experience of cause-and-effect to the repeated successive observations of perceived objects. Although psychologists advancing more recent theories have argued about which of the three principles are important or necessary, subsequent accounts have always included one or more of them.

Hartley's Theory

An ambitious attempt to enumerate the psychological principles of association underlying mental activity was made by David Hartley, whose *Observations on Man,* published in 1749, was a remarkable advance beyond the work of his predecessors towards an acceptable modern theory of learning. For Hartley, experience comprised both *sensations,* which he defined as a person's internal feelings arising from the input of external events, and other internal feelings, which he called *ideas*—there being a corresponding idea for each sensation. Hartley's law of association stated that when sensations occurred together on a number of occasions, one sensation could acquire the capacity to evoke ideas corresponding to the other sensation. He extended this principle to demonstrate that ideas recall each other, and stated that some muscular motions were also subject to these laws of association. Simple associations could combine into larger clusters, thereby accounting for complex ideas. Successive associations were shown to lead to sequential chains of ideas.

Hartley's account of associative learning is not unlike a number of twentieth-century theoretical positions, notably the one underlying Pavlov's research on conditioning in dogs. In one respect Hartley's outlook contrasts with that of David Hume, his contemporary, and is more similar to a twentieth-century behaviorist theoretician, E. R. Guthrie, in that the essential basis of association is restricted to contiguity alone. Unlike Hume, Hartley did not regard similarity or resemblance as such as being fundamental factors. He argued that any ideas which are contiguous in time tend to become connected, their union being strengthened by repetition. Hartley considered that similar principles also applied to the control of motor actions.

Hartley drew attention to a number of the functions that are emphasized in present-day cognitive attempts to explain human learning. For instance, he produced a reasoned account of the function of memory in thought. He also considered the manner in which the contents of memory are influenced by experience. It may seem surprising that neither the serious attempt to explain learning advanced by Hartley nor the detailed theories put forward by his successors, including Thomas Brown (1778–1820) and James Mill (1773–1836), led immediately to a program of empirical investigation. Their accounts contain a number of experimentally testable hypotheses concerning the nature and form of associative learning. Yet it was not until considerably later—toward the end of the nineteenth century—that systematic empirical inquiries were conducted into the role of associative mechanisms in learning.

EBBINGHAUS AND THE FIRST EMPIRICAL INQUIRIES

In the second half of the nineteenth century a number of people were beginning to undertake empirical investigations of learning. Much of the research was directly concerned with the influence of associational factors. In 1879, Francis Galton described some experiments he had carried out in order to investigate the association of ideas. Galton claimed that by writing down the words that occurred to him as associates to a variety of events and other words, he acquired

> an interesting and unexpected view of the number of the operations of the mind, and of the obscure depths in which they took place, of which I had been little conscious before. The general impression they have left upon me is like that which many of us have experienced when the basement of our house happens to be under thorough sanitary repairs, and we realize for the first time the complex system of drains and gas—and water pipes, flues, bell-wires, and so forth—upon which our comfort depends, but which are usually hidden out of sight, and of whose existence, so long as they acted well, we had never troubled ourselves (Francis Galton, 1879. Reprinted in Crovitz, 1970, p. 25.)

Galton himself was not greatly concerned with the quantitative effects of associative factors upon learning. However, around this time J. A. Bergstrom examined the effects of interfering associations during practice, E. A. Kirkpatrick made comparisons between abilities to recall and recognize verbal items, and Alfred Jost examined the effects on learning of massed and distributed practice (Warren, 1921). Mary Calkins investigated the influence on verbal learning of item frequency, vividness, and recency. In a paper published in 1894 she described the phenomenon now known as the *serial-position effect*, whereby the first and last items in a list are most likely to be recalled, the middle items being more easily forgotten.

The work of Hermann Ebbinghaus provided by far the most important contribution during this period to a methodologically sound experimental psychology of human learning. After receiving German scientific and philosophical training, Ebbinghaus spent a number of years in England, and his view of learning was influenced by study of the British associationist philosophers. His experimental research into the psychology of learning consisted of a number of carefully designed experiments to investigate the ability to retain and reproduce verbal items.

Ebbinghaus was acutely aware of the methodological difficulties encountered when one attempts to follow scientific procedures in designing psychological experiments, and he attached great importance to the need to design experiments that included the necessary experimental control procedures. He was quick to see the necessity to develop appropriate statistical and sampling procedures in psychological research. His book *Memory* (Ebbinghaus, 1964; first published in 1885) contains excellent descriptions of the application to psychology of statistical constructs, including normal-curve characteristics, error distributions, and the concept of probable error. In the second chapter of his book there is a discussion of fundamental considerations for the design of experiments on human learning that can still be read with profit by anyone who intends to be a researcher. Ebbinghaus was a highly professional scientist, far removed from the numerous Victorian amateurs who dabbled in scientific research. Not only did he become aware of many of the difficulties associated with designing experimental investigations into human learning, but he was also remarkably successful at developing ways to overcome them.

Today, Ebbinghaus is widely known for introducing *nonsense syllables* to psychology. These are three-letter units lacking apparent meaning (e.g., SOF, XUM). Ebbinghaus' reasons for using nonsense syllables are clearly stated in his book: wishing to investigate associational factors in learning and memory, he was anxious to overcome or minimize the difficulties caused by factors that might affect learning but were outside the control of the experimenter. He realized that one important influence on learning and memory is the meaningfulness of the material being acquired by the learner. The general problem in conducting research was "to keep constant the mass of conditions which have proven themselves causally connected with a certain result."

The difficulties obstructing experimental control that led Ebbinghaus to make use of nonsense syllables were those imposed by the meaningfulness of the material to be learned. It is difficult to study the formation of new links or new associations between items, as Ebbinghaus wished to, if some of the materials presented to the learner are already familiar to him. The learner may avoid or minimize new associative learning by using his existing knowledge, in the form of previously acquired associations, or by using information concerning semantic attributes of the material. The introduction of such strategies on the part of the learner would not pose too serious a problem if one could be sure that each experimental subject learned meaningful verbal items in exactly the same way. However, individuals differ in their knowledge about items. For example, they vary in the extent to which a particular word evokes meaningful attributes or existing associated items. When two people are given identical familiar materials to learn, the experimenter cannot guarantee that each individual possesses equivalent existing pertinent knowledge. Thus it cannot be assumed that the amount and kind of new associative learning is identical.

Ebbinghaus quickly became aware of this kind of difficulty in experiments on associative learning, but he hoped that using nonsense syllables would enable him to deal with the problems. The syllables used by Ebbinghaus consisted of three letters, the first and last being consonants, with a vowel for the middle item. He restricted the choice of consonants in the final position in order to insure that every syllable could be pronounced with reasonable ease by German speakers. He noted that nonsense syllables have a number of advantages for studying learning and memory, not all of them due to their lack of meaning. The syllables provide simple, relatively homogeneous items of uniform length. Some of the influences of factors such as changing context, mood and style, degree of interest, and other striking qualities are avoided. The constant size of the nonsense syllable made it possible to vary at will the length and quantity of materials to be learned; an advantage which was maximized when attention was given to careful control over the timing of presentation. Ebbinghaus was quite aware that nonsense syllables are not entirely homogeneous or meaningless, and he warned that the materials were far from perfect in these respects. The task of systematically measuring the degree of meaningfulness possessed by different items was left to later investigators.

Ebbinghaus knew that any of a number of other factors can create problems of experimental control. For instance, the attention that an individual gives to whatever he is learning may waver and diminish when he becomes tired or bored, and the "capriciousness of mental life" makes it difficult to maintain the entirely constant conditions desirable in experimental research. However, he felt that a degree of control could be maintained over the most important influences, so long as investigators

> . . . try in experimental fashion to keep as constant as possible those circumstances whose influence on retention and reproduction is known or suspected, and then ascertain whether that is sufficient. The material must be chosen so that decided differences of interest are, at least to all appearances, excluded; equality of attention may be promoted by preventing external disturbances. (Ebbinghaus, 1964, p. 12. Originally published in 1885.)

He also perceived that the problems due to momentary changes in attention can be reduced by averaging performance over relatively long periods of time. He anticipated the modern practice of using balanced designs in which the order of presenting the different experimental conditions is systematically varied.

In addition to his work on research design and on the preparation of materials for experimental research into learning, Ebbinghaus attempted to solve a number of problems associated with measurement. Measuring what an individual has learned on a particular occasion is not as simple or straightforward a matter as it might appear to be, and Ebbinghaus saw the need to devise procedures that were both reliable and valid. One ingenious technique he developed requires the individual who has learned something on a previous occasion to relearn it to the original criterion. By subtracting the length of time required for relearning from the time originally taken to learn the task, Ebbinghaus obtained a measure of what he termed *saving* of work or time. The scores thus calculated can be used in a number of ways. For example, the average saving per list repetition and the relationship between the saving and the time required for first learning served as dependent measures which were incorporated in attempts by Ebbinghaus to discover empirically based laws of human learning. The savings method has not often been used by others, possibly because it requires a large amount of time and effort on the part of experimental subjects, few of whom possess the indefatigable quality of Ebbinghaus himself. He served as the sole subject in most of his own experiments.

AN UNSOLVED PROBLEM

It was an enormous achievement to extend the powerful techniques and weapons of the experimental sciences to the study of human learning, an area of concern that was previously considered inaccessible to empirical investigation. Before Ebbinghaus, little thought had been given to the possibility of systematic empirical research into learning, and it must have seemed to some that the methods of science had no place in furthering our understanding of something which only philosophers had closely examined. After Ebbinghaus, there could be no doubting the potential value of an experimental psychology of human learning. His work uncovered major problems, some of which were alarmingly different from any difficulties that had been encountered in those physical sciences that provided the contexts for the growth of modern experimental design and methodology. However, the work of Ebbinghaus on the design and analysis of experiments into human learning indicated that although the problems were great, progress could be made toward solving them.

The advances made by Ebbinghaus were based upon a fusion of the associationist psychology developed within the British philosophical tradition and the fast-advancing German tradition of experimental research into the natural sciences. There are limits to what such a fusion can achieve, and both the successes and the limitations of Ebbinghaus' undertakings reflect the preoccupations of his times. The associationist view of learning, in which human abilities are described largely in terms of the formation and retention of bonds or connections, is one which can lead to an underestimation of the active role of the human learner in organizing, coding and processing information. Active processes on the learner's part are, in the main, equally crucial to learning as are strictly associative events. Associationist accounts of learning do not necessarily deny the possibility that learning may depend upon cognitive processes that cannot be reduced to simple associative elements, but such accounts tend to emphasize those aspects of learning in which the formation of connections is prominent.

In 1931 E. L. Thorndike reported some findings that demonstrate the importance for learning of organizational attributes of material to be learned, a matter which continues to receive much attention in contemporary psychological research into human memory and the acquisition of knowledge. Thorndike's experimental results made it clear that the formation of links based solely upon the associationist principles of frequency or temporal contiguity could not fully account for learned performance. His procedure involved reading a list of 32 sentences six times to a large number of university students who served as experimental subjects. The sentences were similar in structure, for example:

Barney Duke and Ronald Curtis worked today.
Arthur Blake and Thomas Roper listened then.

Thorndike constructed some of the sentences in such a way that they each contained parts in common with some other sentences in the list, for instance:

| Daniel | Bragg | and | Truman | Mason | played | there. |
| Janet | Bragg | and | Truman | Napier | played | apart. |

In this way he was able to vary in a systematic fashion the frequency with which different word items occurred together. Thorndike suggested that if temporal contiguity was the dominant principle governing performance at a task which required subjects to remember specified single words from the sentences, those items that were most frequently contiguous in the sentences presented to the subjects would be the ones most often recalled. The questions posed to Thorndike's subjects required the participant to specify "What would come after_____?" The final word for each question was taken from any one of the different positions in the sentences. For instance, a particular question might be "What word came after *Janet*?" or "What word came after *apart*?" It was thus possible for Thorndike to test what he termed the "strength of the connections" between the different words in the sentences.

Thorndike did not find that level of performance was determined solely or mainly by the frequency with which the different word pairs had occurred contiguously. On the contrary, the probability of a word being recalled appeared to be much more strongly influenced by other factors. For example, twice as many subjects recalled the correct answer to the question "What came after *Janet*?" as remembered the correct word item for "What word came after Bragg and?" Yet the word "Janet" had occurred in Thorndike's repeated lists on just six occasions, followed by the word "Bragg," while all subjects had listened to 24 pairings of the phrase "Bragg and," followed by the correct word. The extreme case is provided by questions asking for the word that followed the final word in one of the 32 sentences, the correct answer being the first word of the following sentence. Less than one percent of the subjects made correct responses to questions of this form.

As Thorndike observed, these results show that the positions of words in the sentence structure partly determine what is recalled. He noted that the degree of *belongingness* of word items in their contexts was just as important as repetition and contiguity. He thus gave a clear demonstration that the associative principles of learning which Ebbinghaus had so effectively begun to explore need to be augmented by knowledge of structural or organizational factors if one is to fully understand human learning.

THE INFLUENCE OF BEHAVIORISM

Since Ebbinghaus, experimental research into human learning has continued without interruption up to the present. However, new developments engendered in other areas of experimental psychology, especially in the early years of the present century, have influenced the form of subsequent investigations of human learning in ways that Ebbinghaus could not have anticipated. To state matters briefly, experimental psychology acquired a strongly and sometimes exclusively behaviorist emphasis. Partly for this reason, the forms of research that were undertaken to investigate human learning began to be influenced in important ways by the activities of psychologists studying animal behavior.

Toward the end of the nineteenth century, at a time when a major goal of empirical investigations in psychology was to describe and analyze the structure of conscious experience, psychologists using the methods and techniques then available to them ran into a number of difficulties. To some, the difficulties appeared to be so overwhelming as to necessitate a radical change in approach for the science or psychology. During that period, psychology was beginning to become a laboratory-based science, largely concerned with attempting to analyze the contents of experience. Much of the research activity was based upon that of the psychological laboratory at Leipzig in Germany headed by Wilhelm Wundt. Wundt thought that it would be possible to investigate the simplest units of conscious experience and then proceed to discover how such units combine, through the principles of association, to form larger and more complex mental functions. It was hoped that analysis of the conscious processes experienced by individuals would lead to discovery of the laws underlying mental activity. The methods adopted by Wundt placed emphasis upon self-observation by carefully trained individuals. As they attempted such self-examination of inner experience, or introspection, under controlled conditions, they reported the mental processes that reached awareness.

Unfortunately, Wundt's introspection-based laboratory approach, known at the time as *structuralism* because of its concern with the structure of mental acts, was not as fruitful as had been anticipated. One source of difficulty lay in the element of subjectivism inherent in the introspective method. The elements of experience reported by one trained introspectionist were not always identical to those reported by another individual, although the objective situation was intended to be the same. Problems of a fundamental nature were raised by doubts about the status of conscious experience in mental processes. Do people's conscious experiences, sensations and images, for example, necessarily correspond to crucial mechanisms underlying mental activities? The findings of research being conducted in another German laboratory, at Wurzburg, indicated that much mental activity was not accompanied by any mental images and occurred without the individual's conscious awareness. Psychologists at the Wurzburg laboratory could not demonstrate any conscious experience to account for the decision making that was required for the task of judging the relative weights of different objects. A variety of sensations and images were reported by introspectionists instructed to make judgments of this kind, but the crucial psychological processes underlying their choices eluded the introspective observations.

The writings of Sigmund Freud provided separate support for the view that the elements of conscious experience cannot adequately account for the psychological processes underlying human learning and thought. Freud gave a number of convincing demonstrations to support his claim that a good deal of mental activity takes place in the absence of awareness. It was hard for the introspectionists to contradict such a conclusion. The accumulating objections to the introspective method inevitably led to a questioning of the ultimate value of the nineteenth-century structuralist approach as a means of discovering basic laws about the events governing mental life.

The unsatisfactory state of affairs revealed by the serious difficulties encountered in introspective psychology served to open the way for an important shift toward the behaviorist approach that has strongly influenced psychology in the present century. The term *behaviorism* in psychology eludes precise definition because it has been introduced by psychologists to mean a number of different things, but use of the word always implies placing emphasis on objectivity and the need for reliable measurement of the variables being investigated. Behaviorist writers have proposed that observations of measurable behavior should be the sole data of experimental psychology. Subjective experiences that cannot be measured or described in a publicly verifiable manner are not premitted. In the context of such usage the word behavior is allowed to refer to *any* observable activity of a person or animal (see, for example, Thorndike, 1931.) The behaviorist objection to dealing with thoughts or feelings was not that they do not form behavior, but simply that they cannot be publicly observed. Implicit in the viewpoints of most behaviorist psychologists is acceptance of the necessity to define the theoretical concepts used in an experimental science of psychology in terms of the precise procedures of operations by which they are obtained. Taken as a whole, the behaviorist movement in psychology, which emphasized precise observation and the exclusion of data and theoretical constructs that cannot be objectively verified, was an attempt to make psychology scientific, by limiting psychological inquiry within certain constraints believed to be obeyed by physical scientists.

In the most extreme forms of behaviorism, unobservable phenomena are completely barred from consideration. Some experimental psychologists thought that such exclusion was essential in order to conform to the practices of the physical sciences. (In reality, a variety of inferred and hypothetical entities are encountered in the different sciences. The progress associated with concepts such as "electrons," "atoms," and "neutrons," would never have taken place had such a limitation been imposed.) Those psychologists who denied the scientific admissibility of data that cannot be observed directly believed in the possibility of creating a science of behavior that is based upon laws which describe regularities between the behavior of organisms and events in the environment.

It is undeniable that the actions of animals or people (their responses) are partly determined by what happens in their environment (the external stimuli). However, it is unlikely that an exclusively behaviorist approach can advance very far toward a full explanation of all human activities. Those aspects of the individuals' environment that are publicly observable form only a limited proportion of the significant influences upon them. Many actions are determined by the mental processes underlying knowledge, beliefs, hopes, attitudes, skills, and thoughts. While the immediate environment undeniably influences every living person, it is the environment *as interpreted by the individual*, through personal mental activities and experience, that affects the person's behavior.

A strongly behaviorist position in psychology implies that psychology should be a science about behavior rather than about human experience or the underlying mental processes. With hindsight, such a retreat from the attempt to create a science about mental life now appears to have been too strong a reaction to the problems and difficulties, grave as they were, that were encountered when Wundt and his followers tried to establish psychology as a laboratory science. A psychology from which reasoning and thinking are excluded has very limited potential. But if the early behaviorists were aware that their redirection of psychology was a retreat, they never admitted it. The behaviorist position, expressed most clearly and vociferously by J. B. Watson, was that psychology ought not to concern itself with mental processes, excepting those intermediary responses produced by peripheral movements, such as subvocal speech movements.

The early behaviorists were convinced that it was possible to build a valid science of behavior that was based upon objective, quantifiable data alone.

Influence of Early Behaviorism on Human Learning Research

For those who regarded psychology as being the science of behavior, research in which animals served as the experimental subjects had a number of important advantages over human research. It would be a sound research strategy to commence a study of behavior by initially investigating organisms that are less complex than man. A body of theory that successfully accounts for animal behavior would provide a good start toward a theory of human behavior. This would be especially true if, as most early behaviorists believed, important basic behavioral laws applied equally to lower species and to man. Another advantage of research using animal as subjects is that closer control can be achieved over environments and experimental conditions than would be either possible or morally permissible in research involving people. It has usually been thought acceptable to deprive or restrict other species for the cause of science.

So it is hardly surprising that the acceptance of behaviorist viewpoints in psychology was accompanied by an increasing emphasis on animal research. The significance of these developments for the psychology of human learning is that the major impetus for research into learning during the first half of this century came from psychologists who used animal subjects and worked within a behaviorist tradition. The instances of learning which were investigated tended to be ones that either were important for the mammalian species (notably the white Norwegian rat) used as experimental subjects, or could be easily observed and manipulated in those species. Similarly, the environmental influences upon learning that were most frequently investigated were ones that could be clearly shown to influence the behavior of the animals being studied. For instance, there were many investigations of the effects of manipulating the amount of food that was provided to animals at various times. The hope was that research in which animal activities were rewarded, or *reinforced,* would make it possible to state general rules or principles about behavior in relation to reinforcing events in general. Such principles were expected to apply to varied species and to a variety of reinforcing events.

Some forms of learning received rather scanty attention. First, there was neglect of those kinds of animal learning that either did not readily occur or were not easily observed in the circumstances provided by the kinds of experimental apparatus that psychologists devised. For instance, perceptual learning, which often takes place in the absence of readily apparent reinforcing events, received relatively little attention until around 1950, although this learning is crucial for the survival of animals in the wild. Second, and of greater direct importance for the study of human learning, varieties of learning in humans that either are not encountered in other species or are less developed in them tended to be neglected. The instances of learning that are most clearly unique to humans depend upon language. They contribute to the acquisition of information and knowledge. Equally important to man are his manipulative abilities. As we noted in the previous chapter, these are more advanced in humans than in other species. The forms of learning that involve modifications of human motor activities and precise motor control are particularly crucial, perhaps the most important activities being those using the hand, which is vital for human survival.

It was never claimed that language-based human learning is unimportant. Yet the dominance of animal behavior studies produced an intellectual climate in which some writers failed to appreciate that principles and laws derived from animal behavior experiments could not necessarily be extended to account for all human behavior, including that which involved language and reasoning. As a result, psychologists brought to the study of verbal learning in humans a range of concepts, methods of observation, and theoretical perspectives borrowed from research on lower mammals, without seriously questioning whether these provided the most appropriate ways for increasing our understanding of human learning.

THORNDIKE AND SKINNER

The early studies of animal behavior that exerted the most profound influence upon psychology in general were those by E. L. Thorndike in the United States and Ivan Pavlov in Russia. Neither of these researchers can be regarded as thoroughly behaviorist in every respect. Thorndike was inclined to describe animal reasoning in terms that J. B. Watson considered to be mentalistic, and both Thorndike and Pavlov speculated at length about the possible ways in which physiological and neural processes might control behavior. Pavlov's work was not widely read in the West before 1927. Nevertheless, around 1910 an account of it came to the attention of J. B. Watson, and from around 1920 the Russian research into conditioning began to exert a major influence upon psychology in the United States.

Thorndike, whose first animal researches preceded the growth of behaviorism as an explicit viewpoint in psychology, worked within the associationist tradition and conceived of learning as involving the formation of new associations, bonds, or connections between sense impressions (which can be called *stimuli*) and activities or impulses to action (which are called *responses*). Thorndike was never reticent in suggesting extensions of his findings to human behavior, or in giving advice to teachers on the basis of his experimental research, which was carried out on cats, dogs, fish, and monkeys. He became convinced that animal learning consisted mainly of connections being formed between sensations and responses and that the fundamental processes underlying human learning were essentially similar. He justified this extension by referring to the similarly shaped learning curves that are obtained from learning experiments involving human and cat subjects.

The Law of Effect

In his early publications Thorndike stressed the importance of exercise or practice upon learning, but it later became clear to him that practice alone does not guarantee that learning will occur. He also emphasized a principle of readiness, by which he meant what we now call *preparedness*, and he noted the necessity for the learner to attend to appropriate events. Most important, Thorndike stressed the importance of motivational factors, in particular those related to the consequences of behavior, which were said to influence future actions through a "Law of Effect." This stated that when a modifiable connection is made and is followed by a satisfying state of affairs, the strength of the connection is thereby increased. Thorndike defined his terms in a way that was broadly acceptable to behaviorism, with a satisfying state of affairs being defined as one which the animal does nothing to avoid. Similarly, the strength of a response was operationally defined as the probability of its occurrence.

The role of the Law Effect was illustrated by a Thorndikian learning task in which a cat made various responses, and the appropriate ones led to the cat receiving a reward. Thorndike believed that the correct responses came to be "stamped-in" through the Law of Effect, forming a bond or connection between the external situation (or stimulus) and the appropriate motor responses. The experimental procedure involved placing the cat in a large box that could be opened only by manipulating a latch on an inside wall. This caused a door to open, giving access to food outside. When the animal was placed in the box for the first time, it did not usually succeed in opening the latch until the latter was struck accidentally, after a good deal of apparently random movement. Over a number of succeeding trials the time elapsing before the latch was opened decreased, and the cat gradually and irregularly made progress toward the state in which the door was opened immediately after the animal entered the box. The relatively slow and irregular initial progress made by the subjects in this task led Thorndike to deny that cats possess any quality of insight or reasoning. He asserted that the learning process was one in which the activities that were followed by rewards tended to be repeated because they somehow became stamped-in as a consequence of trial and error.

Thorndike's Statements About Human Learning

Thorndike believed that his observations of the need for preparedness and the importance of reward had direct implications for the understanding of human learning by children at school. For school learning, he considered it important to identify the particular associative bonds that had to be formed; if teachers were insufficiently explicit about the particular content their students were required to learn, the wrong connections might be strengthened rather than the correct ones. The Law of Effect provided a further source of advice for teachers. In addition to stressing the importance of identifying appropriate bonds to be formed, Thorndike drew attention to the need to specify the states of affairs that were satisfying in classroom learning situations and to the need to provide such satisfying states. He considered that some of the most important influences upon motivation lay in the nature of the task. Thorndike listed interest in the work, interest in improvement, the significance of the learning task, and the student's attitude toward the problems at hand as being among the factors determining success.

Thorndike had much to say about the kinds of learning that are important in education. He believed that many of his statements about human learning were fairly direct applications of the laws he based upon observations of learning in animals. However, he realized that some human learning phenomena are not obviously paralleled in animal behavior. For example, his finding that belongingness was important demonstrated the existence of varieties of human learning that cannot easily be explained in simple associationist terms. They appear to depend upon organizational principles. He also examined the educationally important issue of transfer of training, to be discussed in Chapter 4, and he provided a connectionist explanation based upon the idea that identical elements can be found in different materials.

Skinner and the Concept of Reinforcement

The emphasis Thorndike gave to motivational influences upon learning, expressed in his Law of Effect, is also found in the work of B. F. Skinner. A more thoroughgoing behaviorist than Thorndike, Skinner undertook a large body of experimental research in his early career aimed at the detailed description of the empirical laws governing relationships between the environmental events that follow the responses made by an organism and the future frequency of occurrence of those responses. Whereas Thorndike saw the effects of rewards as producing satisfying states of affairs, Skinner preferred to write more simply of *reinforcement*, a reinforcer being described as an event that raises the probability of a response which it follows. For example, if giving a rat food every time it turns to the right increases the frequency of the animal's turning to the right, the provision of food is said to reinforce, or act as a reinforcer for, the turning-to-the-right response in that animal. Despite any circularity in defining reinforcement in terms of its consequences, the definition is a useful one because it avoids making any assumptions about the nature of those events that can reinforce behavior. A particular event may or may not seem to the experimenter to be intuitively rewarding, but it can be said to be a reinforcer if, and only if, it increases the probability of the preceding responses in the experimental subject being studied. The concept of reinforcement is a central one in the psychology of learning and will be discussed at greater length in Chapter 3.

Thorndike never developed theoretical systems of any great complexity, and Skinner has been even less willing to advance explanatory theories that go beyond the observable evidence. He has bluntly emphasized his opposition to the building of theories in contemporary psychology. Instead, he directed his energy toward building up a body of data concerning environmental influences upon animal performance, and he hoped that it would be possible to express his findings in the form of strong empirical laws (Skinner 1938).

Skinner's aim has been to produce what is unambiguously a science of behavior, making it possible for such behavior to be predicted and controlled. With this end in mind, he has argued against giving priority either to explanations of behavior that involve unobserved processes or to increasing one's understanding of the mental events underlying human activities. He prefers to ignore learners' mental activities and inner states, and has avoided making statements about what might be occurring at any level other than that of the behavior itself. He regards efforts to make physiological or neurological explanations as being a form of reductionism that in the present state of psychological science is fruitless and unnecessary. This view was not shared by Thorndike or by Pavlov, or even by behaviorism's staunchest early advocate, J. B. Watson. It should be noted that many experimental psychologists who disagree with Skinner's views about the place of explanation in behavioral science nevertheless use the procedures and methods he has developed, such as his "operant conditioning" techniques.

Applications of Skinner's Findings to Human Learning

Like Thorndike, after Skinner had undertaken early in life a large body of experimental research on animals, described in *The Behavior of Organisms,* published in 1938), he devoted considerable energy to developing applications and extensions of his research to human learning. For Skinner there has not been any insurmountable problem about extending the findings of animal behavior experiments to man (Boakes and Halliday, 1970). Skinner and his followers have not been deeply interested in animal learning in the sense that learning serves functions in the life of the particular organism participating in the experiment. The aims have been to identify relationships between responses and environmental events and to derive laws about general learning processes that apply to a number of species. However, recent research has indicated that there are severe restrictions on the degree to which it is feasible to consider that such general laws may operate (see Chapter 4). Doubts have been cast upon the wisdom of drawing directly upon observations of animal behavior as a basis for making pronouncements about human learning.

Skinner has written a novel, *Walden Two,* concerning a utopian community which provides a setting for propounding the viewpoint that conditioned associations form a basis for mature human abilities. He has also produced an account of language acquisition (Skinner, 1957), and he has applied the principle of reinforcement to the shaping and controlling of behavior in animals and humans. A variety of practical applications have been introduced in the field of education. Skinner promoted the use of teaching machines and programed learning, in which learners are frequently tested as they attempt to acquire new knowledge or skills, and their responses are followed by reinforcing consequences. In the fields of mental disorder and mental retardation, ways of modifying inappropriate behaviors have been developed. Skinner's name appears repeatedly in future chapters, since he has been influential in several areas of concern in which efforts have been made to use the data and techniques of research into animal behavior to help solve practical human problems. His work has been criticized on a number of counts, but it cannot be denied that Skinner's approach has led to developments having distinct practical value in the modern world.

PAVLOV AND WATSON

Both Thorndike and Skinner considered that the consequences of behavior, as indicated in Thorndike's Law of Effect and in Skinner's account of reinforcement, are centrally involved in learning. Other theorists have inclined toward the view, which was also implicit in much that was written within the older associationist tradition, that contiguity provides the fundamental principle for learning. Reinforcing events are regarded as being crucial only insofar as they either provide instances of contiguity or bring about conditions which include repeatedly contiguous events. Such a view has been endorsed by a number of twentieth-century theorists, and it was largely accepted by two individuals who between them exerted an extremely powerful influence on the psychology of learning, Ivan Pavlov and J. B. Watson.

Conditioning

From about 1912 J. B. Watson was energetically advocating that psychologists should accept a strongly behaviorist position, which would exclude all references to mental states and take the form of a science of behavior alone. Thorndike's work on animal behavior was considered by Watson to include descriptions that were unacceptably subjective. Watson considered, for example, that the place given in the Law of Effect to satisfying states of affairs would be better filled by objectively measurable phenomena. He was anxious to introduce acceptably objective methods of studying behavior, and his interest was attracted by a description of research inspired by Pavlov, involving a kind of learning later to be known as *classical conditioning*, in which dogs were induced to make an automatic response to stimuli that had not previously elicited a reaction.

The experiments that first attracted Watson's attention were undertaken by a colleague of Pavlov named Bechterev, who was interested in using conditioning techniques to study human learning. Watson immediately recognized that Pavlov's work provided an approach to learning that obeyed the constraints imposed by a strictly behaviorist position, and Watson's vigorous publicizing efforts lead to wide acceptance of the concept of conditioning in psychological research. Pavlovian conditioning involves the establishment of a connection or bond, through which an environmental stimulus comes to elicit a response by the organism. American psychologists came to regard the *stimulus-response* (or S-R) *pairs* established by conditioning as forming units of behavior. The S-R bond became for some time an essential part of the descriptive language of behaviorist psychology.

It is easy to see the appeal of Pavlovian conditioning for Watson and like-minded psychologists. The typical experimental situation is simple, with conditioning being achieved by pairing, on a number of occasions, a new (to be conditioned) stimulus with an unconditioned stimulus that already elicits a measurable response by the subject. Eventually, provided that a number of procedural details are followed, the new stimulus evokes the response that was previously elicited only by the unconditioned stimulus. A fuller account will be given in Chapter 3. For the present, an important consideration is that classical conditioning provided a way of examining simple learned changes that might form element of complex forms of learning. The study of conditioning requires neither introspection nor reference to inner states or feelings, the necessary components being observable stimulus events and observable responses. By testing the effects of measurable parameters, such as the intensity, duration, and other physical qualities of a stimulus, it appeared possible to acquire a body of detailed knowledge that would serve as a starting point for scientific laws about varied kinds of learned behavior.

Classical Conditioning and Human Learning

In some respects, research into Pavlovian conditioning has met Watson's expectations. But the applicability of classical conditioning principles to human learning is not unlimited. For example, they do not shed much light on the kinds of learned changes that are involved in the learning of entirely new behaviors. Classical conditioning principles are clearly relevant to those situations in which learned changes occur in the circumstances that serve to elicit a given reaction. Such learning would be important for and animal to gain the ability to respond appropriately to poisonous plants and to other events that signify danger. However, there do not appear to be many applications of classical conditioning research to the kinds of learning that produce new or modified actions. For studying learned changes in active behavior, the techniques developed by Thorndike and Skinner are more useful. They use what is now known as *operant conditioning* or *instrumental conditioning*.

Pavlovian conditioning, (more commonly called classical conditioning), enables an animal or a person to learn about the circumstances in which it is appropriate to make previously established responses, and learning of this kind is valuable for the adaptive capacities of higher animals. However, this type of conditioning is probably of greater significance for other mammals, such as Pavlov's dogs, than for humans. It could be argued that Watson's advocacy of Pavlov's approach encouraged experimental psychologists to direct their interest in learning processes to forms of learning that are relatively unimportant for acquiring advanced human abilities. However, the phenomena observed in studies of operant-conditioning do clearly relate to the direct effects of the organism's actions upon the environment, and operant behavior is prominent in humans.

Nevertheless, the forms of conditioning described by Pavlov do occur in humans, and a good deal of research on classical conditioning in infants has been undertaken. In *behavior therapy,* techniques based upon classical conditioning methods have been introduced to deal with phobic behaviors and other problems of human adjustment. Watson himself, who repeatedly stated his belief in the practical value of animal conditioning research for helping to solve human problems, was no more reticent than Thorndike and Skinner to suggest implications of animal learning findings for human learning. Like Skinner, he was confident that developments in experimental psychology along behaviorist lines would make it possible to predict and control human behavior.

Almost as soon as Watson had read Bechterev's account of conditioning, he began to work out a new approach to psychopathology in which human maladjustment was perceived as being the end product of faulty conditioning. He followed up his speculations with experimental research designed to investigate conditioning in the human infant. For Watson, the term conditioning covered a wide range of phenomena. The procedure of Watson's famous experiment in which conditioned emotional reactions were acquired by a young child named Albert did not strictly adhere to the form of Pavlovian conditioning methods. Indeed, Pavlov's name was not even mentioned in the original report (Watson and Rayner, 1920).

Albert was an 11-month-old boy described as stolid, unemotional, and "one of the best developed youngsters ever brought to the hospital" where the experiment was performed. Watson and Rayner demonstrated that when objects such as a white rat were presented on a number of occasions simultaneously with an unpleasant loud noise, the child's startled and frightened response to the noise was subsequently elicited by presentation of the objects on their own although they had not previously produced any sign of fear in the child. The results of this grotesque experiment left little doubt in Watson's mind that emotional responses to a variety of objects can be acquired through procedures that made use of conditioning. He noted that the responses continued to occur for over a month and suggested that they might persist and modify personality throughout life.

Watson claimed that many of the phobic disorders encountered in psychopathology are actually conditioned emotional reactions that have been acquired directly or through transfer. He took pains to emphasize the differences between his explanation of phobic disorders and those offered by psychoanalysts. He jestingly suggested that had an analyst observed the fearful reaction to a sealskin coat of the child who had participated in Watson's experiment, the analyst's approach would be "to tease from him the recital of a dream which upon their analysis will show that Albert at 3 years of age attempted to play with the pubic hair of the mother and was scolded for it" (Watson and Rayner, 1920, p. 112).

Hull's Attempt at a Comprehensive Behavior Therapy

Whereas Skinner and the early behaviorists took the view that research into animal behavior had relevance for human learning and wrote at considerable length about practical aspects of human learning, later behaviorists have given less emphasis to human applications. In part, the divergence between animal psychology and human learning has reflected increasing awareness of the magnitude of species differences in learning, and of the risk of making erroneous extrapolations. Equally important was the movement toward comprehensive theories of animal behavior, such as that of Clark Hull (1943).

Behavioral scientists in the middle of the century directed considerable energy to testing aspects of Hull's theories or those of his rivals. Hull's approach was more theoretical and made a stronger attempt to be comprehensive than that of his predecessors. Whereas Skinner argued that broad theories in experimental psychology are unlikely to be useful at the present stage, and the theories of neither Thorndike nor Watson and his successors were worked out in great detail, Hull's theory was more detailed, more comprehansive, and more ambitious. It was the product of a time of considerable optimism in experimental psychology.

Hull did undertake some experimental research in human psychology and it was intended that his theoretical system should have relevance to humans. Some attention is given to behaviors that are uniquely human. For example, "Theorem 133" refers to voluntary social acts, and states that "every voluntary social interaction, in order to be repeated consistently, must result in a substantial reinforcement to the activity of each party to the interaction" (Hull, 1952). Hull was also interested in concept learning, and some of his students were encouraged to investigate learning in humans. However, Hull's theory is essentially about animal behavior, and during the period in which it captured the interest of researchers, human learning tended to be left in the cold, outside the mainstream of experimental research.

THE STIMULUS-RESPONSE APPROACH

Watson urged that conditioning be accepted as forming the basis of learning and higher mental processes in humans as well as in lower mammals. He succeeded in gaining widespread acceptance for stimulus-response pairs as fundamental units in the analysis of learned behavior. The notion that one can regard behavior as consisting of a series of responses to external or internal stimulus events was widely accepted among experimental psychologists. It became customary to describe all behavior in terms of stimulus-response units. In research into verbal learning, for example, words and nonsense syllables have often been called *stimulus items* or *response items* in tasks that involve associative learning of lists of item pairs (following the procedure devised in 1894 by Mary Calkins) the terms "stimulus" and "response" were customarily attached to the two verbal items forming each pair. These words are even used in modern research that follows information-processing approaches to learning and cognition, although scientists using such approaches accept few of Watson's views.

The concept of an S-R unit offered a number of attractions to behaviorist psychologists. First, it appears to provide an excellent unit for behavioral analysis and forms a possible building block for complex forms of behavior. For an analytic approach to complex behavior to be possible, it is clearly necessary to reduce phenomena to simple units. Second, the S-R link seems to imply a relationship that is causal and deterministic. It is better to be able to state that event *A* causes event *B*, and possibly to build a body of scientific knowledge from chains of such cause-and-effect links, than merely to know that the two events are somehow related. Making use of the S-R link as a basic unit of behavioral science thus appears to lead to explanation of behavior in terms of causal factors analogous to those that operate in a mechanical system. A third advantage of invoking S-R bonds is that the contact between individuals and their environment is thereby emphasized. The learner can be seen to be not just *in* the world but responding *to* it. A fourth attraction of the S-R unit is that it gives rise to simple explanations and quantitative predictions. J. B. Watson stated that when a stimulus and a response occur together, the connection between them is strengthened to an extent depending primarily upon the frequency with which the stimulus and the response occur together. He thought that the neurological outcome of stimulus-response pairing was to lower thresholds or strengthen existing connections, rather than to form completely new bonds. Finally, an S-R approach deals primarily with observable entities, and one does not have to be a strict behaviorist to appreciate the advantages of this.

Limitations of S-R Approaches

It is now clear that attempts at behavioral analysis based upon S-R units encounter a number of problems. The view that straightforward cause-and-effect relationships exist between environmental stimuli and human responses receives little support. The S-R concept over-simplifies the nature of the relationships between people and the environment on which their life depends, and it implies that there is a clear separation between individuals and their environment. Actually, it is more accurate to regard the learner as being intertwined with the outside world, interchanges taking the form of close "give-and-take" events. The learner's role is a highly active one; far from simply "responding" to the stimuli of an active environment, the organism engages in "stimulus-seeking" and searches for variety and change in order to maintain an optimum state of arousal. The spontaneous, self-organizing and largely self-directed qualities of much behavior, especially in higher species such as humans, make a simple stimulus-response description generally inadequate as a way of conceptualizing the relationship between human learners and their world.

Moreover, it is not true that each measurable response can be tied to an identifiable external stimulus. We cannot assume that a stimulus which leads to a response necessarily causes that response, except in the limited sense that operating a switch may cause an electric motor to operate. While an external stimulus may indeed initiate a sequence of behavior, the nature of the behavior may be not at all predictable from knowledge of the stimulus alone.

Behaviorist theorists recognized this problem from the outset, and devoted much ingenuity to attempting to overcome it. To analyse in S-R terms any circumstances in which mental functions mediate between events in the environment and a learner's responses, it has been necessary to postulate "covert" S-R connections that involve unobservable, hypothetical stimuli and unobservable responses. But to do so introduces serious problems. First, unless one is very careful to include only those unobserved (and therefore hypothetical) stimuli or responses that are directly linked to ones that *are* observable, the account takes on elements of the subjectivity that behaviorists were at pains to avoid. Since it is probably impossible to account for behavior that depends on reasoning without admitting the need for mental processes that are not directly linked to observable events, S-R theorists find themselves in something of a cul-de-sac.

Strenuous efforts have been made to overcome such difficulties, but doing so is only made possible by flouting some of the limitations on the admissibility of data that are essential for a behaviorist approach. Furthermore, the very notion of a stimulus is not so objective as it appears to be. When an animal makes a response to a stimulus, the effective stimulus cannot be defined purely in terms of physical qualities; it is a stimulus *as perceived* (and hence coded) *by* the animal. And if mental processes enter into determining the effective stimulus, there must be doubt whether a behaviorist approach can ever be totally objective.

Observations and Inferences

As we have seen, behaviorist theorists were sometimes willing to depart from strictly observable data and to discuss inferred or hypothesized processes in order to account for otherwise inexplicable behavior. It was common to restrict the form of such inferred processes to ones which closely parallel what can be observed. Interactions between the organism and the environment could be regarded as forming links between stimuli and responses.

Inferred inner processes were likewise described as stimulus-response links, which combine in chains. Such a stimulus-response, or S-R, approach has often been followed in experimental psychology, and it has certain merits. On the one hand, a willingness to break away from rigid adherence to observable behavior as the sole data to be considered can bring about increased explanatory power. On the other hand, there is much to recommend the cautious approach to inference-making, an approach which limits or restricts the kinds of unobservable events that are postulated. This is especially apparent when one surveys the morass of unverifiable theories inhabiting some of the wilder shores of psychology. Scientific verification is virtually prohibited by a profusion of inferred constructs, including id, ego, animus, persona, shadow, self, and a host of others.

BEHAVIORISM TODAY

Most experimental psychologists today would agree that some of the procedures advocated by the behaviorist movement are necessary for sound experimental science. Stress upon objectivity, careful measurement, precise definition of concepts, and careful description of procedures are all seen as being essential for a scientific approach. One needs reliable and replicable findings in order to test theories and ideas, to deduce laws and principles, and gradually build up a body of knowledge about the causes of psychological phenomena. However, some of the rules stipulated by early behaviorists have become too restricting for modern psychology. The refusal to admit inferences about what cannot be observed is a particularly strong brake on progress. Overwhelming evidence exists that human behavior is strongly influenced by mental activities that cannot be directly observed. A science of behavior in which it is not permitted to make any deducations about the form of those unobservable processes cannot advance very far. On the other hand, it may yield some valuable practical generalizations about the behavioral consequences of certain environmental events, as can be found in applications of behavior modification techniques, for instance.

Certainly when scientists make do deductions and inferences about mechanisms that are not observed directly, it is all too easy to give way to unrestrained speculation and to postulate hypothetical mental processes that are not firmly based on reality. Some of the models and systems that have been devised to account for human behavior are based upon little firm evidence and are largely untestable. We cannot afford to ignore caution when speculating about the nature of learning processes. However, despite the dangers, psychology has for many researchers returned to being the "science of mental life" that it was for William James in 1890, and that it clearly was not in the 40 years following 1910. Once we accept that human encounters with the environment are not just matters of being stimulated by stimuli and responding to them, and that self-regulated activities are involved in learning, a departure from the strict tenets of early behaviorist traditions becomes inevitable. Little advantage is to be gained from proceeding as if *all* mental processes take the form of inner stimulus-response bonds. If an attempt to explain human learning is to include inferences about things that cannot be directly observed, it is surely necessary for the inferred mental processes to have properties that could account for learning.

Such a strategy is followed by modern cognitive psychologists. To anticipate the arguments in favor of information-processing approaches to human learning, important higher mental processes in learning must involve functions such as storage, retrieval, coding, and organization. These cannot be reduced to simple links or connections between stimulus and response events. Nevertheless, we should not deny the importance behaviorist approaches and S-R analyses have had for the advances in the experimental psychology of learning that have been made in the twentieth century. Some of the contributions made by experimenters in the S-R tradition will be encourntered in later chapters.

COGNITION AND LEARNING: THE RETURN TO MENTAL LIFE

Most psychologists today would agree that in order for humans to learn, they must engage in some of the active mental processes we have hinted at. Each learner needs to possess adaptable systems for retaining information, with facilities for storage and retrieval, and for relating new information to existing knowledge. As Newell remarks, "the psychological mechanisms are there, confronting us. If we are ingenious enough they will yield up their secrets . . . to believe that we should proceed only with descriptions of regularities (in behavior) and avoid any attempt to see in them the processing that is involved, seems to me almost a failure of nerve" (Newell, 1967, p. 252).

Newell's statement pinpoints a reason for the widespread agreement among contemporary experimental psychologists that mental life cannot be excluded from scientific psychology. They share a belief in the value of trying to discover the nature of the mental processes that underlie human performance. Noam Chomsky (1972) has written that behaviorism imposes "intellectual shackles" which no physical scientist would be willing to accept. While the emphasis on objectivity in a behaviorist approach is entirely acceptable, the restraint of limiting inferences about mental processes to S-R units may preclude accounting adequately for the richness of human abilities. Also, the approach of the early behaviorists involves a view of man as being less independent and more dominated by the external environment than is really the case. Over the years a number of researchers have been unwilling to accept that psychology should only be the science of behavior on which J. B. Watson insisted. They have turned again to cognitive approaches aimed at providing a scientific account of mental activities.

Cognitive approaches have never been entirely absent from recent psychology. Indeed, the best-known psychological theory of our century, psychoanalysis, is essentially a cognitive one. However, not until the 1950s did cognitive approaches that involved the experimental study of learning, memory, and human performance cease to be overshadowed by behaviorist views.

Early Views on Cognition

Some features of cognitive psychology can be traced at least as far back as the work of the philosopher J. F. Herbart (1776–1841). He explained that the manner in which we receive information from the world is strongly influenced by the existing contents of our minds. These form what Herbart called an *apperceiving mass,* containing the conceptions and the stock of ideas determining what each individual does when exposed to new experiences. William Blake's statement, "The fool sees not the tree the wise man sees" might be regarded as a succinct summary of this view. Herbart added that in admitting new experience we disturb as little as possible of our existing stock of ideas. As if hating to accept anything that is absolutely new, mental processes assimilate the new and unfamiliar to what is already familiar and, by assimilating, absorb it.

For Herbart, the cognitive structures that he regarded as having a powerful influence upon perceptions and the acquisition of new ideas were thought to be formed along essentially associationist principles, with the apperceptive mass being an outcome of the association of ideas. Such a belief in the associationist nature of cognitive processes was shared by William James, who claimed that the human mind is essentially an associating machine. James suggested that active mental processing can act upon the materials already in a person's consciousness and make connections with new external impressions we receive. In this manner, he argued "it is the fate of every impression thus to fall into a mind preoccupied with memories, ideas and interests, and by these it is taken in (W. James, *Talks to Teachers,* 1903 edition, p. 158).

As we indicated earlier, a cognitive system confined to principles of simple associationism would have difficulty explaining phenomena such as the organizational abilities implied in Thorndike's principle of belongingness, according to which connections are more easily acquired if the response belongs in the situation. The notion that the human mind has active organizing functions is encountered in a number of early twentieth-century works, some of the more noteworthy being a body of studies within the sphere of influence of "gestalt" theories of form.

Frederick Bartlett's book *Remembering* (1932) also helped to demonstrate the importance of learners' constructive mental activities. In a series of experiments, Bartlett demonstrated that meaningful information is not assimilated in a passive manner. Rather, individuals engage in constructive processes that involve an "effort after meaning" and they search for ways of integrating the new data into their existing structure of knowledge. Bartlett considered that when learners attempted to relate new material to their existing "frame of reference," the new information might be represented in memory in a modified or distorted manner. New inputs to the long-term memory system would retain only those characteristics that could be readily assimilated to the learners' background of past experience.

Cognition in Behaviorist Theories: Tolman's Approach

Even in the heyday of behaviorist psychology cognitive voices were not entirely absent. Hull's theory, with its multiplicity of unobservable inferred processes, inevitably took on some aspects of a cognitive approach. As it became apparent to later behaviorists that intervening processes would have to play a larger part in psychological theories of behavior, and that elements not directly determined by observable stimulus events could not be altogether excluded, a distinction between two kinds of intermediaries was introduced. The term *intervening variable* was adopted for concepts introduced to describe functional relationships. Intervening variables were to have no surplus meanings, that is, implied properties other than those made explicit in the relationship between observables. An example is the constant g, introduced to describe the acceleration of a free-falling body. *Hypothetical constructs,* by contrast, took the form of inferred intervening processes that were less tied to a specific function, having properties of their own and, potentially, a wider range of explanatory powers. Hunger, anger, and discomfort are examples of hypothetical constructs.

Within the behaviorist tradition of research into animal behavior, one psychologist, E. C. Tolman, advanced a theoretical position that was markedly cognitive in content and placed as much emphasis on the purposive nature of behavior as upon stimulus-response connections (see, for example, Tolman, 1932). For Tolman, the function of a reward was not to strengthen a S-R link directly but to influence the learner's knowledge of "means-ends relationships." The individual was said to acquire dispositions such as expectancies and beliefs. Learning was regarded as inducing knowledge about relationships rather than specific response patterns. As a result of experience, an organism formulates provisional expectancies or hypotheses, and interprets events accordingly.

Tolman was not convinced that the S-R unit formed an especially valuable basic unit of behavior. In place of such a "molecular" approach, whereby the investigation of phenomena commenced by detecting their smallest elements, he preferred a "molar" approach that attempted to explain behavior in terms of observable properties. By analogy, he pointed out that understanding the properties of water is not necessarily best achieved by considering it only in terms of the hydrogen and oxygen molecules that form its constituents, since doing so may leave us uninformed about important physical properties.

In some respects Tolman's impact was a constructively negative one: he did not produce an ambitious and closely integrated theory comparable to Hull's, nor did he make a great contribution to detailed empirical knowledge about learning. But he performed an important service in making apparent some of the limitations of S-R approaches, and in demonstrating the adaptiveness, flexibility, and the planning capacity that underlies behavior, even in lower mammals. By showing that it would be difficult for animal behaviorists to proceed far while ignoring animal cognition, he helped to produce a climate in which cognitive views received some attention.

Problems Encountered in Verbal Learning Research

By around 1950 it was apparent to many psychologists investigating human learning that cognitive approaches were necessary. However, research into verbal processes was being advanced along lines that were strictly behaviorist and broadly in accordance with an S-R associationist perspective. The research that was accomplished (much of which was summarized by McGeoch and Irion, 1952) demonstrates considerable powers of ingenuity in defining apparently cognitive and subjective concepts in acceptably objective terms. For example, the meaningfulness of a word was operationally defined in terms of the number of associated words it evoked.

Verbal learning research in the behaviorist mold flourished until the 1960s and is by no means dormant. The present writer's view is that its real contribution to our understanding of human learning is less than the amount of published research might lead us to expect. Verbal learning research has encountered a number of problems that some psychologists consider to be insuperable unless cognitive approaches are adopted. Research on issues raised by some of these problems will be discussed in later chapters, but at this point we can briefly note three difficulties that proved particularly troublesome. First, an attempt by Skinner (1957) to explain language acquisition in terms of a behaviorist account of learning was widely considered to be somewhat unsuccessful. A critique by Chomsky (1959) argued that the kind of approach Skinner had adopted could not be fruitful for investigating language abilities in man. Second, results obtained by researchers who had conducted experiments into the function of organization and grouping phenomena in verbal performance (for instance Bousfield, 1953, and Miller, 1956) confirmed the importance of the organizational phenomena for which Thorndike had advanced the belongingness principle. These results gave further evidence of the inadequacy of simple associationist accounts. (Chapter 10 discusses the functions of organization in human learning.) Finally, just as some S-R animal behavior theorists faced the dilemma of having to introduce hypothetical S-R links that became less and less directly connected to observable events, verbal learning theorists of the 1950s found themselves introducing increasingly numerous and complex chains of mediating links in order to try to account for human behavior. They encountered most of the disadvantages and few of the advantages of an overtly cognitive approach. These and other difficulties provided conditions which have encouraged the recent growth of an alternative tradition, one in which the mental processing underlying cognition has been a major object of interest.

HUMAN LEARNING AND CONTEMPORARY COGNITIVE PSYCHOLOGY

Modern cognitive theories and models have been influenced by some developments that took place around the time of the Second World War. Advances in theories about complex communications systems provided one such influence. For instance, C. E. Shannon conceived of language comprehension as involving human learners using knowledge that they already possess, in order to deal with an incoming sequence of words. Related progress in *information theory,* in which complex systems are analyzed in terms of the flow of information to and between their parts, was also received with enthusiasm. Some psychologists were attracted to the idea of regarding the brain as a highly complex information processor, in which many activities have the function of processing and transmitting data from environmental stimuli and within the system. A measure of the amount of information transmitted by the brain could be obtained by assessing the extent to which information flowing through the system "reduced uncertainty" for the receiver by communicating knowledge about events.

Quantitative measures of information processing were seen as having value for a range of problems in the psychology of cognition. Such measures have been widely used in research into reaction times, selective attention, choice and decision making, and into recall and comprehension of prose text. In the latter case, ways of estimating amounts of information transmitted were developed, such as the "approximation-to-English" method to be described in Chapter 11. The idea that cognitive abilities involve the processing and flow of information in the brain lends itself to representation by flow diagrams and visual "models" in which hypothesized mental processes can be schematically represented. Figure 2.1 shows one such model. It illustrates information flow in humans, and it is taken from *Perception and Communication* (Broadbent, 1958), an influential book in which a variety of concepts from communications sciences and information theory were applied to human performance. The model illustrated in Figure 2.1 indicates that data is received by the senses and transmitted to a "short-term store." Subsequently, the model suggests, the data may be retained in a more permanent store or be used to influence the individual's actions.

Cybernetics, the branch of science that is concerned with control and self-regulation of complex systems, has provided another source of concepts and ideas for recent cognitive psychology. Knowledge of self-regulating mechanisms has been available for many years. Servomechanisms were extensively used in nineteenth-century engineering, and in 1932, W. B. Cannon's *The Wisdom of the Body* demonstrated that the human body makes extensive use of feedback control systems. The period of the Second World War saw major advances in the use of self-guiding feedback loop systems for military purposes, and a number of psychologists found it useful to think of human cognitive activities as a self-regulating system controlled to some extent by feedback mechanisms. The feedback loop receives special emphasis in Mil-

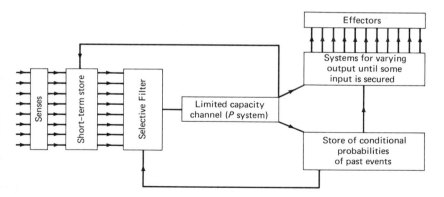

Figure 2.1   A tentative information flow diagram for the human organism. (Source: Broadbent, D. E. *Perception and Communication,* 1958. Reprinted by permission of Pergamon Press Ltd.)

ler, Galanter and Pribram's *Plans and the Structure of Behavior* (1960), in which a simple feedback control sequence forms a unit for the analysis of controlled behavior that partly filled the role of S-R units in the older behaviorist tradition. However, while it is now accepted that control mechanisms must play an important function in human cognitive processes, only a few researchers (e.g., Cunningham, 1972) have made extensive use of the feedback control unit as a basic mechanism in cognitive processing.

For recent cognitive psychologists studying human memory and learning, computer technology has been an important source of analogies and hints about the possible forms and functions of the processes underlying human cognition. Computers are required, as are brains, to store large amounts of information, and they have to function as artificial memory systems. Computers can also be made to perform some of the operations necessary for intelligent human behavior. An outcome of the development of computer systems with very large processing and storage capacities has been to show that human cognitive systems need to perform certain complex functions. For instance, in work on computer design it became clear that when large amounts of information need to be stored it is essential to include procedures insuring that the stored contents are readily accessible. The sheer volume of memory capacity is by no means the sole constraint on the power of an artificial memory. Knowing this has helped psychologists to realize the need for human memory to possess effective input and output mechanisms, and to retain stored information in an organized manner to facilitate gaining access to it.

The science of psychology continues to change, not only through acquiring new data and facts that increase our knowledge, but also by altering its methods, approaches, and some fundamental assumptions about aims and goals. As Kuhn (1962) has made clear, this state of affairs is by no means rare in science, nor is it restricted to the earliest periods of growth.

SUMMARY

1. Throughout the centuries there have been many attempts by philosophers to understand the nature of learning, and a number of scholars have advanced theories in which a central role is given to the formation of associations as basic elements of learning.

2. Hermann Ebbinghaus combined an associationist viewpoint with the adoption of experimental methods. In an ambitious series of investigations, he applied the methods of the natural sciences to the investigation of the psychological phenomena of human learning and retention.

3. At the beginning of the present century, the limited success of approaches to psychology that were based upon attempts to analyze conscious thought processes led many psychologists to accept that their goal should be to create a science of observed behavior, in which hypothesized mental processes had no place.
4. On the basis of research into animal learning, a number of laws and principles of learning were derived, and these were intended to apply to learning in humans. E. L. Thorndike and B. F. Skinner used the findings of animal learning studies for a number of statements about human learning, and they developed methods for investigating learning which continue to influence modern research.
5. The acceptance of behaviorist views was strongly advocated by J. B. Watson. He considered the classical conditioning method, developed by the Russian physiologist I. Pavlov, to offer a means for investigating learning. There was widespread acceptance of the practice of analyzing instances of learning in terms of relationships between a learner's responses and the environmental events that were thought to elicit them.
6. Some attempts were made to construct comprehensive and large-scale theories of animal learning, but these theories have had relatively little influence on research into human learning.
7. The stimulus-response approach and other aspects of behaviorism have been considered by many modern psychologists to be unduly restricting. In particular, many investigators think that scientific progress in psychology is only possible if we are prepared to try to understand the mental processes underlying learning phenomena. In the past 20 years or so there has been increasing willingness to take account of the mental processes that contribute to human cognition, and to derive and test theories about the form of such processes.
8. Nineteenth-century approaches to the understanding of mental activities were based on the assumption that such activities can be discovered by analysis of conscious thought. Modern cognitive psychologists appreciate that encoding precludes our being aware of our cognitive processes, and have introduced concepts from the study of communications theory, from developments in computer processing, and from studies of artificial intelligence.

Suggestions for Further Reading

Kuhn, T. S. (1962) *The Structure of Scientific Revolutions*. Chicago: University of Chicago Press.
Estes, W. K. (1978) "On the organization and core concepts of learning theory and cognitive psychology." In W. K. Estes (ed.), *Handbook of Learning and Cognitive processes*, Vol. VI. Hillsdale, New Jersey: Erlbaum.

CHAPTER 3

Simple Learning and Conditioning

OVERVIEW

Chapter 3 provides a general introduction to experimental research into human learning. The chapter outlines some of the basic procedures used in learning research, describes ways in which experimental methods are used and considers some factors that influence learning. A large number of studies have investigated forms of learned change known as "classical conditioning" and "operant conditioning." A further kind of change, "habituation," is also discussed. The aim of research has been to isolate circumstances of learning that are relatively simple, easily examined, and basic to the acquisition of human abilities. In this chapter we consider some evidence for learning in very young infants. We also investigate the effect of motivational factors that reinforce activities and discuss the role of attention in human learning.

CLASSICAL CONDITIONING IN YOUNG CHILDREN

In this chapter we describe some simple forms of learning and introduce a range of topics that are for various reasons basic to the study of human learning. First, classical and operant conditioning are discussed. Those forms of learning that are known as conditioning have been more extensively examined in experimental research than other kinds of learned change. The chapter will discuss the evidence that different forms of conditioning can occur in young infants. Most forms of learning help the individual to adapt to the demands of the world he inhabits. Classical conditioning contributes to successful adaptation by producing changes in the circumstances that elicit the activities and responses which a person has already acquired.

Classical conditioning was first observed in studies by a Russian physiologist, Ivan Pavlov, who measured salivation in dogs. The alternative terms *respondent conditioning* and *Pavlovian conditioning* have been widely used to describe similar phenomena, the three terms being broadly synonymous. In a typical classical conditioning experiment it is possible to observe the establishment of a simple association. An external stimulus event comes to elicit a response in the learner. The chosen response is not new to the learner but is one that was not previously connected to or elicited by the stimulus event.

Pavlov's experimental procedure provides an illustration of classical conditioning in practice. Conditioning was studied in dogs, and salivation, which Pavlov was able to measure fairly precisely, formed the chosen response. In normal circumstances, when the stimulus of food is presented to a hungry dog, it will salivate. Pavlov's procedure was to pair the presentation of a new neutral stimulus event with presentation of a food stimulus that normally elicits food. The food, which produces a salivation before any conditioning has occurred, functions as an *unconditional stimulus.* Similarly, the dog's salivation response to the food is known as an *unconditioned response.* Presentation of the food is paired on a number of occasions with a new event, typically the sound of a buzzer, and the salivating response continues to occur, presumably induced by the food. The experimenter has previously ascertained that the buzzer on its own is a neutral event which does not lead to the dog salivating.

The next step in the procedure involves presenting the new stimulus on its own, in the absence of the unconditioned food stimulus. When this is done, providing that certain details of timing and procedure are followed, a salivating response may occur. In short, a previously neutral event, the buzzer, has come to elicit a response, salivation, by the animal. Conditioning is now said to have taken place. The previously neutral buzzer stimulus is now regarded as being a *conditioned stimulus,* and the response to the buzzer alone is known as a *conditioned response.*

The classical conditioning procedure provides a demonstration of associative learning, and there has been a good deal of interest in studying classical conditioning in humans. In particular, because it appears to be so simple in form, classical conditioning has seemed to offer a promising approach for studying the earliest manifestations of learning in young infants. If there is a degree of similarity between the forms of human learning that occur at different ages, and if what is learned early in life constitutes the basis for learning in the mature person, we can expect that our discoveries about learning in infants will help us understand the more complex kinds of learning observed later in life. Furthermore, since classical conditioning does not seem to depend much upon previous learning, and does not involve making new responses, procedures based upon classical conditioning avoid some difficulties encountered in investigations of more active forms of learning.

There are a number of ways in which the young child might possibly benefit from associative learning like that observed in experiments on classical conditioning. For example, if a child is repeatedly bitten by a small animal, the sight of the animal might eventually lead to the crying response (which gains the mother's attention) that previously followed the bite. Or, the sight of a bottle of milk may produce the sucking response which initially was delayed until presentation of the nipple. Classical conditioning processes make a major contribution to the autonomic processes associated with bodily functioning, digestion, heart rate, etc. Emotional responses such as fears, anxieties, are also strongly influenced by conditioning. Learned emotional reactions make an important contribution to human personality, although they have attracted relatively little attention in experimental research into human learning. Knowledge about the principles of classical conditioning has made it possible to devise a procedure called *systematic desensitization* for treating human problems that involve debilitating emotional responses to certain situations. In treatment sessions, patients learn to relax in circumstances that previously led to fear or destress.

Early Research into Infant Conditioning

The study of classical conditioning in human infants began as early as 1907, when N. I. Krasnogorski attempted to demonstrate conditioning in 1-year-old children. He used a procedure that was very similar to the one with which Pavlov had studied dogs, measuring salivation as the conditioned response. Krasnogorski was eventually able to demonstrate conditioning in infants aged around 6 months and older, but not in younger infants. However, salivation is not an ideal response to observe and measure in young humans, and it is quite unsuitable for very young infants, since the salivary glands are not fully functional in the first months of life. Later experiments on human conditioning have used responses that are more easily measured.

One of the first infant conditioning experiments outside Russia was conducted in 1931 by Dorothy Marquis, who observed infants during the first nine days of their lives. The conditioning sessions took place at feeding times, and the observed response was sucking, which has often been incorporated in subsequent conditioning studies. To measure sucking, Marquis used a somewhat clumsy device based on a balloon that was fastened under the infant's chin and connected to a recorder. Presentation of a feeding bottle, which elicits sucking by young infants, provided the unconditioned stimulus. The sound of a buzzer was the initially neutral stimulus, and this was paired with presentation of the bottle. Marquis was able to obtain data on eight infants who were observed in a number of experimental sessions that contained between two and five pairings of the buzzer and the presentation of the bottle. The buzzer would be sounded for five seconds, and then the child was given the bottle. Marquis reported that in seven of the eight infants, after the buzzer and bottle had been paired together, sucking movements could be observed whenever the buzzer sounded. It was claimed that conditioning to the buzzer had occurred in these infants.

This early demonstration appeared to prove that simple learning in the form of classical conditioning can be induced in newborn infants. The evidence suggests that the youngest infants are capable of learning, despite the physiologically immature state of the human brain at the time of birth, and encourages us to think that learning may play a part in the infant's life right from the time of birth. However, for a number of reasons, subsequent researchers have been unwilling to accept that this conclusion is inevitable.

One problem is that it is very difficult to undertake experiments on infant learning that are sufficiently controlled to insure that observed changes in the infants' behavior are undoubtedly due to learning rather than other causes. Contributing to the practical difficulties is the fact that infants make rapid and unpredictable changes in their state, from being sleepy and inattentive to being wide awake and active. The experimenter may have to wait until the infant reaches an appropriate state of attentiveness before a learning trial can be commenced. The difficulty does not necessarily end there, since the child may suddenly become drowsy or fretful during the conditioning session. If a changed response is observed, it is hard to know for certain whether the change was due to conditioning or to the child's altered state.

In order to design adequate tests of infant conditioning, it is necessary to include experimental control procedures that make it possible to distinguish between those behavior changes that indicate true conditioning, and any artifacts—that is, changes due to other factors such as the infant's varying state—which may be mistakenly interpreted as evidence of learning. One kind of artifact, *sensitization*, takes the form of an increased responsiveness to a neutral stimulus that is not caused by conditioning but is due to the individual becoming increasingly sensitive to the repeatedly presented stimulus. To insure that any sensitization that occurs is not mistaken for learning, it is necessary to have condition in which the neutral stimulus is repeatedly presented on its own. In order to demonstrate that conditioning has really occurred, an experimenter needs to show that the response to repeated presentations of the neutral stimulus was significantly less than the response to the same stimulus when paired with the unconditioned stimulus.

Another experimental artifact, known as *pseudoconditioning*, can be described as a general increase in sensitivity that results from presenting the unconditioned stimulus. The effect is to make any stimulus more likely to evoke a response than hitherto. In a conditioning experiment an altered responsiveness resulting from a general increase in sensitivity may be mistakenly attributed to new learning, unless an appropriate experimental control condition is included.

The difficulties associated with both keeping the infant subject at an appropriate state of attentiveness and providing adequate controls to insure that it is possible to distinguish between changes produced by learning and those due to artifacts combine to make research into conditioning in young humans a complicated undertaking. Futhermore, some considerations indicate that human conditioning is not necessarily a particularly simple or straightforward type of learning. One problem is that whether conditioning will occur or not occur on a given occasion may be strongly affected by the particular stimulus and the precise response that the experimenter selects. It used to be thought that, providing the infant could perceive the stimulus and produce the response, conditioning would take place, following general principles of learning. It did not seem to matter which particular responses and stimuli were chosen. In fact, this is not the case. Fitzgerald and Brackbill (1976) note that it may be possible to condition response X to stimulus A, as well as response Y to stimulus B, but impossible to condition response X to stimulus B, even when there is no doubt that the infant is capable of perceiving both stimuli and making each of the two responses.

Procedural Issues

In conducting experiments on conditioning in children, it is necessary to attend to certain procedural details that influence the rate of conditioning and the probability of conditioning taking place at all. For instance the time interval between the presentation of the stimulus to be conditioned and onset of the unconditioned stimulus ("inter-stimulus interval") is important. When the gap between the two stimuli is long, it is unlikely that conditioning will occur if events similar to either of them are presented during this period. It is also important that the unconditioned stimulus occurs more often when the stimulus event to be conditioned is present than in its absence. For example, if the unconditioned stimulus of a shock occurs as frequently when a neutral stimulus that the experimenter is attempting to condition is absent as when it is provided, conditioning will not take place. The originally neutral stimulus will not elicit the response (Rescorla, 1968). Also, if the new (to be conditioned) stimulus has been presented to the learner on several occasions prior to the learning session, a larger number of pairings of the neutral and unconditioned stimuli will be necessary in order for conditioning to occur (Estes, 1970). For this reason, if the stimulus to be conditioned was a sound that the learner had previously heard a number of times on the day of the conditioning trials, the sound would not easily become conditioned when it was paired with an unconditioned stimulus.

Despite the various complications, a large number of experimental studies have demonstrated classical conditioning in infants. The events that have been used as unconditioned stimuli have included puffs of air, auditory tones, and a number of other items.

FINDINGS OF EXPERIMENTAL RESEARCH INTO CONDITIONING

To illustrate how modern research on infant conditioning is accomplished, we shall return to the difficulties left unsolved by Marquis' apparent demonstration that newborn infants can be classically conditioned to make sucking movements (the conditioned response) on presentation of a buzzer (the conditioned stimulus). Marquis' procedure and findings present a number of problems. She used a subjective method for scoring the babies' responses, she provided no statistical analysis of her findings, and the actual number of pairings of buzzer and bottle varied widely between subjects, from 100 to 250 occasions. In addition, there were no control procedures to provide a check on the possibility that the responses which apparently indicated conditioning might have been due to the artifact of sensitization. The babies might have become increasingly sensitive to the neutral stimulus (the buzzer) as it was repeatedly presented. Nor can the possibility of pseudoconditioning be ruled out, since repeatedly presenting the bottle might have made the babies more responsive to the buzzer. Another limitation of this pioneer study lies in the fact that the time interval between the sounding of the buzzer and the presentation of the bottle was not carefully controlled, and it might not have been equivalent for all of the infants or for the different experimental sessions in which each child participated. At the time when Dorothy Marquis designed her study, psychologists were not aware of the range of potential experimental artifacts in research of this kind.

L. P. Lipsitt and H. Kaye (Lipsitt and Kaye, 1964; Kaye, 1967) have conducted several studies incorporating precise measures, refined procedures, and careful experimental control procedures in order to determine whether sucking behavior really can be conditioned in very young infants. They studied babies in the first week of life. To check on the possibility that sensitization was the cause of the increased responding observed by Marquis, Lipsitt and Kaye included a control group of young infants for whom the sound of the buzzer was unaccompanied by the bottle. A slight increase in sucking was observed in these infants, but the increase was much smaller than that of the infants who received the full conditioning procedure. One second after the presentation of a tone (the initially neutral stimulus), a nipple (the unconditioned stimulus) was inserted into the baby's mouth. Following four pairings of tone and nipple, the tone was presented alone. At this time infants in the experimental group, who received paired presentations of tone and nipple together, did not respond to the tone when presented on its own more frequently than did the infants in the control group, to whom both tone and nipple had been presented, but not paired together. However, in subsequent trials, when the tone was presented alone, infants from the experimental group did make a larger number of sucking responses, indicating that conditioning had occurred.

In a subsequent study, Kaye (1967) followed the onset of a tone by placing a pacifier in the infant's mouth. The pacifier served as an unconditioned stimulus which elicited a sucking response. The tone commenced one second before presentation of the pacifier, and it was sounded throughout a period of 19 seconds during which the pacifier was present. For infants in the experimental group, tone and pacifier were always paired, while infants in a control group received both stimulus events, but not together. Kaye's findings indicate that conditioning did occur in the infants forming the experimental group; when the buzzer was presented they made many more sucking responses than infants in the control group.

The fact that sucking is a highly organized response in young infants may actually form a complication in some kinds of conditioning research. It is very easily elicited by a number of events, and it is conceivable that by the time of birth sucking may already have been conditioned to certain stimuli (Sameroff, 1972). The fact that different oral stimuli vary in effectiveness in eliciting sucking adds another possible complication.

A number of classical conditioning studies have measured infant responses other than sucking. Some researchers have attempted to condition the *Babkin reflex*, which takes the form of a combined opening of the mouth, or gaping, and turning the head towards the front and raising it, as a reaction to the infant's hands being pressed. Conditioning of the Babkin reflex was first reported by Kaye (1965). The initially neutral stimulus to which he attempted to condition the Babkin response consisted of movement of the infant's arms. Kaye found that after pairing arm movement with the palm-pressing stimulus that forms an unconditioned stimulus, the experimental group made more Babkin responses to arm movement by the experimenter than did a control group who had received palm pressing but no arm movements. A subsequent study by Connolly and Stratton (1969) confirmed this finding, and also demonstrated that the Babkin response could be elicited by an entirely different conditioned stimulus, in the form of an auditory tone. However, Sameroff (1972) had raised doubts about these findings. He noted the absence of a control group in which both unconditioned and conditioned stimuli were presented, but not paired. The results of a further experiment by Sostek, Sameroff and Sostek (1972), which included three different control groups, careful baseline measurement of the infants' initial responses, and systematic observations of the infants' state, provided no evidence of conditioning.

It is clear that attempts to replicate conditioning studies sometimes produce contradictory results. Earlier findings apparently indicating conditioning are not always replicated in further studies that include more refined control procedures. This problem indicates that care is required in interpreting the experimental results.

Extinction

The procedure used to determine whether or not a response has become conditioned involves observing the effects of presenting the initially neutral (unconditioned) stimulus on its own, on a number of occasions. This provides a measure of *extinction*, which can be defined as a weakening of behavior that occurs as a result of repeatedly presenting of the conditioned stimulus alone, without the unconditioned stimulus. Extinction of conditioned emotional responses can be observed in everyday life. For instance, in a child who has acquired a conditioned fear of spiders the fearful response may extinguish after the child sees spiders on a number of occasions in innocuous circumstances. The resistance of a conditioned response to extinction is related to the number of occasions on which the conditioned stimulus and the unconditioned stimulus have been paired. The greater the number of such pairings, the larger the number of times the conditioned stimulus can be presented alone before extinction is complete. The rate of extinction is influenced by a large number of factors: for instance, in many species, spacing the test trials apart tends to increase the length of time it takes for a response to become extinguished.

Stimulus Generalization

When conditioning has taken place, an event that is very similar to the conditioned stimulus is likely to elicit a reaction that is similar to the conditioned response. The greater the similarity between the two stimuli, the larger the response. For instance, in the experiment by Watson and Rayner that was described in the previous chapter, when the child acquired a conditioned fear response to the appearance of a white rat, the response generalized to similar objects. When the child was shown a white rabbit he cried and avoided the animal, and he reacted similarly to a dog and to other objects such as a fur coat. On the other hand, a certain amount of discrimination occurred; thus the child did not cry when shown toy blocks. Evidence from classical conditioning experiments indicates that as the number of pairings between conditioned stimulus and unconditioned stimulus increases, the learner becomes more likely to discriminate between the conditioned stimulus and similar items, responding selectively to the former.

DOES CONDITIONING TAKE PLACE IN NEWBORNS?

Despite the many procedural difficulties involved in undertaking infant conditioning studies, and the difficulty in replicating some findings, there is firm evidence that conditioning can take place in young infants. But interpreting findings concerning the possibility of conditioning in newborns presents some special difficulties. While some researchers agree that newborns (and possibly infants before birth) are probably conditionable, there continues to be controversy concerning whether particular studies provide definite evidence of conditioning. Sameroff (1972) has pointed out that the newborn infant is more complicated in his functioning than many psychologists have believed. He says that it is naive to expect learning in infants to be necessarily simpler or easier to understand than learning in mature individuals, and he also notes that it is wrong to think of infancy as the beginning of life. It is more accurately regarded as a transition, in which the infant changes from a state in which physiological modes of functioning are predominant to one in which psychological factors become important. For Sameroff, birth is a "transition from an existence where space and time are for the most part irrelevant to the organism's immediate adaptation to his interuterine environment to an existence where the spacial and temporal extensions of psychological experience become crucial to adaptive functioning" (Sameroff, 1972, p. 209). From the time of birth, functioning becomes psychological as well as biological. As the infant begins to be conscious and awake, his transactions with his environment start to be extended from the material to include communication of various forms of information.

   The physical immaturity of the newborn contributes to the difficulty of observing whatever kinds of conditioning may take place.

Although much of the physiological development of the human brain occurs before birth, maturation of some of the structures involved in higher mental functioning lags behind the rest. Transmission of information within the brain is influenced by a process known as *myelinization*. Through myelinization, part of the nerves become covered with a fatty tissue that considerably improves the capacity of the nerves to conduct impulses, and thus to transmit signals. Since not all cerebral neurons are myelinized at the time of birth, some of the processes necessary for normal conditioning may not be fully operative. Of course, perceptual and motor abilities are also very restricted in the newborn, but this does not necessarily add to the difficulty of undertaking conditioning experiments, providing one is sure that the infant does possess the ability to perceive the stimulus information and to make the particular responses being studied. Another problem is that formation of connections between stimuli and responses depends upon the infant having acquired separate control over sensory functioning and motor responses. Sameroff has pointed out that the young infant may not yet have developed separate systems for controlling sensory and motor functions.

A fundamental difficulty in studying conditioning in infants at birth resides in the fact that the changes in activities that can be attributed to learning are not easily separable from those that are caused by unlearned biological mechanisms. This is especially so in the case of newborns. Sameroff (1972) claims that one cannot clearly separate the psychological functioning of an infant from the background of physiological activities that maintain life. Partly because of differences in the rate of physiological maturation of various capacities, the infant at birth is better prepared for conditioning that involves some combinations of responses and stimulus events than others.

There is no cast-iron evidence of classical conditioning in newborns, but as infants become older conditioning becomes increasingly easy to demonstrate (Fitzgerald and Brackbill, 1976). Lintz and Fitzgerald (1966) used an "aversive" conditioning procedure to condition infants aged 33 days and older. An apparatus delivered a puff of air (the unconditioned aversive stimulus) to the infant's eye, causing a blink (the unconditioned response). The initially neutral stimulus was an auditory tone that was presented one second before the onset of a three-second air puff to the right eye. There were 25 trials a day, and on a third of the trials, at random intervals, a buzzer was presented without the air puff. The experimenter observed whether or not the infant blinked. The criterion for deciding whether conditioning had occurred or not was a very stringent one, the infant having to blink on nine out of ten trials. Two experimental control groups were included, making it possible to distinguish between genuine conditioning and experimental artifacts. The main finding was that all the subjects in the experimental group reached the criterion, but none of the control group subjects did. These results provide firm evidence of conditioning in infants aged one month and more.

MIXED FORMS OF CONDITIONING IN INFANTS

Although it is customary to distinguish between classical (or respondent) forms of conditioning on the one hand and operant (or instrumental) conditioning on the other hand, some demonstrations of learning in early life have involved aspects of both these kinds of conditioning. In one such study, a Czech psychologist, Hanus Papousek (1967a), used mixed forms of conditioning to produce learning of a kind that has possible adaptative value in the life of the young child. Demonstrating that a young baby *can* learn something early in life does not prove that such learning normally occurs at this stage, nor that learning plays a major role in the changes that occur in the infant's earliest months. Nevertheless, the knowledge that a certain form of learning is possible for the child at a particular age may give us useful clues. This is particularly so if, as in the study to be described, the procedures used to bring about learning in an experiment are not unlike natural events that occur during the child's normal life. Classical conditioning methods have proved effective for discovering whether young infants are capable of learning, but the mixed form of learning to be described may be more typical of the manner in which early learning actually takes place. The changes observed in research into classical conditioning are in the circumstances that elicit a response. The experiments by Papousek are more similar to studies of operant conditioning, since the babies actual responses were reinforced.

The particular response studied in the present experiment (Papousek, 1967a; Papousek and Bernstein, 1969) was head turning. Infants can turn their heads as soon as they are born, and it is relatively easy to measure head movements by constructing a light, foam-lined framework that is attached to the head so that movements are automatically and reliably recorded. Papousek tested healthy infants who varied in age from around 3 days to 5 months of age. The procedure involved the presentation of an initially neutral (to be conditioned) stimulus, typically a tone, followed by a touch to the infant's cheek. The touch often provides an unconditioned stimulus that elicits head turning. However following the head-turning response the baby was given some nutriment, typically milk, as a reward (and at this point the procedure was more like that of operant conditioning than classical conditioning.)

First, observations were made of the amount of head turning that normally occurred in each child, to provide a baseline measure. The experimenter also sounded a bell behind the infant's head, and noted that the sound on its own did not produce head turning. To commence the experimental trials the bell was sounded for ten seconds. If the infants turned their head (to the left) during this period, they were given milk through a rubber nipple that was connected to a bottle. If the head turn did not occur during the ten second period of the bell, the experimenter tried to elicit a turn by touching the infants' cheek. If this was not successful, the experimenter would turn the infants' head. Following the head turn, the children received milk regardless of whether head turning was accomplished by the children themselves, or elicited by a touch of the cheek, or achieved by the experimenter. Training sessions took place during the morning, with each session consisting of ten trials and lasting about twelve minutes in all. A criterion of about 30 degrees was chosen for successful head turns. Conditioning was said to have taken place if on five of the ten trials forming a single session the infants themselves made five head-turning responses that did not require any help from the experimenter.

Either of two kinds of learning might influence a child's performance in Papousek's study. First (the classical conditioning component), the sound of a bell may become a conditioned stimulus after it has been paired with the touch stimulation that normally elicits head turning. Second, (the operant conditioning component), hungry infants who rotate their head immediately receive milk. The sooner they turn their head, the sooner they are fed.

Five-month-old and 3-month-old infants mastered this learning task without too much trouble. They achieved the criterion (five spontaneous head-turns on ten trials) after an average of 28 and 42 trials respectively. Can newborn infants succeed at this task? The findings show that the infants who were newly born at the beginning of the study did eventually achieve the criterion, but only after a much greater number of trials than the older babies. On average, the 14 newborns required 177 trials. At first the experimenter had to move their heads and then deliver the milk. Learning did eventually occur, but the slowest babies required over a month of daily sessions, by which time they were no longer newborn, strictly speaking. There was great variability within the youngest group, and the fastest baby among them learned the task in only seven days. Further recent research into conditioned head turning has produced a somewhat confusing array of findings, but it now seems most likely that head turning can be conditioned in newborns as well as in older infants (see, for example, Clifton, Siqueland, and Lipsitt, 1972).

OPERANT (INSTRUMENTAL) CONDITIONING

Investigations of operant conditioning provide numerous illustrations showing how the activities of humans and other species can be modified by their consequences. Children learn that some of their voluntary actions lead to predictable consequences. When they coo and gurgle, adults respond with delight; when they move their rattle, it makes a noise. In this way children achieve some control over what happens to them, and they may also acquire the general expectation that they can influence important events in their environment (Schaffer, 1977).

Since operant procedures enable the experimenter to manipulate the learner's actions rather than just change the circumstances that elicit responses, as in classical conditioning, operant researchers can parallel varieties of learned change that have widespread importance in human life. Operant conditioning appears to be especially important in social learning, and procedures based on operant principles are widely used in practical attempts to cure certain behavior disorders and inadequacies. Forms of learning that are based upon, or related to, principles of operant conditioning will be encountered in later chapters more frequently than varieties of learning in which classical conditioning principles are closely involved. As I have already suggested, part of the value of research into classical conditioning lies in demonstrating an associative learning ability that is necessary for forming habits and acquiring knowledge.

The terms "operant conditioning" and "instrumental conditioning" are largely interchangeable in respect to human learning, although some writers (for example, McLaughlin, 1971) make a distinction based on the extent to which the learner's activities are restricted. In instrumental conditioning the range of responses possible for the learner is limited, whereas in operant conditioning procedures the individual's actions are less constrained and a variety of responses may be emitted. In the following pages I will generally adopt the term "operant" when referring to procedures involving systematic reinforcement of behavior. The term "operant" reflects the fact that the behavior *operates* on the environment to produce an effect.

Most of the instances of operant conditioning to be described in the present chapter will concern infants and young children, but operant conditioning is also important for older children and adults. In experiments on operant and instrumental conditioning, reinforcement is provided by the experimenter, whereas in everyday life a child's activities may be reinforced by the mother and other people who interact with the child, and also by objects and events in the natural environment. For instance, the consequences of banging a toy or shaking a rattle may be reinforcing, leading a child to repeat this behavior.

The previously described experiment by Papousek, which contained elements of both classical and operant forms of conditioning, indicated that operant conditioning can occur very early in life. It can readily be observed in everyday human activities. Imagine, for instance, the situation in which babies are rewarded with a kiss by their mother for clapping their hands, and they then proceed to clap their hands with increased frequency. The mother's behavior exerts some control over the child's actions. Notice that this situation differs from ones in which classical conditioning takes place. Operant conditioning normally produces a change in the learner's responses, typically in the rate at which responses are made. Operant behaviors are determined less by preceding stimulus events than by the events that follow each response, that is, the *consequences* of the individual's responses. Generally, if a response is regularly followed by an event that can be broadly described as rewarding to the learner, as is the case when milk or sucrose solution is given to a young infant, the response is likely to be repeated. If the reinforcing event that has regularly followed a response is withdrawn, the response tends to diminish in frequency and may eventually cease. This phenomenon is known as the "extinction" of an operant response, and is analogous to the extinction of classically conditioned responses. To cite an illustration given by Seligman (1975), if you regularly push the elevator button when you reach your office building, and on one particular morning the elevator does not arrive (because it is out of order), you do not go on pushing the button forever. Eventually you give up and climb the stairs.

An event which has the effect of increasing the frequency of a response which it regularly follows is known as a *reinforcer*. The meaning of the word "reinforcement" is similar to that of the word "reward," but not identical. If an event that regularly follows an individual's response leads to that response being made with increased frequency, the event is said to reinforce that response, whether or not it appears to an observer to be rewarding. Conversely, however rewarding something may appear to be, if providing it regularly after an individual's response does *not* increase the frequency of the response, the event cannot be said to reinforce that particular response. Strictly speaking, we should not refer to an event as a reinforcer until we know that it does actually increase the frequency of the response we are concerned with. However, since certain events (providing food, for instance) are known to have widespread effectiveness as reinforcers, they are often described as such at a point when the experimenter has yet to verify their actual effectiveness in a particular situation.

Reinforcers can be classified in several ways. Those response consequences that function as reinforcers because of the nature of each person's inherited biological equipment are known as *primary*, or *unconditioned, reinforcers.* Examples are food, water, and warmth. Events that become reinforcers as a result of the individual's experience are known as *acquired,* or *conditioned, reinforcers.* Praise, money, and approval are acquired reinforcers. If a consequence is known to increase the frequency of a response, it is often known as a *positive reinforcer,* as distinct from a *negative reinforcer.* One definition of a negative reinforcer is an event which reliably decreases the frequency of a preceding response. Just as a positive reinforcer is not always apparently rewarding, events that function as negative reinforcers are not necessarily ones that would strike an observer as being unpleasant or punishing, although some of the most effective negative reinforcers are clearly unpleasant or painful ones, such as shocks, burns, and stimuli that produce nausea. An event can also be described as a negative reinforcer if it serves to increase the frequency of behavior that removes or avoids it, as is often the case with pain and shock.

Both positive and negative reinforcers are defined by reference to their influence on an individual's preceding behavior, and what is reinforcing depends largely upon the individual. Milk is an effective reinforcer for many infant behaviors, but it is much less effective for adults. The desire for social prestige may strongly influence the activities of mature business executives, but not those of their 6-month-old children.

Failure to appreciate that an outcome which reinforces the activities of one person will only be effective as a reinforcer for another person's behavior if the two share certain characteristics has led to a good deal of misunderstanding and confusion. For instance, a number of very effective behavior modification experiments have been carried out on school children of around 7 or 8 years of age, using teacher attention as a reinforcer. It is generally found that if the teacher attends only to actions that are considered appropriate to a peaceful and productive classroom, a variety of disruptive behavior problems are reduced or eliminated. Some teachers have attempted to apply the same procedure in classrooms containing much older children. Finding it generally ineffective, they have concluded that behavior modification procedures are worthless. The most likely explanation of the failure is that the event intended to reinforce behavior—that is, the teacher's attention—is inappropriate for, and does not reinforce, behavior in older children. To devise behavior modification procedures that are effective for older children, it is essential to select events that do reinforce their behavior.

OPERANT CONDITIONING IN INFANTS

Operant conditioning readily occurs in infants, and forms of learning that involve aspects of operant conditioning contribute to the child's acquiring the social habits and the motor skills that emerge during the first year of life. Some of the experimental procedures that have been used to demonstrate infant operant conditioning are fairly similar to ones developed for research into animal behavior by B. F. Skinner, following the earlier work of E. L. Thorndike, and make use of primary reinforcers, such as milk. However, there are important differences in operant conditioning between humans and other species. For example, in research on many animals the delay between the animals' responses and the reinforcing event has to be very small, but humans can withstand much longer delays (Boakes and Halliday, 1970).

It is not easy to establish with absolute certainty if operant conditioning is possible in the very earliest days of life. The difficulties are similar to those encountered in attempting to demonstrate classical conditioning in newborns. Recall that in Papousek's investigation, which contained an element of operant learning, the infants who commenced the experiment in their first week did eventually achieve the criterion of success, but that by the time they did so they were over a month in age. However, the youngest child to meet the criterion was only several days old, so it would appear that at least some infants can be instrumentally conditioned in the first week of life. The associative learning observed in classical conditioning may not be possible immediately after birth, but a degree of operant control over behavior can be achieved at this time (Sameroff, 1972). However, Sameroff notes that to claim a specific operant conditioning process exists at birth implies making an unrealistic assumption about the separability of the newborn's psychological information-processing capacities and his unlearned biological functions for adapting to the physical environment. At birth, the already-existing physiological functions and the newly emerging psychological processes are not so distinct as they subsequently become.

At the time of birth, both classical and operant conditioning are restricted by the fact that the infant is in a stage of transition between a state where physiological forms of functioning are all unimportant and one in which psychological processes become significant. As we found to be true for classical conditioning, the probability that operant conditioning can occur early in the infant's life depends to some extent on the degree of the infant's preparedness with respect to the particular response and the particular reinforcing events involved. Thus, operant procedures are likely to be effective when sucking actions form the responses and food is used as the reinforcer. This is due to the infant's relatively advanced preparedness in respect to feeding.

By around 4 months of age, babies are definitely capable of operant learning. Rovee and Rovee (1969) used an apparatus that caused a colorful mobile to rotate whenever the infants moved their leg. There was a three-minute baseline period, during which the number of naturally occurring leg movements was measured. Then a 15-minute conditioning session followed in which leg movements were immediately succeeded by movement of the mobile (the reinforcing event). In a subsequent five-minute extinction period, leg movements were not reinforced. During the conditioning phase, frequency of leg movements rose to three times the original level. In this session and in the extinction period, the infants maintained a much higher response frequency than infants in a control group who were not reinforced and infants in a second control condition whose mobiles were moved, but without the movement being contingent upon leg activity. In another investigation, infants aged 2 months were successfully conditioned by a procedure in which head movements led to the rotation of a colorful visual display. The children reacted with apparent pleasure to the outcome of their actions, cooing and smiling when the mobile moved. Another finding, reported by Bruner (1970), is that the event of bringing a visual pattern into clear focus can serve to reinforce sucking in infants aged less than 4 months. When the apparatus was arranged so that sucking increased visual clarity, the infants sucked at a high rate, and they sucked at a much reduced rate when the effect was to put the picture out of focus.

Shaping

Operant conditioning procedures can produce other changes in behavior, in addition to increasing the frequency of an existing activity. Alterations in behavior can be induced by the use of procedures similar to those used with animals by B. F. Skinner, who was able to *shape* behavior by selectively reinforcing responses that were, as his experiment proceeded, progressively closer to the desired activities. The use of response-shaping procedures to produce alterations in infants' behavior is illustrated by a study by Etzel and Gewirtz (1967). They wished to condition smiling in infants aged 6 weeks and 20 weeks, but at the beginning of the experiment the children hardly smiled at all, partly because they spent much of their time crying. Initially, the experimenters produced smiles by presenting a child with a shining metal saucer, and then they reinforced the smile that was elicited in this manner. At first even this procedure did not lead to a full smile, so the experimenter introduced a "prompting" procedure in which he reinforced any approximations to smiles elicited by the saucer. On successive occasions they only reinforced successively closer approximations to proper smiles, until the presentation of the object regularly led to an open and broad smile. In subsequent trials, presentation of the metal saucer was gradually discontinued, and smiling was maintained by reinforcement alone.

The above examples indicate that operant conditioning can influence the activities of young children. Indeed, operant conditioning principles help us account for many instances of learning that take place in childhood and later life. The addition of procedures that make it possible to shape behavior, by reinforcing successively closer and closer approximations to a desired response, extends the range of learned changes that operant methods can produce.

Conditioning in Research into Perception

We can briefly note that both classical and operant forms of conditioning, especially the latter, make a number of contributions to psychology apart from furthering our knowledge of learning processes as such. Conditioning methods are valuable for the study of perception, for example, and procedures involving selective reinforcement of responses can be used to gain knowledge about perceptual capacities and discriminative abilities. In a preverbal infant or in an animal the information might otherwise be impossible to obtain. McKenzie and Day (1971), for instance, wished to measure the abilities of infants aged between 6 and 12 months to discriminate between visual patterns. The infants were trained to turn their heads in different directions according to the pattern they were shown, and appropriate head turning was socially reinforced. It was found that the children did vary the direction of headturning, according to which of the patterns was shown. This indicates that the children were able to discriminate between the two patterns. It is also possible to use operant procedures to investigate children's auditory discrimination. An experimenter might reinforce responses to one tone but not to another, or reinforce one response to the first tone and a different response to the second tone. In both cases, responding appropriately would demonstrate that a child could tell the tones apart.

Classical as well as operant conditioning procedures have been used for measuring the sensory capacities of young children. Sheppard and Willoughby (1975) describe a study by J. E. Bordley, who conditioned a response to a particular tone. He then lowered the intensity of the tone until the response disappeared, and raised it again until the response returned. This procedure was used to establish the infant's auditory threshold for the tone.

The Concept of Conditioning in Learning Research

In recent years there has been some debate about the value of the concept of conditioning. One question is whether the word "conditioning" has a meaning that is more precise than "learning" or even "experience." In the main, those phenomena to which the word "conditioning" is customarily applied are forms of learning in which the establishment of associations between events is relatively prominent, in which extinction can occur, and in which the contribution of memory and existing knowledge appears to be relatively small. The term "conditioning" usually refers to instances of learning in which forming a new connection or a new association is crucial. Associations as such cannot directly be observed. It is usual to *infer* an associative change after observing a changed response, but the fact that we have to infer that such changes have occurred, since we cannot observe them directly, causes difficulties (Hamlyn, 1970). Furthermore, the different instances of learning to which the term "conditioning" is used do not all have similar effects on the learner. Nor, so far as is known, are the underlying mechanisms similar.

THE CONCEPT OF REINFORCEMENT IN PSYCHOLOGY

Reinforcement is crucial for human learning, and investigations in which reinforcers are manipulated have shed light on some interspecies differences in learning. In animal research it is generally found that those stimuli that function as reinforcers in one situation are also reinforcers in a variety of other circumstances (Boakes and Halliday, 1970). This is less true in human learning, although some reinforcers undoubtedly have wide effectiveness, as do milk for infant learning and money for adults. As children develop, there are marked changes in the nature of the events that reinforce their behavior. In people, especially adults, there is greater individual variation in the events that reinforce behavior than is found in nonhuman species.

Schedules and Timing of Reinforcement

Animal conditioning studies have included numerous investigations of the effects of varying the contingencies, or *schedules*, of reinforcement. In consequence, some widely applicable statements can be made about relationships between schedules of reinforcement and the frequency of responding in animals. There has been less research into the effects of different reinforcement schedules on human learning, but relationships between reinforcement schedules and learning appear to be less straightforward in humans than in lower mammals. This is partly due to the greater number of factors influencing the behavior of humans, and it is also related to the fact that one cannot usually exert as much control over the reinforcement history of a human learner as is possible in the case of, say, a Norwegian rat. Human subjects cannot be deprived of primary reinforcers to the extent that laboratory rats are deprived of food in the days before study of conditioning. For this reason it is difficult to provide large numbers of reinforcers without encountering the problem of the human learner becoming satiated.

Any of a number of reinforcement schedules may be used. Every single response may be reinforced, and this schedule is known as *continuous reinforcement*. Schedules in which not every response is reinforced are known as *intermittent schedules*. If every nth response is reinforced, the schedule is known as *fixed ratio*. When reinforcement follows every nth response on average, but it is not possible to predict which particular response will be followed by reinforcement, the procedure is known as *variable ratio* reinforcement. Alternatively, behavior can be reinforced the first time a response occurs after a given interval of time has passed, irrespective of the number of responses. This is called *fixed interval* reinforcement, and a similar schedule, *variable interval* is similar except that the first response is reinforced after a specified average time interval, but the particular time intervals vary. The outcome, like that of using variable ratio rather than fixed ratio reinforcement, is to avoid exact predictability. A number of other schedules of reinforcement have been used. *Multiple, chain*, and *tandem* schedules all involve combinations of the schedules described above. *Differential* schedules may be introduced, in which a response is reinforced only if a specified amount of time has elapsed since the previous reinforced response (Reese and Lipsitt, 1970).

Continuous reinforcement schedules (in which every response is reinforced) are not frequently used, since experimental subjects easily become satiated, and when this happens if is impossible to obtain satisfactory conditioning. A study by W. C. Sheppard (Sheppard and Willoughby, 1975) illustrates the effect of varying reinforcement schedules on a young infant's behavior. A conditioning procedure that followed a fixed ratio reinforcement schedule, in which touching the infant's hand served as the reinforcing event, was found to be effective in increasing the rate of a child's vocalizations during the first month of life. In the following months the infant was reinforced for kicking, and it was observed that a schedule in which one response in five was reinforced resulted in greater frequency of response than the continuous reinforcement schedule. (However, the findings of an investigation by Bloom and Esposito (1975), to be discussed in Chapter 5, raise some doubts about the interpretation of this result.) A study by Rheingold, Stanley and Doyle (1964) showed that older children, aged 2 to 5 years, responded more frequently with higher fixed interval ratios. The most effective ratio was higher (reinforcing one response in ten) for the children aged over 3 years than for the younger children, for whom a ratio in which one response in three was reinforced was most effective. The task required children to touch the end of an adjustable rod, and this response was reinforced by a three-second filmed sequence. Children were not immediately placed on an intermittent reinforcement schedule, but were continuously reinforced at first. After one minute of stable responding, they were transferred to a fixed ratio schedule of three responses per reinforcement, and successively higher ratios of 5, 8, 10, 12, 15, and 18 responses per reinforcement were progressively introduced as soon as a stable response rate was achieved at each ratio. Most of the children were able to work effectively with the higher ratios, but at the highest ratios pauses following reinforcements became increasingly common.

An experiment by R. J. Seltzer (Resse and Lipsitt, 1970) attempted to investigate the effects of varying reinforcement schedules on very young infants, initially 10 days of age. Strong sucking responses were reinforced by delivery of a small amount of milk. The infants were divided into three experimental groups which received different reinforcement schedules in a training period, with each group receiving a total of 50 reinforcements. The first group received continuous reinforcement on the first 25 occasions, followed by intermittent reinforcement on a fixed ratio for the remaining trials. The second group received fixed ratio intermittent reinforcement on the early trials, followed by continuous reinforcement. The third group received continuous reinforcement throughout. When the three groups were compared over a five-minute extinction period following their respective training schedules, it was found the subjects in the first group (who received continuous reinforcement followed by fixed ratio intermittent reinforcement) made more than twice as many sucking responses as infants in the other two groups. The differences between the first group and the others in the number of sucks per minute was as great in the final minute of the extinction period as in the beginning of the period, indicating greater resistance to extinction of conditioned sucking.

Seltzer's findings suggest that even in very young babies intermittent reinforcement leads to greater resistance to extinction than continuous reinforcement. The relatively poor resistance of subjects in the second group indicates that the youngest infants may require a period of continuous reinforcement training, in order to become familiar with the procedure, before an intermittent schedule can be successfully introduced. However, to verify this suggestion it would be necessary to add a further condition to Seltzer's basic design: incorporating intermittent reinforcements throughout the training session.

The finding that intermittently reinforced behavior resists extinction more effectively than continuously reinforced behavior can also be observed in older children. Bijou (1957) conducted an experiment in which children aged between 2 years and 5 years were instructed to place a small ball into a hole that was positioned in the upper part of a wooden box. Subjects in a continuous reinforcement group received a trinket each time the ball was placed in the hole. Children in the other group were reinforced on a variable ratio schedule averaging one reinforcement per five responses. In the first session all the children received an equal number of trinkets. The number of responses they made during an extinction period was observed, and in this phase the children who had received the variable ratio schedule made twice as many responses as children in the continuous reinforcement group.

The Functions of Reinforcing Events

The definition of a reinforcing event as one that increases the frequency of a preceding response, while admirably straightforward, leaves a number of unanswered questions about the way in which reinforcers exert an influence. This definition introduces the important fact that future behavior is influenced by the consequences of previous behavior, a generalization which indicates one of the ways in which experience affects a person's behavior. When Thorndike put forward the "Law of Effect," he considered that the function of a rewarding event was to "stamp in" associations, producing direct and automatic strengthening of the connection between a response and the preceding stimuli. Subsequent research has provided little support for such an account. One theory is that associations as such are formed by contiguity of events. The function of reinforcers, according to this theory, is to provide information that helps learners become aware of the consequences of their actions (Estes, 1970).

Most events that provide effective reinforcers are ones that fill a useful function for the organism. Reinforcers may contribute to the needs of the individual learner in any of a variety of ways. For instance, they may meet bodily requirements or they may provide necessary stimulation of the brain. A particular event or input is likely to function as a reinforcer if it has value, in the broadest sense, for the learner. Reinforcers need not be events that meet any tissue needs or supply an obvious reward. They may simply provide information that contributes to the individual's well-being. Such information may concern significant environmental events, or it may give useful feedback about the learner's own activities.

Just as an internal combustion engine requires a number of separate inputs—gas, oil, water, air, electricity, and so on—so does a living organism. Some of the requirements (food and air, for example) directly influence the physiological operation of the organism, but in higher animals a large proportion of the inputs necessary to insure well-being are ones that serve to provide forms of information. Inputs of information contribute through psychological rather than directly physiological mechanisms. Those reinforcing events that provide social stimulation, approval, knowledge of results, interesting sights, or sounds all supply the human learner with needed information.

The suggestion that certain events are reinforcing because they meet requirements that extend beyond obvious physical needs helps us to account for some instances of animal learning in the absence of *apparent* reinforcement. It is found, for instance, that if young rats are allowed to move about in a maze, without receiving any reward, for sessions of half an hour per day over a period of ten days, and are then tested at learning the maze, they perform much better than animals in a control group who lack previous experience of the maze. Learning must have occurred during the daily sessions, despite the fact that the experimenter did not reinforce behavior at that time. Although the experimenter provided no rewarding event to reinforce the animals on the daily sessions, it is not necessarily true that the animals' activities in the maze were not reinforced at all. Animals need to be able to find their way about in their natural environments, and it is quite possible that exploratory behaviors provide a useful function for the animal and can be considered to be reinforcing.

Human behavior can be reinforced in many different ways. Whether or not some particular consequences of a person's actions will be reinforcing to him depends on a number of individual qualities. For example, the sight of the mother is often reinforcing to children aged about 1 year, but in babies aged 1 month it is less likely that seeing the mother will be more reinforcing than seeing a stranger, simply because at that age infants cannot recognize their mother.

Developmental changes affect the reinforcement value of various events. Some of the most noticeable changes in the effectiveness of particular reinforcers occur in the first year of life. This is partly because of early changes in children's ability to recognize things. At birth, infants can respond to simple physical stimuli, and as they get older they become increasingly responsive to qualities embedded in stimuli. They gain the ability to perceive objects, and can do so because they are able to detect qualities that are abstracted from the actual physical events detected by their sensory organs. If we wish to describe the way in which reinforcers exert an impact on behavior both in young infants and in older individuals, it may be necessary to describe the events involved at two different levels, corresponding with differences in children's ages. Thus, aspects of the mother's presence may be reinforcing both to a 9-month-old child and to a baby aged 1 month, but only in the case of the older child might it be correct to state that the "presence of mother" is reinforcing as such. For the younger infant the effective reinforcing event may be provided by some physical stimulus, milk, for example, that happens to be provided when the mother is present.

Because it is often difficult to specify the crucial components of some reinforcers, unless we take account of characteristics of the individual whose activities are reinforced, it is not possible to make a simple classification of the numerous events that can be reinforcers. In young children, tones, patterns, touch stimuli, smiles, and visual movement are often effective. As a child gets older, the number of things that can serve a reinforcing function increases, and individual factors have an increasing influence in determining whether a given form of behavior will be reinforced by a particular event or not.

A number of the different items that can function as reinforcers share the function of providing novelty. For young children, new toys are especially effective. Corter, Rheingold, and Eckerman

(1972) found that babies aged 10 months who were left in a strange environment would normally follow their mother after less than a minute, but if there was a new toy to play with the average delay before going to the mother increased to three minutes. Further evidence of the reinforcing qualities of novel events is provided by Parry's (1972) observation that 12-month-old children who were allowed to choose between entering familiar and unfamiliar rooms often chose the latter. When allowed to choose one of two toys they usually selected the one that was most novel to them (Ross, Rheingold, and Eckerman, 1972). According to Kagan (1972), items that are partly but not entirely novel are particularly attractive to children. Kagan considers that there is an optimal level of discrepancy from the familiar. An item has optimal novelty if, in Piaget's terms, it is sufficiently unfamiliar to necessitate the child accommodating in order to incorporate it within existing mental structures, but not so unfamiliar and meaningless to the child. In the latter case the item does not gain attention for long.

Another way to reinforce some activities is to allow an individual to practice or "run through" behaviors that are in the process of being acquired. Kessen and Mandler (1961) have suggested that, for species highly dependent upon learning, it would be advantageous if having the opportunity to practice newly learned activities or habits was reinforcing, since practice improves the efficiency of performance. Other events that reinforce behavior in young children are ones that have the effect of making interesting sounds or sights last (Piaget, 1970).

Yet another function of some reinforcers is to reduce the learner's uncertainty about crucial events. Gibson (1969) considers that much perceptual learning contributes to this. Reduction of uncertainty is achieved by many of the activities that individuals repeatedly engage in. However, some writers make a contrast between "reinforcing" consequences of actions and those consequences that serve the purpose of providing useful information. For instance, Eleanor Gibson suggests that perceptual learning is controlled by "laws of the reduction of uncertainty, not laws of external reinforcement" (Gibson, 1969, p. 47). Similarly, Fantz (1967) claims that learning which takes the form of acquiring new knowledge is a fundamentally different kind of learning from that which is based on changes in response tendencies following reinforcement. These views show that our broad usage of the concept of a reinforcer to include not only things that meet physical needs but also requirements for information necessary for psychological functioning is not one that is universally accepted.

One contemporary psychologist, Gewirtz (1969), advocates that if we are to classify reinforcers at all, we should avoid doing so in the way that we have attempted here, that is, by trying to reflect the processes through which a particular event exerts a reinforcing function. Gewirtz argues such an approach is bound to be largely a matter of guesswork, and unlikely to be fruitful. Gewirtz and other strict behaviorists take the view that simply knowing what events reinforce an individual's responses cannot lead to an understanding of the processes underlying the behavior, since the relationship between the observed behavior and the nature of the individual who emits it is not at all simple. The present author does not agree with this conclusion. Knowing about the events that serve to reinforce certain activities does at least give fruitful clues to psychological processes that directly or indirectly influence learning. The resulting inferences may sometimes be wrong, but the approach illuminates more often than it obscures.

MOTIVATION

The facts discovered from operant conditioning research concerning the consequences of reinforcement for future behavior demonstrate that learning is as dependent upon its success in meeting human needs as it is upon more narrowly defined learning variables. We cannot ignore the value of what is learned to the individual person. The importance of motivation is illustrated by a comparison of learned foreign language abilities in the citizens of small countries, such as Holland and Denmark, on the one hand, and in English-speaking people, on the other hand. Performance is clearly superior in the former people, yet no one would claim that the Dutch or the Danes are innately superior at acquiring languages. They simply have more incentive to learn.

I noted in Chapter 1 that the effects of human learning upon the individual are cumulative. New learning builds upon what has been acquired already, previous learning being an important determinant of what a child can learn at any time. Previous experience may also influence the probability that a particular event will serve to reinforce a person's behavior. Imagine a situation in which two children are engaged in the same task, and each of them is informed he has been responding correctly on fifty percent of occasions. Ostensibly, it would appear that giving this identical information to each child would affect them equally. But let us assume that the two children have experienced markedly different past histories of success and failure. One has been consistently successful during most of her life, has learned things easily and has become accustomed to a high level of reinforcement. The other child has consistently failed in many situations over the years, and is consequently unaccustomed to success.

Confronted with the situation in which each child is told he or she is responding correctly on 50 percent of occasions, it is likely that the two children will put very different interpretations on this information and react differently. The child who is accustomed to failure may consider that he is doing noticeably well at the present task. He may be pleased with his level of performance, and happy to continue in much the same manner. The other child, however, for whom the present rate of success is appreciably lower than what is customary, is likely to be dissatisfied with her performance and therefore strive to improve. She will succeed in doing so, and surpass the first child's level of performance. In this example, although the two children are in an apparently identical situation, their past experiences have led to their having different levels of aspiration. Therefore, they place different interpretations on the feedback they receive about their performance, and, in consequence, their actual behavior will be different.

An account by Staats (1971) gives a further illustration of the possible effects of motivation over a period of time. He considers the hypothetical case of the child who is not very successful at school, and whose achievement test scores are low. However, the child does not appear to be generally retarded, and manifests no major emotional problems or perceptual difficulties. To account for such a child becoming less successful than others, Staats provides a possible case history. Perhaps, he says, the child did not acquire the habit of regularly paying the close and sustained attention that is evident in successful children. In the child's earliest days at school he did not attend to what the teacher was saying, preferring to give his attention to matters that were less relevant to success at school tasks. Consequently, he would seldom have been rewarded for attempts at academic achievement, and if, as a result of his failure to learn, school lessons became incomprehensible, boring, and unpleasant for him, he might have gained the habit of evading lessons by disruptive behavior. As a result of failing to make normal progress, the child may have suffered from other children laughing at him or making rude remarks about his ignorance, leading him to make further attempts to remove himself from the classroom.

Classroom situations that are pleasant and interesting for children who are making good progress can be aversive for a child whose school achievement is unsatisfactory. Experiences of failure by an individual can lead to him avoiding certain situations. Over a long period, the chain of events produced by the cumulative effects of many failures may profoundly affect what a person learns and produce marked differences in levels of achievement.

The developmental changes that take place in the nature of the events that reinforce an individual's actions are not restricted to a child's earliest years. The motivational influences on learning may continue to change throughout childhood and adolescence. Ausubel (1968) has suggested that there are at least three separate components of motivation for achievement at school, and that the relative strength of the different components alter with increasing age. One component, *cognitive drive*, refers to the motivational effects on a student of the interest inherent in what is being learned. The second component is *ego-enhancement*, and includes motivational aspects of status, self-esteem, and success. Achievement motivation also has a third, affiliative component, which involves indications that individual learners are receiving the approval of a person or group of people with whom they identify. People acting in a particular way to prove they are "one of the boys" would be demonstrating the role of the affiliative component. According to Ausubel, there are changes in the relative strengths of the three components as a person becomes older. Young children need the attention and encouragement of adults, and affiliative factors may be especially important. With increasing age, ego-enhancing and cognitive factors become prominent. Motivational factors contribute in a number of ways toward individual differences in what people learn. We can note in passing that if it was established for certain that hereditary factors influence learned human performance, it would be conceivable that the relationship between inheritance and achievement was due to hereditarily transmitted motivational factors rather than to factors that directly affect learning processes.

HABITUATION PHENOMENA

In addition to classical and operant conditioning, we can identify a further broad class of basic changes in an organism's behavior, related to experience. The term *habituation* is applied to a variety of phenomena, some of which can be regarded as being forms of learning. Habituation is defined as a relatively long-lasting decrease in responsiveness that follows from repeated stimulation which is not followed by reinforcement (Thorpe, 1956). It shares with other kinds of learning the fact that responses are influenced by experience, but the above definition also includes some changes in behavior that are produced by sensory mechanisms.

The fact that repeated presentation of a stimulus leads to a reduction in responsiveness makes it possible for an organism to cease responding to repeated stimuli. This ability is of vital importance for all animals. It is often useful for an animal to respond to a new stimulus (Estes, 1978), but the sensory organs are constantly bombarded with signals from the environment, and it is simply impossible to process in depth all the incoming information. For the individual to be able to respond to those events that do carry significance, it is essential to be able to ignore stimuli that are insignificant and to attend selectively to ones that are important. Habituation makes this possible. It insures that the individual gives priority to things that are novel, unfamiliar, and unexpected. This is an especially useful facility for the survival and well-being of species that live in environments where new events often signal danger.

Superficial observation of an adult person may not provide evidence that the person is habituating, but it is nonetheless important. Habituation can occur to any of a variety of events, from very early in human life. Engen, Lipsitt and Kaye (1963), for instance, demonstrated rapid conditioning to odors in infants who were 2 days of age. The experimental technique involved placing a cotton swab that contained a solution of the odorous substance next to the baby's nose for a ten-second period. At first the babies reacted by increasing their physical activity, but when an odor was presented on ten successive trials the responsiveness diminished. This was a clear demonstration of habituation. Initially, smelling a substance known as "asafetida" led to increased activity in the infants on 100 percent of occasions. By the tenth trial, however, only 25 percent of the presentations led to increased activity. The experimenters ascertained that the infants in this study were not simply becoming less responsive to *any* odor through fatigue or adaptation of the smell receptors. When asafetida was presented again following ten trials in which a different odor had been presented, the infants once more increased their activity levels.

In all, four separate smells were presented, and it was found that the infants habituated to each of them. In addition to giving evidence of habituation, experiments of this kind can be used to provide information about infants' discriminative abilities. Thus, the present finding that after habituating to one odor, very young infants immediately responded at a much higher level to a new odor proves that they could discriminate between the different smells.

Habituation also occurs to auditory tones. Bridger (1961) observed that the presentation of a loud tone initially produced a marked acceleration in heart rate, but when the tone was repeated, heart rate acceleration reduced considerably. In addition, a number of studies have demonstrated visual habituation in young children.

However, there are a number of awkward procedural difficulties. It is essential for experiments to include conditions that control for possible experimental artifacts similar to the ones that have led to findings of classical conditioning studies being misinterpreted.

Procedures that are similar to the ones devised for measuring simple habituation have also been used by a number of investigators to examine the effects of unfamiliar events. For instance, Fantz (1964) showed pairs of visual patterns to young infants. Each pair was presented for a one-minute trial, after which one item would be changed, and the new pairing displayed for a further minute. A ten-minute session contained ten pairs, each of which contained one item that remained constant throughout all the trials and one item that was changed between each trial. Fantz found that over the ten trials infants of 2 months and older attended progressively less to the constant stimulus and more to the new items, but babies aged less than 2 months did not exhibit such a trend. Preference for novel rather than familiar items has also been observed in a number of studies involving older children. They often react more strongly and more quickly to items that are new. For instance, Cantor and Cantor (1964) observed fast reaction times by kindergarten children to light and buzzer signals that were relatively novel. Response times to each kind of stimulus became slower as the items became more familiar. Cantor and Cantor (1965) found that both the novelty of a new stimulus and the change from one stimulus to another contributed to faster reaction times. These were fastest when a new stimulus followed a familiar item, and the slowest reaction times occurred when there were successive presentations of a familiar stimulus.

ATTENTION

Habituation helps to free individuals to direct their attention to those environmental events that are likely to be important. Among the many factors that influence learning, attention is one of the most crucial. However effective the individuals' learning processes, however highly motivated they are, and however well equipped they are through previous experience, little or no new learning will occur if they do not direct their attention appropriately.

State Variables in the Young Infant

In the transition from the womb to the more varied environment of the outside world, infants enter an existence where awareness, alertness, and the ability to give sustained attention to the messages that their sensory apparatus now convey to them suddenly become important. The fast and unpredictable changes taking place in the newborn's state, indicated by rapid alterations between sleep and alertness, are an indication of the infant's first efforts to become adjusted to the extra-uterine world. At this time in life, attentional skills are at a rudimentary stage of development. Strictly speaking, it would be incorrect to state that attention as such influences the very young infant's learning, and more accurate to say that learning is affected by a number of changes in the baby's state. Some of the state changes are related to degree of arousal and alertness, and broadly analogous to attention in the mature learner. You may recall that we have encountered state variables previously in this chapter, since they are a source of experimental artifacts in research into infant conditioning.

The influence of state variables on learning in the young infant is even greater than that of stimulus characteristics (Kessen, Haith, and Salapatek, 1970). Close relationships exist between learning and measures of arousal, such as heart rate (Gottlieb and Simner, 1966). A complication is that there are a number of different components of an infant's state. Prechtl (1969) suggests that as many as 16 separate measurements of neurophysiological and other functions have to be taken in order to make a proper assessment. It is necessary to record functions such as heart rate, respiration, and electroencephalographic and electromyographic responses. Unfortunately, none of these measures on its own provides a reliable general index of the child's state, since the various contributing factors are partly independent of each other (Ashton, 1973). However, a cardiac deceleration (heart rate) measure does give a useful rough guide to the infant's attentiveness.

Attention and Learning Deficiencies

The ability to give careful and sustained attention to particular events is essential for success in a wide range of tasks. As we have suggested, children who have failed to acquire the habit of giving careful attention to, say, the teacher's voice, are at a disadvantage in the classroom learning situation, campared with their peers. Failing to learn something on one occasion may be a trivial matter, but the cumulative effect of many such failures is often appreciable.

More severe instances of inability to attend selectively when it is necessary to do so in order to learn can be observed in individuals who are classified as being subnormal or mentally retarded. The evidence suggests that failure to attend selectively is not simply a side effect of mental retardation, but a crucial factor that underlies many instances of failure to learn. This view is supported by in the findings of a number of studies in which the performance of normal and retarded individuals has been compared, first under ordinary conditions, and later in circumstances in which care has been taken to insure that both groups of subjects did actually attend to the same stimulus events. Typically, it has been found that the differences between normal and retarded learners in the first condition are markedly reduced, and sometimes eliminated altogether, when attention is carefully controlled (Estes, 1970). Recall that even among "normal" children, the effects upon learning of not attending may accumulate, so that failing on one occasion may prevent an individual from acquiring a mental skill that can be used on future occasions by those learners who do gain it. Conceivably, deficits in retarded individuals' ability to give sustained selective attention to appropriate events, and switch attention when necessary, may be among the most crucial of the factors contributing to a retarded child's learning disabilities.

The Orienting Response

Research originating in Russia with the work of E. N. Sokolov and his colleagues (described by Lynn, 1966) has given emphasis to the contribution to learning of processes involved in habituation and attention, in conjunction with the contents of memory. In simple organisms, and perhaps in very young human infants, habituation occurs only to simple mechanical stimuli, but mature people make similar reductions in response to repeated complex stimuli and to events, such as verbal ones, that are deeply processed by the individual (Estes, 1978). Each person is said to acquire a *neuronal model* containing information about the attributes of a number of events. As individuals experience new events, these events are compared with the contents of their neuronal model in memory. If the new inputs match information stored in the model, they are recognized. If not, there is a "mismatch" between the actual input and the expectancy induced by the neuronal model, and individuals are said to react by making an *orienting response*, enabling the new input to receive full attention. The orienting reaction may include any of a number of separate components, such as pupil dilation, turning the head toward the source of stimulation, increasing in muscle tonus, galvanic skin response and heart rate changes, modification of the cerebral activity indicated by electroencephalogram recordings, and vasoconstriction in the limbs. Clearly, a mechanism that enabled the contents of memory to control a person's orienting responses would have the valuable function of insuring that unfamiliar information was given full attention. It would enable a person to habituate to relatively complex events as well as simple physical stimuli. This would increase the individual's effectiveness in dealing with the external circumstances of life, since unexpected events are often particularly important.

According to Sokolov, the neuronal model to which incoming sensory data are compared includes a chain of neural cells that retain information about various aspects of stimuli, such as their duration, quality, and order of presentation. Sokolov assumed that the mechanism for selecting the events which are to receive attention is based upon high-level central processing in the cortical areas of the brain, and there is some physiological evidence to support this assertion (Lynn, 1966). Habituation phenomena occur more readily and more speedily in species with highly developed cortical areas. Thus monkeys habituate more quickly than dogs, and habituation to visual and auditory stimuli requires ten trials in dogs, around 40 trials in pigeons, and up to 170 trials in carp (Reese and Lipsitt, 1970). Habituation to relatively complex events does occur more rapidly in higher than in lower species, and takes place more quickly in mature individuals than in the very young. These observations are consistent with the view that some kind of memory model controls orienting responses.

SUMMARY

1. Classical conditioning, a relatively simple kind of associative learning, can occur in young infants, although it is difficult to establish exactly what infants can learn in their earliest months. Classical conditioning phenomena may account for the generalization of human emotional responses.
2. Young infants can learn useful activities under circumstances that involve aspects of both classical and operant conditioning.
3. Operant conditioning, in which the frequency of an activity is influenced by its consequences, contributes widely to human abilities. Babies are capable of operant learning by around 4 months of age, and possibly younger.
4. A variety of events can function as reinforcers. Behavior is influenced by the timing and scheduling of reinforcing events, and there are differences in the effectiveness of particular reinforcers. In young children, food and social attention are widely effective. Events that are effective as reinforcers appear to be ones that meet needs and requirements of learners.
5. Motivational factors have important effects on learning, and severe deficiencies may be caused in part by abnormal patterns of motivation in childhood. Motivation to achieve has a number of separate components, and their relative strengths vary with age.

6. Habituation, which can be defined as a decrease in responsiveness after repeated stimulation that is not followed by reinforcement, enables learners to ignore repetitious and unimportant environmental events. People can concentrate on attending to events that do involve change and are likely to be of significance.
7. Attention strongly influences the probability of something being learned, and is at the root of many individual differences in learned performance. Attention variables have a particularly crucial influence during the earliest months of life, when the infant's state is highly unstable and subject to unpredictable changes.

Suggestions for Further Reading

Fitzgerald, H. E., and Brackbill, Y. (1976) Classical conditioning in infancy: development and constraints. *Psychological Bulletin*, 83:353–376.

Reese, H. W. and Lipsitt, L. P. (1970) *Experimental Child Psychology*. New York: Academic Press.

Sheppard, W. C., and Willoughby, R. H. (1975) *Child Behavior: Learning and Development*. Chicago: Rand McNally.

CHAPTER 4

Some
General Issues

OVERVIEW

Chapter 4 introduces a number of issues that relate to the applicability of our knowledge about learning to various circumstances. We start by asking questions about the extent to which what is learned is transferable, and proceed to investigate ways in which relatively complicated forms of learning are related to simpler and more basic learned abilities. Later, questions about the generality of derived principles and laws of learning are introduced. In this chapter we also consider the evidence for the view that various species are biologically prepared to learn some things more easily than others and discuss some of the difficulties of defining human learning.

THE TRANSFERABILITY OF LEARNING

Something that is learned on one occasion is likely to influence future learning. Research investigating the "transfer" of learned skills was undertaken during the early days of experimental psychology. The activities of the researchers ranged from memorizing large numbers of poems in order to ascertain if a transferable memorizing ability could be acquired, to discovering whether practicing a skill (for example, mirror writing) with one hand would improve performance using the other hand. Transfer refers to the influences of preceding activities upon present tasks, and can be distinguished from "retroaction" which is the effect of an intervening activity upon the retention of something learned previously (Osgood, 1953).

The term *'transfer of training'* has been applied to a wide range of phenomena. There are few principles of transfer that apply to all the different circumstances in which something learned on one occasion influences a person's learning in the future. It is more realistic to regard the phrase "transfer of training" as a kind of umbrella term for questions about the applicability of learned abilities. Transfer is assumed to have occurred if some prior learning influences subsequent learning (Kelly, 1967). This makes for a somewhat broad definition of transfer, since most, if not all, instances of learning by an individual might influence subsequent learning, and it is questionable whether the term has a meaning that is clearly distinct from that of "learning."

People who are concerned about practical outcomes of learning, especially in relation to education, make a number of assumptions, some of them explicit and some implicit, about the transferability of what has been learned. Such assumptions are implicit in the old belief that the human mind has certain mental faculties—reasoning, the will, memory, and so on—which can be improved by training, in a manner not unlike the way in which muscles are strengthened through exercise. In fact, such a view rests upon an over-simplified account of mental activities, and it is not surprising that the findings of early experiments provided no evidence for this kind of transfer. William James (1890), for instance, undertook an investigation to determine whether memorizing large amounts of poetry would lead to a general improvement in the ability to learn poems. In one experiment James and his students started by learning a poem by Victor Hugo, and they measured the amount of time required to do so. Every day for the next month they practiced learning poems, and at the end of the month they memorized another Victor Hugo poem, identical in length to the original one. There was a tiny decrease in the average time required, but it was hardly sufficient to support the claim that training can improve memorizability. James had to conclude that each person's native retentiveness is unchangeable.

Most modern investigations of transferability attempt to answer questions about outcomes of learning. The particular questions that are asked and the generalizability of the answers are usually confined to the particular kinds of learning that are being studied. Asking how a motor skill involved in tennis may influence performance at badminton makes a very different question from asking if learning certain reading skills will help a child with other aspects of reading. Nevertheless, the broad generalization that learning builds upon abilities that have already been acquired is true for many human skills. Some kinds of transfer take the form of straightforward generalization, involving events and responses that are similar to ones encountered in prior learning. In more complex instances of learning, transfer may depend upon the learner having acquired rules or principles that apply to variety of different circumstances.

Gagné (1970) considers that to acquire advanced abilities the individual learner needs to apply increasingly complex rules. He regards the acquisition of knowledge as a process in which new capabilities are built upon foundations established by abilities learned previously. A person may not be able to learn a particular rule until certain basic abilities have been mastered. According to Gagné, different instances of learning that are necessary for gaining an advanced human skill can be represented as a hierarchy of learned elements. Figure 4.1, for instance, illustrates some of the steps from which a child acquires skills that are necessary in arith-

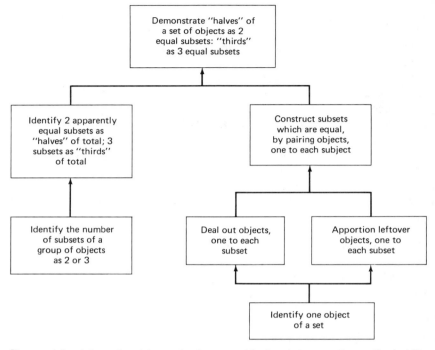

Figure 4.1   A learning hierarchy for a prekindergarten mathematical skill. (Source: Gagne, R. M. *The Conditions of Learning*, 1970. Reprinted by permission of Holt, Rinehart and Winston.)

metic. On the top level are some abilities that are to be attained. The lower levels show progressively simpler skills that the individual must first possess. To be successful at learning the skills on each level, the learner needs to be able to perform the tasks at the level immediately below. This, in turn, depends on prerequisite achievements at the lower levels.

Learning to Learn

There is a large difference between the simple kinds of transferability of learning implicit in generalization of conditioning effects and the more complex transfer phenomena encountered in hierarchically organized skills. Among the instances of transfer at levels intermediate between these extremes are the *learning-to-learn* abilities, or *learning sets,* described by Harlow (1949). Harlow conducted a number of experiments that typically included three objects, of which two were identical or similar, and one was different. The learner was required to respond consistently to the different, odd, item, and after the subject had achieved the criterion performance level on the first task a new set of three objects would be introduced. Once again, two would be identical and the third would be odd. Harlow found that after the first few problems children could solve subsequent ones very quickly, often needing only one response. The individuals had not only learned the solutions to specific tasks but they had also acquired a general skill that was applicable to a whole class of problems.

The subjects in Harlow's studies (monkeys as well as children) had acquired a simple rule or code. Bruner (1966) notes a similar transfer effect in rats who learned their way through mazes. After a rat has learned to travel along a maze by a route that involves a series of turns in alternate directions—left, right, left, right—it will take a substantially shorter time than previously to learn the reverse sequence—right, left, right, left. In short, the animal has learned to alternate. Bruner notes that although this might be described as an instance of transfer of training, in actuality nothing is being transferred. The animal is simply *applying* the rule to new situations.

In one experiment investigating learning-to-learn, Levinson and Reese (1967) compared the abilities of people of different ages at solving learning-set problems. Two items were presented at a time, the one that was correct having been selected by a toss of a coin, so there was no way for the subject to be sure that the first choice would be correct. However, when the first choice was found to be wrong, the effective response was always to choose the other object on the next occasion. To be entirely successful, an individual only had to make one incorrect choice on a pair of items. The experimenters adopted a criterion that was achieved by a subject making no more than one error (excluding the errors on the first choice with each pair) on a sequence of five problems, each of which involved a new pair of objects. The results are shown in Figure 4.2. The college and fifth grade students quickly achieved the criterion on around 90 percent of the blocks of problems, indicating that they usually made correct choices as soon as it was possible to do so. The preschool children made slower progress, but they did eventually acquire a learning set, giving them near-perfect early choices. The average performance of the elderly group was inferior, and the authors point out that different samples of old people varied considerably. The number of problems before reaching the criterion level was 20.4 for preschool children, 10.8 for fifth grade children, 6.7 for college students, and over 100 for elderly people.

Parameters of Transfer

Research on the transferability of particular learned capabilities will be discussed in later chapters and I shall describe some general

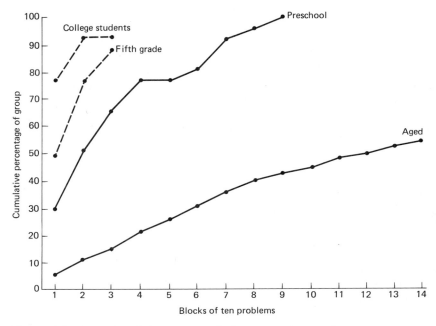

Figure 4.2   Learning to learn: cumulative percentages of groups reaching criterion. (Source: Adapted from Levinson and Reese. *Monographs of the Society for Research in Child Development,* 1967, 32:115.)

strategies of learning that enable people to acquire and to retain knowledge. Experimental psychologists are less sanguine today than in the past about the possibility of deriving general principles of transfer, but there are good reasons for continuing to undertake research into the transferability of what is learned. For instance, one difficulty with many retarded individuals is that what they learn is more firmly wedded to the particular context in which it was acquired, and less likely to transfer to different circumstances than in learners of high ability. Some experiments by Campione and Brown (1974) were designed to investigate the possibility that transfer deficiencies are a major cause of learning disabilities.

In a typical study, subjects had to press one of two translucent panels. The correct choice depended on which values of certain dimensions were present in the display. For instance, one series of display items contained a red T, a blue T, a red X and a blue X, and the relevant dimension was color. To respond correctly, the subject pressed one panel when each of the red displays was shown and the other panel when the letter was colored blue, irrespective of whether the letter in the display was a T or an X. Subjects were given some training trials followed by a number of tasks. The aim was to discover to what extent different kinds of similarity between the training task and the new task facilitated learning. In the new task, colors might be relevant (as in the training trials) or irrelevant, and the form of the letter could be irrevelant (as in the training trials) or relevant. The two displays in the original task might be presented at the same time, or successively. In the new task either the same procedure or the alternative one was followed.

One study by Campione and Beaton (1972), in which kindergarten children served as subjects, showed that fewer errors occurred when the training procedure and the new task were similar. However, the extent of transfer was not determined only by the number of similar elements in the training task and the subsequent task. When the same presentation procedure (simultaneous or successive) of the training tasks was followed in the new session, there were fewer errors than when it was changed. When the same dimension was relevant, fewer errors occurred than when the dimension was changed. However, when training and subsequent tasks both involved either successive or simultaneous presentation, changing the dimension after training led to a much larger decrement in performance. The most errors on the new task, indicating the least amount of transfer, did not occur in situations involving the greatest change from the training task, but in those where the procedure was retained but the relevant dimension altered. Degree of similarity in the physical stimulus was more important than similarity in the presentation procedure in determining the amount of transfer. On the whole, the more similar the training and the subsequent tasks, the greater the transfer of learning.

Questions about transferability arise whenever learning is discussed. The variety of situations in which transfer may occur is considerable, and makes it impossible to derive universally valid, simple laws. Yet the well-worn concept of transfer of training does remind us that effects of learning are cumulative; that which we have already acquired has a large influence on future learning.

CONTINUITY BETWEEN SIMPLE AND COMPLEX FORMS OF LEARNING

Among the issues that a concern with transferability of learning brings to the fore is the relationship between simple and complex kinds of learning. In what ways are relatively advanced and complicated kinds of learning related to, say, the learning observed in experiments on simple conditioning?

One answer that has been given to this question is that simple forms of conditioning form "building blocks" for advanced learning. Superficially, the metaphor is a convincing one; it suggests that many small elements combine to form a bigger, more complicated structure. However, it is doubtful whether the different learned achievements are actually related to each other in quite so straightforward a way. As Figure 4.1 showed, advanced human abilities may be regarded as being hierarchically organized, with the acquisition of each ability being achieved only if the learner already has the necessary lower-level skills. As Gagné points out, such a schematization can help us to understand how relatively simple and easily acquired capabilities might contribute to the acquisition of advanced abilities. It also provides an indication of the steps through which an individual might proceed in the course of learning advanced human skills.

Do the simplest forms of associative learning make a direct contribution, either as building blocks or in some other way, to the acquisition of higher-level abilities? Gagné has attempted to deal with this problem, and although his account does not answer all the questions that can be asked about the relationships between different forms of learning, he has made an effort to discover what forms of continuity do exist between simple and less simple varieties of human learning.

Gagné's Eight Types of Learning

Gagné (1970) distinguishes between eight types of human learning. He calls them signal learning, stimulus-response learning, chaining, verbal association, discrimination learning, concept learning, rule learning, and problem solving. The earlier items in the list are relatively simple and are similar to the associative learning phenomena that are observed in conditioning experiments. Thus in *signal learning*, the person learns to respond to a signal, as in an anecdote reported by the learning theorist E. R. Guthrie. He told of two mischievous boys who lived in the country in the days before motor cars. Once a week the local pastor paid a visit, and the boys were supposed to unharness, groom, and feed his horse. To amuse themselves they made the horse undergo a number of what we would term conditioning trials, in which one boy would shout "whoa" while the other would stand behind the horse and give it a sharp jab with a hay fork. The signal learning that resulted must have puzzled the unfortunate pastor.

As the anecdote indicates, Gagné defines signal learning as the establishment of a simple connection in which a stimulus ("whoa") takes on the properties of a signal. Gagné's second type, *stimulus-response learning,* is essentially a form of operant conditioning, and involves making voluntary movements. In this kind of learning, the learned connection is regarded by Gagné as being instrumental in satisfying a need or motive. A single connection is said to be formed between a stimulus and a response.

The above two forms of simple learning are thought by Gagné to form essential prerequisites for the others. Thus for *chaining,* the third type, it is essential that the individual has already learned the single stimulus-response connections which are to be joined. Chaining is described as the connecting of a sequence of two or more previously learned stimulus-response connections. As examples of chaining, Gagné describes instances of learned chains of responses, such as a dog who has learned to shake hands by offering its paw after barking, and a child who joins together simple verbal responses. Similarly, a child who has learned one connection between her doll and the spoken word "doll," and another connection between the experience of hugging the doll with that of lying down in a bed, may ask for the doll when put to bed. Gagné claims that this demonstrates that connection between the doll object and the word representing it is linked to that between the doll and the experience of lying in bed.

Chaining and a fourth kind of learning, *verbal association,* are necessary for further learned achievements. Verbal association involves the learning of chains that are specifically verbal. It is thought by Gagné to be important for the acquisition and use of language. It enables a number of learned connections involving words to be emitted in a single sequence.

If a person can form chains and make verbal associations, he will be capable of Gagné's fifth type of learning, *discrimination learning.* This enables the individual to make different responses to similar stimuli. It involves more than simply making isolated stimulus-response connections, because it is necessary to deal with the problem of interference between similar items. People have to be able to distinguish between different stimulus items and between different responses. Learned discriminations are involved in learning the names of people, and distinguishing between plants, animals, chemical elements, colors, and shapes.

Gagné considers that discrimination learning is a prerequisite for a sixth kind, *concept learning,* in which the individual learns to make a common response to stimuli that form a class or category but differ in their physical characteristics. For concept learning, the person has to represent information in memory, classifying events and discriminating between them on the basis of abstracted properties of them. Those who can do this will be capable of applying simple rules, and will be ready for Gagné's seventh type of learning, *rule learning*. A rule is said to consist of a chain of two or more concepts. If a person has learned concept *A* and concept *B*, rule learning will enable him to apply them together in a relationship such as "if *A* then *B*."

Finally, a learner who can form and apply rules will be capable of Gagné's eighth and final type of learning, *problem solving*. Problem solving is said to involve the process of recombining old rules into new ones, making it possible to answer questions and solve problems. The process of forming new rules is regarded as especially important for human problem-solving situations in real life, ranging from replanning a work schedule as a result of a new appointment, mapping one's way as a driver through rush-hour traffic to marshaling arguments in order to present a point of view, and designing laboratory experiments.

A brief summary cannot do justice to Gagné's book length account. Gagné would admit that he has not described *all* the ways in which advanced learned abilities depend upon simpler learning having taken place. The relationships between different kinds of learning remain incompletely mapped, but the fact that instances of simple learning do contribute to the acquisition of advanced abilities is well established.

DISCRIMINATIVE LEARNING

It is often important to discriminate between similar events, as we mentioned when discussing human attention. The fact that Gagné includes discriminative learning among his eight basic types is another indication of the importance given to discriminative abilities. People have to be able to isolate those properties of perceived events that are particularly significant to them, and to detect those aspects of similar events that enable them to discriminate between those events. Not surprisingly, a large quantity of research using humans and other animals has investigated forms of learning that involve discriminative abilities. In Chapter 4, some perceptual aspects of learning to discriminate will be discussed in more detail.

Some of the experimental research investigating human abilities to make discriminations has been conducted in circumstances in which subjects have chose between two similar items. The procedures followed in the experiments, described above, by Harlow, and by Brown and Campione, are examples of the tasks used in experiments on discrimination learning. In research investigating learning in children, it is customary to make a distinction

(Reese and Lipsitt, 1970) between "perceptual" discrimination learning, which involves discriminating between physical stimuli, and "conceptual" discrimination learning, in which distinctions depend upon abstracted properties of stimulus events. In a third category, "dimension" discrimination learning, individuals learn to respond to particular aspects of the complex events they encounter. In everyday life it is often important to know which of the many things we experience convey the most useful information. We notice this when we are in a new situation, in which the dimensions we normally use for discriminating are ineffective. For example, the reason why Caucasian people find it hard to distinguish between individuals whose physical characteristics are not European ("All Chinese people look alike.") may be that the particular aspects of faces that we have learned to use to identify people—hair and eye color, and shape of the nose, for instance—are not the ones which are the most effective for identifying individuals whose facial features are non-Caucasian.

Children can learn to make auditory discriminations between sounds of different pitch. Children aged 11 to 13 years who were unusually poor at auditory discrimination were selected for an experiment conducted in 1933 (Reese and Lipsitt, 1970). They were trained over a three-month period. Subsequently, all of the children were able to discriminate between semitones at every point within a four-octave range, and half of them learned to discriminate between tones as little as one-half cycle apart. This finding clearly contradicts the widespread assumption that deficits in musical ability caused by tone deafness and poor pitch perception are irreversible by middle childhood.

In much of Papousek's research into human conditioning the infant has to learn tasks that involve perceptual discrimination between physical events. In one experiment (Papousek, 1967b), babies aged 3 months and older were given milk if they turned their head to the left after hearing an auditory tone, or turned to the right after hearing a buzzer. Children could discriminate between the two sounds by the age of 3 months, but their learning to do so necessitated over 100 trials on average, spread over several weeks. Five-month-old children responded correctly after only a quarter as many trials. Afterwards, the experimental situation was altered, and in order to receive milk reinforcement the babies had to reverse their responses to the two sounds. Again, the older children needed appreciably fewer trials. Findings obtained by Siqueland and Lipsitt (1966) show that newborn infants may be able to make auditory discriminations. However, an additional tactile stimulus was necessary to elicit a response. This makes it difficult to interpret their results, and some subsequent experiments have failed to confirm the findings. By around 3 months of age children can visually discriminate between items on the basis of a dimensions of shape and form (Bower, 1967). By the age of 8 months children can learn to respond discriminatively according to the colors of objects.

PREPAREDNESS, BIOLOGICAL CONSTRAINTS, AND THE GENERALITY OF LAWS OF LEARNING

The forming of associations between a learner's representation of events is an important aspect of many instances of learning, and in classical conditioning it is the central function. Psychologists have tended to believe that any pair of events can be connected with approximately equal facility. Seligman (1970) quotes statements by Pavlov, Estes, and Skinner, demonstrating that the view that all events are equally associable has been widely accepted among experimental researchers investigating the psychology of learning. Pavlov, for instance, considered that any stimulus the experimenter chooses can become a conditioned stimulus. If this were the case, it would be possible to produce general laws of learning that do not have to take account of the particular content of what is learned or of the particular organism in which learning occurs.

On the basis of the assumption that there is equivalence of associability between different events, a number of researchers have tried to produce general laws and general theories about learning. A main concern of B. F. Skinner, for instance, has been to identify relationships between an animal's responses and the events in its immediate environment, and thus derive laws of learning. Laws of behavior were thought to be very broadly applicable, and it was considered unnecessary to display interest in the particular organism being observed or to take much account of the particular form of behavior that was emitted.

If the equivalence of associability assumption were correct, it might indeed be possible to derive some very general, species-independent laws of learning. But is the assumption valid? A number of findings from experimental research have indicated that the ease with which associations can be formed depends both upon the particular events to be associated and the particular species in which learning is observed. Some observations appear to be incompatible with the view that all stimulus events and all responses are equivalently associable. Breland and Breland (1966) noticed that the behavior of animals that had been taught, through reinforcement, to act in one way tended after some time to drift back toward activities that were natural or instinctive to that animal. For instance, they tried to condition a racoon to pick up a wooden egg and then drop it into a chute. Following an operant procedure, the racoon was reinforced with food after making correct responses. At first things went very well, but later the racoon appeared reluctant to drop the egg. It would look at the egg, fondle it, and put it into the chute and take it out again, spending some time on this activity instead of repeating the reinforced response of dropping the wooden egg down the chute.

Other animals have been seen to act in similar ways. The Brelands found that otters trained to drop a ball into a chute became reluctant to let it go. A similar phenomenon was observed in pigs which had been successfully conditioned to put large coins into a box. After several weeks, their behavior began to change. They would manipulate the coin and put it into the box, but they had great difficulty in dropping it. Monkeys can be equally reluctant to let go of small objects such as coins, despite the fact that they are promptly reinforced or rewarded as soon as they do deposit them. Breland and Breland consider that these instances indicate that the natural behavior of the animal may come to dominate recently conditioned responses. When an animal already possesses instinctive forms of behavior that are similar to ones that are being conditioned, the animal's activities tend to drift back toward instinctive behavior.

Whether or not one accepts the Breland's explanation, their findings present a serious challenge to the view that we can account for all behavior in terms of general associative laws that apply to a variety of species. Other observations from research into learning introduce further difficulties. For instance, responses in many species are known to extinguish more slowly in operant conditioning procedures that involve partial reinforcement than after a 100 percent reinforcement schedule, but the opposite is observed in fish (Bitterman, 1965). Unless we assume that there are inter-species differences in the mechanisms underlying learning, it is hard to see how this finding can be explained.

A review by Seligman (1970) surveys other findings that appear to contradict the equivalence of associability assumption. Some of the findings suggest that animal species, including humans, are by virtue of unlearned processes "prepared" to differing extents to form particular learned connections. Seligman suggests that individuals are naturally prepared to learn associations that involve some particular pairs of events and responses. Learning will partly depend upon the learner's level of preparedness for a particular association. If this is correct, it will not be possible to derive general laws that predict the outcomes of learning trials in all circumstances, irrespective of the particular species, the particular responses and, the particular events that are involved.

Some findings that appear to contradict the equivalence of associability assumption emerged from a study by Garcia and Koelling (1966). Rats were given sweetened water to drink, and while they were drinking three things happened to them, all at the same time. Lights flashed, a noise sounded, and the rats were exposed to X-radiation, which had the effect of making them ill, the sickness setting in about one hour later. The authors next presented the different happenings one at a time, in order to discover to what extent the rats had learned to associate illness with each of the different events. As a result of sickness, the rats might have become classically conditioned to avoid all three of the stimulus events that were present—taste, light, and sound. In fact, only one of the three became aversive, the flavor of the sweetened water. The rats avoided the sweet taste, indicating they associated it with the illness, but they did not learn to avoid either the light or the loud sound. This result suggests that rats learn an association between nausea and a taste more readily than they acquire learned connections between nausea and light or nausea and noise. The rats appear to be prepared for learning the association involving taste and nausea, but not the others.

Seligman considers that rats are prepared by virtue of their evolutionary history to associate tastes with illness. Such preparedness would have clear survival value for rats and other small animals living in similar natural habitats, enabling them to learn very quickly which substances they should avoid eating. It is known that rats who recover from poisoning by an unfamiliar food afterwards carefully avoid new tastes. These observations are consistent with a theory advanced by Herbert Spencer in 1870, to provide an account of the influences of consequences on future behavior, some 30 years before Thorndike's Law of Effect. According to Spencer, natural selection works during the course of evolutionary development of a species to produce correlations between feelings of pain and injurious actions, and between feelings of pleasure and actions that promote well-being. Such a mechanism would aid survival, since animals that experience pain following injurious actions and pleasure following beneficial ones would tend to live longer than others.

It is conceivable that preparedness has an indirect rather than a direct effect upon learning. One possibility is that some events, perhaps including taste, are more closely attended by rats than other events, or are more distinctive. However, this particular explanation is contradicted by the findings of an experiment to be mentioned shortly, in which shock and light became effectively conditioned. Another possible explanation is that tastes linger longer than the effects of other stimuli, and for this reason are more likely to become associated with subsequent nausea. There are in fact a number of ways in which Garcia and Koelling's results might conceivably be explained. The findings do not provide proof of evolutionary preparedness, and, in any case, the concept of evolutionary preparedness does not give a detailed explanation of the observed phenomena. It remains to be discovered exactly what is prepared and how it becomes prepared.

Whatever the correct explanation, the findings of Garcia and Koelling's study do show that not all of the pairs of events presented in a conditioning experiment are equally likely to become associated. The findings of nonequivalent associability are not just a stray outcome of a solitary experiment. In another experiment, Garcia and Koelling gave rats electric shocks instead of X-radiation, and on this occasion the rats were subjected to bright flashing lights, noise, and electric shocks to the feet, while they drank flavored water. This time the animals did not learn to avoid the flavor, but they did subsequently avoid the noise and the light. Thus, once again, associations were formed between some of the simultaneous events but not others. On this occasion, however, the particular associations learned were different than the ones acquired in the previous study.

Again, the idea of evolutionary preparedness suggests a plausible account. It would be useful for animals to readily learn to associate illness with tastes, thereby enhancing their chances of survival by avoiding poisonous materials. It would be equally useful to associate pain to the foot with environmental objects, since external events are more often than not the cause of foot pain. Painful feet are rarely caused by eating poisons, and learning an association between pain (or shock) and taste would have little survival value. The explanation appears to be a reasonable one, but again we need to bear in mind that no clear proof exists at this stage.

Nonequivalence of associability in learning is apparent in many instances of operant conditioning. When E. L. Thorndike was developing procedures for investigating learning by cats he used a number of different puzzle boxes. Escape from the boxes was achieved by various responses, including pulling a string, pushing a button, and depressing a lever. In one puzzle box procedure the experimenter would simply open the door whenever the cat scratched itself. The latter procedure might appear to present the easy way for the cat to get out of the puzzle box, but it was the one that gave the cats the greatest difficulty, as indicated by the time taken to escape on successive occasions. Another pertinent finding is that it is very difficult to train dogs to yawn (a response which they make quite often in normal circumstances) in order to obtain food (Konorski, 1967). Also, although monkeys can be taught to explore when a sound is presented, they cannot learn to groom themselves on hearing the same sound. Conversely, certain operant behaviors are elicited very easily in the absence of the reward schedules usually necessary for high levels of performance. Brown and Jenkins (1968) found that when pigeons were shown a lighted key and food was given to them in a lighted food hopper placed below the key, the pigeons began pecking the key. They continued to do so at a fast rate even when the food was delivered, regardless of whether the key was pecked at all. It appears that these birds are highly prepared to make pecking actions in order to obtain food in the form of grain.

Preparedness in Humans

The instances we have described all concern learning in animals and not in humans, and we might expect preparedness to be less important for human learning. Compared with other species we are especially good at learning and especially dependent upon learning, so human ability to learn may be less constrained by built-in attributes formed by evolution. Ability to learn may be more "general purpose" in man than in other animals, and less tied to particular associations.

There may be some truth in this view, but there is firm evidence that elements of preparedness are not entirely absent in humans. The child is born with a number of already-formed structures that influence perception and behavior. A number of experimental findings suggest human preparedness. When Watson and Rayner (1920) were conducting the studies of conditioning in a young child, described in Chapter 2, they found it fairly easy to condition the child to respond fearfully to animals, such as a wild rabbit, after pairing presentation of the rabbit on a number of occasions with a loud and startling noise. Subsequently the child responded fearfully when he saw the rabbit. But in another experiment, inanimate, non-furry objects such as blocks of wood were paired with the noises, and no conditioning occurred. If all events were equally associable, the child would have learned to associate any kinds of item with the unpleasant noise.

Research described by Sameroff (1972) has shown that conditioning in young infants is strongly influenced by the child's degree of preparedness to learn particular associations. Sameroff notes that the newborn infant may be able to orient to stimuli and to make a particular response, and yet be unprepared to associate the two.

Two months later, conditioning can be undertaken with considerable ease. Whether the child is prepared to form a connection depends upon a number of factors, some of them directly related to learning, some of them to physiological development, and some reflecting the nature of the human species. Sameroff asserts that for classical conditioning to occur in infants, the bond that is formed between the to-be-conditioned stimulus and the unconditioned response might have been prepared by the evolutionary history of the species, but the bond between the conditioned stimulus and the conditioned response is prepared in the life history of the individual child. As we have remarked earlier, various constraints on infant learning, including state variables and maturational levels, limit the applicability of general principles of learning. Maturational and biological factors cannot be ignored (Haith and Campos, 1977).

Even in adult humans some kinds of conditioning are more easily acquired than others. Many people have experienced conditioning through which a taste comes to evoke feelings of nausea for months or even years after an incident in which that tase has been followed by illness. After such an incident some people avoid a particular food for their whole lifetime. The practical technique of *aversion therapy* involves using similar conditioning in order to help a person rid himself of a habit that he wishes to eliminate, for instance drinking, smoking, or overeating. The conditioning procedure involves pairing events associated with the habit with a highly noxious experience, such as chemically-induced nausea.

The fact that such techniques are effective does not prove that the adult is prepared to make a connection between taste and nausea, and it is not known for certain that such connections are more resistant to extinction than associations between tastes and other aversive stimuli, such as electric shock, which is also sometimes used in aversion therapy. Yet there is little doubt that humans are well prepared for certain forms of learning, for instance acquiring a language. It is more than likely that human nature makes us better equipped for learning associations between some perceived events than others.

PROBLEMS OF DEFINING LEARNING

Having considered a number of instances of human learning, we might seem well placed to give a precise definition of learning. Yet some awkward problems remain. It is not easy, and perhaps impossible, to define learning clearly and unambiguously, and in a way that makes it always possible to distinguish between learning in its varied forms and some other causes of change.

Some of the many definitions that have been advanced commence with the phrase "Learning is a change in behavior. . . ." Here we immediately encounter a difficulty. The first five words are acceptable enough, since all kinds of learning involve a change of some form, but the word "behavior" in this context introduces problems. "Behavior" implies something which is observable, quantifiable, and measurable, all of which are admirable attributes in science, combining objectivity with the advantage of being able to define concepts operationally, that is in terms of precise measurements and exact procedures.

But can we really say that learning *is* a change in behavior? There are two possible objections to this. First, there may be instances of learning that do not involve changed behavior. Imagine that I read the fact that Lima is the capital of Peru. It is reasonable to say that I have learned this fact, but I may never give evidence in my observable behavior of having learned it. I may never tell anyone this information, or make use of it. So can we really assert that all learning is a change in behavior?

Behaviorist psychologists might reply by reminding us that the meaning of "behavior" in psychology does not always coincide with the everyday meaning of the term. Simply thinking that Lima is the capital of Peru or being aware of this knowledge can be regarded as instances of behavior. One cannot argue with this reasoning, but we should note that if the concept "behavior" can include phenomena that are not observable and not directly quantifiable, a major advantage of a behaviorist approach to psychology is lost.

The second objection to defining learning in a way that begins "Learning is a change of behavior" is more fundamental. What does it really *mean* to say that learning is a change in behavior? Is not learning a change in the *person* who emits or produces the behavior? Behavior is something learners do, but not an enduring part of them; a behavioral act is ephemeral, gone as soon as it is completed. In short, behavior is not an attribute of people, rather it is something they do. Behavior can provide evidence of learning, but that is not to say that the behavior *is* the learning, and a definition based on such an inference is logically unsound. However, it might be argued that although, strictly speaking, it is illogical to define learning as a change in behavior, behavioral evidence may be the only reliable indication that learning has taken place. In that case there may be no practical alternative to the above definition.

The task of defining and measuring learning is in one respect similar to assessing the quality of a phonograph record. This is usually done by listening to the sound the record makes, but in terms of strict logic, just as behavior is something produced *by* the learner rather than a part *of* the learner, the sound emitted by a record is something it produces rather than part *of* it. But no one would deny that the true measure of a record's quality lies in its sound, and it is difficult to imagine how else we might measure the quality of one of these black discs. So it is with learning and behavior. Behavior is not learning, but it often forms the most appropriate indication of learning.

Additional difficulties are encountered as we try to proceed further with a definition of learning. It is customary to qualify the phrase "change in behavior" by words such as "relatively permanent" or "enduring," to distinguish between learning and more transient changes that can take place as a result of sensory adaptation, fatigue, attentional shifts, or other temporary influences on behavior. However, terms like "relatively permanent" and its synonyms are not precise enough to form a basis for distinguishing between learned changes and other changes. Furthermore, the longevity of a change simply does not provide a reliable guide as to whether or not the change was a result of produced by learning.

It is customary to end definitions of learning with a statement about the conditions under which it is acquired. Examples are, "as a result of practice" and "as a result of experience." Phrases of this kind are ambiguous. There is no simple definition of "experience." "Practice" appears to imply repetition, but it is not certain whether the presence of either of these words is intended to suggest that repetition is necessary for all forms of learning.

Definitions like those above do not provide unambiguous specifications of human learning, but they do give a guide to the kinds of changes to which the term "learning" can aptly be applied, and this may be the most we can expect definitions of learning to achieve. They indicate the kinds of circumstances and the kinds of changes for which psychologists have used the word. Seen in this light, the function of available definitions is unquestionably a modest one.

Most definitions of learning give little or no place to the individual learner's role, and seem to imply a somewhat passive learner. Learning is not a passive process for the person concerned. The learner's activity is not limited to receiving information and assimilating it. On the contrary, learning is "a complex construction in which what is received from the object and what is contributed by the subject are indivisibly linked" (Furth, 1969, p. 239). Human learning is essentially a constructive process.

SUMMARY

1. What is learned on one occasion may influence future learning. Research into "transfer of training" has been undertaken to investigate the effects

of prior acquisitions on subsequent learning. Such research has considerable practical importance for educational issues. Transfer appears to involve specific skills and knowledge rather than broad improvements in abilities such as reasoning and memorizing.

2. The ability to acquire concepts and rules depends upon the learner having previously learned certain simple abilities. Forms of transfer are indicated by "learning to learn" phenomena and by the ability to apply learned rules and codes to new situations. In general, there is less transfer in very young learners than mature people, mentally retarded learners transfer less than individuals of normal ability.

3. It has been suggested that learned skills are hierarchically organized. Gagné distinguishes between eight types of learning, ranging from simple associative learning to problem solving. He claims that the acquisition of abilities at each level in the hierarchy can only be achieved if lower-level skills have already been mastered.

4. An important kind of learning involves making discriminations between events. Discriminative abilities are improved by learning, and discrimination learning tasks can be used to assess the manner in which people encode stimulus items.

5. For many organisms, not all stimuli and all responses are equally associable, and animals may be biologically prepared to acquire certain learned associations more easily than others. Learned activities in some species may drift back toward instinctive patterns. Evolutionary preparedness may help an animal survive if it facilitates the acquisition of some particular associations rather than others. The nonequivalence of associability rules out the possibility of deriving general detailed laws about associative learning that are appliable to all species.

6. In humans, compared with other species, learning is in some respects less constrained by built-in attributes, but there is evidence that differences in preparedness can influence some kinds of human learning, especially in infants.

7. The definition of learning presents a number of problems. Logical difficulties arise when learning is defined in terms of changes in behavior. However, practical definition and measurement has to depend upon observation of behavioral changes.

Suggestions for Further Reading

Sameroff, A. J. (1972) "Learning and adaptation in infancy: A comparison of models." In H. W. Reese (ed.), *Advances in Child Development and Behavior*, Vol. VII. New York: Academic Press.

Seligman, M. E. P. (1970) "On the generality of the laws of learning." *Psychological Review*, 77:406–418.

CHAPTER 5

Social Learning in Childhood

OVERVIEW

Having introduced some basic research procedures and general issues in Chapters 3 and 4, we are in a position to consider particular forms of learning in greater detail. In this chapter we examine social learning. We start by considering how basic social abilities are acquired by young children, and we note the various ways in which mothers, as they interact with the children, help them to acquire skills that are essential for functioning in a social environment. The chapter discusses a variety of social learning processes that contribute to a person's well-being, and includes a brief survey of evidence concerning the role of learning in human aggressiveness.

INTRODUCTION

The human environment is inhabited by other people, and we depend upon them in a number of ways. People respond to us and communicate with us, and as a result of interactions with others we acquire skills and abilities that cannot be learned from our encounters with the inanimate world. We have to learn to interact socially, and the acquisition of social skills begins in the first six months of life as a result of encounters between infants and their caretakers.

The term *social learning* can be applied to instances of learning that influence actions and experiences of a person that concern other people, but there is no hard-and-fast dividing line between forms of learning that are described as social and ones that are not. Most instances of social learning involve acquiring new actions or habits. The individual either learns to do something, or learns about the circumstances in which certain actions are appropriate. Such learning often depends upon the individual communicating or interacting with other people, and differs from the learning that takes place when individuals acquire knowledge. In the latter, many new acquisitions take the form of learning *about* something, rather than learning *to* act in a certain way.

The fact that "No man is an island" is clear from the beginning of human life. Babies depend upon others to supply many of their needs. Among the capacities they possess at birth, at least one, crying, has the social function of communicating to others, especially to the mother, that something is required. Through social learning, individuals equip themselves with abilities that enable them to communicate and cooperate with the other people who share their cultural environment, cooperation with others being virtually essential for human survival. The skills people acquire through social learning do more than simply extend their powers; indeed, the ways in which an individual acts toward others are seen as an integral part of the person, and on this basis others judge the individual's character and personality. When we appraise the personality of someone we know, we do so largely on the basis of our observations of how that person has learned to react to others in the social world.

An Example of Social Learning

The briefest experience can influence our behavior in social situations, as the following experiment indicates. It was conducted by Drabman and Thomas (1974) as part of a research program designed to investigate the effects of television violence on children. The authors produced an ingenious experiment which was highly artificial but designed to convince the participating children that they were in a realistic social situation. When the experimenter met each of the 9-year-old and 10-year-old participants on their own in the school classroom, he mentioned that he was ahead of schedule and proposed that the child should spend the several minutes of spare time visiting his new trailer. The trailer was a large mobile caravan that had been equipped as a playroom for younger children and placed in the school yard. On arrival, opening the door of the caravan revealed a good supply of children's toys and kindergarten equipment. At one end there was a television camera, and the children were informed that this was permanently switched on, to record everything that happened in the room.

Following the visit, the investigator explained to the child that the trailer was used by a friend who was working with children of kindergarten age. The pair then returned to a room in the main school building to participate in the game activities that provided the ostensible purpose for the investigation. At one stage, a television in the room "happened" to be turned on, and some of the children watched an eight-minute violent Western film. Others watched a nonviolent film during the equivalent period. Immediately after the film finished, the experimenter casually looked at his watch and said that he had to make an important telephone call. There was a slight problem, he explained, because he had previously promised the friend who had to look after the children in the portable kindergarten unit that he would keep an eye on some of the children for a short period while the friend had to be away. Then the experimenter pointed to a television set in the corner of the room and said that this was monitoring the kindergarten unit, which was still empty. He showed relief that no children had yet arrived, and explained that it was just possible that some kindergarten children might arrive before the telephone call was finished. In case he did not return in time, he asked whether the child would mind keeping an eye on the television. The participants invariably agreed to do this, and the experimenter repeated the instruction to keep an eye on any young children who did arrive. He finished by saying,"I imagine they will be O.K., but sometimes little kids can get into trouble, and that's why an older person should be watching them. If anything does happen, come and get me. I'll be in the principal's office."

Then the experimenter left the room and at this point each child saw a videotaped sequence on the television set. Since the children had seen the T.V. camera working in the kindergarten unit, there was no reason for them to believe that what they now saw was not live. On the videotape, the unit is initially empty, but after a few seconds a man and two children enter. The adult explains that he has to leave, and tells the children that they can play with the toys. For a minute or so the children play quietly and each makes a building of wooden blocks, but finally one starts to criticize the tower built by the other, and an argument develops in which they insult each other. Next, the boy maliciously kicks over the building the girl has made, there is continued argument and destruction of the brick buildings, and the children begin to fight. They start with pushing and threatening, and this leads to the girl crying and chasing the boy, while he shouts "You can't catch me." They struggle and hit each other and eventually it appears that the camera has been knocked to the floor. The sound channel continues to transmit accusations as the visual signal disappears. The last thing heard is a shouted "Watch out," followed by a loud crash and, eventually, silence.

While all this was happening on the videotape with the child subject watching, the experimenter waited outside the room, stop watch in hand, to measure how much time elapsed from the moment the kindergarten children began knocking buildings down until the participant left the room to call the experimenter's attention to the mayhem in the trailer. The experimenter measured the length of time each participant watched the young children's aggressive behavior before reporting it. The findings showed that children who had previously watched the violent Western delayed considerably longer than the others, their average time being 112 seconds, compared with 69 seconds. There were no appreciable differences between boys and girls. In a further analysis of the results, children who sought help before the more extremes of aggression and actual fighting began were compared with those who did not. Eleven of the children who saw the nonviolent film went to report the event before this point, and eight did not, but of the children who saw the violent film, only three out of the eighteen sought help before the point at which fighting commenced.

These results strongly suggest that brief experiences can lead to important modifications in social behavior. Numerous events in our everyday lives contribute to social learning, each person being influenced by an individual pattern of experiences. In real life, numerous social events are experienced each day throughout childhood and beyond.

OPERANT PRINCIPLES IN EARLY SOCIAL LEARNING

As early as the first 6 months of life some forms of learning involving the principles of operant conditioning may influence social behaviors. Children at birth are not quite so helpless, unformed, or passive as they might appear to be, and they begin life well equipped for social interactions (Howe, 1975a). Much early learning has a social aspect, since people will be prominent among the environmental stimuli that gain children's attention. An outcome of their own responses, such as crying and smiling, is to affect the manner in which people behave toward them.

Among the activities of the young child that have social effects, two that have been examined in operant research into learning are smiling and vocalization. Each of these, like crying, has the function of enabling the young human to communicate with others. Since young children are heavily dependent upon their protectors, any kind of learning that increases the effectiveness of communication makes a real contribution to a child's well-being. We do not have to learn to smile, and smiling can be elicited in infants aged around 2 months by the human voice, by a face, and sometimes by the simple visual pattern comprising two shapes similar in size and form to the mother's eyes (Schaffer, 1971). In the first months of life spontaneous smiling also occurs. Emde and Harrison (1972) established that infants smile spontaneously at a rate of eleven smiles per 100 minutes, on average, throughout the day. As a result of learning, the circumstances in which a child will smile gradually change. In the case of vocalizing, an effect of operant learning is to increase the frequency of vocalizations, ranging from the first noises that a child emits to later sounds that are used in speech.

We have remarked that it is difficult to establish for certain that an observed change in the behavior of a young infant is due to learning rather than to other influences. The study of early social learning has been plagued with difficulties of this kind. For a long time it was widely accepted that results published in 1959 by Rheingold, Gewirtz and Ross provided firm evidence that operant conditioning of vocalizations can take place in infants as early as 3 months of age. By that time infants are beginning to acquire ways of signaling their needs that are more refined than crying, they are socially responsive to their environment, they smile when people are present, and are attentive to other humans.

The experimental design of the study by Rheingold, Gewirtz and Ross included a baseline period in which the frequency of vocalizations was measured prior to operant procedures being used. To assess the reliability of their observations, the authors had two observers separately rate the infant's responses. Then they calculated the interobserver agreement, and the reported 96 percent level of agreement indicates that the measures adopted were highly reliable. For reinforcing vocalizations, the experimenter simultaneously performed three social acts: a broad smile, "tsk" sounds, and lightly touching the infant's abdomen. In providing these three events together, the experimenters were acting in a way not unlike that of a typical mother in the true-to-life circumstances of early social interaction and play. Following a two-day baseline period, in which an adult was present but did not respond to the child in any way, there was a conditioning period, also lasting two days. During the conditioning period the social events described above, which were intended to reinforce behavior, were provided by the experimenter whenever the infants made a vocalization, but at no other time. The two final days formed an extinction period in which no further social reinforcement was provided. As Figure 5.1 shows, the frequency of vocalizations by the infants at the end of the conditioning period was around twice that occurring during the previous baseline period. During the extinction session the number of responses declined toward the previous level.

Conditioning or Elicitation of Responses?

The above result appears to prove that the operant conditioning procedure produced marked changes in the frequency of vocalization of infants at the age of 3 months. However, we cannot rule out the possibility that the increase in vocalizations was not due to operant conditioning but to some other effect of the social events that were intended to reinforce vocalizations. When an adult acts in this way the infant might be stimulated to respond. If this were the case, the increases in vocalizations observed in the above study might simply be an indication of the infants' responsiveness to the social stimuli. The suggestion is that the social events influenced behavior

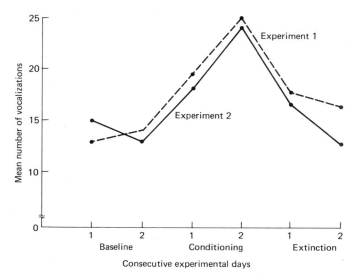

Figure 5.1   Mean number of vocalizations by infants on successive experimental days. (Source: Rheingold, H., Gewirtz, J. L., and Ross, H. W. "Serial conditioning of vocalizations in the infant." *Journal of Comparative and Physiological Psychology,* 1959, 52:68–73 © 1959 American Psychological Association. Reprinted by permission.)

by eliciting greater responsiveness rather than by reinforcing the infants' own vocalizations.

To check on this possibility it is necessary to undertake further experiments that include appropriate experimental control groups. If the increases observed by Rheingold, Gewirtz, and Ross were due to a social eliciting effect rather than conditioning, we would expect to find that the effects of the experimenter's social events would be undiminished if their timing was altered so that they were not contingent upon a subject's vocal responses. However, if the above result was caused by genuine conditioning, disrupting the timing, so that vocalizations ceased to be followed immediately by reinforcing events, would markedly influence the results.

In one experiment that included a control group in which non-contingent social stimuli were provided (Weisberg, 1963), it was found that noncontingent social stimulation produced no increase in social behavior over performance in the baseline period, a finding that appears to confirm the conclusion by Rheingold, Gewirtz, and Ross that their results demonstrated social conditioning. However, recent findings by Bloom and Esposito (1975) prompt us to question this conclusion. A limitation of Weisberg's study was that the total amount of social stimulation given to subjects was not equivalent for the babies in the experimental and control groups. It is quite likely that the amount of stimulation is important, and possibly so is its density and the patterning of its occurrence. An ideal experimental design would control these factors. In the study by Bloom and Esposito, subjects in the control conditions were "yoked" to experimental group subjects. This was achieved by the procedure of giving some of the control subjects noncontingent social stimulation that was identical in frequency and timing to the social "reinforcement" received by those infants in the experimental group who produced the highest number of vocalizations during the conditioning period. A further five control subjects were similarly yoked by pairing them with infants in the experimental condition who made the lowest number of vocal responses. Under these circumstances it was found that although babies in the experimental group did have a large increase in vocal responding during the conditioning period and a corresponding decrease in the extinction period, an equally large effect was observed in the yoked control subjects for whom social stimulation was not contingent upon, and was therefore unrelated to, their own responses. This result suggests that the earlier findings, which appeared to show that social conditioning occurs in 3-month-old infants, could have been due to the elicitation of greater vocal responsiveness by the social stimulation, rather than to conditioning based upon reinforcement of the infants' activities.

To demonstrate eliciting effects is not to deny that conditioning may also occur. Both reinforcing and eliciting outcomes of social stimulation could have contributed to the findings of a study by Routh (1969). Infants in three groups were socially reinforced for vowellike sounds, consonantlike sounds, or for all vocalizations, and all three groups were observed to vocalize more frequently during the conditioning sessions than during a previous baseline period, irrespective of the kinds of vocalization that had been reinforced. Ramey and Ourth (1971) provide another demonstration of increases in vocalizations by infants aged 3 months and older, as a result of conditioning. The social stimulation procedure used in the previous studies was provided in order to reinforce vocalizations, but there were delays of zero, three, and six seconds between infants' responses and reinforcement. The duration of the experiment was shorter than usual, and it included a half-minute baseline period, six minutes of conditioning, and two minutes for extinction. Ramey and Ourth found that when reinforcement immediately followed responses there was the usual increase in responsiveness, but when the reinforcing events were delayed, no increases in vocalizations occurred. Since the infants in the delayed groups did receive some of the social stimulation provided for the other group, the present result would seem to favor a conditioning rather than elicitation interpretation. However, the delayed reinforcement groups did not receive quite so frequent social stimulation as the nondelayed group, so the possibility of the social events having had an eliciting effect on infants' behavior cannot be ruled out.

There is some evidence to suggest that if the training period is sufficiently long, infants aged appreciably less than 3 months can be socially conditioned to increase their rate of vocal responding. Sheppard (1969), who tested an infant at home over 67 daily sessions beginning when the infant was 2 weeks old, provided two distinct forms of reinforcement in order to shape two kinds of behavior. In early sessions flashing lights and a recording of the mother's voice were separately used to establish operant control over a motor response, leg kicking. Later, either vocalizations or leg kicking responses were reinforced, but not concurrently; one or the other of the two responses were selectively reinforced in alternating five-minute periods. Thus, for the first five minutes, vocalization would be succeeded by both forms of reinforcement (lights plus voice) but leg kicking was not reinforced. For the following five minutes, kicking would be followed by the reinforcers, but vocalization was not. Subsequently a red light was introduced to indicate which of the two behaviors would be reinforced, and under this condition it was found that the infant was able to respond discriminatively. This finding shows that each of two infant behaviors could be controlled by the reinforcement procedure. The infant could learn to respond discriminatively, according to which of the behaviors was currently being reinforced.

The weight of evidence suggests that operant conditioning of social behaviors can take place in young babies. This is true despite the fact that Bloom and Esposito's results cast real doubt on the evidence for conditioning in 3 month olds produced by Reingold, Gewirtz, and Ross. It should be emphasized that not all studies of infant conditioning lack the necessary control identified by Bloom and Esposito, and it is not seriously questioned that older children can learn from social conditioning procedures. However, the objection raised by Bloom and Esposito to earlier claims to have demonstrated conditioned vocalization in the first months of life may apply to some other studies apparently demonstrating infant conditioning of social responses, notably smiling. For instance, social conditioning of smiling in babies averaging 4 months of age was reported by Brackbill (1958), who used an experimental design and a form of reinforcement that were broadly similar to the procedure of Rheingold, Gerwitz and Ross's (1959) study of vocalizing. Brackbill found that frequency of smiling increased during conditioning sessions, and that variable ratio reinforcement produced greater resistance to extinction than continuous reinforcement. Other findings indicate operant conditioning may occur in infants as young as 2 months (Etzel and Gewirtz, 1967). When the different components of the reinforcing stimuli were provided separately, a combination of smiling with picking the baby up was found to be most effective, and just touching the infant was the least effective. Again, however, it is difficult to interpret the experimental results, because the studies lack the control conditions that would make it possible to rule out the interpretation that the events used as reinforcers were eliciting behavior without actually reinforcing it.

In the study by Brackbill (1958), the fact that smiling by infants under ratio reinforcement schedules was more resistant to extinction than smiling in continuously reinforced infants, although the latter group were socially stimulated more often, gives some support to the view that conditioning, rather than elicitation, was the primary cause of the findings. As Millar (1976) points out in an article on the problems of conducting research into infant conditioning, a further complication is added by the possibility that habituation phenomena, which can influence infants' responses, may affect the results of studies of this kind. Taking the evidence on social conditioning in young infants as a whole, it seems likely that conditioning most probably can and does contribute to the developing abilities of young babies to respond to others and communicate with them. However, findings such as those obtained by Bloom and Esposito (1975) show that it is not easy to demonstrate social conditioning in the very young. Experiments need to incorporate control procedures that are more refined than those of the early studies which appeared to offer convincing evidence for social forms of operant conditioning in young infants.

Negative Reinforcement (Escape)

Negative as well as positive forms of reinforcement play a role in human learning. Negative reinforcement is said to occur if the frequency of an operant behavior is increased whenever that behavior is followed by the removal of an aversive stimulus. For instance, consider the mother's behavior when her child screams. The mother might attend to and calm the child, or she might cover her ears. In either case the effect of her action is to remove the aversive stimulus (the sound of screaming), and this consequence serves to reinforce her action. The mother thus escapes from the aversive stimulus. Similarly, a parent may escape from an unpleasant situation in which her child is behaving in a demanding manner by giving in to the demands. Incidents such as this may account for some people learning to act in a manner that is more deferential and less assertive than is normal.

Avoidance

Avoidance is similar to escape, but while escape involves the negative reinforcement effect of terminating an unwanted stimulus situation, avoidance postpones or prevents an unpleasant situation. A person may avoid a punishment by complying with orders, or avoid a blow by running away. The fact that the consequences of a person's acts do influence future behavior is of great importance for human life, and operant research into human learning makes it possible to investigate the functioning of such consequences. The future actions of people are influenced by the results of their present behavior, that is, by reinforcing events and by the timing and scheduling of reinforcers. Furthermore, since the precise consequences of the acts of individuals are partly unique to the particular circumstances, the particular people, and the particular objects that form the environment of their life, different individuals will respond to reinforcers differently. This contributes to individual variability in human habits and capabilities.

OBSERVATION AND HUMAN LEARNING

The consequences of our own actions do not comprise the only factor influencing what we learn. If reinforcement of operant behaviors provided the sole means of learning about the outcomes of firing a gun at another person, eating poisonous plants, jumping over a cliff, or falling into a stormy sea, few people would live for long. The human species could not survive a state of affairs in which experiencing the consequences of actions provided the only mechanism for learning how to do things. If all learning depended upon the reinforcement of existing responses it would be difficult for a person to acquire new behaviors. Fortunately, mechanisms for learning exist that are less expensive in life and limb, making it possible for new things to be learned without it being necessary to wait for each activity to be produced by the individual learner. One way to learn is through watching other people behave, and in this way we can acquire habits, skills, and knowledge without having to directly experience the consequences of every single action. In the present section we shall introduce some instances of observational learning and imitation, and subsequently discuss attempts to explain how these kinds of learning are possible. People are able to learn from what they observe, and they thereby gain access to a much wider range of abilities than would be possible if all learning depended upon the reinforcement of behaviors. Learning through observation often involves finding out things that are not directly experienced. In this respect, observational learning is half way between learning through direct experience and learning that depends upon symbolic communication, through spoken or written language. We might learn to cook through direct experimentation, or through observing others, or through reading a recipe book. Most literate people will experience all three of these kinds of learning. If we were restricted to direct experimentation our achievements would be very limited.

The consequences of activities may exert as much influence on behavior that is based on observation as they do in instances of operant conditioning. If we watch people doing something, what happens to them will influence the probability of our repeating their action. However, although the consequences of their behavior will influence the likelihood of our *repeating* it, the consequences to them may not affect our *learning about* what they do. In this respect, instances of learning that take the form of acquiring information are less dependent upon consequences than the learning studied in operant conditioning research.

Many experimental investigations of human learning through observation have been conducted in the laboratories headed by Albert Bandura at Stanford University. A number of the experiments have examined social learning in fairly young children, and in a large proportion of observational learning studies the activities investigated have been ones associated with aggression, such as hitting and striking. Aggressive responses are not the only kind of behavior that is learned through observation, but aggressive responses do tend to predominate among the activities measured in experiments on observational learning. This is not because the researchers all believe that aggressive responses are more important than other social activities. Experiments investigating aggressive acts have considerable relevance to social activities in general. One reason for the fact that a high proportion of observational learning studies concern aggressive behavior is that, compared with other social behaviors, aggressive actions are easy to discern and convenient to measure objectively. Objective measurement of helping behaviors may be difficult, but it is not difficult to observe one child kicking another!

A simple experiment by Bandura, Ross, and Ross (1963a) illustrates the observational learning of social behaviors. The participants were 96 children in a nursery school, aged between 3 and 5 years. Each child was assigned at random to one of the experimental conditions and taken into a room and encouraged to settle down with some toys. Subsequently an adult who was in the same room began to play with the toys, which included an inflated clownlike doll that was about five feet high and weighted at the bottom. The adult began to hit the inflated doll with a mallet. He was careful to introduce aggressive actions that were both highly distinctive and new to the children. As each child watched what was happening, the adult repeatedly performed the distinctive aggressive actions on a number of occasions. In another experimental condition the children also saw an adult acting aggressively toward a doll, but in a film version rather than live. In addition, there was a control group containing children who did not witness aggressive behavior.

Following the session in which the adult was observed, each child was directed to another room where there were a number of very attractive toys, which the child was told could be played with. But just as soon as the child had begun to do so, the experimenter interrupted to say that she had decided to reserve these toys for a different group of children. The child was then taken to yet another room, where there were a number of ordinary toys and also a doll like the one the children had seen in the first room, together with a mallet. Individual children were observed for 20 minutes in this room to see how they would behave in the frustrating new circumstances.

The results of this experiment showed that prior exposure to the adult acting aggressively markedly influenced behavior. The average number of aggressive responses made by children in the control group, who had not watched the aggressive adult, was 54. Those children who had watched the adult hitting the inflated doll made an average of 82 aggressive actions, more than half as many again, and children who watched the adult on film acted slightly more aggressively than children who saw the live person. The form of the aggressive acts was influenced by what the children had observed, the particular actions being copies of the adult's behavior. The findings show that children can and do learn new forms of social behavior through observation, and they imitate the aggressive acts they see performed by adults.

A second example shows that in observational learning the consequences of social behavior to the person being observed are important, just as in individual operant conditioning the consequences of a person's own actions influence that person's future behavior. Child subjects averaging just over 4 years of age watched one of two films, both of which involved two men. (Bandura, Ross, and Ross 1963b). One film starts with one of the men, called Johnny, playing with some attractive toys. The other man, Rocky, asks Johnny if he can play too. Johnny refuses, whereupon Rocky starts to act very aggressively toward Johnny and his toys. The particular forms of aggression used by Rocky were highly distinctive so that it was possible for the judges who rated the children's subsequent actions to distinguish between aggressive actions that were within a child's existing repetoire and new acts that directly imitated the adults in the film. As the film continues, Rocky, as a result of his aggressive behavior, is victorious over the unfortunate Johnny, who is last seen sitting dejectedly in a room. In contrast, Rocky is announced as the victor as he plays happily with his toys, simultaneously consuming food and drinks that he clearly enjoys.

This film was seen by some of the children. Others watched a film that started in the same way and contained the identical two characters. In the second film Rocky is less successful and the outcome of his aggressive behavior is that he is beaten up by Johnny. This time it is Rocky who ends up dejected, without toys, while Johnny is the victor. Some other children formed a control group, and they saw no film at all. The next part of the experiment involved observation of the children for a 20-minute period as they played in a different room containing a number of toys, some of which were identical to ones displayed in the film. Again, judges rated the children for the number of aggressive actions, the average score being 75 by children who watched the film in which Rocky was rewarded for acting aggressively, 54 by the children who saw the film in which he was less successful, and 62 among children in the control group who did not watch any film at all. A greater amount of imitative aggression occurred after observation of a person who was rewarded for aggressive acts than after watching someone who was not rewarded for being aggressive. The fact that participants in the latter group made lower scores than the control group children indicates that the effects of watching the unsatisfactory consequences of the aggressive adult's behavior negated any influence of viewing aggression in the early part of the film.

This result supports the view that rewarding people who behave aggressively influences the likelihood of their actions being imitated, but it does not necessarily indicate that rewards to the model affect observational learning as such. If children do not imitate an act we cannot conclude that they have not learned it. Children may be as likely to retain, and subsequently act upon, information about activities that are not rewarded when the children first observe them. This possibility was investigated in a third experiment. Again, the child subjects were around 4 years of age, and each child saw one of three films on a television screen. In one film an adult acted aggressively toward a large doll in the form of a clown. He was rewarded by being told he was a "strong champion" and receiving large quantities of sweets and fizzy drinks. The second film also depicted the model behaving aggressively, but the consequences were less successful. He was called a bully, sat upon, and struck. The film ended with him running away while he was being threatened with a spanking if he was caught acting in the same way again. In the third film only the first part of the sequence was shown. This depicted the adult person acting aggressively, but the film ended without showing any consequences of this behavior. Next, the children were observed in a play situation and, as the findings of the previous experiment might lead us to predict, those individuals who had seen the film in which the adult was punished after acting aggressively displayed less imitative aggression than the other children. Girls imitated the aggressive behaviors somewhat less than the boys. Then a further stage of the experiment was introduced, in which all the children were told they would be rewarded for showing what the model had done on the television film. Under these circumstances one might expect the children to display responses which they had learned from the film but had not previously displayed (after seeing the negative consequences to the adult in the film). At this stage of the experiment, children in all three groups were found to be able to perform a greater number of imitative acts than they had previously demonstrated. The previous difference between the groups in the number of aggressive actions disappeared and so did the differences between the sexes. The girls now displayed virtually as many aggressive acts as the boys.

These findings show it is necessary to make a distinction between learning and performance. In some circumstances the way in which experimental subjects act does provide a reliable indication of what has been learned. However, in circumstances like those of the first part of the present experiment, this was not the case. Spontaneous imitative activities are not always a good guide to what has been learned through observation.

Observational learning and imitation do not usually involve mimicry of what has been observed. Observations may lead to a person acquiring a rule that can be applied to new and partly unfamiliar situations (Zimmerman and Rosenthal, 1974). Observers *may* copy a particular response they have seen, but among mature individuals learning is not limited to the acquisition of specific responses. Through observing others, we can acquire new concepts, rules governing the use of language, and new strategies and ways of coding information. For example, Guess, Sailor, Rutherford, and

Baer (1968) taught a 10-year-old mentally retarded girl to use language in order to give appropriate singular or plural words when she was shown the objects they represented. The experimenter would demonstrate the required performance, and when the child performed the task correctly she was reinforced with praise and food. The child's behavior indicated that she had learned a rule rather than simply acquiring particular responses; she learned to supply appropriate plural labels for new items that had not appeared in the experimenter's demonstrations. Also, when the experimenter presented three objects at the same time, the girl gave a plural response, although there had never been more than two objects in the demonstrations. The fact she learned rules rather than particular responses is also demonstrated by some of her mistakes, for instance "mans" instead of "men."

Terms and Concepts in Observational Learning

Bandura and Walters (1963) used the word *model* to denote the person whose behavior is observed and subsequently incorporated by the learner, and the term *modeling* to refer to the performance by the model of the behavior observed by the learner. They pointed out that although social learning is frequently based upon observation of real-life models, symbolic models have become increasingly important in recent years. People can also pattern their activities after verbal accounts of behavior, for instance those in handbooks describing appropriate actions for dealing with practical problems.

A number of different terms are used, to some extent interchangeably, to describe forms of social learning that are based on observation and involve some kind of matching activities. In addition to modeling, the terms imitation, observational learning, vicarious learning, identification, internalization, introjection, incorporation, copying, social facilitation, contagion, and role taking can all be encountered in descriptions of social learning. While not denying the value of any of these words, Bandura (1969) chooses to use "modeling" as a general term, prefering it to "imitation" because he thinks that the latter seems to imply simple mimicry of responses, and Bandura is concerned with a broader range of effects. Other terms, for example, "identification," are considered by Bandura to be too diffuse in meaning.

Bandura distinguishes between three separate effects of modeling. The first, an *observational learning effect*, is demonstrated when an individual who has watched a model exhibit a response that is novel to the viewer reproduces the response in substantially the same form. Second, *inhibition effects* can occur, in which individuals become less likely to display a behavior already in their repertoire or become generally less responsive as a result of observing a model's behavior that has led to punishing consequences. Third, *disinhibitory effects* are evident when an individual observes a model undertake, without punishment, acts that the observer has regarded as threatening, frightening, or prohibitive. As we shall discover in Chapter 6, using modeling procedures to bring about disinhibitory effects toward threatening objects has had very beneficial effects in the treatment of certain phobic conditions, in which a person is inhibited about approaching particular objects or situations.

All three of the above phenomena depend upon the observer being able to imitate what is modeled. Attempts to explain observational learning try to account for the person learning to match the perceived actions. For children to learn by imitation, they must first learn to imitate.

EXPLAINING OBSERVATIONAL LEARNING AND IMITATION

A number of explanations have been advanced to account for the acquisition of imitative skills. Early investigators believed imitation to be an instinctive capability. This view is incorrect, but some findings by M. K. Moore and A. N. Meltzoff (Parton, 1976) suggest that infants as young as 2 weeks of age may be capable of primitive imitative responses. Alternative explanations of imitation have invoked principles of association. Stated simply, such theories claim that stimuli which have been associated with an act are likely to become ones that lead to the act being performed. Imitation is said to be possible when people can match observed responses that are similar to the feedback to their own previous actions. Individuals may acquire a fairly small repertoire of responses, but combining responses in different sequences produces a variety of behaviors.

Associative explanations of imitation are limited in that they cannot account for the fact that while some social stimuli associated with an act elicit a repetition of the act, other stimuli that have just as often been associated with the activity have no such effect. Nor can a purely associative account explain how people come to produce a response that they have not made previously. It can give a possible explanation of the fact that acts which can already be performed may be elicited by seeing other people perform them, but the acquisition new activities remains unexplained.

A number of alternative attempts to explain imitation, emphasize the importance of matching responses being reinforced. Miller and Dollard (1941), for instance, suggested that when imitative acts are repeatedly rewarded, the act of imitation acquires the status of a secondary (learned) drive, so that individuals will regularly imitate what they observe. Furthermore, as a result of conditioning, many parental behaviors acquire a reinforcing function for the infant. Imitating parental acts has reinforcing consequences, and the future likelihood of imitative acts is thereby increased. In addition, Staats (1968) has suggested that the more similar the infant's responses to those of the parents, the greater the probability of reinforcement.

Accounts that emphasize the role of reinforcement help to explain how children become motivated to imitate and to act in ways that become increasingly similar to behaviors of their parents. However, the origins of imitative behavior remain unexplained. A satisfactory explanation may necessitate looking beyond principles of association and reinforcement and considering the cognitive processes of the learner. In a theory advanced by Bandura (1977), it is noted that a person who observes a model does not just acquire specific stimulus-response associations, but gains information about the model's actions. Four related processes are necessary for this to happen. The first is attention. The observer not only has to be exposed to modeled acts, but he must also attend to them and discern the distinctive features of the behavior. A number of factors influence how people will attend to modeled behavior. For instance, individuals will be especially likely to attend to a model's activities if they expect to be rewarded for imitating them, or if the model is especially attractive, distinctive, or possesses desirable attributes, such as success, money, or political power. So far as observing live models is concerned, the circumstances of a child's life will determine which people serve as models who are regularly observed.

Second, Bandura points out that as well as attending to modeled activities, a person must form a memory representation of the observed acts. Information about the activity is retained in a form that is more schematized or abstract than the original physical act itself. Bandura notes that the ability to perform learned responses on occasions removed from the time at which they were first observed necessitates the retention in memory of information about the observed events. He claims that most attempts to explain imitative learning have ignored this difficulty. Bandura draws attention to two representational systems in which information from observational learning can be retained. These are the "imaginal" and "verbal." Imaginal representations, are used when the observed event involves highly distinctive physical activities, as in sports, for example. Verbal coding is used for observed events that are relatively lengthy or complex or do not involve distinctive physical acts. For example, a verbal coding would be adopted for learning the route transversed by an observed model, since the instruction "Take third turn on the right then the second left turn" is more effective than depending upon a visual image of the itinerary.

The effectiveness of symbolically representing information acquired in observational learning is demonstrated by an experiment of Bandura, Grusec, and Menlove (1966). Children watched a film in which people performed complicated sequences of activities, and some of the children were instructed to describe the behavior sequences in words as they saw them performed. Others had to count rapidly while they watched the film. This activity was designed to prevent any verbal coding of the responses that the children observed. Later, observational learning was tested. It was found that those children who had verbally coded the events they had seen in the film could reproduce significantly more of the observed responses than children who had seen the models but had been prevented from describing them in words. These children who gave verbal descriptions retained more than twice as high a proportion of these filmed activities that they had coded in words than of the activities they had not coded verbally.

On the whole, older children and adults are more likely than young children to give spontaneous verbal descriptions when they are observing visual events, and learning is influenced by their doing so (Gerst, 1971). As we might expect, explicit instructions to provide verbal descriptions as events are being observed are more likely to increase observational learning by younger children than by older children. The habit of verbalizing perceived events is a kind of strategy that enables mature people to learn more than less able learners. In later chapters we shall have more to say about the influence of strategies used by individual learners.

In addition to the attention and retention processes that are needed for observational learning, Bandura lists a third component, "motor reproduction processes." Motor processes are required for the actual performance of the activities, and are guided by stored information about them. Bandura considers that producing responses similar to ones that have been observed is achieved by mechanisms similar to those necessary for copying the actions of models at the same time they are performing them, or for following direct instructions. However, symbolic representation is especially valuable if previously observed activities are to be imitated. Of course people cannot copy activities they have observed unless they can carry out the necessary motor actions. At the outset of learning they may be unable to do so, for instance, in circumstances in which complicated new action sequences are required, as in skilled crafts and sports. At sporting events, spectators sometimes feel that they could perform as well as the golf or tennis stars they are watching, but these experiences usually turn out to be illusory. When the skill to perform a sequence of activities is lacking, learning may be helped by methods of instruction in which the component actions are modeled one at a time. In this way the learner can acquire the elements separately, before attempting the whole sequence of activities.

The final component of observational learning and imitation listed by Bandura is provision for motivational factors. Reinforcement variables can influence observational learning in a number of ways. As was noted earlier, the attention paid to models is influenced by the perceived reward value of imitating their behavior and by attributes of the model, such as attractiveness or other desirable qualities. Motivational factors exert a further influence after the behavior has been observed. Even if a person has learned to act in a particular way, the acquired ability may never be performed if conditions are unfavorable. If learners are not motivated to act in the way they have learned to do, the performance will not be activated. This is often fortunate, for example in respect to the horrific forms of behavior that are learned from observing violent television programs.

Babies frequently imitate. They need to acquire imitative skills and to gain habits of matching observed behavior. Young children sometimes engage in the game of repeating everything a parent does or says, and the reaction of the imitated parent may reinforce the imitative behavior.

Bandura's account of the processes of observational learning and imitation gives a more detailed description than the earlier theories, primarily because it takes into account the mental processing by the learner. This is especially important when events are being represented in a person's memory. The interpretation of observed events largely depend upon the cognitive capacities of the individual. What is perceived by two separate observers may be surprisingly different. The skilled enthusiast who watches a game of football, or the musically educated person who listens to a Beethoven symphony, perceive things very differently from naive observers. In this context, Blake's statement that "The fool sees not the tree the wise man sees" is quite literally true.

First Attempts at Imitating

Some aspects of learning to imitate have yet to be adequately explained. Bandura's account illuminates some of the conditions and processes that are necessary for imitation to occur, but it has little to say about the way in which the ability to imitate originates in the very young infant. Parton (1976) points out that observations made by Piaget give some useful clues. Piaget observed that when young babies watched a facial response that they could not yet imitate, they would sometimes make movements that, while not matching the observed response, displayed a functional similarity to it. For instance, Piaget noticed that all of his own three children would at some stage open and close their hands or mouth on seeing a model opening and closing his eyes. The children appeared to be able to produce behavior that matched the model's actions in some way, before they could imitate the particular physical response. Similarly, an infant, after watching the model close his eyes, was seen to pull a pillow over his own eyes. Parton suggests that children search through their repertoire of behaviors to find a response that matches the observed activities.

Even simple forms of recognition require some kind of search. What is perceived has to be matched with something stored in memory. Also, a decision must be made concerning the equivalence of the observed behavior and the baby's own actions. This is difficult for young infants, and early attempts at matching the behaviors of others are inaccurate. Infants' responses may be only grossly similar, or similar in just one dimension. The difficulty of matching is increased by the fact that the precise stimuli received by the infants from their observations on the one hand, and from their own imitative behavior on the other hand, may be very different. The need for observed events to be matched on a number of separate dimensions adds to the children's difficulty.

Normally, the search process preceding imitative behavior is a covert one. It is not usually so readily apparent from the infant's actual behavior as it was in the instances described by Piaget. Certainly, whatever the precise nature of the search processes that underly the matching required for a response to be imitated, it is clear that imitative behavior does depend on active mental processing by the individual. The essential searching, matching, coding, and retention functions cannot be achieved by mechanisms of simple associative learning.

THE MOTHER'S ROLE IN EARLY SOCIAL LEARNING

During the first year of life, the child's social world is a highly restricted one. The immobility of young babies limits them to a fairly uniform environment, except at those times when their caretaker, usually the mother, is attending to them. In the first months, the mother is the major source of social events, and indeed the main source of most forms of stimulation. She not only provides the material needs but she gives her infant visual stimulation often combined with movements, sounds, and touch sensations. All of these are provided at close proximity and are appropriate to the incompletely developed sensory capacities of the young infant. The mother acts in ways that are responsive to the baby's own behavior; mother and child engage in sequences of interaction, and signal to each other in a manner that is undoubtedly social. Interactions and exchanges between mother and infant lead to the child acquiring learned social skills and social habits that form the beginning of a repertoire of behaviors for dealing with social aspects of the human world.

The mother helps to make it possible for her infant to acquire a sense of mastery and control by creating situations in which the child's responses have predictable outcomes. The child learns that his actions matter: they have a tangible effect upon the environment. Children's growing sense of mastery rather than helplessness emerges from their early experiences of predictable outcomes to their own responses. Synchrony between responses and outcomes is basic to the child's gaining a sense of being in control. Observing his own child, Seligman (1975) notes,

> "He sucks, the world responds with warm milk. He pats the breast, his mother tenderly squeezes him back. He takes a break and coos, his mother coos back. He gives a happy chirp, his mother attempts to chirp back. Each step he takes is synchronized with a response from the world" (Seligman, 1975, p. 139).

The Freudian View

Freud recognized that early social encounters with the mother are important for the formation of adult character and personality. He considered that two social situations, feeding and toilet training, are especially crucial. Both of these begin early in a child's life and both involve frequent, close and sustained interaction between mother and infant. Freud stated that the way in which children adjust to feeding and toilet-training situations has a large influence on personality development.

The young child's progress through the stages in which these events are first encountered is affected by the way in which the mother behaves, and by the mother-child relationship that is established. If there is harmony and progress is satisfactory, all is well. For various reasons, strains and traumas may occur, leading to a child's fixating at a particular stage or regressing to an earlier stage in which there was greater harmony. Such deviations from smooth progress through the different stages were thought by Freud to provide the roots for personality disorders in later life.

Even if we reject most of the detailed content of Freudian theory, we can note that Freud was absolutely right to draw attention to the importance of early social interactions with the mother. In the young child's daily routine feeding and toilet training provide two periods in the day when the child is awake, away from the inanimate world of the crib, and cooperating closely with another human being, the mother. At feeding and toilet-training times, the infant communicates with the mother at length and is reinforced by her. These social situations, in which both mother and infant depend upon the cooperation of each other, provide the child's first regular and frequent experiences of working with another person. Since both kinds of situations take place regularly and frequently, and their duration is quite long, each member of the pair has the opportunity to become fully aware of the other. The mother responds in a way that becomes increasingly predictable as she learns to adjust and time her own behavior in the light of a sensitive reading of the communications of her baby. Thus, it is small wonder that feeding and toilet training are important, since they provide the stage for important early social learning. Freud was right to stress their importance.

Early Social Interaction with the Mother

There is considerable evidence about the ways in which mothers contribute to their children's learning and development. In the present chapter we shall be limited to the specifically social forms of learning that are caused or directly influenced by mother-infant interaction. However, we can briefly note that the caretaker's influence is also crucial for the acquisition of intellectual abilities, such as the capacity to recognize and remember objects, and for the development of an awareness that perceived objects have a separate identity and permanence. Investigations by Piaget have shown that very young children are only aware of the existence of objects in the world when they are directly experiencing them. Regular interaction with the mother contributes to a growing awareness of the permanent identity of objects. Children become increasingly able to recognize previously perceived objects on the basis of attributes of them that have been retained in memory. The fact that the infant sees the same mother, day after day, rather than a succession of constantly changing caretakers, is almost certainly important for these developments. In impersonal and under-manned orphanages and institutions for babies (see Dennis, 1960, for example) lack of regular mothering is a cause of retarded develpment.

As I have said, circumstances in which mother and infant regularly and frequently engage in close communication provide an excellent setting for early social learning. Successful feeding is helped by social skills not unlike those that are apparent when two people are engaged in a conversation (Schaffer, 1977). The two participants need to be attuned to each other's signals, and their excahnges must follow shared codes. As in a conversation between adults, harmonious communication depends on the two members of the pair being able not only to understand the same verbal language, but also to produce and react to a variety of nonverbal signs. As Schaffer (1977) points out, the two participants have to integrate their contributions in a way that enables the conversation to flow satisfactorily. A number of rules or conventions are followed. Although neither partner may be able to express or articulate the rules, the necessity for them becomes apparent when people attempt to converse in circumstances where conversational rules and conventions are not shared, as in the embarrassingly stilted conversation that takes place when people with extremely different cultural backgrounds try to converse.

Observations of interactions between mother and young children demonstrate some surprisingly complex integrations and temporal synchronisations between the responses. Preverbal infants have an admittedly limited range of responses for signaling their needs and for communicating with their mother. However, in addition to being able to cry and (by around the second month) to smile, their patterning and timing of certain other responses, for instance sucking and swallowing, have communicative functions that the mother learns to "read." Changes in alertness and general responsiveness can provide the sensitive mother with further information about her child's needs.

Findings of Observational Research into Mother-Infant Interaction

Observations by Jaffe, Stern and Peery (1973) led them to suggest that the time patterns of the looking and gazing that occur when mothers and infants communicate with each other are the same as those found in verbal exchanges between adults. Stern (1974) discovered that when 3-month-old infants and their mothers were observed in a face-to-face situation, and their head movements were carefully timed, each turned toward or away from the other person in close time with the head movements of the other, almost as if they were dancing a waltz. The partners followed a basic pattern but carefully adjusted their own behavior to the detailed moves of the other person.

Dialogue is evident in many mother-infant social situations. Mother and infant take turns at acting different roles and reciprocating, with the interaction being sustained by both partners rather than just one of them. Kaye (1977) noticed that when mothers were feeding their infants, the mother was most active during the pauses between the infant's bursts of sucking. The mother would stimulate and talk to her baby during the pauses, but as the baby started to suck she would become more passive. Thus the mother and the infant took turns at being the more active partner, and the mother allowed herself to be paced by her baby and responded quickly to the signals in the infant's behavior. Kaye also observed similar "dialogues" between mother and infant in play situations in which the baby was acquiring new motor skills. Typically, the mother would remain relatively passive while her child was giving full attention to the task, but when the baby stopped attending, she would do something to maintain the baby's interest. Again, mother and infant took turns at playing the active role, and mothers who were responsive to their baby's signals would dovetail their own actions with those of the baby to form a harmonious sequence.

In early life, the social dialogue is slightly one-sided. The mother is the more sensitive, responsive partner, and paces her behavior to match that of her baby, who does not yet possess the capacity to act similarly. However, young infants soon become sensitive to the signals implicit in the mother's behavior, and by the time infants are 1 year old it is possible to observe extended and complex chains of interacting behaviors. David and Appell (1969) found that the exchanges that took place in each of the mother-infant pairs they observed were strikingly consistent and similar from one occasion to the next, although there were large differences between pairs. One kind of response chain, in which mother and child successively responded to the actions of the other, is illustrated by the following example.

> Molly, under a table, is playing peek-a-boo with the observer and smiling at her. Her mother says to the observer, "You see she is copying Susan," and to Molly "Come along, let's go and fetch Susan" → Molly (forgetting her game with the observer) promptly comes out of the hiding place, responds to her mother with happy sounds, takes her hand → they both go towards the door → mother asks Molly to say good-bye to the observer → Molly ignores this but tries to open the door → mother, wishing her to stop doing so, picks her up → Molly protests strongly—mother says, "Come along, it isn't time yet" and to

distract her gives her Susan's doll → Molly takes hold of the doll and speaks to it → mother puts Molly down → but Molly goes back to her mother and wants to be picked up → mother says cheerfully, "Always Mummy" and gives her another doll → Molly smiles broadly at her mother → mother announces reluctantly, "I won't look any more" → Molly seems content and retires to play under the table → mother looks down at her and asks, "What are you doing there?" → Molly comes out and stands up . . . etc. (from David and Appell, 1969, p. 174).

The patterns of interaction in five mother-infant pairs observed by David and Appell differed in a number of ways. Three of the five pairs were judged to interact in a consistently intense manner, but the tone of the dialogue between another pair was described by David and Appell as being flat. In two pairs, the interactions were regularly happy and pleasurable for each of the partners, although the pairs differed in the tone of the exchanges, with the dialogue in one pair being described as "happy and boisterous" while the other pair were described as interacting in a "happy and quiet" manner. In another pair, David and Appell considered that the pattern of interaction between mother and infant displayed mutual dissatisfaction on the part of each partner. Even in pairs who usually interacted in a harmonious way there were occasional moments of disharmony, anger, and conflict being displayed by mother, infant, or both.

The evidence from studies in which mothers and children are observed as they interact with each other suggests that the mother-infant situation provides an excellent starting point for the learning of a number of important social skills, although we cannot be certain that this is so. Further research is needed to establish whether or not early exchanges with the mother do lead to the child learning essential social skills. Useful evidence about the effects of different patterns of early interactions would be provided by showing that individual differences in adults' social skills and habits are consistently related to their early interactions with their mothers. Unfortunately, few hard facts are available concerning the long-term influences of early mother-infant social interactions. Another way to discover if early patterns of mother-infant interactions are likely to have a large influence is to find out if what is observed in early mother-infant exchanges is predictive of the child's concurrent behavior in different situations. David and Appell (1969) provide some evidence of this kind, and the findings of a number of studies by Mary Ainsworth and her her co-workers provide further confirmation.

Observations by David and Appell show that the manner in which mother and infant interact together is related to the behavior of the child when the mother is not present. These authors noted, for instance, how the children reacted when they saw a stranger. One child they observed enjoyed a very close and intense relationship with her mother, and mother-infant exchanges customarily consisted of lengthy chains of responses involving each partner. There was considerable physical contact and the child would often follow the mother in order to avoid separation. When this child was confronted with a stranger, her reaction was to scream and cling to her mother, but at the same time to display intense interest in the new person. Gradually she would start to look up and leave her mother, slowly approaching the stranger but leaping back to the mother again if the new individual moved toward the child.

When a second child was confronted with a stranger, she showed much less sign of disturbance and would approach the stranger cautiously but with some confidence, observing the stranger from a distance at first, before she walked up to him and began to play. Observation of this child with her mother revealed a pattern of interaction between the pair that was different in a predictable way from what had been observed in the previous pair. The exchanges between the second child and her mother were less intense in tone and shorter in duration, and the lengthy responses observed in the first pair were largely absent. The second pair touched, kissed, and cuddled less, and their exchanges depended to a greater extent on visual cues and on visual attending by both mother and infant. David and Appell state that the different ways in which the two infants responded when confronted with a stranger were in line with what might have been predicted following observation of situations involving mother and infant together.

On the basis of a large number of observations, David and Appell claim that all areas of a child's personality, not just the area of social learning, are deeply influenced by interactions with the mother, and that over the period of early childhood her reactions to the infant's responses progressively influence the baby's social behaviors and habits. Indeed, however one interprets the detailed activities of mother and infant when they are observed together, it is undeniable that the mother's actions do a great deal to shape the infant's behavior by selectively reinforcing some responses, and by serving as a model whom the child can regularly observe and imitate.

Research by Mary Ainsworth

The evidence provided by David and Appell for their view that early mother-child exchanges form a basis for social learning is somewhat impressionistic. Objective measurement and quantification tend to be subordinated, quite appropriately in view of the aims of the research, to the desire to observe mother and infant together in circumstances that are as natural as possible. Investigations by Mary Ainsworth have also examined the relation between the contents of mother-infant, and Ainsworth has emphasized objective measurement of behavior. A study by Bell and Ainsworth (1972) examined the relation between mother-infant interactions and crying. This, as we have seen, is a form of social behavior that is present right from birth, and has the important function of communicating the individual's needs to the mother and to other people. Normally, the amount of crying decreases after the earliest months, as the child gains communicative skills that are more precise and more effective. Mothers usually respond to their young infants when they cry, even though the view is sometimes expressed that responding to the cries of young babies is likely to make them spoiled and fussy.

Bell and Ainsworth measured the frequency and duration of crying over the first year of infants' lives, in order to discover whether there was any relationship between the mother's responsiveness to episodes of crying and the amount of crying that occurred. A number of mother-infant pairs were seen at home for four-hour sessions. The authors found large individual differences in the total amount of crying. On the whole however, the less a mother attended to her infant's cries during one 3-month part of the year, the greater was the amount of crying during the following three months. This result suggests that ignoring crying will increase rather than decrease the likelihood that the baby will cry frequently in the future. A policy of not attending to a young baby's cries seems unlikely to be successful in reducing the frequency of crying. We must note, however, that the above findings are in the form of correlations. They do not provide firm proof of a cause-and-effect relationship between the mother's actions and her child's crying.

The fact that infants' behavior affects how their mothers respond, as well as vice versa, might partially account for the results of the above study. However, it was found that the frequency of a baby's crying during one 3-month period was not so closely related to the mother's tendency to ignore cries in the succeeding period. When we combine this observation with the finding reported above, that a mother's responsiveness is related to the infant's crying in future months, we are encouraged to conclude that mothers' responses to infants' cries influence their babies' behavior to a greater extent than babies' activities influence their mothers. It is interesting to note that no clear relationship was observed during the first few months of life between the extent to which crying was ignored and the frequency of crying during the same period. Since during the earliest months the infant has yet to develop more effective means of communication, a fair amount of crying is necessary and desirable.

Those infants in the study by Bell and Ainsworth whose mothers were most responsive not only cried less frequently than the others but advanced further toward acquiring social skills in the form of more mature methods of infant communication, involving facial expressions, gestures, and vocalizations. The sensitive mothers' actions, in responding to their infants, contributed to the acquisition of the more advanced social abilities that replace early crying.

The effectiveness and the harmoniousness of mother-infant exchanges may also influence the learning of additional social habits and skills. Stayton, Hogan, and Ainsworth (1971) undertood an investigation to discover whether a mother's responsiveness to her infant contributes to the child's becoming socially compliant and obedient. Previous observations had suggested to the authors that infants having harmonious and secure relationships with the mother tended to be compliant to the mother's commands and that training specifically directed toward the learning of obedience was unnecessary. The infants were observed by Stayton, et al., for four-hour periods over the first year of life. Observers measured a number of potentially important factors including the sensitivity of the mother to her infant, her use of procedures explicitly designed to teach the baby to be obedient (such as verbal commands and prohibitions), and discipline-oriented physical interventions, including slapping the baby and jerking the child away from forbidden objects.

In fact, neither verbal commands and physical interventions were positively related to measures of the infants' obedience. The babies of mothers who made numerous commands and interventions, did not become any more obedient than other babies. However, when the mothers were divided into two groups according to their rated sensitivity to their infants, it was found that the infants of the more sensitive mothers obeyed on 86 percent of observed occasions, whereas infants of the less sensitive mothers obeyed only 49 percent of the time. Thus the development of those skills necessary for the infant to be able to obey the mother appears to be related to a mother's relationship with her infant. Furthermore, the acquisition of internalized social controls by infants (indicated by self-inhibiting and self-controlling behaviors) was also related to the mother's sensitivity, her acceptance of her child, and her cooperation with the infant. The children's ability to control their own behavior was unrelated to the frequency of deliberate attempts to impose discipline.

In brief, the findings indicate that for infants in the first year of life both obedience to others and self-control are more closely related to the existence of a harmonious, cooperative, and mutually satisfying relationship with the mother than to the use of any procedures explicitly designed to teach the child to be obedient. There is no reason to suppose that fundamentally different principles govern the acquisition of other social skills required for cooperating with others and establishing mutually rewarding social relationships in later life.

ATTACHMENT

Since the mother is a very important figure in the child's early life, it is not surprising that separation from her causes hardship and distress. A report appearing in 1951 by John Bowlby claimed that maternal deprivation was a root cause of mental disorder in later life and of personality inadequacies. In particular, Bowlby suggested that prolonged separation from the mother lay behind the behavior of *psychopathic* individuals, who exhibit social deficiencies such as an inability to form bonds with others, a lack of feelings of responsibility, and an absence of a normal conscience. Psychopathic behavior is exhibited in apparently illogical and thoughtless acts, often violent or delinquent, and commonly physically or socially destructive.

Research findings published since Bowlby's 1951 report indicate that the link between maternal deprivation in early childhood and serious psychological problems in adult life is not so clear as it originally appeared to be. It is not easy to identify the chains of cause and effect that link adult personality to the circumstances of life in early childhood. The task of tracing such links is made more difficult by the fact that maternal deprivation in real life is often tied to other social problems and sources of disharmony that are known to contribute to maladjustment and social inadequacy, such as poverty, drunkenness, family strife, divorce, and battering of wife and children. However, the balance of evidence strongly indicates that normal development depends upon the infant having the opportunity to interact regularly over a long period with one person, or a small number of individuals, so that the infant is able to establish a close human relationship. The disruption of mothering contributes to problems of adjustment in later life.

One outcome of research into maternal deprivation has been to introduce the widespread use of certain psychological terms that have considerable relevance to social learning by children and adults. Three terms, *attachment, bonds,* and *identification,* are frequently encountered, and each refers to mechanisms that are thought to underlie social learning. Matters are complicated by the fact that not all users of these words appear to agree on their precise definitions, and by the fact that some psychologists are more willing than others to admit that inferred constructs such as these can help to explain social behavior. In general, researchers who incline to strongly behaviorist views, such as Bandura (1969), Staats (1971), and Gewirtz (1969), tend to be unwilling to concede that much explanatory value can be found in terms of this kind. They would argue that such terms refer to processes that are unobservable and of doubtful real substance. Other psychologists, for example Ainsworth (for example, Ainsworth, Bell and Stayton, 1974) and Bowlby (1969), are more inclined to claim that social behavior and social learning cannot be adequately explained unless we introduce concepts such as these.

Early Attachments

"Attachment behaviors" can be defined as acts that seek or maintain proximity to another individual. Behavior toward objects of attachment is different from behavior toward other people in the same location. Bowlby points out that all primate species cling to certain objects with great tenacity, but he notes that attachment also necessitates learning to discriminate between different individuals and becoming tied to a particular one. In some monkey species, attachment behavior toward a preferred individual may be evident within the first week of life, and once established, the preference is extremely strong and persistent. Attachment behavior in man takes much longer to become established, largely because some time is required before infants can reliably recognize their mother and become aware of her as an individual person. Furthermore, the physical locomotion that is necessary for some kinds of proximity-seeking actions is absent in humans during the earliest months, although the baby's ability to communicate by crying and by other forms of signaling behavior provides some compensation. Unlearned or instinctive factors may have been involved in the evolution of human attachment behaviors. In many species, activities by the mother or the infant, or by both acting together, that function to maintain proximity have survival value for the infant through providing protection from predators (Bowlby, 1969).

The vast majority of children form strong attachments to their parents. The strongest attachment is usually directed to the mother, but most children also display attachments to other people, such as the father. The development of specific attachments depends on there being regular contacts between the child and the other individual. Schaffer and Emerson (1964) found that 29 percent of the infants they observed formed several attachments as soon as they became capable of making specific attachments. By the age of 18 months, 87 percent of the children had formed multiple attachments, five or more in the case of a third of them. The contact needs to be reasonably prolonged, but the intensity of the interaction appears to be equally important (Rutter, 1972). Children display stronger attachments toward mothers who play with their infants frequently and give them a good deal of attention than to mothers who interact infrequently (providing only routine physical care). Attachment develops most readily between infants and those adults who are sensitive to the individual child's signals and who adapt their behavior to meet the needs of the individual child.

The Secondary Reinforcement Account of the Development of Attachment Behavior

The central role that is attributed to attachment in modern research investigating the origins of social behavior contrasts with the earlier view of psychologists influenced by stimulus-response accounts of learning. According to the latter, the close relationships that exist between mother and infant are caused by a conditioning process. Stimuli that are associated with primary reinforcers (ones which meet an organism's basic needs for sleep, food, and so on) acquire the status of a secondary or conditioned reinforcer, thereby gaining reward value. Since the mother's presence is encountered by the child at the same time as food, this presence is said to acquire reinforcing properties via a process not entirely dissimilar from that in which a buzzer became a sign for food in Pavlov's dogs. As an outcome of generalization, according to this view, children also begin to approach the mother for other needs, and they generalize their social approaching behavior to include other people. However, as it happens, nonreinforced or punished attachment responses by human infants get stronger rather than diminish. Bowlby cites this finding as an argument against the secondary reinforcement explanation of attachment behavior.

A body of evidence that appears to contradict the "cupboard love" explanation of a child's becoming attached to the mother was obtained by Harlow and others (for example, Harlow, 1958) in work with infant monkeys. In one study Harlow placed infant monkeys in cages that contained two very different kinds of surrogate mothers. One of these was made of wire, and there was a bottle attached to it through which the infant monkeys were fed. The other surrogate mother was covered in soft toweling, but it did not provide food. Contrary to a secondary reinforcement theory of attachment behavior, the infant monkeys approached the cloth-covered mother frequently and clung to it, and they spent much less time with the wire mother. The tactile qualities of the surrogate mother appear to have been important, irrespective of the fact that the wire model was the one which was associated with satisfying the need for food. Furthermore, when monkeys were fearful they more frequently approached the cloth-covered mother than the wire mother. For instance, if a large model spider was placed in the cage, infant monkeys would run to the cloth mother. But although the cloth-covered monkeys were clung to and sought after by the infant monkeys in preference to the wire models, they did not by any means provide all the essential qualities of a real mother. The development of monkeys brought up with surrogate mothers was markedly abnormal.

Attachment Behavior in Children

Attachment behavior can be seen in young infants who are left by their mother in an empty and unfamiliar room. The infants will follow their mother out of the room with the least possible delay. However, it may be relatively easy to modify this behavior, and Corter, Rheingold, and Eckerman (1972) found that if the unfamiliar room contained just one new toy, infants aged 10 months would remain there, apparently without distress, for an average period of three minutes. Furthermore, at around this age children display great interest in strangers, and are not by any means always fearful of unfamiliar people. The tendency to approach the mother may, in part, reflect the fact that not only does she represent comfort and security that satisfy the infant's need for attachment and dependency, but she also provides that part of the child's environment which is most stimulating, most responsive, and most interesting for the infant.

Schaffer (1977) considers that attachment behavior develops in three basic steps. First, an initial attraction to other human beings (perhaps related to their qualities of mobility and responsiveness) makes children prefer them to inanimate features of the environment. Second, children learn to distinguish between different people, and they become able to recognize their mother as a familiar person. Third, they form lasting bonds with particular individuals, and they seek their company and their attention. The third stage must await the earlier developments, since it is essential for the infants to be able to recognize their mother before they can become attached to her. It is not until children are around 6 months of age that they display clear signs of missing the absent mother and are seriously distrubed by being separated from her.

Although social attachments are customarily formed between the young child and other individuals, the breakdown of normal attachment relationships is not particularly rare. Schaffer (1977) notes that the number of children who are the victims of cruelty, neglect, or desertion, or who are even battered to death by their parents is too great for such instances to be written off as exceptional aberrations. Schaffer also mentions the Ik, a "loveless society" reported by Colin Turnbull (1973). With these people social disruption, partly caused by the removal of the people from their traditional hunting ground and the consequent erosion of their habitual way of life, has led to the disintegration of social organization. As a result, the institution of the family has been virtually destroyed, and people emerge from the struggle for basic survival lacking the emotions of love and tenderness, especially toward the very young.

Turnbull observed that children in the Ik society receive no parental love and affection, that hunger is completely ignored in all but the very youngest children, and that the parents do not attempt to protect their babies from danger. It appears from Turnbull's report that the consequences to the individual child of an upbringing in a human society that lacks the conditions in which attachments may be formed are similar to the consequences found in particular families (within a generally nurturant society) which fail to provide adequately for the social and emotional needs of their young children.

BONDS

The word "bond" is sometimes encountered when social learning and attachment are discussed. The process of attachment is said to involve the acquisition of bonds between a mother and child. As a concrete metaphor the concept of bond formation suggests the physical, proximity-seeking aspect of the mother-child relationship. This aspect is illustrated by the sight of a sheep with her lambs, who run after her whenever she moves away, as if connected to her by an invisible thread. The idea that a bond exists between mother and infant is a metaphorical one. It is probably wrong to assume that there is a specific mechanism for bonding. Rather, bonding is an outcome of attachment, and the broader concept of attachment is more likely to indicate possible underlying processes.

Researchers who have wanted to account for the harmful effects of maternal deprivation have suggested that deprivation effects may be due either to a failure to establish mother-child bonds, or to the disruption of already established bonds. Disruption of bonds arises from the separation of the child from the person (normally the mother) to whom a strong primary attachment has been formed. There is ample evidence to show that such separation does cause considerable distress in infants aged around 6 months and older, the age from which the mother is consistently recognized as an individual. It is hard to say whether relatively brief separations of periods of up to a month or so have any permanent effects, as the evidence on this question is inconclusive.

The effects of separation partly depend upon the precise reasons for the separation, and upon the home and family circumstances. To assume that the outcome of a situation that involves separation is simply a result of the separation *per se* is to oversimplify the real state of affairs. Rutter (1972) notes that delinquency in adolescence is strongly associated with broken homes and separation from the mother in early life, but the particular causes of the separation are important. For instance, children from homes disrupted by divorce and separation do tend to become delinquent, but children from homes broken by the death of a parent do not have a higher rate of delinquency than other children.

Turning from the circumstances that lead to the disruption of bonds to those in which mother-infant bonds fail to develop, for one reason or another, it is more than likely that such failures will have serious consequences. The findings we have previously surveyed indicate that the origins of the social learning involved in establishing relationships with others, communicating with other people, and acting responsibly toward individuals, lie in habits and skills that are formed in the course of early mother-child interactions.

Circumstances in which bonds fail to develop may give rise to severe inadequacies in adult personality and especially to the psychopathic traits of adults who lack normal ties of affection and conscience. Bowlby claimed such inadequacies result from the rather broadly defined problem of maternal deprivation. Children reared in impersonal institutions that do not provide opportunities to form attachments with specific individuals do show unusual patterns of social life. For instance, they display clinging and unusually dependent behavior in infancy, followed by indiscriminate friendliness to all adults, and attention-seeking in later months. The suggestion that the problems are caused by failure to develop a "bond," provides an illuminating metaphor, but it does not necessarily correspond with an underlying process, and the explanatory value of the term is therefore limited.

As we have noted, psychologists differ as to the extent to which they perceive constructs such as attachment, bond, and identification, and related concepts such as "dependency" as being conducive to increased understanding of social behavior. Among behaviorists, Gewirtz (1969) has suggested that concepts of this kind should be used only as abstractions to denote classes of functional relationships in which stimuli provided by an individual exert stimulus control over responses in another individual (as in attachment). He is against using these terms as though they represented unitary processes. However, we could argue that there are likely to be common elements in the differing circumstances which display evidence of attachment. The different instances of attachment may well have more in common with one another than the fact that a person exerts stimulus control over another person's responses.

IDENTIFICATION

Primitive manifestations of attachment do not survive early childhood, but as we become more independent with increasing age, we remain dependent in many respects on other individuals. Attached by bonds of love and affection, we continue to be influenced by other people. The concept of "identification," which was introduced to psychology by Freud, refers to the fact that people internalize attributes or behaviors associated with others. Children typically identify with a parent or with other people to whom they are attached. For instance, a 6-year-old boy may identify with his father, and thereby regard himself as possessing some of the parent's characteristics, including his maleness. Children vicariously share the experiences of the parent, behaving as if events that have happened in the parent's life are happening to themselves. Thus, a girl experiences pride at seeing her mother being successful, and she copies some of her actions and shares her attitudes. A young child may assume the role of her mother in the kitchen, engaging in the activities she sees her mother performing and experiencing feelings associated with her awareness of the mother. In these circumstances the child appears to have internalized some characteristics of the parent, and experiences feelings or emotions that derive from identification with that other person.

Freud's explanation for the emergence of identification is in reasonably close accord with modern views on social learning. Coinciding with the growth of the superego, needs and motives that were initially manipulated and controlled by external factors become internalized, according to Freud, within the child. After learning that certain activities result in approval and that other behaviors meet disapproval, children gradually begin to avoid behaving in a particular way because they identify with the source of the disapproval rather than becuase they fear punishment or disapproval of such behavior. Young children thus become socialized, taking into themselves important conventions, laws, and values of society. Such internalization of values through identification is clearly invaluable for the smooth running of any large human group in which individuals depend upon each other and have to cooperate with one another. The fact that people can internalize approved attitudes and can share taboos and social sanctions drastically reduces the need for aversive external controls and punishments. Hence identification reduces interpersonal friction and human conflict. However, the internalization of behavioral controls can also be regarded in a less favorable light. Leonard (1968), who writes of "internalizing the whip," argues that

> too often, indeed, such terms as conscience, dignity, stoicism, heroism, or even glory have constituted ultimately undefinable variations on a single theme: man's endeavour to act and speak in a manner aversive to him without the prod of external punishment. During the entire period of civilization, a large measure, perhaps a majority of an individual's education was devoted to teaching him how to be less than he could be and to perform this feat with the aid of no external taskmaster whatever. The whip securely tucked inside, Lord Raglan's rider could charge the cannons at Balaclava with a narrow smile and a quip (Leonard, 1968, p. 76–77).

It has been suggested by some writers that, contrary to the views of Freud, the processes to which the term "identification" are normally applied are essentially those of observational learning from adult models. The tendency of children to identify with parents and with other objects of attachment is explained by the facts that the parents provide the most frequently available models for young children to observe. Also, by virtue of parental status, they control a number of the resources that function as effective rewards or reinforcers.

An account along these lines provides a satisfactory explanation of some, if not all, aspects of identification. The social significance of identification for human life is considerable, irrespective of whether identification phenomena are caused by mechanisms that are basically similar to those underlying social learning or whether different processes are involved. It would be surprising if identification phenomena were not affected by the variables that have been found to be influential in research on observational learning and imitation. However, in identifying, a person not only imitates particular observed responses, but regularly and consistently reproduces the actions of particular individuals, and internalizes attitudes and emotions associated with the model. These facets of identification set it apart from simple forms of imitative learning.

Separate Aspects of Identification

Some authors have regarded identification simply as an interesting phenomenon, and others regard it as an explanation of many human behaviors. Research by Bronfenbrenner (1960) and Mischel (1970) indicates that it is necessary to distinguish between three aspects of the concept's meaning. Identification can first refer to the behavior observed when one person acts like another individual, although behavioral similarity alone does not provide proof of identification. Second, identification can refer to a motive, by which one individual has a disposition to act like or be like another person. This may involve standards of behavior, and it may refer to desires to possess attributes possessed by a particular valued category of people, as in the wish to "be a man" and act in a masculine manner. Identification may also involve people believing that they share characteristics or dispositions of the identified individual. Third, identification can refer to processes or mechanisms through which the imitating or sharing aspects of identification are said to have been acquired. The scores that a person obtains on alternative measures of identification may be very different (Sears, Rau, and Alpert, 1965) indicating that it would probably be wrong to assume that a unitary process underlies all identification phenomena.

Bruner (1966) describes identification as the strong human tendency to model one's self and one's aspirations upon some other person, so that we feel pleasure when we think we have succeeded in being like that figure and suffer when we feel that our behavior has let that person down. Bruner considers that identification is not limited to strong attachments that involve considerable emotional investment. He notes that although children's early identifications may be with parents, individuals do also identify with others. The phenomenon of hero worship by young people is common. Heroes tend to be attractive, glamorous, and successful, combining a number of qualities that are highly valued, but identification can have undesirable consequences, as in Nazi Germany. The ubiquity of the cult of the person in political as well as religous ideologies (Stalin, Mao, Ché Guevara, the Virgin Mary, for example) bears witness to a widespread human need for particular individuals with whom to identify.

Bruner points out that milder forms of identification may be important in everyday life, particularly at school. He emphasizes the influence of competent people with whom we can interact directly, in contrast to the inaccessible popstar or the distant hero. The milder identifications may involve individuals who possess some desired ability that can be acquired through interacting with them. Thus, a good teacher may not only help a child to gain a necessary skill, but may also impart certain attitudes toward the subject of instruction, and possibly attitudes toward learning in general. This is one reason why the effectiveness of teachers cannot be measured simply by assessing their ability to impart knowledge. If Bruner is correct in thinking that the process of education is affected by the identification phenomena he describes, a view which accords with many people's reflections on their own education, it may be that identification processes make a large contribution to decisions about a person's education, career, and lifestyle.

LEARNING AND HUMAN AGGRESSION

The studies of observational learning described earlier in this chapter show that children learn to behave aggressively. An important question is whether human aggression is acquired solely through learning, or whether innate factors also contribute. Since aggression and violence are at the heart of many of the world's problems, it would be valuable to know for certain whether or not human beings are inherently aggressive.

A number of writers have expressed the view that learning is not essential for the emergence of aggressive human acts, and that it simply directs the forms of aggression that occur. Lorenz (1966) and Tinbergen (1951), for instance, consider that aggressive activities in humans are due primarily to innate biological factors, with all forms of human conflict being subject to laws of phylogenetically developed instinctive behavior. They believe that the function of learning and cultural factors is simply to trigger off such instinctive acts. Morris (1967) has expounded a similar view in his book *The Naked Ape*, and Ardrey (1966) has claimed that human beings are instinctively a killer species, possessing an "aggressive imperative" that frequently leads to acts of violence.

Accepting such views can have important social consequences. Eisenberg (1972) has pointed out that what we choose to believe about the nature of humans may influence our own social actions. If we believe that humans are by nature an aggressive, territorial species, we are likely to consider that the more destructive actions of humanity are an inevitable consequence of human nature, and we are likely to be pessimistic about the value of trying to reduce the incidence of human destructiveness through improved education or by other means.

The view that human aggression is innate is not firmly based on valid evidence. The writers cited above are very knowledgeable about certain animal species but less so about the mechanisms underlying human behavior. They have justified their views by introducing observations of aggressive animal behaviors, some of which are known to be controlled by partly innate factors. It is claimed that since some aggressive behaviors in humans parallel forms of aggression in other animals that are influenced by innate mechanisms, the aggressive behaviors of humans must also be innate. In reality, however, the fact that parallel forms of behavior are observed in humans and other species by no means always indicates that similar underlying mechanisms are involved.

Considerable evidence indicates that human aggression is largely the outcome of learning. The sheer range of variability in the extent to which different societies exhibit violence provides a strong counter-argument against the claims that have been made for instinctive determinants. Anthropologists have observed that neighboring cultures sharing similar physical and genetic characteristics can differ very markedly in the extent to which they display violence and aggression. If aggression was innately determined, it would be very difficult to explain why it is absent from so many human societies. Feshbach (1970) notes that even in species that depend much more upon instinctive mechanisms than humans do, learning has an important role as a cause of aggressive activities.

It is not at all hard to understand why children learn to act aggressively. Bandura (1973) has described a large number of ways in which social learning leads to children acting in an aggressive manner. Aggression is observed by some children in their own homes, and the amount of violent behavior children display is closely related to the extent to which their parents act violently (Cohen, 1971). Battered babies tend to grow up to be battering parents. Patterson, Littman and Bricker (1967) suggest that a starting point for aggressive habits may be made by reinforced actions in children as young as 7 months of age. They observed, for instance, that the attempts of an infant to reach for a glass of milk were ignored until the infant began to pummel his mother's arm, and this action was immediately followed by milk being provided. Furthermore, interviews with parents have made it clear that in many families love and rewards, especially from the father, are given when a boy behaves aggressively (Bandura and Walters, 1959). Even when aggressive acts are not rewarded by the parents and the parents themselves never act aggressively in front of the child, television programs provide excellent opportunities for observational learning of violent actions (Howe, 1977b). In addition, other young children may reinforce an individual child's aggression. Patterson Littman and Bricker found that three-quarters of the aggressive acts toward other children they observed in 3 year olds and 4 year olds resulted in the other child acting in a way that rewarded the attacker, for instance, giving him a toy. Clearly, aggression pays!

As Ashley Montagu has remarked, we are not the creatures but the creators of our destiny. Man has evolved as "The most educable of creatures, released from the constraints of a limited learning capacity into the freedom of an unlimited educability" (Montagu, 1976, p. 320). Violent as we may be, there is no justification for regarding human aggression as the inevitable outcome of irreversible instinctive causes.

SUMMARY

1. Each of us depends upon other people, and we learn the skills required for interacting with others. Other people are at least as important a part of our world as are inanimate objects.
2. A number of examples demonstrate that children's own activities are strongly influenced by the behaviors they observe in others.
3. Social learning is influenced by the factors involved in operant conditioning. Conditioning procedures involving reinforcers that take the form of social events can help infants aged 6 months and under to acquire social skills necessary for communicating. However, some findings of earlier research that appeared to demonstrate social conditioning in very young infants may have been produced by eliciting effects of the social events administered as reinforcers.
4. Observation makes a major contribution to social learning. Reinforcing an observed model influences the possibility of the behavior being copied by the learner, but it does not necessarily influence the acquisition of the ability to act in the way observed.
5. Learning that follows observation includes an element of imitation. Imitative learning is not normally restricted to simple mimicry. To imitate, it is necessary for the learner to retain some representation of what has been observed. The ability to imitate is increased when the learner retains events symbolically.
6. The mother plays an important role in early social learning. She provides a source of social and perceptual stimulation, and she interacts with the child, responding sensitively to the infant as an individual. As a result, even the preverbal child engages in complex and closely synchronized chains of communication with the mother, leading to a dialogue in which each member of the pair takes turns to respond.
7. The importance of mother-infant interaction is indicated by the fact that the behavior of babies in various social situations parallels that which is observed when they are with the mother. Furthermore, the babies of mothers who are highly sensitive and responsive to them cry less than

others and advance more quickly toward gaining more advanced communicative abilities.

8. Infants develop social attachments to individuals with whom they regularly interact, and they develop bonds and identify with others. A result is to make social learning and behavior less dependent upon the presence of external reinforcing events. Social learning mechanisms contribute to the establishment of harmonious relationships in human societies. Their absence in individuals is associated with psychopathic behaviors and personal destructiveness. A society in which there is widespread breakdown of social learning is characterized by disintegration of social organization and social responsiveness toward others.

9. It has been suggested that aggressive behavior in humans is controlled by innate mechanisms, and is largely independent of learning. However, there is no firm evidence for such a view. Early childhood provides numerous opportunities to learning aggressive actions.

Suggestions for Further Reading

Ainsworth, M. D. S., Bell, S. M. and Stayton, D. J. (1974) "Infant-mother attachment and social development: 'socialization' as a product of reciprocal responsiveness to signals." In M. P. M. Richards (ed.), *The Integration of a Child into a Social World*. London: Cambridge University Press.

Bandura, A. (1977) *Social Learning Theory*. Englewood Cliffs, New Jersey: Prentice-Hall.

Millar, W. S. (1976) "Operant acquisition of social behaviors in infancy: Basic problems and constraints." In H. W. Reese (ed.), *Advances in Child Development and Behavior*, Vol. XI. New York: Academic Press.

Montagu, A. (1976) *The Nature of Human Aggression*. New York: Oxford University Press.

Parton, D. A. (1976) "Learning to imitate in infancy." *Child Development*, 47:14–31.

CHAPTER 6

The Modification
of Social Behavior

OVERVIEW

In this chapter I continue to examine social learning, and discuss the application of principles of learning in order to enable people to change maladaptive social behaviors. A number of procedures for modifying behavior are mentioned, some of them designed to induce relatively minor alterations in the activities in normal individuals, for instance, in classroom circumstances. Other procedures have been designed to produce changes in cases of severe disorder or deficiency. Other behavior modification techniques are used to aid mentally retarded individuals to acquire social skills that help them to be independent. The chapter also introduces a number of procedures in which emphasis is placed on self-control by individuals who wish to change their own behavior.

SOCIAL LEARNING AFTER CHILDHOOD

Throughout our lives, learning continues to contribute to the way in which we behave in social situations. Reinforcement plays a part in such learning, although as we become older and more sophisticated the simple rewards that are effective with young children need to be replaced by reinforcing events that meet the needs and desires of mature individuals. However, we should not overestimate age-related differences in the nature of effective rewards: in many circumstances approval and attention continue to be remarkably effective well beyond childhood. Moreover, items that can be exchanged for alternative rewards, or which represent a variety of reinforcers, such as money, have a wide effectiveness that is not at all diminished by the fact that people differ.

Modeling and related influences on observational learning and imitation also continue to be important for social learning after early childhood, although the older learner is less confined than the infant to direct imitation of observed models. Language makes it possible to follow instructions which describe activities in symbolic form, since learners who can read are able to acquire and modify their social responses through reading descriptions of how others behave in a social situation. A person's abilities to think and to imagine things play a part in social learning. The fact that social learning is influenced by what people observe and by the reinforcing consequences of their actions does not imply that the learners' own knowledge and cognitive abilities are not closely involved in social learning. Of course, observational learning may take place in the absence of a deliberate intent to learn. This is often evident from the behavior of a young child who has been watching television.

When circumstances involve face-to-face contact with other people, there tends to be a greater degree of responsiveness to the individual's actions than when learning occurs in an inanimate environment. If the learner is with others who behave toward the person as an individual, opportunities will be present for transactions and communications, and for chains of behavior in which people react to each other. As we have remarked earlier, the large impact of early interactions between mother and child is partly due to the fact that she responds to the child as an individual. In the mature learner, learning that follows from contact with others remains important for social actions. In the young child, learning based upon social interaction also appears to be important for many nonsocial aspects of intellectual development, but this is less true in older learners.

PRINCIPLES OF BEHAVIOR MODIFICATION

The ways in which behaviors are gained and altered through social learning have been studied in literally thousands of experimental investigations. The umbrella term *behavior modification* is widely used to describe procedures in which principles that are based upon knowledge of social learning are applied in order to bring about desired behavior changes. Behavior modification procedures often involve elements shared by studies of operant conditioning, and the use of reward or reinforcement is very common. However, they may also involve classical conditioning procedures (notably in behavior therapy), modeling procedures and a reliance on observational learning; and sometimes learning principles are applied in conjunction with relaxation techniques, as in "desensitization" procedures.

Some investigators have applied the term "behavior modification" exclusively to techniques based on operant procedures, contrasting it with "behavior therapy." However, we shall follow the widely accepted custom of using "behavior modification" as a blanket term to refer to procedures for changing behavior that are based on principles of learning.

Behavior modification procedures have been introduced to produce changes in many forms of human activity. Customarily, the procedures have been designed to modify the kinds of behavior that are broadly social, and involve interactions between people. For instance, some investigations have involved techniques that aim to help disruptive school children to act in ways that are more conducive to classroom learning. Behavior modification methods have also been applied in order to produce intellectual changes in an individual. For instance, A. W. Staats (1971) carried out a number of investigations in which social learning procedures were used to help children to learn to read. Other procedures have had narrower aims, for example, to help people combat phobias and fears, such as fear of snakes or of spiders.

The activities which behavior modification methods are designed to modify may lie within or outside the range of normality. Generally speaking, procedures have been introduced when some kind of behavioral problem is evident. Typically, a relatively specific behavioral change is desired in order to produce necessary improvement. In some instances the procedures are intended to deal with normal everyday problems, for example that of managing unruly children in a classroom. In other circumstances, the problems to which behavior modification procedures have been applied are ones that indicate more extreme forms of maladaptedness, perhaps associated with mental abnormality or retardation. For instance, behavior modification techniques have been applied to the remediation of self-destructive behaviors in autistic children, and to changing hoarding activities in schizophrenic hospital patients.

Note that the "normal" and the "abnormal" kinds of behavior to which behavior modification procedures are applied form a continuum of relative abnormality, and are not clearly separate or distinct. Furthermore, many maladaptive behaviors are neither rare nor indicative of severe pathology. Mild phobias provide an example of a class of common problems of adjustment that can often be solved by making changes which can be induced by behavior modification techniques.

SOCIAL LEARNING OF NORMAL AND ABNORMAL BEHAVIOR

The findings of research into social learning support the view that positive social behaviors are acquired through learning processes which are essentially the same as those leading to social behavior that is described as being maladaptive, deviant, bizarre, delinquent, negative, or even criminal. Undoubtedly, what has been learned is strikingly different, nevertheless the underlying principles and learning processes are basically similar. To account for the observed differences in behavior, social learning theorists would point to detailed differences in the circumstances in which learning occurs rather than to differences in the principles by which social attributes are acquired.

Differences in the kinds of behaviors that are and are not rein-forced in early childhood may account for some of the differences between the social behaviors of two adults. One person may behave much more aggressively, because, in the past, he was more often reinforced for acting aggressively. The other individual may be more likely to respond in a friendly and unaggressive manner, be-cause she has been more frequently rewarded for doing so. In addi-tion, past experiences in relation to the behavior of observed models, particularly the parents, will affect a person's social beha-vior. An individual who, as a child, observed his parents custom-arily reacting to frustrating circumstances by acting aggressively or violently is more likely to behave aggressively in similar circum-stances than will a person whose childhood observational learning has been very different.

The above summary description of the influence of an individ-ual's past history of reinforcement for social behaviors and observa-tional learning of social activities is clearly over-simplified. The present behavior of an individual cannot be predicted by simply adding together ther person's past experiences involving rein-forcement and observation of others. As I have remarked earlier, individual social learners are not simply a passive assimilators of environmental events. As they observe events, they do not just ab-sorb the contents of their perceptions, they make use of them. A person's mental life is regulated as much by internal cognitive pro-cesses as it is by environmental events. Furthermore, as I have also noted, much social learning occurs in situations that involve lengthy communications and transactions of give-and-take between people, and cooperation between the learners and other individuals who respond to them as individuals. However, these considerations do not alter the fact that maladaptive, deviant and unsuccessful forms of social behavior are acquired through basically the same princi-ples of social learning as are forms of social behavior that are condu-cive to the well-being of individuals and those with whom they interact. Maladaptive instances of social learning are often indica-tive of an abnormal early social environment, in which the people from whom the individuals learn social behaviors act toward them in ways that do not promote social learning of normal behaviors.

It has been suggested that many of the disorders to which the term "mental illness" is applied are explicable in terms of failure to learn effective ways of adapting to the circumstances of life and to deal with the problems of daily living. The observations of psychia-trists such as R. D. Laing and T. Szasz are broadly consistent with this view. It is opposed to the notion that mental disorders parallel physical illnesses in being discrete diseases with clear signs and symptoms and with specific causes and treatments. As MacKay (1975) points out, most of the various states of unhappiness, anxiety, and confusion we term "mental illness" fall short of these criteria. Bandura (1969) considers that many forms of abnormal behavior are best considered "not as manifestations of an underlying pathology but as ways, which the person has learned, of coping with environmental and self-imposed demands" (Bandura, 1969, p. 62).

Bandura argues that when people are labeled as being mentally ill, on the assumption that they are suffering from a specific disease, they tend to be treated in ways which intensify rather than ameliorate the difficulties which led to them to be diagnosed as ill. Labeling people mentally ill and placing them in institutions often leads to suspension of the kinds of normal environmental conditions that may lead to beneficial changes. Moreover, "the attendant stigmatization, the patient-role requirements of the mental hospital culture, the limited opportunities to perform behaviors that are necessary in community life, and the develpment of institutional dependency produce further impediments to successful readjustment to typical environmental demands" (Bandura, 1969, p. 17).

Seligman (1975) considers that many instances of depression and severe anxiety are largely the outcome of what he terms *learned helplessness*. The results of a number of experiments on human and animal subjects show that when an organism learns that it has no control over what happens to it, it becomes unresponsive, has difficulty in learning, displays fewer aggressive and competitive responses than normal and is generally passive. Seligman regards many of the symptoms of depression as being indications of learned helplessness. He draws parallels between the "paralysis of the will" of a depressed person, and the accompanying isolated, withdrawn, slow, retarded, passive and indecisive behavior, and the behavior of animals who have acquired learned helplessness by being placed in circumstances in which their own actions do not exert effective control over the environment.

Learned helplessness is not always acquired through experience of failure. Seligman describes the case of an attractive and previously successfull young woman who became severely depressed. In her case, the cause of helplessness lay in the fact that, as the coddled only child of doting parents, all her behavior had been followed by what she wanted. When she arrived in the demanding environment of a university, she was simply helpless to act effectively. Since all her actions in childhood had been followed indiscriminately by happy consequences, she had not experienced the synchronies between actions and their outcomes that are essential to the learning of mastery over important aspects of life. A child whose every response is followed by success becomes as helpless as one who is always unsuccessful.

The Acquisition and Modification of Undesirable Behavior: An Illustration

It should not be supposed that the individuals who provide the social learning environment in which a person acquires maladaptive or deviant forms of social behavior necessarily act in a manner that is grossly deviant. There are some instances where parents and other significant adults consistently behave in a child's presence in a manner that does provide models of highly violent or criminal acts, or deliberately reinforce their children for acting in ways that most people would consider wrong, criminal, or even mad. It is more common, however, to find situations in which parental patterns of reinforcement are simply inconsistent, or in which the parents acquire the habit, without being aware of it, of reinforcing undesirable forms of child behavior.

It is alarmingly easy for this to happen. For instance, imagine the following chain of events affecting the parents of a 2-year-old child. The child was very ill in his first year, and required constant attention. When he was ill, he whined a good deal and became alarmed and inclined to cry when adults left his presence or ignored him. Gradually, a state of affairs has developed in which the child, although he has by now recovered from his illness, continues to demand constant attention, and to whine, cry, or scream whenever he is left on his own. The parents are concerned about the child, and they react to his whines and cries by giving more attention, thus inadvertently reinforcing the habit of crying whenever the child wants them to attend to him. Note that this state of affairs has not arisen through any grossly abnormal behavior on the part of the parents; rather it is only too likely to occur as confused normal parents try to cope with the difficulties of life.

A behavior modification study reported by C. D. Williams in 1959 was designed to deal with the problems arising in circumstances like these. It demonstrates how disruptive behavior was initially maintained by reinforcement, and how it was subsequently modified by alterations in the reinforcing behaviors of the parents. The child observed in the study was a boy aged 21 months who for much of the first 18 months of his life had been ill, and had consequently received close care and attention from adults. At the beginning of the study his physical health had recovered, but he continued to demand the almost continuous attention to which his early life had made him accustomed. The child was especially demanding at bedtime, when he would engage in violent and lengthy tantrums. If a parent left the child's room he would scream and fuss until the parent returned. This behavior was successful in making the parents feel unable to leave the room until the child was asleep. Even if a parent simply picked up a book, the child would scream and scream until the book was replaced. The parents found the child's behavior at bedtimes particularly distressing because they had to stay in the room for periods of over an hour, waiting for their son to go to sleep.

Devising a behavior modification procedure for changing this state of affairs involved first analyzing the existing situation, to ascertain why the unsatisfactory behavior was being maintained, and then introducing changes that would lead to the behavior being altered in desirable ways. It was thought that the child's crying and tantrums were being reinforced by the parental attention and the signs of concern it produced. The behavior modification procedure that was devised was based on the view that if the parents ceased to reinforce the crying and tantrum behaviors, these would diminish, by a process broadly analogous to extinction in studies of operant conditioning. A very simple procedure was chosen. After making sure that the child was comfortable and safe the parent would bid him goodnight, leave the room, and not return. On the first occasion the child cried for a total of 45 minutes. However, as Figure 6.1 shows, over the subsequent four nights the average duration of crying decreased very quickly to around five minutes, and by the seventh night the boy did not cry at all when his parents left his room at bedtime. About a week later, the child screamed and fussed when an aunt was putting him to bed, and she reinforced this behavior by staying in the room. This made further extinction sessions necessary. Again, the tantrums were soon eliminated and no further bedtime tantrums were reported during the next two years.

Strategy of Behavior Modification Procedures

The above example illustrates the basic strategy followed by investigators using behavior modification procedures. First, the existing state of affairs is examined, to discover what is maintaining the present undesirable state of affairs. Second, on the basis of knowledge of principles derived from research into learning, the environmental circumstances are altered (in the present case by simply not reinforcing tantrums) so as to bring about a desired change in behavior. Of course, it is often necessary to introduce procedures that are not so simple or so straightforward as the minor change in

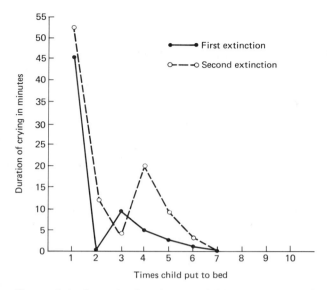

Figure 6.1   Length of crying by child aged 21 months in two extinction series after being put to bed. (Source: Williams, C. D. "An elimination of tantrum behavior by extinction procedures." *Journal of Abnormal and Social Psychology,* 1959, 59:269. © 1959 American Psychological Association. Reprinted by permission.)

the pattern of reinforcement that was effective in the instance described above.

   The fact that the particular behavior modification procedure I have been describing was aimed at the elimination of crying should not be taken to imply that behavior modification techniques can or should be used indiscriminately for the reduction or crying behaviors. The impressive success of some behavior modification procedures have led unwary and naive enthusiasts to consider that modification techniques should be applied in any situation where change is desired. Such procedures will certainly not eliminate crying in all children of all ages, and applying similar techniques to an infant aged, say, 2 months, would not only fail to reduce crying but might harm the child. This is apparent when we recall that crying in the young infant has a signaling function that is vital until more advanced ways of communicating are developed. Apart from the distress caused to the infant by the mother's failure to satisfy the need signaled by crying, her failure to respond to such signals may retard an infant's acquisition of more advanced communicative systems, as research by Mary Ainsworth and her colleagues has shown.

If a person regularly acts in any manner, however destructive or undesirable, to obtain reinforcement that is provided as consequences of such actions, it is likely that a real need for the reinforcer exists. Changes that are made in introducing behavior modification techniques should take this into account. It is often essential to insure that the individual is provided with an alternative way of gaining for himself the reinforcing events that previously followed the undesirable behavior.

BEHAVIOR MODIFICATION IN THE SCHOOL CLASSROOM

The practical necessity to provide children with the reinforcers that initially followed undesirable activities is apparent in a number of classroom applications. A common problem in schools is that children behave in a noisy or disruptive manner that is not conducive to learning. Many teachers worry about problems of control and discipline in the classroom. Granted that children need to have reasonable opportunities for free expression and movement, some degree of control may be essential in order to create a classroom atmosphere that is sufficiently quiet and relaxed for effective communication and learning to be possible. Teachers who are using much of their energy in struggling to maintain order cannot concentrate on helping children to learn.

Having identified the classroom behaviors (for example, shouting, hitting, running about) that need to be altered, the next step is to identify the reinforcing events that have been maintaining them. With young children, especially up to the age of around 10 years, the attention of the teacher is a powerful reinforcer for a variety of behaviors. This is not too surprising when one considers that, compared with the familiar circumstances of family life, the classroom situation is one in which adults are in short supply. For each individual in a class of 30 children, the teacher's attention is a valued commodity, and highly effective as a reinforcer.

Attention as a Reinforcer

Note that it is the *attention* of the teacher that is reinforcing. One might expect that the teacher's response would need to be a definitely positive one, incorporating praise or encouragement if it is to have a reinforcing effect. As it happens, however, attention is reinforcing even if it does not include these positive aspects and takes the form of censoring remarks, threats, or verbal criticisms. This is a major reason for a teacher of young children experiencing difficulty in obtaining order. Suppose a 7-year-old boy at the back of the classroom starts shouting, and the teacher responds by telling him to be quiet. As the teacher sees it, the effect of this response should be to quieten the child. Certainly this would be the expected effect on an adult, and the immediate effect on a child will probably be for him to stop shouting. But, seen from the point of view of its effect on the child, the incident is somewhat different: a behavior (the shout) has been followed by a reinforcing event (attention), and therefore the frequency of this behavior is likely to increase rather than to decrease. It is true that the reinforcing event was not *intended* by the teacher to have a reinforcing function, and it would be regarded by an adult as anything but rewarding. Nevertheless, if an effect of the teacher's responding is to provide attention, and if the attention of the teacher is a powerful reinforcer, the teacher's action will increase rather than decrease the undesirable behavior it followed.

It follows that in introducing behavior modification procedures to reduce undesirable behaviors, it is customary to emphasize the necessity to avoid reinforcing such behaviors. Classroom teachers are made aware that actions on their part that they regard as being not at all rewarding or encouraging may nevertheless exert a reinforcing function. If a teacher's attention is highly reinforcing, it follows that the children do have a need for it. Therefore it is important that the teacher, in addition to not attending to undesirable behaviors, does attend to individual children, but only when their behavior is acceptable. This insures that the reinforcement (teacher attention) follows desirable rather than undesirable classroom activities. A number of investigations have demonstrated that if the teacher does ignore undesirable behaviors and also gives frequent praise and encouragement to young children for acting in ways that are appropriate for learning, behavior problems decrease considerably.

Classroom Experiments

In one classroom experiment, Becker, Madsen, Arnold, and Thomas (1967) used a behavior modification procedure that involved selective teacher attention and praise in an urban school. Ten children were studied, all of whom had behavior problems that made classroom learning difficult for themselves and for others in the class. The teachers had participated in a workshop and seminar that was designed to help them learn to apply principles based on social learning research. Before introducing any experimental changes, the investigators measured the initial frequency of disruptive activities. The precise behaviors that were measured differed somewhat from one child to another, but in general, disruptive behaviors were defined as being ones that interfered with classroom learning or violated rules established by the teacher. One boy aged 7 was very noisy and often fought with other children, and seemed unable to stay seated for any appreciable time. Another 8-year-old boy hit other boys and children smaller than himself, reacting loudly and angrily whenever he was reprimanded for his aggressive activities.

The teachers involved in the study were trained to do two things. First they were required to ignore activities that they considered to be undesirable or disruptive, except when it was impossible to do so, for instance when one child was hurting another. Second, the teachers were trained to give frequent praise and attention to any kind of behavior that facilitated or contributed to learning. Children were told why they were being praised, and the teachers attempted to introduce the two aspects of the behavior modification procedure (ignoring disruptive behaviors and praising positive ones) simultaneously, so far as was possible. Examples of the kind of positive encouraging statements to be used were "You are doing fine" and "That's the way I like to see you work."

The teachers' changes produced striking results. At the onset of the study, the ten children whose behavior was measured displayed disruptive activities on 62 percent of the occasions on which they were observed. When the new procedures were introduced, the average decreased to 29 percent, and remained at this much lower level throughout the period of the investigation. A description of a particular child observed in this experiment illustrates some of the findings. Alice, who was 7, usually seemed to ignore her teacher and she moved around the classroom a good deal and sulked a lot. Before the experimental procedures were introduced, disruptive behavior was observed in Alice on about 50 percent of the observations that were made over a 20-minute period each day. When the teacher introduced the new procedures the frequency of Alice's disruptive activities dropped to 20 percent, and it stayed at the reduced level. The considerable improvement was reflected in a number of useful ways, and at the end of this study Alice was described by her teacher as a responsible, hard-working student who smiled, made jokes and played with others. The same individual had previously been described as a sulking child who gave a good deal of concern to the teacher.

In the course of this experiment the teachers observed that certain practical techniques were especially helpful. For instance, most teachers found that praising a child who was behaving in an appropriate and positive way at the same time as another child was misbehaving, was particularly effective. In addition, acting in this way made it easier for the teacher to ignore the disruptive activities. Quite apart from the fact that a child who is behaving sensibly is likely to be reinforced for so doing, the fact that the children can observe their peers gaining attention for positive, but not for disruptive, forms of behavior provides opportunities for useful observational learning.

One problem with interpreting the findings of the above investigation is that we cannot be absolutely sure that the change in behavior following the introduction of behavior modification procedures was really due to the procedures as such, and not to any additional factors that might be involved. What is required is an experimental design that includes a subsequent condition in which there is a return to the circumstances existing prior to the introduction of the behavior modification procedure. If the effect of this is to reintroduce the preexperimental level of disruptive behavior, we can be reasonably certain that the original change really did follow from the behavior modification procedure and was caused by it rather than by other new factors that happened to be present at the time it was introduced, such as the presence of observers in the classroom.

An investigation by Hall, Lund, and Jackson (1968) shows how such an additional experimental condition can be incorporated. One 8-year-old boy was rated at the outset as being engaged in study on only 25 percent of the periods in which his behavior was measured, and the remaining 75 percent of his time was spent in playing, talking, and other activities that were not conducive to learning. The purpose of the behavior modification technique was to increase the proportion of his time that was spent in effective study. It was noted that much nonstudy behavior had been followed by teacher attention, and the investigators suggested that his behavior might improve if the teacher combined giving encouragement, praise, and attention to studying with ignoring nonstudy activities. This procedure was apparently successful, raising the frequency of study behavior from 25 percent to 71 percent. However, the change in behavior might conceivably have been due to other causes, or it could have been purely coincidental, and to provide a check on these possibilities, the experimenters added a "reversal" condition. This replicated the classroom situation that had existed before the behavior modification procedures were introduced. The effect was to reduce the frequency of study behavior to below 50 percent, a change toward the previous behavior which indicated that the original improvement had been caused by the behavior modification procedures. Next, the procedure was reintroduced, and once more the frequency of study behavior increased to about 75 percent. This experiment involved six children in all, and the detailed methods adopted varied somewhat between the different children. However, the reinforcement procedures did produce desired changes in every child, and in each case a reversal condition, in which the new procedures were temporarily suspended, led to changes back toward previous levels of behavior.

The Effects of Rules, Praise, and Ignoring

In most classroom applications of behavior modification, a number of changes have been introduced at the same time, for example, reinforcing desired behaviors, ignoring inappropriate or disruptive activity, and specifying explicit rules for the children to follow. When a successful procedure involves a number of separate elements, a question arises concerning which elements or combinations of elements are directly responsible for the effect that is observed. It is conceivable that the findings would occur only if all the different elements were present together; alternatively there might be one or two key elements, the remainder having little effect. A report by Madsen, Becker, and Thomas (1968) describes an experiment that was designed to investigate this question. Teachers in an elementary school were required to vary their behaviors systematically in order to measure the effects of various procedures that were administered separately or in combination. Three procedures were introduced. In the first procedure the teacher specified explicit rules of classroom conduct, making it very clear to the children what was expected of them. Each teacher was instructed to produce a list of about five or six easily remembered short rules, and care was taken to insure that the children did learn the rules and were reminded of them from time to time. The second procedure was to ignore inappropriate behaviors. The teachers were carefully instructed to give no attention at all to activities that interfered with learning, unless a child was being hurt by another. The third procedure provided praise and encouragement for appropriate behaviors. The teachers received careful instructions (including specific examples of appropriate comments) to follow the general principles of giving praise and attention to behaviors that facilitated learning, at the same time telling the children why they were being praised. The teachers were also instructed to try to reinforce behaviors that were incompatible with ones that they wished to decrease.

The children were around 6 years of age, and they were observed for 20 minutes a day. On the first days some observations were made of the children's behavior prior to the introduction of any new procedures. Next, explicit rules were introduced and their effects measured by the observers. On subsequent days the provision of clear rules was combined with ignoring inappropriate behaviors. Observations of the children during these days enabled the experimenters to assess the effects of this combination of procedures. Subsequently, praise was added to the other two procedures to provide a combination of rules, ignoring, and praise. After this, the experimenters introduced a reversal procedure for several days, in which the teachers were instructed to revert to their original ways of managing the classroom. Finally, the combination of rules, ignoring, and praise was introduced again. The findings of this experiment are summarized in Figure 6.2.

It is apparent from Figure 6.2 that merely introducing clear rules in the classroom had no appreciable effect on the level of inappropriate activities. When rules were combined with ignoring such activities the outcome was an increase in inappropriate behaviors in some children and little change in others. However, the next condition, which combined rules, ignoring, and praise, produced clear improvements. The frequency of activities such as acting noisily and turning around to talk to others declined to less than half the original level. It is clear that success relies on a combination of measures.

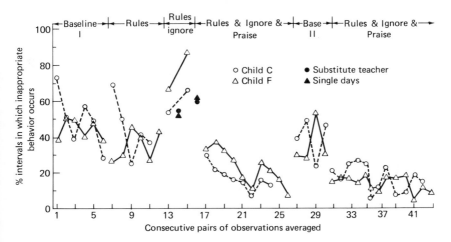

Figure 6.2 Inappropriate classroom behavior of two problem children as a function of experimental conditions. (Source: Madsen, C. H., Becker, W. C., and Thomas, D. R. "Rules, praise, and ignoring: elements of elementary classroom control." *Journal of Applied Behavior Analysis,* 1968, 1:139–150. © 1968 Society for the Experimental Analysis of Behavior, Inc.)

THE INFLUENCE OF THE CLASSROOM TEACHER

Some teachers have reacted adversely to reports advocating the classroom use of behavior modification techniques that are based on attending to appropriate behaviors and simultaneously ignoring disruptive activities. One common reaction is that this kind of procedure could not possibly work. However, it really is effective and has been demonstrated to be so time and time again on literally hundreds of occasions. Another assertion is that ignoring disruptive behavior in young children, letting them "get away with it," must lead to all kinds of problems. Yet the fact of the matter, as results of controlled experimental investigations clearly show, is that when ignoring inappropriate behavior is combined with a strategy in which the teacher gives increased praise and encouragement to desirable behaviors, disruption does decrease.

A possible reason why some people find it hard to accept that these findings can be true is that the effects of different kinds of classroom management may be easier to see in the very short run. Actions by teachers that have an immediate effect appear to be more effective than those which have no immediately apparent result, and teachers might understandably regard the immediate outcome of their control procedures as being the best indication of their effectiveness. When teachers punish or threaten a child who is misbehaving, the immediate effect will probably be for the child to obey. It is hard to realize that control procedures like this, despite their immediate effects, may in the long run be quite ineffective. Yet the findings of the experiments we have considered leave no doubt that a strategy which combines attending to desirable behaviors and ignoring inappropriate activities has far greater long-term effectiveness. This is usually apparent within a day or two of introducing the new procedures.

Adults often underestimate the extent to which they influence the behavior of young children. People often think that whether or not children behave well in class is largely governed by factors outside the teacher's control. A particular class may be regarded as "tougher" or more difficult to manage than others, and it is widely accepted that problems of classroom discipline are more severe in poor urban areas than in affluent suburbs. Undoubtedly, more difficulties are encountered in urban schools. The reasons for this are numerous and complex, but one contributing factor is the belief that children are likely to be disruptive, which can act as a self-fulfilling prophesy. Teachers who are confronted with a class that they anticipate giving discipline problems may adopt what they consider to be a firm approach, in which emphasis is placed on frequent reprimands and threats, and little encouragement is given for desirable behaviors. Social learning principles suggest that this is exactly the kind of approach that will lead to the problems of behavior that it is intended to eliminate. If little attention is given to positive forms of behavior, the children will be confronted by a situation in which the most effective way of gaining needed reinforcement (in the form of teacher attention) is to be disruptive. Hence the children are noisy and difficult to control, fulfilling the teacher's expectation.

Of course, the above account is not a satisfactory explanation of *all* difficult classroom situations, but the findings of an interesting experiment by Thomas, Becker, and Armstrong (1968) suggest that it contains a sizeable measure of truth. They undertook a behavior modification program in a well-behaved elementary school class containing well-adjusted children from middle class homes. At the beginning of the study the children were well-behaved, and they presented no major problems. The behavior modification procedures adopted in this experiment involved requiring the teacher to alter her methods of classroom control in ways that were opposite to the changes introduced in the other studies we have described. Initial observations showed that the teacher consistently gave praise and encouragement for desired behaviors.

She was told to stop giving approval and praise, and to increase the number of occasions in which she made disapproving, threatening, or scolding remarks. If the children's good behavior was mainly due to their backgrounds, and largely independent of the teacher's influence, one would expect that this newly introduced procedure would not make much difference to the children's classroom activities. In fact, the outcome of the change was to produce a dramatic increase in the amount of disruptive behavior. This rose from 9 percent in the period before the new procedure had been introduced to 25 percent in a condition in which the teacher stopped giving approval and praise, but did not otherwise change her actions, and to 31 percent when she combined giving no approval with making frequent disapproving and reprimanding remarks. When she resumed her usual, largely positive methods of control, the amount of disruptive behavior returned to the original low level. These findings clearly demonstrate that changes in the way a teacher acts can increase as well as reduce disruptive behaviors by children at school. The behavior of young school children is very strongly influenced by their teachers.

Classroom Reinforcers

In all the classroom studies I have described, the attention of the teacher proved to be an effective reinforcer. However, the children participating in these experiments were young, and the behavior of older students at school is not so easily controlled by reinforcement in the form of teacher attention. Nevertheless, the basic principle remains valid, that identifying effective reinforcers makes it possible to alter behavior. It is important that the behavior modifier should be able to control those events that function as effective reinforcers for the particular individuals in whom behavior changes are required. It is not always easy either to specify or to control the events that provide effective reinforcers for adults and adolescents.

Even with young children, teacher attention on its own may be an insufficiently powerful reinforcer. Although most young children find adult attention and praise reinforcing, some do not. In certain situations additional reinforcers may be required, for instance tangible rewards, such as chocolate or small toys. A study by Orme and Purnell (1968) was designed to improve teachers' control of a classroom that was initially chaotic. The school was situated in a ghetto district of Boston, the children were around 9 years of age, and the situation was much more extreme than any we have mentioned previously, as is indicated by the fact that during a 20-minute period every single child was observed to have been struck by another pupil at least once. The children tore up paper, threw books around, yelled, and shouted; they took the desks apart, ran around the classroom, and outside it when they were not fighting each other.

The behavior modification procedures that were adopted in order to improve matters included praising desired behaviors, and, so far as was possible, ignoring undesired ones. In addition, however, children could earn tangible rewards. The system worked by providing points for good behavior, and the points could be exchanged for articles such as sweets and balloons, or saved and spent later on a desirable treat such as an interesting outing or project. Care was taken to insure that the children understood the rules they were expected to obey and the system of rewards. A hidden television camera was used to observe behavior, making it possible for the behavior ratings to be made at leisure, away from the noisy classroom. The new procedures resulted in marked improvements. At the outset of the study the ratings indicated that between 40 and 50 percent of the time was spent in behaviors that were disruptive or inappropiate for learning. The new system proved to be very effective, and the average frequency of disruptive behaviors decreased to around 20 percent. The frequencies of all the categories of behavior judged to be compatible with learning increased and all the activities judged to be incompatible with learning decreased.

SHAPING PROCEDURES

A problem encountered by Orme and Purnell was that at the beginning of the study so few desirable behaviors occurred that it was difficult to give any rewards. To deal with this problem the experimenters introduced a "shaping" procedure, similar to ones used by B. F. Skinner for teaching new behaviors in animals. To shape behavior, one starts by reinforcing actions that are at least not totally incompatible with the desired behavior. Consequently, there is an increase in the number of actions that are similar to the desired ones, and the experimenter proceeds by reinforcing only those behaviors that are progressively more and more similar to the desired ones. With selective reinforcement of only those activities that are increasingly close to the behavior that is required, the learner eventually produces the target behavior, and subsequently only that behavior is reinforced.

A similar procedure for increasing an activity that initially occurs too infrequently to provide adequate opportunities for reinforcement is to constantly reinforce a related response. Nordquist and Bradley (1973) devised an educational program to increase speech in a 5-year-old girl who rarely spoke. It was not practical to reinforce speech as such, since she spoke so infrequently that it would have been necessary to give constant close attention to the child, and the experimenter wished to avoid doing so. It appeared that a policy of reinforcing related responses might be more successful than attempting to reinforce only speech. The procedure that was adopted was to reward the child, by verbal approval, for any play in which she interacted with other children. The program was markedly successful, since as the child communicated more and more with her peers in nonverbal ways, she also began to speak with greatly increased frequency.

The practice of shaping behavior in order to teach new activities is illustrated in a description by Sheppard and Willoughby (1975) of procedures through which a father may teach his son to catch a ball. The father begins by using a large soft ball, which he throws to the infant who is two feet away, and the child is shown how to hold his arms so that the ball will land there without failure. Both success in catching the ball and gaining the father's praise are reinforcing for the child. Subsequently the father increases the distance and begins to reinforce more selectively, praising only when effective catches are made. Later a smaller ball is introduced, and distance is once more gradually increased. By this stage the behavior is beginning to approximate the desired final performance. Progressively, only those responses that are closer and closer to the final criterion level are selectively reinforced, until a satisfactory standard is achieved. Care is taken to avoid advancing either too slowly or too quickly: if advancement is too slow, the child may become satiated by the reinforcers or bored; if it is too fast, insufficient reinforcement is received.

This above description undoubtedly over-simplifies the actual process of learning to catch a ball. It underestimates the essential skill acquisition element, which demands considerable practice and depends upon the integration of different sub-skills. It also underestimates the degree of conscious thinking, planning, and understanding that is often necessary. Furthermore, the modeling element is also important, as the child learns a good deal simply from watching the more skilled behavior of the parent. Nevertheless, the above account does communicate the essential quality of shaping. Behavior is gradually altered, so that it approaches closer and closer to a desired end product as increasingly accurate responses are selectively reinforced.

An investigation reported by Harris, Wolf and Baer (1964) provides a final illustration of shaping. The experimenters wanted to help a young boy to make use of a climbing frame, since he hardly ever engaged in physical play activities and lacked normal strength and dexterity. At first the child never approached the frame, and simply stood quietly in the play yard, although the other children around him climbed on the frame, ran about, rode on bicycles, and were physically active. The teachers started by reinforcing the child (by giving attention) for simply being close to the climbing frame. Subsequently, as he began to approach the frame, they reinforced him only when he touched it, and later only when he began to climb a little. Finally they attended only to the more ambitious climbing attempts that the boy was making by then as a result of the procedure of reinforcing progressively closer approximations.

Over a nine-day period, the result was to raise the proportion of the child's time spent in climbing activities from less than 10 percent to over 50 percent. Following a brief reversal period, which demonstrated that when reinforcement for climbing was removed the boy's climbing activities decreased, the child was reinforced for all forms of climbing and vigorous play, and he consequently gained the habits and skills required in vigorous play. A check-up one year later confirmed that this level of activity had been maintained.

BEHAVIOR MODIFICATION AND INTELLECTUAL SKILLS

The experiments I have described show that behavior modification procedures which are based on reinforcing desired behavior can help children to acquire useful skills. In some instances, it appears likely that intellectual abilities would have been influenced, albeit indirectly. Alternatively, intellectual habits and skills can be directly taught, using behavior modification techniques in which reinforcement follows the performance of intellectual tasks. Thus Staats (1971) describes a project in which children learned to write letters. One of the children was a 4-year-old boy with an I.Q. of 89. His training sessions totalled 17 hours in length, made up of short trials of between five and eight minutes, and the boy learned to copy single letters and letter sequences. The child was rewarded with a token following each appropriate response, and the tokens could subsequently be exchanged for various desirable objects.

The short sessions proved to be very effective. By the end of the training program, the child had acquired reading and writing skills that were advanced for his age, despite the fact that, having a low I.Q. and a culturally deprived home environment, he might have been expected to perform poorly. The same training procedure was followed with another child whose I.Q. was 130. Again, the training was effective, but learning was not noticeably faster despite the marked difference in intelligence test score. Staats argues that the lack of a difference demonstrates that when training procedures are appropriate, children generally learn quickly "without the large differences we generally attribute to some inner personal quality that we call intelligence" (Staats, 1971, p. 112).

USING NEGATIVE REINFORCEMENT AND PUNISHMENT

Modification of behavior can be achieved by punishment and by negative reinforcement methods based on escape or avoidance as well as by positive reinforcement. Procedures based entirely on positive reinforcement of operant behaviors are sometimes ineffective with serious problems, for example self-injurious head banging by mentally disturbed individuals. In such cases, negative reinforcement procedures and ones that involve punishment have often been found to be effective. However, when the problem behavior is less extreme, negative reinforcement and punishment methods are usually avoided, since they introduce ethical problems and may also lead to other difficulties. The effects of punishment are less predictable than those of positive reinforcement, especially in respect to long-term influences and side effects, and punishment may lead to increased aggression. However, it can be effective for temporarily supressing destructive activities and redirecting attention. For this reason, procedures that include punishment in conjunction with positive reinforcement of desirable behavior are valuable for dealing with some severe problems.

SOCIAL LEARNING AND SERIOUS DEFICIENCIES

A variety of behavior modification procedures have been used to reduce behavioral difficulties that are more serious than the ones encountered in the investigations already described, in which the problem behaviors were broadly within the bounds of normality. Problems that are especially serious are encountered in: first, the behaviors of psychotic individuals diagnosed as being schizophrenic; second, in the cases of extremely obsessive, compulsive, and highly anxious people suffering from fears and difficulties that prevent a normal life; and third, in retarded individuals whose learning ability is very restricted. To deal with the more extreme disorders it has been necessary to introduce a wider range of behavior modification procedures than have been used to solve problems that involve relatively normal behavior.

Using a behavior modification technique in order to produce desired improvements in the behavior of people who are diagnosed as having a mental illness need not imply a belief that such changes in behavior constitute a cure of the illness. Psychologists differ in the extent to which they make distinctions between observable abnormal behavior and the underlying disorder. Some professionals argue that the superficial behavior can be regarded as no more than a symptom of a deep-rooted disorder. They consider that merely altering behavior does little or nothing to solve the basic difficulties, which are likely to cause new problem behaviors as soon as the original ones are eliminated. Others (for example, Albert Bandura, 1969) states that to form a clear distinction between the individual's underlying problems on the one hand, and the behavior of that person on the other hand, is to make a false separation. Bandura argues that behavior is an important aspect of people, and that what they *do* cannot be distinguished from what they *are*. We cannot develop this issue here, except to note that the extent to which a behavior abnormality is seen as being *the* problem, rather than being regarded as a symptom of a more deeply rooted difficulty, will depend both on the disorder involved and on the views of the therapist.

I remarked earlier that many deviant or abnormal social behaviors are acquired by the same principles as adaptive social behavior, the differences lying in patterns of reinforcement and in the models available. Thus, "crime breeds crime"; battered babies may grow up to be baby-battering adults, and Scottish children subject to physical punishment as a method of control at school become more violent than their English peers south of the border. There is little doubt that the actual behaviors displayed by maladjusted individuals are learned according to principles of social learning, irrespective of whether inappropriate learning is the root cause of the maladjustment, or whether there is a deeply based underlying pathology. The degree to which social learning procedures are successful in alleviating a problem provides some indication of the extent to which social learning contributes to it. The fact that procedures based on social learning principles have been more successful than Freudian psychotherapy in curing snake phobia gives some support to the view that inappropriate social learning caused the phobia in the first place, rather than the conflicts in infancy postulated in Freudian theory. Such a conclusion is reasonable, although not logically inevitable.

Whether a particular form of behavior is considered to be desirable or undesirable depends to some extent upon the particular society in which it occurs. Ullman and Krasner (1965), state, as does Bandura, that there is no discontinuity between desirable and undesirable modes of adjustment or between healthy and sick behavior, and they consider that maladaptive behavior is often maintained by more direct and more immediate forms of reinforcement than those controlling effective human activities. Successful adaptive behaviors tend to exhibit a greater degree of independence on the part of the individual. These authors note that a major reason for people being admitted to a mental hospital is that someone else wants to change them. Once there, people learn to take the role of the patient.

REINFORCEMENT TECHNIQUES FOR SEVERE DISORDERS

Among the many studies using behavior modification procedures to change the behavior of individuals suffering from severe disorders, some have involved new patterns of reinforcement as the primary agent of change.

Other studies have incorporated alternative factors, as are found in therapy based upon classical conditioning, desensitization, and modeling procedures. We shall first consider some instances in which reinforcement was the crucial agent of change.

Behavior Modification in a Psychiatric Institution

A report published in 1959 by Allyon and Michael demonstrated that a variety of simple procedures, administered by relatively untrained personnel, could produce large beneficial improvements in the behavior of mental hospital patients who had been thought to be beyond hope of improvement. The people administering the procedures were selected from the regular nurses, aides, and attendants in a large Canadian psychiatric hospital. The authors were especially interested in changing those activities by patients that were particularly disruptive. In some instances the behaviors were ones that had led to the individual being admitted to the hospital (as in the case of a patient who regularly attacked other people), but other troublesome behavior had been acquired while the patient was living in the institutional hospital environment. The kinds of activity that it was considered especially desirable to modify included hoarding objects, hitting, punching, spitting on other patients, failing to eat, dress, bathe, and interact socially, upsetting chairs, constant attention seeking, breaking windows, damaging walls and scraping paint from them, stuffing paper in the mouth and ears, and walking in a squatting position. Actions like these necessitated the nurses giving time and attention that might have been better spent in promoting patients' well-being. The disruptive activities also made life noisy and chaotic for everyone, producing an environment more reminiscent of Bedlam than of the kind of relaxed setting in which people can regain mental health.

Some of the behavior modification procedures followed by Allyon and Michael (1959) depended upon nonreinforcement of undesirable behaviors, the aim being to extinguish them. In the case of a woman who, despite continually being told not to do so, made frequent visits to the nurses' office and interrupted their work, the nurses were instructed not to reinforce the woman by paying attention to her when she entered the office. They were told to ignore her at these times, so far as was possible. The participating nurses and attendants had been instructed in the basic principle of withholding social reinforcement as a means of changing disruptive behaviors. They had been told that attention was an especially powerful reinforcer for maintaining undesirable activities. The nurses were also instructed to record the occasions on which the woman entered the office. It was found that she did so 16 times per day, on average. The behavior modification procedure reduced the average figure to about 12 times a day after two weeks and eight times a day after four weeks. By the eighth week following introduction of the nonreinforcement procedure, she went into the office no more than twice a day, which was acceptable to all concerned.

Another woman patient engaged in endless, repetitive psychotic talk centered around the men she claimed were constantly pursuing her. The other patients found the talk annoying to the extent that several had struck her in an attempt to keep her quiet. Her influence upon the general atmosphere of the ward was very upsetting and not at all conducive to the normal social interaction desirable in a therapeutic community. The procedure followed by the authors was similar to the one which had been effective with the other woman. The fact that some nurses had listened to this patient, and even encouraged her to talk in an effort to help her, suggested that her psychotic talk might have been maintained by the nurses' attention. The nurses were told to encourage this patient to talk normally about matters other than her delusions, but to avoid reinforcing any psychotic talk. The effect of the new procedure over a five-day period was to reduce the percentage of occasions in which she engaged in psychotic talk from 90 to 25. However, the figure subsequently rose again, although not to the original level. There was a large increase in the ninth week, which the authors attributed to the fact that the woman had been talking to a social worker, who, without the nurses' knowledge, had been reinforcing the psychotic talk. Difficulties of this kind often occur with behavior modification procedures that involve withdrawing reinforcement for undesirable behavior, unless one has complete control over all the possible sources of reinforcement. The authors report encountering what they called "bootleg reinforcement." In the above case it came from a lady volunteer hospital visitor and from a hospital employee who was not aware of the program in operation. Organizing a behavior modification program may necessitate gaining the cooperation of a large number of individuals who have contact with the patients, and this is not always easy to arrange.

Some of the procedures introduced by Allyon and Michael, like the ones we have described earlier for dealing with school problems, incorporated a combined strategy of not reinforcing disruptive activities and also strengthening (by reinforcing) behaviors incompatible with the undesirable ones. This procedure is called "counter-conditioning." One violent woman patient was prone to attack other patients and hospital staff for no apparent reason. E.C.T. (shock treatment therapy) aimed at reducing her violence was not successful. After trying to strangle her mother during a visit, the patient was given a leucotomy (surgical removal of part of the brain), but she remained so violent that she had to be isolated for much of the time to avoid serious injury to others. In her case the experimenter decided to reinforce one of her existing activities, sitting on the floor. Although this was not a totally desirable form of behavior, it had the advantage of being incompatible with fighting. The authors decided to reinforce the activity of sitting on the floor by giving attention to it, and also to attend to any other nonaggressive approaches by the patient, thereby reinforcing her for adaptive social behaviors.

Since sitting on the floor is not an activity within the range of normal social behavior, the plan was to cease reinforcing sitting after the fourth week. It was hoped that the early procedure would by then have produced a marked reduction in aggressive activity. Subsequently it was intended that nonaggressive social approaches to the nurses would be reinforced, but being on the floor would not be. However, the behavior modification procedures were only partly successful. The patient made only one attack on another person during the four-week period during which sitting on the floor was reinforced, but in the subsequent weeks she attacked others on eight occasions. Although her social approaches increased in the first four weeks, they subsequently decreased despite the fact that they were still being reinforced.

Negative Reinforcement and Feeding Behavior

With two female patients, Allyon and Michael introduced negative reinforcement procedures that involved escape and avoidance conditioning. These patients regularly refused to eat without assistance and consequently they had to be spoonfed by the nurses. Since both women were relatively indifferent to the attention of the nurses, it seemed unlikely that a procedure based upon social reinforcement of desired behavior would be successful. It was noticed that both these patients were very concerned about neatness and cleanliness in clothing. Allyon and Michael designed a procedure that combined escape and avoidance conditioning. The spilling of food on the patient provided the aversive stimulus, which she could avoid by altering her behavior.

The nurses were told to insure that whenever the patient was spoonfed a few drops of food would fall on her dress. They were asked not to overdo the food dropping, but to indicate to the patient that it is impossible to spoonfeed a person as cleanly or efficiently as the individual can feed herself. The patient was thus placed in the position of having to choose between feeding herself and keeping her clothes clean, or risking getting them soiled. The nurses reinforced the patient whenever she ate on her own, staying with her and giving her attention. The first part of the procedure can be regarded as a form of escape training, in which cessation of spoonfeeding stopped an aversive event (food on the clothes). Subsequently, the patient developed avoidance behavior (self-feeding) and she thereby prevented the spilling of food.

During an eight-day observation period before the new procedures were introduced, one of the women ate five meals on her own, refused seven meals, and was spoonfed for twelve meals. When the treatment began, she soon started reaching for the spoon after a few drops had fallen on her dress and after a while she would eat on her own from the beginning of each meal. The result of the behavior modification procedure was to increase the amount of self-feeding very considerably and to markedly diminish spoonfeeding, as is shown in Figure 6.3.

As Figure 6.3 indicates, there was a relapse, lasting for about five days around the sixth week, for reasons which were not entirely clear. Over the eight-week period, the patient's weight rose from 99 pounds to 120 pounds, and she was able to leave the hospital. Allyon and Michael report that the other patient required a little longer to become completely self-feeding, but that in both of them the program eventually resulted in complete self-feeding. This was maintained throughout the succeeding ten-month period, up to the time when the report was produced.

Changing the Behavior of Mentally Retarded People

One of the techniques used by Allyon and Michael involved a satiation effect, induced by providing vast quantities of the objects that some patients were accustomed to hoard. The satiation aspect of the procedures was loosely analogous to a phenomenon observed in animal learning experiments. A reinforcer that is provided in large

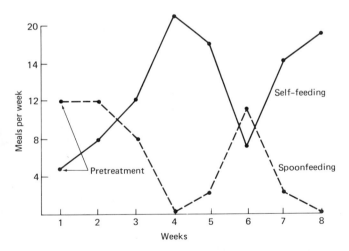

Figure 6.3   Escape and avoidance conditioning of self-feeding in an adult. (Source: Allyon, T. and Michael, J. "The psychiatric nurse as a behavioral engineer." *Journal of the Experimental Analysis of Behavior,* 1959, 2:323–334. © 1959 Society for the Experimental Analysis of Behavior, Inc.)

quantities eventually ceases to have the reinforcing qualities that it possessed when the learner was first deprived of it. Allyon and Michael observed that several mentally defective male patients had the habit of collecting large quantities of papers, magazines, and rubbish, which they carried around with them inside their clothing. This hoarding behavior produced severe skin rashes in one individual, and he had to be "de-junked" several times each day. The authors reasoned that hoarding was being maintained by two factors: first, the actual scarcity of printed materials, and second, the attention patients gained by hoarding. It was decided to flood the ward with large quantities of magazines, in the belief that such a situation would tend to decrease hoarding behavior. Also, social reinforcement, in the form of attention to hoarding, was withheld. As a result of these changes, hoarding gradually decreased in all the patients to a point at which, after nine weeks, it ceased to be a problem.

The report by Allyon and Michael (1959) provided a useful guide to some of the ways in which principles of social learning might be applied in modifying problem behaviors in mentally retarded people. Behavior modification principles have since been applied, often very successfully, in a variety of other circumstances in which inappropriate, deviant, destructive, or inadequate forms of social behavior are encountered.

The possibility of using principles of learning to help severely retarded individuals was demonstrated by Fuller (1949), who reported on a very seriously retarded 18-year-old individual whose behavior appeared to be limited to small movements in his arms, head, and shoulders, blinking and opening the mouth. He never moved his legs, could not roll over, and prior to the experiment was reported never to have made any sound. His repertoire of activities was described as being that of a "vegetative idiot." An operant conditioning procedure was introduced in which a solution of sweetened milk served as the reinforcer. This was provided when the right arm was moved towards a vertical position. After several daily sessions the frequency of this behavior increased from around one response per minute to three responses per minute. In the course of a 70-minute extinction period, arm responding decreased again to the original level. The procedure was successful in conditioning the patient's behavior despite the fact that the physician responsible for him had considered him to be totally incapable of learning and thought that he had never previously learned anything in his life.

Reinforcement procedures have often led to progress in people whose behavior is retarded or extremely restricted. To give one more example, Metz (1965) devised a program to increase imitiative behaviors in autistic children. The children he studied rarely imitated other people, and since imitating is important for social learning, they were placed at a serious disadvantage. Metz applied operant conditioning methods to teach generalized imitation behavior to two autistic children, a boy and a girl, each aged 7, who were mute, resisted change, and were socially isolated and unresponsive. Training sessions took place at lunch times. The children had been deprived of breakfast, and the reinforcers took the form of food, tokens, and verbal praise. The desired imitations were defined as behaviors that were similar to those of an adult model who demonstrated a number of separate responses.

The subjects were trained to imitate discriminately. For instance, they had to imitate either of two observed responses according to which of them had been demonstrated most recently. The activities to be imitated included a variety of distinctive nonverbal responses such as picking up books, hopping on one foot, hugging a doll, throwing a ball, opening a paint box, and inserting a peg in a board. Different activities were modeled in the training and testing sessions to insure that general imitative ability was being measured and not just imitation of the particular responses observed in the training sessions. Both subjects showed marked increases in imitation, indicating that such children could learn to imitate. Their learning generalized to similar but new behaviors without specific training. Imitative activities persisted, without the particular responses being reinforced, so long as some imitative behaviors were reinforced. It was noticed that the improvements were accompanied by other signs of progress. For example, they showed expressions of joy that had never been seen in the children before, there was a reduction of temper tantrums, and they made social approaches to the experimenters.

Choosing Effective Reinforcers

In the Allyon and Michael study, social reinforcement was not thought likely to be effective for the two women who had to be spoonfed at meal times. Milk was used as the reinforcer in the case of the very severely retarded 18 year old who was the subject of Fuller's (1949) investigation. Such instances remind us that although social attention and encouragement do provide widely effective reinforcers, they are not universally reinforcing.

In some situations nonsocial reinforcers may be more appropriate. It is often useful to discover what activities patients decide to engage in when they have a choice, and to incorporate opportunities for these *high probability behaviors* as reinforcers that are made contingent upon a required behavior change. In children, for instance, the opportunity to play freely may be an effective reinforcer. Osborne (1969) designed a program to increase the amount of time a school class of deaf girls remained in their seats. For every 15 minutes they stayed seated, the girls earned five minutes free time. Those who did not remain in their seats had to continue working. As a result, all the girls increased the amount of time spent in their seats. In another effective application, an adult woman was helped by the reinforcer of being allowed to spend time in therapy. She was initially unable to concentrate, complained of lack of energy, and was concerned that she would be unable to study during the final year of her university course. The woman was told to keep a close record of the time spent studying. She earned time in weekly therapy, her high probability behavior, the duration being determined by the amount of time she had spent studying. Sixteen weeks after introducing the new procedure, her study time had increased from two hours per week, on average, to around ten hours per week. In a case like this, which includes self-rating of behaviors, one cannot be certain that the designated reinforcer was the sole cause of change. Also, the very act of recording study time may have contributed to the increased time spent studying. Nevertheless, it is likely that using a high probability behavior as a reinforcer was a major reason for the effectiveness of the procedure, if not the sole cause.

Punishment and Avoidance Techniques

Allyon and Michael's success in changing feeding behavior in the two spoonfed women patients indicates that procedures involving negative reinforcement principles can be effective in cases where positive reinforcement alone is ineffective or inappropriate. Kushner (1968) describes the use of electric shocks in a procedure designed to reduce sneezing in a girl who, despite strenuous attempts to cure the problem, sneezed about once every 40 seconds throughout her waking hours. The technique that was eventually successful delivered an electric shock, via electrodes taped to the girl's fingertips, whenever she sneezed. This led to a rapid decrease in sneezing. It disappeared entirely by the fourth 30-minute session, and there was no uncontrollable sneezing in the following 16 months.

Shock has been incorporated in some procedures designed to eliminate or reduce the self-destructive behaviors that may occur in psychotic and severely retarded individuals. For example, Bucher and Lovaas (1967) administered shock to a boy aged 7 who constantly struck his own head as many as 3000 times in a 90-minute observation period. The self-injurious behavior had been going on for five years, but a procedure in which shock was delivered whenever the boy hit himself led to the elimination of the hitting activities after only 12 shocks. Risley (1968) describes a similar use of punishment to help a 6-year-old hyperactive girl whose bizarre activities included dangerous climbing that had led to severe injuries. After a number of unsuccessful attempts to modify her behavior, a procedure was devised in which whenever the girl began to climb, the experimenter would sing "oh" and at the same time deliver a shock to the child's leg. This procedure considerably reduced climbing, and it was successfully applied to the girl's other injurious behaviors, such as attacking her siblings. When lower rates of climbing had been achieved, it proved possible to substitute a more humanitarian system of control in which the child could avoid receiving shocks by sitting in a chair for ten minutes as a punishment.

Nonaversive Treatment of Self-injurious Behavior

The above findings show that aversive procedures involving punishment may eliminate or supress behaviors that are injurious or destructive, but punishment does introduce a number of problems. In addition to the problems with the use of punishment that we have mentioned previously, there is the fact that social relationships can be negatively affected by punishments, and the punished individual may avoid or attack the person administering them. Since social attachments and the kinds of interaction that depend upon close relationships between individuals are important for social learning, the side effects of punishment can be very damaging. It would be valuable to have a method for reducing self-destructive behaviors that did not include punishment. Peterson and Peterson (1968) describe a project in which an extinction procedure involving positive reinforcement was used to control self-destructive activities in a retarded boy, aged 8, who had been placed in a state institution because he was unmanageable at home. He could move around but had no speech and was not toilet trained. When not lying or rocking on his bed, he spent much of his time slapping his head, hitting his teeth, banging his head against his arm, or striking his head and hands against the wall or any available objects, crying loudly while he did so. Consequently much of his body was covered with bruises and scratches.

Following a baseline period in which the child's behavior was measured, an initial experimental period began. At meal times, whenever the boy refrained from self-injurious activities for as long as four seconds, the experimenter said "good" and at the same time delivered a quarter of a teaspoon of food. Each week there were between one and 11 mealtime sessions, lasting around 15 minutes. Any self-injurious act was followed by the experimenter removing the food and waiting for a period of ten seconds without such behavior before giving more food. In a second series of experimental sessions, the procedure of removing the food from the table whenever a self-injurious response occurred was stopped. Instead, the child was instructed to walk across the room and sit on a chair. If he did not make any injurious actions while walking to the chair, the experimenter would immediately give him some food and say "good." The child was not actually prevented from making self-injurious responses, since walking across the room did not hinder him from doing so. Following the series of mealtime sessions and 37 subsequent sessions, there was a temporary reversal period in which the experimenter reinforced self-injurous behaviors. The main findings are shown in Figure 6.4.

The findings depicted in Figure 6.4 show that following the introduction of the treatment procedures in the first experimental

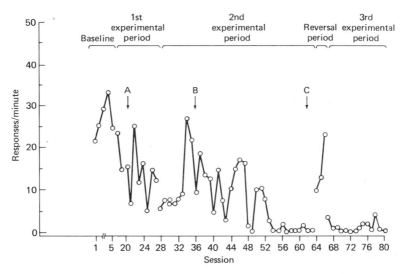

Figure 6.4   Self-injurious behavior of a retarded 8-year-old boy. (Source: Peterson, R. F. and Peterson, L. R. "The use of positive reinforcement in the control of self-destructive behavior in a retarded boy." *Journal of Experimental Child Psychology*, 1968, 6:351–360. Reprinted by permission of Academic Press, Inc.)

period, there was a drop in the number of self-injurious responses from the baseline rate, but there were considerable variations from session to session. The average number of self-injurious behaviors per minute was 14.2 in the first experimental period, compared with 26.6 in the baseline period. At the beginning of the second period of sessions, there was an immediate drop in self-injurious responses. After six daily sessions, however, the pattern of considerable variability from one day to the next resumed. Subsequently there was a gradual reduction in the rate of self-injurious responses, which disappeared almost entirely during the final ten sessions. In the reversal period, self-injurious behaviors rose again to a high level, demonstrating the effectiveness of reinforcer control over the boy's activities. When the experimental reinforcement procedure was resumed in the final period, the rate of self-injurious activities dropped toward zero again.

DESENSITIZATION

An alternative technique that is used quite extensively to modify inadequate or maladaptive social behaviors is *desensitization*. Wolpe (1968) used the term to denote a procedure he devised for reducing anxiety and fear. The procedure is loosely derived from classical conditioning. It involves pairing presentation of initially mild forms of stimuli feared by an individual (for example, spiders, cats, snakes, heights, enclosed spaces, aeroplanes), with stimuli that elicit incompatible positive responses. For instance, weak fear-eliciting cues might be presented at the same time as deep muscle relaxation is induced. In therapy, a person may be shown how to relax, and at the same time is told to imagine a scene that includes events which would normally produce mild anxiety. Gradually, scenes that usually induce progressively greater anxiety or some other emotional response can be imagined without the person experiencing distress or extreme arousal. If the individual does experience any unpleasant emotional response, the aversive scene is withdrawn, and, after relaxation has returned, the items are gradually reintroduced. Over a number of sessions the person becomes increasingly able to experience events without the anxiety they originally produced.

The term "counter-conditioning" can be applied to procedures of this kind, in which fear-arousing and positive stimuli are presented together. As Bandura (1969) points out, counter-conditioning is not fundamentally different to forms of simple extinction in which repetition of a stimulus without reinforcement may elicit responses that compete with the previous one. The basic difference between

simple extinction procedures and the counter-conditioning procedures involved in desensitization techniques is that in the former,
competing responses may occur spontaneously, whereas in
counter-conditioning they are deliberately introduced.

Desensitization procedures have been used both for dealing
with personal problems that are relatively common and not very
serious (for example, a mild fear of snakes) and for more severe
difficulties in which extreme fears of common everyday events
(leaving one's home, for example) make normal life impossible. The
report of a study by Davison (1968) illustrates the use of a desensitization procedure based on counter-conditioning. Students who had
a fear of snakes were matched on the basis of the strength of their
avoidance behavior in the presence of a snake, and they were each
allocated to one of four conditions. Some of the students received
counter-conditioning; they watched pictures of snakes that were
increasingly more threatening, and at the same time muscular relaxation was induced. The second group of subjects, who formed one
control condition, were given relaxation exercises, but these were
not paired with pictures of snakes. A third group saw the snake
pictures but did not experience relaxation procedures. A fourth
group, providing the final control condition, received no intervening treatment between the pre-test of snake phobia and a final post-
test. It was found that the students who received the relaxation
exercises in conjunction with depictions of progressively more
threatening interactions with a snake made substantial increases in
snake-approach behavior, but none of the other students improved.
This finding suggests that both elements of the desensitization training, the relaxation and the depiction of relevant interactions, are
necessary for success. An earlier study (Lang and Lazovik, 1963)
indicated that the improvements are likely to be maintained for at
least six months, although there are large individual differences in
the effectiveness of brief forms of training.

Group Desensitization Techniques

In some circumstances desensitization techniques can be administered on a group basis. Lazarus (1961) successfully treated groups of
people whose disorders included fear of heights, claustrophobia,
and sexual phobias, as well as a mixed group containing individuals
having pathological fears of sharp objects, physical violence, dogs,
and, fear of being a passenger in a moving vehicle. The desensitization method produced 13 recoveries and five failures, whereas alternative forms of treatment (an "interpretation" method aimed at
achieving insight, and the interpretation method in conjunction

with relaxation techniques) led to only two recoveries and 15 failures.

A number of demonstrations of desensitization have involved the modeling of a desired behavior (for example, interacting with a snake) by a live person, rather than simply presenting pictures of the feared object. Observing a live model may help the individual who is suffering from a phobia to acquire new ways of responding. To treat children's snake phobias, Ritter (1968) used a desensitization technique in which subjects watched adequate responses being modeled. She had observed that fear of animals is common and often intense in children, tending to persist into adulthood. The subjects participated in groups and were trained either by a *contact desensitization* method or by a *vicarious desensitization* technique. The contact group started by watching the experimenter remove a snake from its cage and hold it. The experimenter then played with the snake until one of the older children appeared willing to join in, at which time the child was told to put on a glove and to place a hand on the experimenter's hand while the latter was stroking the snake. Gradually the child progressed to stroking the snake with a hand gloved, and later with a bare hand. All the children were encouraged to participate by gradually approaching the snake and contacting it. Later, some of the children engaged in further interactions with the snake, lifting and holding it in addition to stroking it. The children in the vicarious desensitization group watched these things being done by the experimenter and by other children, but did not participate themselves.

Both groups of participants became significantly less fearful of snakes than children in a control group, but contact desensitization was significantly superior to the vicarious desensitization procedure. Since the contact procedure was successful in treating a group of 12 children with a total expenditure of 140 minutes of the therapist's time, it was considered to be a powerful and economical procedure for eliminating children's animal phobias. Similar group methods have been applied to the treatment of stage fright in children and adults (Kondas, 1967). Children who suffered from anxiety about examinations showed marked improvements in their scores on a reading test after receiving either individual or group desensitization. Desensitization procedures have also been successfully applied in cases of school phobia (Lazarus, Davison, and Polefka, 1965) and *anorexia nervosa* (Hallstein, 1965).

As Hallstein points out, a basic tenet of social learning approaches to behavior modification is that the acquisition, maintenance, and alteration of all activities, both adaptive and maladaptive, follow essentially the same principles. This does not mean that different people acquire each form of maladaptive activity in exactly the same way or that there is one best way of changing a given kind of undesirable behavior. Thus, whereas Hallstein (1965) found that a treatment based on desensitization was effective in the case of one 12-year-old girl suffering from anorexia nervosa, who had a strong phobia of foods that she associated with weight gains, Bachrach, Erwin, and Mohr (1965) decided on a treatment based on positive reinforcement of operant behaviors for treating another anorexic woman, and in her case the latter treatment was effective. Had the methods applied to the two patients been reversed, it is open to question whether they would have been equally successful. The fact that alternative methods have been successfully applied in order to change self-injurious behavior, as we have shown, gives a further demonstration that behavior changes may be induced by following procedures based upon any of the principles that govern human social learning.

SELF-CONTROL

Operant and classical conditioning procedures were originally developed in the context of research into animal learning. The early behaviorist psychologists who undertook such research quite properly took the view that so far as animal phenomena were concerned, questions about the role of awareness and self-control in conditioning were not amenable to scientific investigation. It has been suggested that animal conditioning can be regarded as a kind of "stamping in" of new responses or new associations upon a relatively passive organism. Such a view has sometimes been extended by implication to circumstances in which human behavior is modified by procedures akin to those of animal conditioning.

Awareness in Social Learning

Awareness and some degree of conscious control are present in the majority of situations in which human behaviors have been altered by procedures based on knowledge of social learning. Humans think, make decisions, and exhibit a fair degree of autonomy and self-control. It would be absurd to suggest that these abilities go into abeyance as soon as anyone introduces a behavior modification procedure based on learning processes that are in any way similar to ones observed in nonhuman species. Neither the fact that similar events may serve a reinforcing function for both human and other animals, nor the fact that similar kinds of circumstances may lead to the extinction of a response both in man and in other species justifies leaping to the conclusion that precisely the same mechanisms are involved in the human and animal phenomena. The processes underlying reinforcement or extinction effects in man need not be identical to those underlying the actions of, say, a rat or a pigeon. Apart from other considerations, the fact that events may have complicated symbolic functions for man sets human conditioning phenomena apart. Reinforcing events do provide important feedback for nonhuman species, but, for humans, symbolic processes add an important degree of precision.

As it happens, psychologists following procedures intended to change human behavior have often found it not only desirable but necessary to inform participants reasonably fully about the precise aims, methods, and rationale of the procedures being used. The object of a procedure may be to change overt behavior, but it does not follow that unobservable thoughts play no role in determining that behavior. Successful modifications often depend on the subject understanding and cooperating with the experimenter's aims. Azrin (1977) has remarked that although the primacy of overt behavior, rather than insight or subjective events, is often assumed in learning therapies, in all the many treatments he used it was necessary to question the individuals concerned in order to discover what events were reinforcing to them. Similarly, Peterson and London (1965) suggest that because behavioral problems are evident, and the aim of treatment is to produce changes in behavior, psychologists have wrongly concluded that insight and awareness are unimportant. They admit that insight is not always essential for learning new behavior patterns but they also note,

> "Pigeons can be taught, paramecia can be conditioned, and planaria can be trained through ingestion of their educated forebears—all without apparent benefit of awareness. But in human beings, it seems equally that insight, that is, cognition, can significantly facilitate the acquisition of adaptive skills. Insight may not be necessary, but it appears to be very helpful" (Peterson and London, 1965, p. 290).

Some investigators would insist that insight is not merely helpful, it is essential in many circumstances. Spielberger and DeNike (1966) consider that the function of reinforcement is not to strengthen a response directly but to convey information that the learner uses to guide subsequent behavior. To assess the role of awareness in a verbal conditioning task, DeNike (1964) asked subjects to write down their thoughts about the experiment after each 25-word block in a task in which they were reinforced for giving nouns referring to people as response items. Subjects who were aware of the reinforcement contingency made marked increases in appropriate responses, but those participants who were not aware did not improve their performance at all.

Demonstrations of the importance of awareness in ostensibly behavioral procedures have shown that the learner's role is be neither so passive nor so dependent as descriptions of behavior modification may appear to suggest. It is frequently wise to encourage the learner to play an active part, and to give emphasis to awareness, insight, and self-control rather than to control by an external manipulator. Such an approach may be ineffective in certain circumstances, for instance, teaching elementary social skills to severely retarded people, but in numerous situations it is advantageous to encourage the individual who is being helped to contribute to the administration of the procedures.

The increased use of self-control methods does not obviate the need for specialist skills and knowledge about the application of social learning principles to behavior modification, but the function of the expert becomes that of an adviser or consultant, rather than a manipulator. Apart from the increase in human dignity accompanying a change toward individuals taking on increased responsibility for the acquisition, maintainence, and modification of their own activities, there is the advantage that, once acquired, behavior that is largely under one's own control does not require external agents to administer the reinforcers that maintain it. The individual is, in a word, independent.

Following Self-control Procedures

A number of practical reasons favor using procedures that are based upon self-control to deal with personal problems. Sometimes personal difficulties are not apparent in overt responses. Difficulties may involve covert or private events that can only be observed by the individual in whom they occur. For example, a person may be troubled by uncontrollable "bad thoughts," fantasies, hallucinations, or dreams. For the behavior therapist, these do not provide any clearly observable responses that can be followed by appropriate reinforcing or nonreinforcing consequences. The individual who experiences these phenomena is in a far better position to introduce appropriate reinforcers, if these have been planned as part of a procedure in which he is participating.

Other problem behaviors may be similarly inaccessible to an external therapist or helping agent. For instance, sexual problems tend to occur on occasions when the therapist is unlikely to be present. Over-eating, marital discord, and many phobias affect people at times when the external helper is unavailable to administer reinforcing events or any other procedures. Making the individuals responsible for organizing procedures designed to control or modify their own activities also avoids another problem that is sometimes encountered with behavior modification procedures. This is that the person who administers reinforcers may become a necessary cue for the performance of the desired behavior, so that it occurs only when that person is present.

The range of self-control procedures that have devised for changing social behavior varies from ones that are similar to modification techniques that are normally used by external modifiers (for example, techniques involving the use of positive reinforcement) to ones which are quite different from any methods that can be applied except when the learner is responsible for administering the procedure himself. A number of self-reinforcement techniques have been used. For example, Mahoney, Moura, and Wade (1973) describe a self-reward method aimed at achieving weight reductions. Overweight individuals started by depositing money with the experimenter, and every time they weighed themselves they were allowed to reward themselves by retrieving some of their money. Other subjects were instructed to fine themselves if they had not lost any weight. After four weeks of treatment the self-reward group showed a large weight reduction, and the loss had been maintained when it was checked four months later. In another study, male college students who found it difficult to form social relationships with girls were instructed to reinforce themselves by allotting points for activities that involved social interaction with girls. Reinforced actions included sitting next to a girl, asking for a date, and expressing feelings of affection. At weekly sessions the students reported the number of points they had given themselves, and the therapist delivered praise accordingly. The men who followed this procedure increased their social interactions and also reduced their anxiety, and the improvement was found to be maintained when it was checked at a follow-up nine months later.

Self-punishment provides another procedure for self-control of a behavior the individual wishes to eliminate. Punishment can take the form of imagining the aversive consequences of an activity. For example, people trying to control over-eating might be told to imagine aversive consequences, such as social rejection or physical difficulties, whenever they prepare to eat a fattening food. In this way, it is claimed, the unpleasant consequences of eating, which are normally delayed, are brought closer to the actual act. Alternatively, more direct forms of punishment can be used, such as self-administered shock or having to give money away. Another self-control technique that has been applied successfully in a number of situations is known as *stimulus control*. It is reasoned that when a behavior regularly occurs in particular circumstances, items that are present in the immediate environment may take on the properties of cues for the behavior. Thus, if drinking coffee serves to cue smoking, it may be especially difficult to refrain from smoking in a coffee-drinking situation. Individuals can help themselves by carefully avoiding the situations that provide cues for the behavior they wish to eliminate. Contrariwise, if people want to strengthen behaviors, they may do so by establishing circumstances that do provide cues for the behavior. For instance, students who find it difficult to study may lack particular settings, times, and cues that are regularly associated with studying. It is useful to develop regular study habits so that particular circumstances, locations, and times become associated with studying and take on the property of cuing study activities (Kazdin, 1975).

CONCLUSION

The success of the behavior modification procedures that have been described demonstrates that consistent application of a small number of principles relating to social learning can be extremely effective in bringing about desirable control over social behavior. However, there are limits to the effectiveness of the procedures, and not all human problems can be solved by changing behavior. Depression, for instance, may not be amenable to behavior modification techniques. Furthermore, since an individual's opportunities, well-being, and effects on other people are largely determined by the person's own knowledge, thoughts, and attitudes, the outcomes of behavior modification are bound to be limited. Even when social inadequacies or difficulties are manifest as behavior problems, such as smoking, alcoholism, drug addiction, or over-eating, it does not necessarily follow that behavior modification methods will be effective. Although there have been a number of cases of successful treatment of all of these by procedures based on social learning principles, it has not yet proved possible, despite considerable efforts by psychologists, to devise behavior modification techniques that produce durable improvements in a majority of cases.

Straightforward behavior modification procedures have been very effective with those behaviors that are governed by factors external to the individual, such as the presence of models, and by externally provided reinforcement. A notable achievement of social learning research in general and of behavior modification studies in particular has been to demonstrate just how influential environmental factors can be, even as the determinants of activities that have commonly been regarded as being caused by, and only by, internal sources of disorder. Nevertheless, it remains true that internal factors, unique to each individual person, are responsible for important aspects of human experience. Most people are independent of their environments in some respects. The distinction between external and internal control is a relative one, of course, and the environmental events a person experiences are events as perceived by that particular individual. A number of internal factors—knowledge, attitudes, and so on—influence how they are perceived.

The limitations of behavior modification techniques reflect the fact that human actions are only to a limited extent under the direct control of environmental circumstances. It is probably for this reason that behavior modification procedures have been relatively unsuccessful in dealing with problems of obesity, alcoholism, drug addiction, and so on, all of which are partly maintained by factors within the individual. Using self-control methods represents an attempt to deal with this difficulty by getting inside the individual, so to speak. But since the internal controls of behavior are by their nature difficult to observe, it is much harder either to identify them or to devise appropriate procedures for producing change. Just as the patient who is treated by behavior modification techniques that rely on external controls may be unaware of the way in which his inadequate activities are being maintained, so the individual whose problems are largely due to internal factors may also lack insight into the causes. Mechanisms of behavior control are less accessible when internal rather than external factors are dominant. When a psychologist introduces a conventional behavior modification procedure that is based on social learning principles, he is, in effect, advancing a possible explanation of how the behavior is being maintained. The degree of success of the procedures the psychologist introduces may give some indication of the adequacy of the explanation.

SUMMARY

1. The term "behavior modification" has been applied to a number of procedures that are based on knowledge of social learning principles and are designed to induce desired changes in behavior.
2. Evidence indicates that much behavior that is described as being abnormal, deviant, or disruptive is acquired through basically the same learning principles and processes as normal social behavior. Many abnormal ways of acting appear to have been learned as partially adaptive responses to abnormal circumstances in early childhood.
3. Many undesirable activities in relatively normal children are maintained by reinforcement. The attention of adults is a powerful reinforcer, especially when few adults are available, as in school situations.

Classroom behavior modification procedures that involve the teacher ceasing to attend to disruptive behaviors and attending only to desirable activities have been markedly successful, and these procedures show that teachers can exert a high degree of control over the classroom behavior of young children.
4. Behavior modification methods for serious disorders and deficiencies have made use of a variety of learning procedures. Negative reinforcement is sometimes used, observational learning has been included in some procedures, and shaping may be used. Classical conditioning principles are sometimes introduced. Reinforcement procedures can be used to improve intellectual as well as social skills.
5. Procedures derived from social learning principles have been applied to a number of behavior disorders in hospital patients. Some techniques involve withdrawing social reinforcement and others use avoidance conditioning methods based on negative reinforcement. A satiation procedure has been successfully applied to reducing hoarding behavior in institutionalized mentally retarded individuals. Reinforcement of imitative behaviors has led to increased social activities in autistic children. Opportunities to engage in those activities that people spontaneously choose has proved to be widely effective as a reinforcer.
6. Punishment and avoidance techniques using electric shock have been successful in eliminating self-destructive activities.
7. Desensitization techniques, based on classical conditioning principles, have been successfully applied to the treatment of a variety of disorders involving anxieties, fears, and phobias. Emotional responses are counter-conditioned by pairing an initially aversive stimulus with the experience of pleasure or relaxation and the modeling of appropriate responses. Some desensitization procedures have been successfully applied on a group basis.
8. Some behavior modification schemes involve learners controlling their own behavior and taking a relatively independent role. Awareness and conscious self-control have been emphasized in a number of investigations.

Suggestions for Further Reading

Bandura, A. (1969) *Principles of Behavior Modifications.* New York: Holt, Rinehart and Winston.
Mahoney, M. J. (1974) *Cognition and Behavior Modification.* Cambridge, Massachusetts: Ballinger.
Seligman, M. E. P. (1975) *Helplessness: On Depression, Development, and Death.* San Francisco: Freeman.
Ulmann, L. P. and Krasner, L. (1965) *Case Studies in Behavior Modification.* New York: Holt, Rinehart and Winston.

CHAPTER 7

Aspects
of Perceptual
and Motor Learning

OVERVIEW

It was remarked in Chapter 1 that an important difference between learning in humans and other species lies in the capacity of humans to acquire the controlled movements that are necessary for exploring and manipulating physical objects and gaining the degree of control necessary for using implements and making tools. This chapter surveys some kinds of learning that contribute to our ability to control our limbs, to perceive the world, and to integrate and coordinate actions and perceptions.

PERCEPTION AND MOVEMENT

In everyday life we are constantly using skills that were acquired through learning. We rise in the morning, wash, dress, make and eat breakfast, turn off the light, drive to work, open the door, and so on. All these activities are learned, although they depend to a greater extent on skilled movements and coordinations of perceptions and movements, and to a lesser extent on acquired knowledge and social behaviors than most of the instances of learning we have previously discussed. As we remarked in Chapter 1, the superiority of human achievements over those of other species is due as much to skills that depend upon perceptual and motor forms of learning as it is to our ability to acquire knowledge and communicate.

In practice, different forms of learning are often encountered together. In order to read and write, which are regarded as being primarily intellectual skills, children have to be able to discriminate between different letters and to recognize them, and they also must be able to undertake coordinated motor activities necessary for writing. Young infants do not possess the motor and perceptual skills these tasks involve; considerable experience, involving opportunities for regular practice, is necessary for their acquisition. Even language, which might appear to be a purely intellectual ability, necessitates the child's possessing a knowledge of the world at a sensory-motor level. As a result of coordinating their actions and their perceptions, children gain a rudimentary understanding based on what they do, how they act, and on the physical consequences of their actions. Research with cats has demonstrated that impairment of perceptual abilities can result not only from sensory deprivation but also from restriction of self-produced movements (Hein, Held, and Gower, 1970). As will be explained in Chapter 8, European psychologists have drawn attention to the fact that children only begin to acquire language after they have gained a rudimentary structure of nonverbal knowledge that is based upon their experiences in perceiving, moving, and learning to control their movements. In some instances specific training at motor skills and at making discriminations can facilitate language acquisition. Sheppard and Willoughby (1975) describe an attempt to teach positional concepts such as "on," "behind," and "under," to a boy, aged 6, whose language development was seriously retarded. Learning was most successful when the actual movements and physical activities demonstrating these concepts were carried out in a highly discriminative manner. To learn "under," for example, the child would be induced to crawl under a table. This form of training led to the child being able to use the words appropriately.

The child at birth is receptive to a range of sensory stimuli, but sensation alone is not sufficient for mature perception. As a result of perceptual learning, the child becomes able not only to receive environmental stimuli, but also to extract information of value from a mass of available stimulation. The child has to learn to select information that is significant. Children learn to discover structure in the world, to notice distinctive features (Gibson, 1969), and to monitor predictable signals at a low level or even to discard them (Kay, 1969). Habituation and orienting reflexes provide useful ways of freeing the central processing capacity to deal with the less predictable and more significant stimulus events.

Learning makes perceived stimuli take on organization and structure, and in one sense it is true to say that structure is formed by the child. Perceived structure is an outcome of active selecting and processing by the individual. The signals that we perceive are grouped and coded forms of the data that reached our sensory organs. The ability to structure perceptions is acquired gradually, through experience. Reducing the mass of incoming data to match their processing capacity is achieved partly by the perceivers being highly selective and partly by their using strategies to group and integrate part of the incoming data.

LEARNING TO DISCRIMINATE

As was remarked in Chapter 7, as children get older they become more sensitive to differences and similarities and increasingly able to make discriminations among stimuli. The young infant's primitive experience of apparently random signals is replaced by the mature individual's perception of differentiated and distinctive events. A number of selection processes contribute to reducing the large mass of received sensory data to manageable amounts. Some data are filtered at an early stage in perceptual processing. If one message is transmitted in a man's voice and a separate message in a woman's voice, the listener can listen and respond to one, while ignoring the other. Selection can also be achieved if one message is louder than the other, if the messages come from different locations, or if separate messages are transmitted to each ear. The evidence indicates that unattended items are mentally processed, despite the individual not being conscious of such processing. Thus, when a person receives separate messages to each ear, through headphones, and pays attention to one ear but ignores the other, the individual perceives occasional items from the ignored message, particularly if they are significant to that person. This indicates that mental processing takes place on the content received by the nonattended ear.

The contribution of learning to the ability to select perceived items and discriminate between them is illustrated by an experiment reported by Gibson and Gibson (1965). Children were shown drawings in the form of scribbled lines. There was a standard scribble, consisting of four coils, and there were 18 variations of it, formed from the standard by altering its orientation, compression, or the number of coils. They were sufficiently similar to the standard scribble to appear at first to be identical to it. In addition to the variations, there were 12 other drawings; each of these bore some degree of similarity to the structured scribble.

Each child was given a pack of 34 cards, consisting of four copies of the standard scribble, 18 variations, and 12 other drawings. The children were told to look through the pack and say which of the drawings on the cards were the same as the standard. The intended procedure was to require the children to go through the pack repeatedly until an entirely correct performance was achieved, in which correct items, and only those items, were judged to be identical to the standard scribble. In fact, only two out of ten children aged between 6 and 8 years old reached the required standard. At this age, the average number of errors diminished from over 13 on the first trial to four on the sixth trial. Children aged between 8 and 11 years did better, making eight errors on the first trial and achieving a perfect performance after going through the pack five times. The probability that an incorrect item would be chosen was related to its similarity to the standard item.

The experimental findings indicate that perceptual learning had occurred, and as a result the children became able to discriminate between the standard scribble and the variations from it, although the experimenter provided neither reinforcing events nor feedback information. Perceptual learning was faster in the older subjects than in the younger children, but at both ages practice led to clear improvements in the ability to make discriminations. As children get older they are able to perceive with greater sensitivity, both in respect to the ability to make an appropriate choice on a single stimulus dimension, and in being able to deal with an increased number of stimulus dimensions.

In everyday life, experiences that provide practice in comparing and contrasting perceived objects lead to the kind of perceptual learning observed in the above experiment. It is hardly surprising that Gibson, Gibson, Pick, and Osser (1962), reporting the findings of a similar experiment, found that the greatest improvements at making discriminations between patterns and shapes occurred at around 5 to 6 years, just when children were learning to read in school. The authors suggested that there was transfer between the kind of discriminative learning that took place in the children's daily lives and their performance in the form discrimination tasks of the experiment. Practice in looking at objects and comparing them leads to the individual perceiving things more precisely, and objects are perceived increasingly accurately. This kind of perceptual learning is not restricted to childhood; adults who gain experience in looking at fine furniture come to find that what first appeared to them to be two almost identical old chairs are instantly recognized as examples of distinct Hepplewhite and Sheraton styles.

In many practical situations the individual who has learned to attend to those dimensions of a situation that are significant has a big advantage over a person whose attention is less effectively directed. In one investigation, Zeaman and House (1967) reported that the differences usually found between normal and retarded individuals at performing tasks that involve learning to make discriminative responses are mainly due to differences in the extent to which subjects attend to appropriate cues.

Learned improvements in children's ability to make perceptual discriminations appear to result from increasing ability to attend to the distinctive separate features of an item, rather than to forming images that represent the whole item. A number of experiments reported by Pick and Pick (1970) show that successful learning to differentiate between perceptually similar items typically involves comparisons being made between the particular features in which the items differ. For instance, Pick, Pick, and Thomas (1966, see also Chapter 9) performed a "cross-modal recognition" experiment, in which children had to recognize similarities in some objects that were first presented visually and then in tactile form, or vice versa. The children were asked to decide whether each of a number of letterlike objects was the same or different from a standard item they had previously inspected. The objects that were different from the standard were made by changing the linearity, the orientation, or the size. After discovering which kinds of form changes were most readily identified in the cross-modal tests, Pick, Pick, and Thomas reached the conclusion that children do not rely on images of whole items to any marked extent, and are more likely to make use of information they have retained about particular distinguishing features of the objects.

PERCEPTUAL INTEGRATION

It is essential for a person to be able to make perceptual discriminations, but other kinds of perceptual learning are also important. In many instances we need to integrate perceptual information that comes from a number of separate sources. These may be from the same sensory modality, as in the case of a complex visual display, or from different modalities, such as vision and touch. In addition to integrating perceptual information, it is also necessary for people to be able to perform activities that involve coordinating their perceptions and their own movements.

Perceiving a complex display of visual information is facilitated by the fact that an individual who is able to detect regularities can make inferences about much of the detailed content. This point is illustrated by a simple task described by Welford (1976). The experimenter used a number of grid patterns, such as those shown in Figure 7.1, and each participant was given a blank grid. The task of the participants was to discover the pattern on the experimenter's grid, which the participants could not see. They were told to guess whether each square was white or black, and after each guess they were given the correct answer, which they recorded on their own grid. In this way the subjects gradually built up their own copy of the experimenter's grid. The probability of any guess being correct was strongly influenced by the nature of the grid pattern. With a

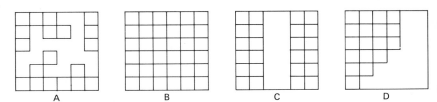

Figure 7.1   Grid designs used in guessing game. (Source: *Skilled Performance: Perceptual and Motor Skills* by A. T. Welford. © 1976 by Scott, Foresman and Company. Reprinted by permission.)

random pattern, such as A, only 50 percent of guesses were correct, on average. But in patterns such as B or C, as soon as regularities were detected the errors rapidly dropped toward zero. In the case of D, where there is a change in the pattern, a number of errors were made in the location of the change, but on the other parts of the display responses were usually correct. This particular task was not solely a perceptual one, but it serves to illustrate the point that when regularities do exist, the amount of information processing necessary for success is greatly reduced.

Detecting regularities also contributes to the perception of three-dimensional gradients. Consider the pattern depicted in Figure 7.2.

One way of perceiving the visual display is as a number of lines that differ in length, thickness and distance from each other, forming a relatively irregular display. But as soon as the perceiver becomes aware of perspective in the display a number of regularities become apparent. The display ceases to look like a mass of short lines, and is seen to form a regular pattern, governed by a small number of rules. Welford (1976) cites this as an instance of an "economy principle," in which the amount or "cost" of processing required in order to perceive the display as forming a gradient is offset by the amount of information that is thereby made invariant or regular and seen to make a simple pattern. As soon as the gradient is apparent to the viewer, certain perceptual ambiguities are resolved. For example, if a large figure of a man was placed at the bottom of Figure 7.2 and a

Figure 7.2   Perspective gradient. (Source: *Skilled Performance: Perceptual and Motor Skills* by A. T. Welford. © 1976 by Scott, Foresman and Company. Reprinted by permission.)

small figure placed at the top, the form of the perceived gradient would give the viewer information enabling him to judge the relative sizes of the figures.

When people look at a large display, they are able to integrate the different pieces of visual information that are obtained from successive glances, and the total perception is the result of their putting together the various sensory data which reach them. This construction process is most readily achieved when all the data are available simultaneously. When they are not, it may still be possible to achieve perceptual integration, but only if the delays between successive parts of the display are less than one second or so (Welford, 1976). As the time between exposure of the different parts increases, the accuracy of integration rapidly falls. The ability to integrate successive visual phenomena clearly depends on the visual information being retained briefly in a visual memory store.

ADAPTATION TO PERCEPTUAL DISTORTIONS

In addition to the need to integrate different perceptions within one sensory modality, it is also essential for people to integrate perceptual information from one modality, for example, with data from a different source. For instance, in the case of visually guided reaching, the child has to reach out for an object, coordinating the movements of an arm with the perception of the object, so that the hand reaches the appropriate position. Some of the difficulties involved in integrating information from more than one sensory modality are demonstrated by experiments in which vision is distorted. If a person wears spectacles that distort perception of the visual world, the normal relationship between visual information and information from other sensory modalities is altered. Considerable readjustment and new learning is required before the person can move around and function effectively in the distorted environment. Readjustment appears to necessitate the individual learning new integrations between the nonvisual sensory information and the changed visual perceptions.

In order to investigate perceptual integration, a number of researchers have systematically distorted the visual input and then observed how people deal with the resulting problems. As early as 1897, G. M. Stratton reported the results of an experiment in which one of his eyes was blindfolded and inverted lenses were placed over the other eye, so that everything was seen upside down and left and right were reversed. Objects moving to the left were seen as moving to the right, the feet were seen as pointing towards the body, although they were felt to be pointing away. Objects and activities that are normally seen below the eyes were viewed as being high up. A pencil tap on the knee was felt at one place and seen at another, and grasping at an object that appeared to be nearby was invariably unsuccessful.

Not surprisingly, disrupting the normally harmonious relationship between vision and the other senses produced feelings of helplessness, but Stratton persisted in wearing the lenses, for three days on the first occasion, and, later, for over a week. Even within the three-day period, a great amount of new integration was achieved, and Stratton was able to report that he could make some actions that were appropriately related to his visual perception, without the conflicts and misinterpretations that occurred at first. After persisting with the lenses for a whole week, Stratton noticed that he sometimes felt that his visual messages were appropriately related to the information from his nonvisual senses. He reported seeing some objects where he felt and heard them to be, and was able to achieve a certain amount of realignment and new integration between the different senses.

A later investigator, I. Kohler, participated in a number of experiments that involved systematic distortions produced by attaching mirrors or prisms to goggles that were placed on the head. Mirrors that reversed the visual image initially led to the difficulties and the sense of helplessness that were experienced by Stratton, but after three days Kohler could ride a bicycle without assistance. By the sixth day he could even ski while wearing the goggles. During the first few days, he found that things usually appeared upside down, but sometimes the perceptual world appeared to right itself, and objects that were simultaneously seen and touched sometimes appeared to be appropriately positioned. Afterwards, removal of the goggles temporarily made things appear upside down again, and this aftereffect persisted for some minutes.

The coordinations involving other senses that were achieved in order to adjust to the distorted visual world had certain interesting consequences. When wearing the goggles, Kohler had to raise his head in order to see, and he gradually began to accept the resulting head position as normal rather than as unusual. Consequently, when the goggles were removed, he felt that he was looking down whenever his head was actually in the normal position. His perception of the position of his head had become distorted as a result of the previous adaptation of felt perception that had taken place in order to coordinate it with the changes in the visual world that were produced by the goggles.

Resolving Perceptual Conflict

Another way to examine how people coordinate different forms of perceptual information is to design circumstances where there are definite conflicts between two sources of perceptual information. In an experiment designed by Rock (1966), subjects saw a one-inch square and touched it at the same time. However, the object was seen through an optical apparatus which changed both its size and its shape, and subjects were unable to see their hands. When they were required to demonstrate how they perceived the size and the shape of the object, by drawing it or by matching it with another square, their judgments of both size and shape were dominated by visual perception of the object. That is, the drawings and the matchings were closer approximations to what they saw than to what they touched. Touch had less influence than vision even in a condition in which subjects were allowed to touch but not see some objects against which the square could be matched.

Subjects in another experiment were required to point at visual objects, but the apparatus prevented them from seeing their arms and their hands. For a three-minute period, the participants wore distorting prisms over the eyes, and were able to see their hand as they pointed to a target. By the end of the period, accurate pointing was achieved despite the prisms. Next, the subjects were tested without the prisms, still without being able to see the hand. There was a large shift in pointing as a result of the subjects having previously adapted to the prisms, but the shift was specific to the particular hand involved. When subjects were subsequently told to point the hand that had not been used in conjunction with the prisms, there was no shift from their performance prior to wearing the prisms. Both this finding and that of Rock's experiment indicate that adaptation took place primarily in perception of the hand's position, rather than in the visual perception of the target. Had the latter adapted, hand pointing would have been influenced by viewing the target through a prism, irrespective of the particular hand involved. Again, it appears that visual perception tends to dominate over the other sensory modalities. Alterations take place in the latter rather than in the former whenever some adaptation is necessitated by an apparent perceptual conflict.

Nevertheless, visual adaptation certainly can occur, as the findings of the early research by Stratton and Kohler suggest. In some instances of sensory adaptation it may not immediately be apparent precisely where the changes lie. For instance, if after wearing a prism for some time subjects are asked to point in the direction of a sound, and there is a change from the previous direction of pointing, it would be hard to tell whether the alteration was due to a change in the subjects' visual experience of where they are pointing, or to an alteration in their felt perception ("proprioception") of the position of the pointing hand and arm. This difficulty was examined in an experiment by Pick, Pick, and Klein (1967). They established that both kinds of adaptation, visual and proprioceptive, contribute to the changed direction of pointing. The combined evidence of studies in which perceptual rearrangements were used to produce conflict necessitating perceptual adaptation, indicates that adaptation can involve changes in the way any of the conflicting sources of information are represented within the processing systems of the brain.

The movements that people make for themselves provide an important source of perceptual information. In some situations such active movements may contribute to perceptual learning. Held and Hein (1963) required subjects to look at their own hand while they wore distorting prisms. In one condition the hand was stationary and in another it was moved by a mechanical device, the subjects remaining passive. In a third condition each subject actively moved the hand. Subsequently the participants were asked to mark points on the visually perceived display. It was found that substantial adaptation occurred in those subjects who made active movements, but those whose hands were passively moved did not adapt; their performance was similar to that of the subjects in the condition where no movement was permitted. This finding indicates that it is important to make a distinction between the output (efferent) information resulting from the activities involved in making a movement, and the perceptual information that is transmitted by the movement as such, the former being especially important. And, just as successful integration of different forms of perceptual information depends upon the data being received, either simultaneously or in close temporal succession, adaptations that involve coordinating information from active movements with the visual feedback from motor actions depend upon the two kinds of information arriving together. If the visual feedback accompanying a movement is delayed by more than a quarter of a second, the person is unable to adapt to an induced visual displacement.

The findings of Stratton, Kohler and later investigations indicate that humans have a remarkable ability to make perceptual adaptations in order to accommodate to changes in the received patterns of sensory information. Yet there are limits to the adaptive capacity of human beings. Humans were designed to move around on their own legs at around three miles per hour and under normal gravity conditions (Reason, 1977). When we are transported passively in modern vehicles at great speed, the various senses that indicate position and motion cannot function together in the normal way to give us information about our orientation. The problems are accentuated in space travel, where the effects of gravity may be entirely absent. One effect of the disharmony that occurs when the human body is moved passively at high speed is the unpleasant experience of nausea.

MOTOR LEARNING

Motor learning takes place whenever a person gains new skills and abilities that usually involve limb movements. Acquiring new learned movements often involves new perceptual coordinations, and for this reason instances of motor learning are typically accompanied by perceptual learning. Accounts of research in this area frequently use the joint term *sensory-motor learning* to refer to the two forms of change that are thus harnessed to each other.

Some of the motor and sensory-motor skills that any normal person acquires are exceedingly complex, requiring fine manipulations, complicated coordinations, and the temporal organization of series of events. The speed and coordination that are characteristic of complex skills like playing the piano are achieved largely through processes that are internally controlled and planned. The individual does not simply make a number of separate actions to external events. Even in those instances where something in the environment does trigger off a response, the environmental event has often been anticipated in advance. When a person has to make separate responses to events that cannot be predicted or anticipated, the rate and accuracy of responding is very markedly reduced.

If we measure how long it takes for a person to react to a single stimulus event, we find that the reaction time is as much as a quarter of a second. When it is also necessary to choose which of a number of possible responses to make, according to which particular stimulus events or signal is presented, the reaction time is appreciably longer. This would appear to make the pianist's task impossible. How might a pianist possibly play over ten notes per second if the reaction time for making one single choice response is over a quarter of a second? Furthermore, in reaction time experiments it is observed that after a person has responded to one stimulus there is a, short refractory period during which responses to subsequent events are delayed. This phenomenon would seem to make the pianist's skills even less attainable.

Fortunately for piano playing and for numerous other human skills, it is not often necessary to make a succession of fast single responses to stimuli that come at unpredictable times. People performing a skilled routine can predict both the form and the timing of events to which they have to respond; that is, they can anticipate events. The notes that pianists strike as they read the music are not made at random but form a predictable series. Consequently, musicians are able to execute an internally controlled plan that enables a large number of motor responses to be made without large reaction time delays between every successive note that is played.

The ability to execute a planned sequence of ordered events, precisely timed, underlies all skilled performance. Activities that depend upon a person making a number of separate responses are less smooth and less rapid than a series of actions that can be achieved when signals from the environment are anticipated (Kay, 1969). Coordinated patterns of skilled movements cannot be achieved by any simple mechanism, and very complex mental processing is required. We humans tend to look upon our intellectual achievements as being more impressive than mere motor abilities, but as Kay (1977) has pointed out, if we were to devise a system that could learn a classical language and another system that could learn to play football, it would not necessarily be easier to design and construct the latter than the former.

The fact that skilled movements form series of integrated events, and not just successions of simple actions, is one reason for human skills being less easy to analyze than they might appear to be. What motor skills and language skills have in common is the fact that the person who learns them and uses them is following a set of rules, or plans. Often, the rules cannot be described by the person who follows them, any attempt at verbal communication of the rules being woefully inadequate. As Reason (1977) notes, the most articulate tennis coach may find it impossible to express in words the various activities that go into an effective serve. Learning is achieved by observing and copying, and in the course of this students internalize, in the form of a plan of action, the information that serves to guide their own actions. When such internalization has been achieved, it is possible for individuals to judge the effectiveness of an action by whether it "feels right" or not. Except in the early stages of learning, it is not usually necessary to have visual information or verbal feedback about the degree of success achieved.

Acquisition of Skill

To illustrate what is involved in acquiring a learned skill, Reason (1977) makes some comparisons between the skilled craftsman and the unskilled apprentice. Reason draws attention to an extract in

Arnold Bennett's novel *Clayhanger,* describing a typesetter at work in a printing office:

> Big James held the composing stick in his great left hand, like a matchbox, and his great right thumb and index picked letter after letter from the case, very slowly in order to display the movement, and dropped them into the stick . . . He was revealing the basic mysteries of his craft, and was happy, making the while the broad series of stock pleasantries which have probably been current in composing rooms since printing was invented. Then he was silent, working more and more quickly, till his right hand could scarcely be followed in its twinklings, and the face of the apprentice duly spread in marvel (Bennett, 1910, p. 114).

Reason notes that the apprentice, in contast, makes large and uncoordinated movements, using up a great deal more energy than Big James, but wasting it through inaccuracy. The apprentice concentrates on individual movements, trying to guide his actions by watching what he is doing and talking himself through step by step as he struggles to remember Big James's instructions. Because Big James has fully learned the skill, the instructions have become internalized, so that he never has to ask himself whether his arm is in the correct position, or watch to see if he is performing the task properly. He does not need to think about the details of the task, and he can concentrate on planning some later stage, or let his mind wander, without the skilled actions breaking down. But for the apprentice, who has not yet acquired a fully internalized plan of action, the task is not comprised of a smooth and continuous series of precise movements but rather of a number of separate reactions. Big James does not have to think closely about what he is doing, but the young apprentice cannot perform the task at all unless he conscientiously attends to every single movement.

With practice, the apprentice's typesetting becomes increasingly similar to Big James's performance. From his first attempts to compose type, in Arnold Bennett's words, "with his feet, his shoulder, his mouth, his eyebrows, with all his body except his hands, which nevertheless traveled spaciously far and wide," the apprentice gradually becomes more precise and dexterous at the task, achieving the smooth timing and the economy of movement that is possible as patterns of movements become more automatic, governed by an internal plan rather than by verbal instructions and visual feedback. His responses become coordinated and automatic, since the skilled person is "restructuring the flow of information from his nervous system so that its handling capacity is maximized" (Reason, 1977 p. 44).

As a smooth series of coordinated actions is gradually achieved and individuals no longer have to give close attention to every single movement, they can attend to increasingly larger series of responses, planning their actions at a higher level. By way of illustration, Reason mentions the classic experiment by Bryan and Harter (1897), which investigated the acquisition of skills by trainee telegraphers learning to operate in Morse code. In the early days of training the learners concentrated on single letters, but with practice words became the unit of attention in receiving and transmitting messages. As the trainees became even more experienced, single words were eventually replaced by phrases.

The fact that skilled performance depends upon the execution of organized plans rather than single responses is reflected in the form of the errors that do occur. If activities are undertaken regularly and frequently, and are performed automatically, with little conscious attention, a number of things may go wrong. Reason calls these "actions-not-as-planned" and gives a number of illustrations. There may be a failure to retrieve stored instructions, part of a plan temporarily lost but later recalled, as when one forgets to mail a letter during a shopping trip. Another kind of memory failure involves forgetting the substance of the plan, for instance, opening a drawer but forgetting what one is looking for. A planned sequence may be terminated too early or too late, an example being getting into the bath with one's clothes on. Classification error may occur, in which an input is wrongly identified as being appropriate for initiating a particular planned sequence. Examples are getting out one's own front door key when approaching a friend's house, attempting to press the clutch pedal on a car with automatic transmission, and approaching the driver's seat when offered a ride in a car. Selection errors may be made, for instance when two different outcomes have initial actions in common. An example reported by Reason is that of a man who, on passing through his back porch on the way to his car, put on the gardening clothes and boots that were standing there.

Most readers will find it easy to remember similar errors made in carrying out planned activities. The point to emphasize is that mistakes such as these are not simply random errors, but indicate failures in the operation of highly organized plans.

FOUNDATIONS OF MOTOR ABILITIES

Complex motor skills and finely coordinated movements rest on a foundation of basic abilities. The child is born capable of some motor actions. These are extensions of movements that can be observed in the unborn child, often as reflexes to proprioceptive stimulation. Some movements in young infants are complicated, such as

the walkinglike action that may take place when a baby is held with
the feet just touching the ground. This reflex movement drops out
after a few months, as movement comes under the control by the
brain's cortical areas, and the spinal cord mechanisms responsible
for the newborn's walkinglike behavior cease to function indepen-
dently of the higher parts of the brain (Kay, 1969).

Mobility

The important motor achievements that are acquired in the first year
of life include the ability to move around and the capacity to pick up
and manipulate small objects. Locomotion is not possible until a
child is able to make a number of controlled movements and can
control the positions of the head and the body. Newborn babies can
control head movement to some extent, and by around 12 weeks
infants lying on their front can raise the front part of their body on
their arms and lift their arms and lift their head until it is almost
vertical. At about the eighth month babies can sit without support,
and they may be able to stand unsupported for short periods. Walking commences around the beginning of the second year, but as Kay
points out, it is not until a long time later that a child is able to run.

Walking is not a simple skill. Anyone who has seen the clumsy
motion of a "walking" doll knows that the movements of walking
cannot be adequately duplicated by any single mechanical device.
As Kay remarks:

> If we think of walking as a series of sub-skills, neatly coordinated, then
> in a case of the adult, each sub-skill is sufficiently well practiced to be
> preprogrammed and run off with the minimum attention . . . it is only
> when signals arrive which are totally unexpected that he attends to
> them (Kay, 1969, pp. 40–41).

Reaching for Objects

Locomotion is essential for humans, and so, too, is the ability to pick
things up and manipulate them. We remarked in Chapter 1 that this
ability is basic to human capacities for using objects as tools, and for
making tools. These skills have made it possible for humans to
extend their control over the environment to a degree which is quite
unlike anything achieved by other animals. Visually guided reaching depends upon a person's perceptual abilities and motor abilities
functioning together in a closely integrated fashion. To pick objects
up one has to make arm movements that are not only precisely
controlled, but are also coordinated with the information received
by the eyes concerning the position of an object and the relative

locations of the object and the hand. Considerable empirical research has been conducted into visually guided reaching, sometimes known as "prehension," from the 1930s onward.

By the age of around 6 months, most children can pick up a small wooden cube that is placed in front of them. The magnitude of this achievement is apparent if one tries to imagine how a machine might be designed to perform the same functions. Walking dolls are poor enough at copying human locomotion, but the possibility of a simple doll's mechanism that could reach out and pick up objects placed in arbitrary positions in the vicinity is quite inconceivable. This human skill requires highly complex communication and control systems.

Like walking, reaching out for objects and picking them up depends upon modified forms of movements that originated in simple motor reflexes. As activities become increasingly subject to control by the cortical areas of the brain, they become more highly organized and used more selectively. There is a primitive grasp reflex which disappears at approximately three months after birth. By the fifth month, the hands are normally open and babies can voluntarily grasp any object they encounter. At this stage, arm movements are still limited to what some researchers have called "swiping actions." At around 20 weeks of age, touching an object may be followed by a hand-closing movement, although finger coordination is restricted, and by approximately 28 weeks, the baby grasps the cube in the palm. Gripping objects between thumb and forefinger is not usually possible until the child is about 1 year old. A great deal remains to be learned before the delicate finger control characteristic of adults is achieved. Gradual improvement takes place, as a result of frequent practice of hand and finger control movements in the course of everyday life.

Learning any skill that involves coordinated movements requires considerable practice. The need for and repetition of particular actions is more apparent in motor abilities than in intellectual learning, but the latter depends upon mental skills that almost certainly require a fair amount of practice. As any sports instructor knows, increasing the amount of practice of a sensory-motor skill tends to improve the level of performance, confirming the validity of Thorndike's Law of Practice (Chapter 2). Several factors which influence other kinds of learning have similar effects on motor learning. Thus, motor performance is affected by a variety of reinforcers, and selective attention is also important; attention to appropriate cues is essential for the acquisition of controlled movements.

When people raise the possibility of accelerating learning or developing ways to compensate for learning deprivations, they normally have verbal forms of learning in mind, in which language skills predominate. However, nonverbal skills are equally basic to human achievement, and until the child has learned to talk, learning and knowledge remain at a sensory-motor level. It is conceivable that giving increased opportunities during the early years for motor and perceptual learning would be especially effective for accelerating learning generally.

Such is the view of B. L. White, and he has tried to identify points in child development at which interventions providing additional experience or practice in perceptual and motor skills can be beneficial. It is not simply a matter of providing extra stimulation in the belief that more is better. What can be learned by the developing child at any one time partly depends upon the stage of physiological maturation achieved and upon the child's previously learned skills that are basic to ones now being acquired. These considerations account for the fact that young children who had been carefully taught to climb stairs were found to be no more successful a week or two later than children of the same age who did not receive training.

One of White's (1971) concerns has been to discover if it is possible to accelerate infants' learning to reach out to objects and pick them up. As we stated in Chapter 1, he conducted a series of experiments that were designed to give opportunities for infants to gain increased practice in some of the component skills that are known to be necessary for guided reaching. One important ability is to be able to give prolonged visual attention to small objects in the environment. A child who cannot do this and is easily distracted will be at a major disadvantage. Accordingly, White decided to display attractive visual stimuli that could be seen while the infants were lying in their crib. I remarked in Chapter 1 that this procedure was successful, and infants who were given the visual displays made longer visual fixations than infants not exposed to them. Thus the experimental intervention had the genuinely enriching effect of improving performance at a skill that is vital for visually guided reaching. But when the babies' eventual success at reaching out at objects was compared, those infants who had received additional visual stimulation were found to be slower rather than faster than the others at reaching a fixed standard of performance.

Paradoxically, then, it seems that practice at an essential subskill delayed progress toward the acquisition of reaching skills. Why should this be? One possibility is that the intervention interfered with the normal sequence of learning. Acquiring a compound skill is not simply a matter of adding together the component abilities. In learning complex human abilities, the precise sequencing of the different elements is also crucial. As I mentioned in Chapter 1, we take it for granted that some kinds of learning are cumulative and that concepts can only be mastered if simple rules have been acquired first. For this reason teachers try to make sure that students are adequately prepared for each new task. It is equally important to insure appropriate sequencing of the learned components of sensory-motor skills.

To return to White's unsuccessful attempt, although the visual stimulation was appropriate to the infants' needs, it was provided at an inappropriate time. Inspection of the evidence gained from observational research revealed a clue to the failure of White's intervention. Young infants spend a great amount of time looking at their hands, particularly during the third month of life, coinciding with the time at which White provided visual enrichment. Hand-regarding activities give infants practice in keeping track of the hands. Since attractive visual stimuli distract the babies from looking at their hands, they may prevent them from gaining practice that is essential for normal development. White's problem was to find a way of giving opportunities for increased visual attention without interfering with the infants' looking at their hands. You may recall that the solution was to provide brightly colored patterned mittens, which stimulated visual attending but directed vision toward the hands rather than away from them. Placing the mittens on the babies' hands at appropriate times led to both an increase in visual attention and accelerated development of the ability to reach out to objects and pick them up.

OBSERVATION AND PRACTICE IN LEARNED MOVEMENTS

Activity and practice are so important in most forms of sensory-motor learning that it is easy to imagine that activity is invariably indispensable and to think that the amount of learning which takes place is always directly related to the learner's level of activity. Some findings of an experiment by Von Wright (1957) demonstrate that this is not so. Von Wright's task consisted of a kind of maze which subjects watched, a small part at a time, through the slit in the screen of a memory drum. At any one time the subject could see a small segment of a line route, and as the line moved, junctions came into sight, one at a time, as shown in Figure 7.3.

The subjects' task was to hold a stylus in the slit as each junction came into view and move the stylus to the left or the right according to which they considered to be the correct choice of route. If the choice was incorrect, soon afterwards the subjects would encounter some double lines that crossed the line they were following

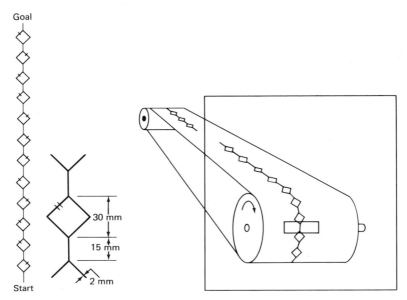

Figure 7.3 Moving maze used by Von Wright. (Source: Fitts, P. H. and Posner, M. I. *Human Performance,* 1967, p. 107. Reprinted by permission.)

with the stylus. If the choice was correct, the line being followed continued uninterrupted to the next junction, at which point the subjects had to make another choice about which line to follow.

When people begin this maze-learning task they make a number of errors on their first few trials. Subsequent performances indicate that errors tend to persist, and subjects find it very difficult to erase or forget their incorrect responses. Von Wright thought that performance might be improved if it were possible to eliminate some of the early errors. He tried a procedure in which some subjects could see the correct route for the first four trials and simply followed it, without the possibility of making errors. These subjects learned the maze, to the criterion of two errorless runs, in half as many trials as the subjects who had to make decisions at each junction from the very first learning trial. Furthermore, the subjects who were shown which direction was correct on the first four trials made only a fifth of the number of errors as the other subjects on subsequent trials.

The above findings indicate that learning of motor skills can be improved by guidance during early training. Further support for such a view is provided by the results of a study by Holding and Macrae (1966). Their subjects had to move a knob a given distance along a steel rod. It was found that if during early training the apparatus automatically stopped when the correct distance was reached, the improvement in performance over a number of trials was greater than in conditions that did not provide such guidance.

Guidance normally provides learners with some kind of information about their performance, in the form of feedback or knowledge of results. The importance of feedback for learned movements is sometimes obscured simply because it is often provided naturally, as an inherent part of the task. In visually guided reaching, for example, it is quite apparent to individuals whether they have succeeded or not, and without knowing about the degree of success of their efforts to pick up an object, it is hard to imagine how any child would acquire the compound skill. Feedback information is most effective when it indicates to the learners the discrepancy between what they have achieved and what is required, rather than simply giving a broad indication of performance (Fitts and Posner, 1967). The more precise the knowledge that is available about one's own actions, the greater the accuracy that can be expected. Removing either visual feedback or motor feedback (for example by anesthetics) leads to marked deterioration in performance. Absence of touch or feeling can be particularly detrimental, as any one knows who has tried to eat after being injected for dental treatment.

Information that provides useful feedback at an early stage in the learning of a difficult task may be less effective at a later stage. Fitts and Posner reported that an indicator placed on the side of an industrial sewing machine, showing the speed of its operation, was found to be helpful to beginning trainees, but it was not useful for more advanced operators because it diverted attention from the article being sewn. Similarly, West (1967) observed that people who were beginning to learn to type performed better if they were allowed to see what they were doing, but that at later stages it was important for them to become independent of vision and to rely on tactile and kinesthetic cues alone. If visual feedback continues to be given beyond the early stages of training, the person may become dependent on visual cues rather than on those inherent in the task, and progress will be restricted.

SUMMARY

1. Movements and motor skills are acquired through learning, and motor skills require coordinations between perceptions and movements.
2. People learn to discriminate and to perceive the significant aspects of objects. Learning increases the ability to distinguish between similar objects.

3. The integration of information from different sources is frequently necessary. It is facilitated by the ability to detect perceptual regularities.
4. The role of perceptual learning is illustrated by experiments in which individuals learn to adapt to perceptual distortions and resolve perceptual conflicts between different sources of information. The fact that major adaptations can be achieved in perception shows that human perception is strongly influenced by experience.
5. The motor learning underlying skilled movements leads to the acquisition of organized sequences of skilled actions. A person who performs a motor skill is essentially following a set of internalized rules or plans. The fact that skilled performance depends upon the execution of organized plans rather than simple responses is illustrated by the nature of the errors people make.
6. Basic human abilities, such as walking and picking things up, depend upon gradually acquired increases in control over movements and the integration of a number of simpler skills.
7. Practice is necessary for acquiring skills that involve learned movements, but in some circumstances learning is improved by the opportunity to observe correct actions before attempting the activity oneself. Prior observation may reduce the tendency of the individual to make and retain early errors.

Suggestions for Further Reading

Fitts, P. M. and Posner, M. I. (1967) *Human Performance*. Belmont, California: Brooks/Cole.

Reason, J. T. (1977) Skill and error in everyday life. In M. J. A. Howe (ed.), *Adult Learning: Psychological Research and Applications*. London: Wiley.

Welford, A. T. (1976) *Skilled Performance: Perceptual and Motor Skills*. Glenview, Illinois: Scott, Foresman.

CHAPTER

The Contribution
of Learning to
Language Acquisition

OVERVIEW

The previous three chapters have been largely concerned with learning *to do* various activities. Much human learning takes the form of acquiring knowledge and gaining skills that are primarily intellectual rather than behavioral. That is, we learn *about* various things. This kind of learning depends upon the ability to use the medium of language, which itself has to be acquired. In the present chapter we examine the role of learning in the acquisition of human language. Some psychologists have claimed that the ability to use a language is gained solely through learning. Others have argued that learning processes cannot account for all of the language abilities humans possess, and that innate mechanisms must exist to facilitate language acquisition.

INTRODUCTION

The achievement of acquiring the use of a language is shared by almost every member of the human species. To learn a language it is necessary for a person to incorporate numerous rules governing the use of word items to communicate with others and to give expression to conscious thoughts.

Some aspects of language acquisition follow associative learning principles. For instance, repetition of pairs of items presented in close temporal contiguity leads to the formation of connections between nouns and the objects they represent. B. F. Skinner (1957) attempted to account for language acquisition in terms of relatively simple kinds of learning. According to his account, principles of reinforcement explain how the child's earliest sounds are gradually modified, the eventual outcome being adult human speech. Language is regarded as consisting of a large number of learned responses, each of which is fundamentally no different from other learned responses. Skinner did not really attack the problem of how thoughts and meanings are transmitted in language, since he considered that investigating mental processes does not contribute to knowledge of the laws of behavior. For Skinner, verbal responses are learned in the same way as other responses, through reinforcement. If a language response that is emitted when an individual needs something is reinforced, that response will be repeated. Skinner called that kind of response a *mand*, an instance being when a person is reinforced for saying "Pass the salt." Another kind of verbal response, termed a *tact*, occurs when an individual is reinforced for naming something appropriately. For instance, a young child sees a dog, says "dog," and the mother immediately reinforces the child's response, smiling encouragingly and saying "That's right."

These illustrations suggest that reinforcing appropriate responses may make a useful contribution to the child's acquiring a vocabulary. Some language can be acquired simply by imitating observed responses, providing the imitative responses are reinforced; the performance of talking birds is based on this kind of language. However, although reinforcement does contribute to language acquisition, it is not possible to account for a child's learning to speak solely on the basis of reinforcement principles and the simple forms of associative learning described in Skinner's account of verbal behavior. Among the many problems encountered is the fact that it is difficult to see how an entirely new sentence could ever be emitted if language utterances depend upon what had previously been reinforced. Language is too complicated to be acquired through associative learning alone. The vast number of meaningful word combinations that exist in any human language precludes the possibility of all of the utterances a person can emit having been acquired through the kinds of learning described by Skinner. There would be simply far too many combinations for any one person to learn. Furthermore, as Greene (1976) notes, although simple responses might be acquired on the basis of operant conditioning procedures that involve reinforcement and the modification of verbal behavior through shaping procedures and stimulus generalization, the ability to comprehend lengthy and complex sequences cannot be explained in this way. One source of difficulty is illustrated by the inability of Skinner's account to indicate why the following two very different sequences of verbal responses mean very much the same thing:

The eye doctor fancied the blonde.
The girl with fair hair attracted the oculist.

Greene also points out that when people are shown sentences like these two, and can detect the similarity in their meaning, they cannot usually remember the actual sequence of the words. Being able to use language is not principally a matter of uttering particular verbal responses.

RULES AND STRUCTURE IN LANGUAGE ACQUISITION

Our ability to generate a vast number of language sequences, some of which we have never previously encountered, is only possible because we can use a number of rules for combining words in a variety of different ways. Such rules enable us to generate word sequences that express the meanings to be expressed. The rules that specify how words can be combined constitute the grammar of a language. Examination of the speech patterns of a young child who is learning to speak reveals that the words are not uttered randomly but obey certain rules that constitute the grammar of the child's speech. Such a grammar is considerably simpler than that of an adult whose language development is complete. Because we know something about the way language is structured, we can immediately recognize whether a particular sentence is grammatical. Thus, "Colorless green ideas sleep furiously" is perceived as a grammatical sentence although the semantic content (that is, the meaning expressed by the sentence) is somewhat dubious, and despite the fact that there is little possibility that we will have 'learned' this sentence from previous exposure to that particular sequence of words.

Using a human language involves following a large number of rules governing linguistic sequences. For young children to be able to discern the rules and regularities that govern a language to which they are exposed, they must possess mental processes that are more highly organized or structured than is necessary for associative learning. The brain mechanisms involved in learning to talk have to be arranged so that young children can analyze the language to which they are exposed and extract the rules that govern it. This is not a conscious process; the children need not be aware that they are extracting rules from the flow of language, and they will never be able to articulate all the rules that they follow when they talk. (People are similarly unaware of many important bodily functions.) Although people may appear to be totally ignorant of the rules that govern their language, at some level the mechanisms that underlie mental processing do "know" the rules; otherwise, it would not be possible to discriminate between a new sentence and an unfamiliar random ordering of the identical words, and we would not be able to produce new sentences that obey the rules of language.

The fact that we do have some awareness of our own mental activities should not mislead us into believing that we are conscious of all important aspects of mental processing. Nor do the contents of awareness necessarily match the processing by which our brains actually undertake the mental processing that is achieved. As I remarked in Chapter 2, this fallacy led the European introspective psychologists of the late nineteenth century into a blind alley.

THE POSSIBILITY OF INNATE LANGUAGE STRUCTURES

We can learn to use a language because we possess cortical structures that are arranged in a way that enables regularities to be detected in the language to which we are exposed in our earliest years. The rules of a language cannot be detected unless organized mental structures exist to detect regularities. Chomsky (1971) claims that since there is no apparent way in which the necessary mental structures can be acquired by simple kinds of associative learning, humans must be born with mental structures so formed as to enable children to learn any human language to which they are exposed. Chomsky stated that children possess an innate *language acquisition device* (LAD) which contains the mental structures necessary for learning the rules of a language.

The view that the human brain is innately "wired in" for language learning received considerable support in the 1960s. One reason was that attempts to account for language acquisition in terms of the processes studied in research into learning and conditioning were inadequate. An entirely different kind of explanation seemed to be required. The failure of Skinner's attempt to account for language acquisition appeared to indicate that approaches of that kind could not be successful.

The conclusion that the mental structures necessary for acquiring rule-governed speech must be innate appeared to be supported by the fact that prior to the 1960s, none of the attempts that were made to teach animals those aspects of human language that are more advanced than simple vocabulary acquisition was at all successful. But animals that were apparently clearly incapable of acquiring even the rudiments of human language were undoubtedly capable of learning many things very effectively. It did not seem likely that the failure to acquire language was due to a limited learning capacity; some other explanation was necessary. The suggestion that language acquisition in humans depends not only on ability to learn but also requires mental mechanisms that are unique to humans provides a possible account.

Some further forms of evidence, listed by Lenneberg (1966), appeared to give additional support for the view that humans possess an innate language acquisition device. One kind of evidence is that human languages all have certain common features, or *language universals*, even though the speakers live in entirely different cultures that are isolated from each other. Lenneberg believes that this fact indicates the existence of biological mechanisms underlying language. However, it could be argued that since different human groups share many kinds of experience, the language similarities are not altogether surprising. Lenneberg also notes that there exists a number of anatomical and physiological correlates of language in the human brain, and verbal behavior is regulated by specialized brain mechanisms. He points out that the developmental onset of speech is a very regular phenomenon, in which principles are learned before unique items, and the first words refer to classes rather than to single objects. Furthermore, the acquisition of language is not easily disrupted, even when a child faces major handicaps, such as deafness, or is subject to gross neglect in a deprived environment.

It might appear that a reason humans, but no other animals, are able to acquire speech is that humans have an especially large brain in relation to body size. However, Lenneberg describes a form of dwarfism in which, due to a genetic abnormality, individuals attain only about half normal height and yet preserve the bodily proportions of ordinary adults. The adult brain size and weight of these dwarfs barely exceeds that of a normal newborn infant, but since the size of their brain cells is normal, these people have only around a third of the usual number of brain cells. Not surprisingly, they do exhibit mental retardation, but they can usually acquire the rudiments of language, the majority mastering verbal skills to at least the level of a 5-year-old child. This evidence clearly contradicts the suggestion that human language ability is simply a function of having a large brain.

It is hard to dispute the view that for children to acquire language, they need to possess mental structures arranged in such a manner that as the children listen to spoken language they can extract the rules by which word sequences are governed. They can then be said to have a language device that is absent in other species. Of course, animals do have ways of signaling information, but such communicative systems lack some essential features of human language. In particular, animal languages do not have the generative capacity that is necessary to produce new statements. They can only convey specific kinds of information about events.

However, the fact that language depends upon mental structures that only humans possess does not make it inevitable that such structures are innate, despite Chomsky's claim. Piaget (1970) accepts Chomsky's view that language in humans necessitates the possession of a language-acquisition device with a strong inner structure, but he disagrees with the assumption that such a structure must be innate, or genetically preprogrammed. Piaget points out that there is an alternative explanation that Chomsky has not considered. It is that the structures are themselves acquired, through learning that occurs in the course of the child's early experience.

CONTINUITY BETWEEN LANGUAGE AND PRELINGUISTIC ABILITIES

Piaget believes that the mental structures that children need in order to learn a language are acquired by the children in the prelinguistic stage of their life, when the children are gaining a preverbal understanding of their world, based on sensory-motor knowledge. Piaget notes that although a child's early language is in some respects distinct from the behavior that precedes it, language ability is nevertheless dependent upon mental structures that are gained early in life. Language undoubtedly does involve mental processes that are different from those underlying nonverbal skills, and language skills reflect a greater degree of biological specialization in our species than is apparent in other forms of behavior. Nevertheless, important continuities exist between speech and a number of nonlinguistic abilities that the child has previously acquired.

Some of the behaviors that are observed before children begin to speak have close similarities to language and symbolic behavior. For example, the fact that children can imitate indicates the ability to form a kind of representation, through actions rather than through symbols. An important aspect of language is that it is representational. It is conceivable that in the course of acquiring early nonlinguistic representational skills, children equip themselves with mental structures that form a basis for the representative skills necessary for language. The ability of children to form mental images might be regarded as evidence of an internalized form of imitation. This enables the individual to think about events that are not being perceived, but are represented in memory. Some of the early games that mothers play with their babies, "pat-a-cake" for example, include imitative events that have a primitive representational function.

Early Representational Skills

Children's first words are spoken at an age when their play activities demonstrate delayed imitation of things that have been perceived (Sinclair-de-Zwart, 1969). The symbolic functions conveyed by language do not suddenly emerge from nothing. They are preceded by previously acquired forms of representation that enable children to experience mental imagery, to retain information in memory, and to imitate things they experience, well before they are able to speak. There is definite continuity between language and the earlier representational skills that language builds upon. In the course of gaining the representational skills, children may acquire those structured language acquisition mechanisms that Chomsky rightly demonstrated to be essential for language. Thus, the structures may be acquired rather than innate.

To illustrate the young child's prelinguistic representational abilities, Inhelder (1971) cites a number of Piaget's observations.

Deferred imitation is demonstrated by the actions of a little girl, aged 1 year and 4 months, who is visited by a boy of similar age. She observes him as he gets into a temper in the course of the afternoon. He tries to get out of his play pen, and screams and stamps his feet as he pushes it around, while the little girl watches in amazement. The next day, when she is standing in her own play pen, she starts to scream and stamp her feet, although she has never acted in this way before. This instance of imitation, which takes place about 20 hours after the observed event, is only possible because the little girl possessed some kind of inner representation of the boy's actions.

Piaget uses the term *semiotic* to describe forms of behavior that have a broadly representational function. Semiotic activities imply knowledge of a distinction between behavior and the action or object that it signifies, and simpler forms of semiotic behavior are regarded by Piaget as being basic to the advanced kinds of symbolic representation encountered in human language. The symbolic representational abilities required in using a language build upon the simpler semiotic functions involved in imitation and other representational activities. In turn, the simpler forms of representation depend upon the child having previously acquired certain basic cognitive abilities and elementary forms of knowledge at the sensory-motor level. Inhelder reasons:

> We think it possible to trace continuous links between the first sensory-motor coordinations and truly cognitive structures, and to hypothesize that language, and, in a more general way, the semiotic functions of which it is the most obvious expression are not suddenly constructed, but prepared by the elementary development of knowledge at the sensory-motor level (Inhelder, 1971, p. 142).

Edmonds (1976) has provided some evidence to support this view. She found that children did not begin to talk until they had already reached a point at which they demonstrated an awareness of object permanence. This involves knowing that objects have a separate and independent existence that is not tied to the child's directly experiencing them. Children gain awareness of object permanence after a gradual process of acquiring knowledge about the world. At first, infants have no understanding of objects except in relation to their own actions, and their concepts of space and time are tied to immediate experience. Edmonds' evidence tends to refute the hypothesis that language acquisition is controlled by innate mechanisms. If the latter assertion was correct, we would expect language acquisition to begin right at the start of life, or no later than the time at which children demonstrate they are capable of other instances of learning.

There is further evidence that the content of a child's early language is closely intertwined with the content of nonlinguistic cognition. Bloom (1973) showed that the very earliest uses of language refer to actions in relation to objects. This is exactly what we would expect to find at this stage, when stable object permanence is emerging. The meaning of a young child's utterance may differ according to the context. When one of the children observed by Bloom said, "Mummy sock it," the words sometimes implied that Mummy was dressing the child, but on other occasions it meant that the child had found a sock which Mummy was looking for. Similarly, young children observed by Edmonds (1976) used language to accompany their actions in relation to objects, saying "do" as they placed a toy car in its garage, or naming an object being manipulated.

In summary, early speech closely matches and depends upon aspects of the child's thinking that are not specifically linguistic. The symbolic behavior necessary for language rests upon similar but more primitive representational functions that are acquired in the course of sensory-motor development. Mastering a first language depends upon the child having previously gained certain basic cognitive abilities. We can accept Chomsky's claim that the language user must possess complex and stable mental structures, but reject the view that such structures must be governed by innate mechanisms. Piaget (1970) points out that Chomsky has considered only two alternatives, either simple associative learning or an innate language acquisition device. Having shown the former to be inadequate, Chomsky accepts the latter. But, as Piaget remarks, there is a third possibility. The regulatory processes that are involved in the infants' early sensory-motor operations are progressively modified to form the inner structures that are necessary for acquiring a rule-governed language.

The mental structures gained early in life are necessary for subsequent linguistic skills, and language does not emerge until towards the end of a long sensory-motor period in which the child acquires a practical knowledge of the world of objects and events. Language and symbolic activities do not appear out of the blue, but come after a long period of preparation through the growth of the basic cognitive structures that guide the young child's understanding.

LEARNING RULES AND MEANINGS

Since language acquisition is closely tied to the child's prelinguistic mechanisms, the child's learning of a first language is not independent of general developmental processes. Most kinds of learning are influenced by developmental factors, and the artificiality of any distinction between learning and developmental processes is especially apparent in relation to learning to talk.

Much early language learning takes the form of children discerning that there are relationships between samples of language and accompanying meanings that are already evident to them. That is, children know the meaning of what is said to them, and they learn that a pattern of words expresses that meaning. Young children use meaning as a clue to language, relating the meaning and the language forms in which it is expressed (Macnamara, 1972). As Macnamara explains, although children must possess appropriate nonlinguistic cognitive processes before they can learn language signals, cognitive structures are not entirely developed prior to the start of language learning. Language acquisition is spread over a long period, and during this time nonlinguistic cognitive abilities continue to develop. To simplify matters, we can say that children who are learning their first language have to gain two kinds of competence, although in practice these are largely inseparable. First, they must develop the cognitive structures that make possible an understanding of meanings. Second, they must learn rules and language elements for relating such meanings to the language that is used to convey it.

Evidence of Rule Learning

The fact that young children learn language rules is demonstrated by some of the errors that children make as they learn to speak. Brown (1973) points out that many children learning English use the form *hisself* rather than *himself* when they are around 4 years of age. This error occurs because the child constructs a reflexive pronoun by following the rule that successfully yields other reflexive pronouns. Combining *my, you,* and *her* with *self* produced *myself, yourself,* and *herself.* Following the same rule with *his* yields *hisself,* and this is incorrect only because the general rule does not apply to that particular case.

Young children often say *mans* for *men, digged* for *dug, mouses* for *mice,* and *sheeps* for *sheep.* Again, what the children are doing is to use the learned rules that are applicable in the majority of circumstances involving these word forms. Absence of such errors may give a clue to inadequate speech development. Brown and Herrnstein (1975) state that the speech of some autistic children lacks rule-induced language errors. Their language imitates the particular linguistic sequences they have heard, and is less rule governed than the speech of normal children. Children who do not use rules to form linguistic utterances will not be able to generate new sentences to communicate meanings. Their language will be subject to some of the same limitations as that of a jackdaw; it can mimic language but cannot use it to communicate.

REINFORCEMENT AND THE ACQUISITION OF SPEECH

Speech, like any other activity, is affected by its consequences, and the availabilty of reinforcers influences the child's use of language. Children who are consistently encouraged to talk will gain opportunities to practice their language skills. Most of the programs that have been designed to help children with retarded language abilities take this fact into account. As we found in Chapter 5, the development of simple communicative skills involving vocalization is related to the mother's responsiveness to her child's early signaling behaviors. The mother who is responsive to her infant's early vocal acts reinforces such behavior more effectively than a less responsive mother. It is hard to specify the precise age from which the frequency of vocalizations can be increased by conditioning, since recent findings by Bloom (1975) and Bloom and Esposito (1975) question the validity of earlier studies that apparently demonstrated social conditioning of infant vocalizing at the age of 3 months (see Chapter 5). Even at that age, however, the rate of vocalizations can be modified by environmental events, possibly through some kind of social elicitation effect rather than reinforcement.

Some increases in children's vocalizations observed by Ramey and Ourth (1971) were almost certainly due to reinforcement. They studied infants aged 3, 6, and 9 months. First, there was a short period in which the infants' baseline vocal activity was measured. In the conditioning sessions of which followed, each vocalization was recorded and reinforced. Three components of the reinforcement procedure were delivered simultaneously: a light touch on the abdomen, a smile, and saying "That's a good baby." At each age, when a vocalization was followed immediately by the events designed to reinforce behavior, the frequency of vocalization rose to about three times the baseline level. That this was a genuine reinforcement effect, and not caused by an alternative outcome of the events provided as reinforcers, is indicated by the finding that if the events were delayed by as little as three seconds they had no effect at all. Had the social events provided by the experimenter as reinforcement been influencing the infants through a social elicitation effect, the effect of a small delay would not have been serious.

Dodd (1972) found that a procedure in which the experimenter himself emitted sequences of consonants and babbling sounds, and also placed the infant on his knee, effectively increased both the number and the length of vocal outputs in infants aged between 9 and 12 months. However, if he provided either the social or the auditory component without the other, by playing a recording when the adult was absent, or by engaging the infant in social play while remaining silent, there was no increase in the child's vocalizations.

Operant Procedures in Language Training

These above findings indicate that the frequency of vocal acts can be modified by the social events which function as reinforcers for other social behaviors. It would seem likely that an infant's early experience in vocalizing influences subsequent speech. In girls, high levels of babbling during infancy in response to the sight of human faces has been found to be associated with high intelligence test scores and attentiveness in later years. The relationship between early vocalization and subsequent language development in boys is less clear.

The influence of reinforcing events on language acquisition is not unlimited. Because of constraints set by cognitive development and by the necessity to acquire basic language rules before more advanced ones can be learned, reinforcement by the parents has little effect on the actual order in which a child masters grammar structures. Language learning is essentially a cumulative process in which the child's acquisition of rules forms a base for subsequent gains. Nevertheless, reinforcers do make a substantial contribution. Staats (1971) has described a simple instance in which a verbal stimulus came to exert control over the behavior of his own daughter, then aged 6 months. He would kneel a few feet away from the child, say "Come to Daddy," and at the same time hold out a key ring that was known to be highly reinforcing to her. When the child approached her father he gave her the ring to play with, and as a result of this training the child would reliably follow the instruction "Come to Daddy" on future occasions.

An instance of the use of an operant procedure to help a child acquire rules necessary for language is provided by the study (mentioned in Chapter 4) by Guess, Sailor, Rutherford, and Baer (1968) in which they taught a mentally retarded child lacking speech to apply the rule for forming the plural forms of nouns she was learning. Following a procedure in which the child was reinforced for imitating an adult model, she learned to generate the plural of each new word in a single trial. However, Guess (1969) found that mentally retarded subjects who learned the rule for distinguishing between singular and plural words were unable to apply this knowledge in expressive speech, unless they received additional specific training in saying singular and plural words. If language acquisition in mentally retarded subjects does parallel its acquisition in younger people of normal intelligence, it would appear that early stages of expressive and receptive language are to some extent independent of each other. Guess and Baer (1973) obtained further evidence that the rules acquired for receptive language may have to be learned again for use in expressive language, and vice versa. They observed that children found it easier to apply rules to new words than to apply rules in a different mode of language (receptive or expressive) than that in which they had been acquired.

OBSERVATIONAL LEARNING OF LANGUAGE SKILLS

Language acquisition following observation may involve either direct imitation or the learning of rules. Acquisition of imitative speech was observed in a study conducted by Lovaas, Berberich, Perloff, and Schaeffer (1966). These authors worked with mute schizophrenic children, and at first they rewarded them with food for emitting any sounds at all. Subsequently, reinforcement was made contingent upon the children making a sound shortly after the experimenter had spoken. Later still, the children were reinforced only for imitating the experimenter's vocalizations. In this way, increasingly similar sounds were required as the experiment progressed, and the children learned to match a series of sounds and words. The rate of learning to match new sounds increased in the course of the experiment, and it was not necessary to reinforce every matching response that was made to the words provided.

Direct imitation has a restricted role in language acquisition, but observational learning through which children acquire rules after observing a number of instances of language use has much greater value. Much is learned by children from observing samples of adult language. What children actually learn as they listen depends not only upon the language they hear but also upon their existing knowledge of language. This determines the kinds of principles they can extract when they are exposed to human speech.

Bandura and Harris (1966) found that after children had observed a model who talked in passive sentences, they could construct passive sentences themselves. The sentences they produced were varied in content and only rarely duplicated the particular sentences produced by the model. Children in an experimental condition that provided modeling, reinforcement for appropriate sentences, instructions to give close attention to sentences that were followed by reinforcement, and the reward of a star for each passive construction were more successful than children in conditions that included only some of these elements. It is also possible to teach retarded children to generate appropriate past and present tense verb inflections after they have observed appropriate samples of language. The children acquire appropriate rules, and they learn to produce appropriate verb endings for verbs that have not been encountered in training sessions.

It is clear that following observation of speech, children, even retarded ones, do not only acquire directly imitative responses but also learn rules for making correct responses when unfamiliar items are presented. In the course of learning to talk, children often imitate the precise language utterances they observe (Sherman 1971). However, this should not mislead us into thinking that the learning is confined to imitative responses that mimic observed behavior. Of course, children who regularly make use of rules in constructing and understanding language sequences may be completely unable to specify the rules, and as Brown (1973) points out, even their parents will be unable to articulate many language rules. Parents do not explicitly invoke language rules to help a child learn. The state of affairs is somewhat analogous to most people's understanding of music. We can reproduce tunes and detect errors in notes and rhythm, thereby demonstrating an implicit knowledge of the principles by which music is structured, without having any formal knowledge of music.

Observing adult speech may lead to children acquiring quite complex rules, providing their existing language competence is sufficiently advanced. Thus, when an observed model wrote complex sentences involving the pluperfect tense (e.g., "He had seen"), seventh grade students produced significantly more complex sentences and verbs in the pluperfect tense. Increased use of lengthy sentences following observation of a model was also reported by Harris and Hassemer (1972). In a study by Wheeler and Sulzer (1970), a child who at first spoke English in a compressed, telegraphic form, lacking articles and auxilliary verbs, learned to produce lengthier sentences from a procedure in which correct English communications were demonstrated and correct responses were reinforced. Fygetakis and Gray (1970) obtained similar findings.

Some of the observed improvements in speech following training procedures may reflect increased use of abilities children already possess, rather than new learning, but the effectiveness of the procedures that we have mentioned suggests children's speech is strongly influenced by the forms of language to which they are exposed in the circumstances of their daily lives. Most of the specific contents of language learning depends upon what a child observes in adult models (Moerk, 1972). A child's own speech is heavily influenced by the particular language content that is addressed to the child at home.

TALKING WITH THE MOTHER

The circumstances in which a child interacts and communicates with the mother are especially important for language acquisition. Children hear numerous samples of correct speech, carefully directed toward them, and they are frequently reinforced for their own speech and for demonstrating that they can understand what they hear. Observation of a mother and her young child together makes it possible to discover what the child learns from this important adult model. Both mother and child imitate each other, but in neither case is narrow mimicry involved. The parent tends to expand the child's utterances, typically expressing what she perceives to be their meaning, in a form that is structured by the rules of adult grammar. The child reduces the mother's words and expresses an approximation to their meaning, within the simpler structure of the language principles that the child has already acquired. For example, after the child says, "Baby highchair," the mother replies with the expanded sentence "Baby is in the high chair" (Brown and Bellugi, 1964). Following the mother's "Oh, just like the cowboy's," the child offers a reduced version, "Just like cowboy" (Slobin, 1968).

Taken together, the mother's expansions and the child's reductions may produce a sequence like the following:

CHILD: Pick 'mato.
ADULT: Picking tomatoes up?
CHILD: Pick 'mato up.

In such exchanges, the mother imitates her child but she also adds something to the child's utterance. Middle-class parents typically expand their children's statements by about a third. Working class parents tend to expand less frequently, and since children's imitations of the parents' expansions of the original utterances are often more grammatically advanced than the original speech (as in the example above), the parental differences may influence the rate at which children acquire mature grammatical language. However, when C. Cazden (Dale, 1972) tested this suggestion in an experiment in which all the utterances of a group of linguistically deprived children were expanded by an adult speaker, the children did not display unusually large advances. The failure of the expansion condition might have been due in part to the fact that the experimenters, who were not the children's parents, sometimes expanded a child's speech on the basis of incorrect guesses about the intended meanings. Furthermore, since *all* of a child's utterances were expanded in the experiment, the adult speech may have been more uniform, less varied and less interesting to the children than the speech of adults who are not constrained to limit their statements to expansions of what the young children say.

Brown, Cazden and Bellugi (1970) observed that the particular forms of language a child produced were related to the mother's talk toward the child, and the more often a mother's expansions included prepositions, the more frequently the child would use prepositions correctly. The order in which a child began to use word inflexions (plurals, possessives, simple tenses, etc.) was related to the frequency with which the parent used inflexions.

A large number of language exchanges between mother and child were observed by Moerk (1972). He reasoned that since the mother is the main adult model for language behavior and often provides feedback for the child's attempts at speech, she is probably the most important person in the child's acquisition of language. Moerk distinguishes between the inanimate environment of things and events and the animate environment in which people are notably influential. The inanimate environment can affect language acquisition in either of two ways, by "structuring" or "eliciting". Eliciting effects lead to a verbal reaction but do not induce the child to produce any novel language structure. For instance, those situations in which children provide the name for an object they are watching involve the elicitation of established language by environmental stimuli. Young children are very good at learning the words that represent particular objects, thereby acquiring a word vocabulary. In an experiment by Vincent-Smith, Bricker, and Bricker (1974), children aged around 24 months were shown 100 pairs of objects in which the name of one of the items was known, and the name of the other item was known in some instances but not in others. On the first trial, the children could match the first object with the correct word label only if they already knew the name of the second item. By the fifth presentation, they could recognize the items from the names. It appears that at this age children rapidly learn the names for unfamiliar objects.

"Structuring" influences of the environment induce the child to produce more than a single word, and to make a statement that translates the perception of a structured environment into a language sequence. For instance, pictures depicting activities may lead children to make statements that are essentially new productions. When a child watches a car disappear from the television screen says, "Allgone car," speech is being structured by what is seen in a way that is different from when the child simply names an object in the room. The precise utterance is elicited or structured by the inanimate environment, but the mother plays an important facilitatory role, as in an observation by Moerk in which the mother said, "What's all over your face?" to which her daughter replied, "Ice cream on it."

According to Moerk, it is more common for the child's speech to be directly induced by animate parts of the child's environment, particularly by people, than by inanimate things. Often the mother will model an activity, accompanying her actions with words. For instance, she will say, "pat-a-cake" and clap at the same time. The function of the human environment is generally one of structuring rather than simply eliciting speech, since people and their activities are usually too complicated to be encoded by the word names that children may produce as they look at objects. A mother might say, "I'll have to put your pants on," while she does so; or she might say, "Let me hold the doll," as she takes it. She thus provides numerous translations of nonverbal acts into structured verbal sequences.

Moerk considers that children acquire language skills through a fourfold relationship between language structure and the environment. First, children's early primitive speech enables them to name inanimate objects they see. Second, the mother and other adults provide numerous demonstrations of the process of translating the structure of events and actions into word patterns. Such instances may occur on literally thousands of occasions, and often involve events and situations that are highly familiar to the children. Third, the children begin to talk themselves, translating nonverbal relationships in the inanimate environment to expressive language. When children make their first attempts, the parents provide reinforcement and feedback, and they expand the children's utterances in the direction of mature language. Fourth, according to Moerk, children attempt translation into language of events that involve the more complicated animate environment, and their attempts also elicit the contribution of the parent in a helping capacity.

Conversational Exchanges Between Parent and Child

As further progress is made, exchanges between parent and child take the form of increasingly lengthy chains. Language ceases to be just a vehicle into which nonverbal mental operations are translated, and it functions increasingly as the medium of thought. The change is not entirely unlike that which takes place when people who are learning a foreign language stop having to translate each word from their first language into the less familiar one, and begin to think in the new language. Thus in the following sequence,

> NANCY: "In a bred one."
> MOTHER: "A red one?"
> NANCY: "Yeah."

it would appear that the child's language and her thought are no longer entirely separate. When the sequence of events is of the form,

1. Child sees object.
2. Child produced language utterance.

a degree of separation can be seen to exist between thought and language, the transmission from one to the other being accompanied by a deliberate process of translation. However, in a conversation with the mother, involving a sequence of events such as,

1. Child's utterance.
2. Mother's utterance.
3. Child's utterance.
4. Mother's utterance.

the child who customarily makes deliberate translations between language and meaning would be very slow to respond.

In practice, talk between mother and child typically includes a mixture of the different phenomena I have discussed separately. A conversational chain may include expansions by the mother, reduction by the child, modeling and imitation of correct language, and correction by the mother of inadequate child language. Several of these processes can be discerned in the following episode, reported by Moerk (1972, p. 243);

> MOTHER: I think those are soldiers.
> MONICA: I think those are soldgineers.
> MOTHER: Can you say "soldier"?
> MONICA: Sold—.
> MOTHER: Can you?
> MONICA: Sold—, Soldier.
> MOTHER: That's better.

One kind of conversational exchange sequence commences with the child producing an utterance that contains errors, whereupon the mother provides a corrective statement that partly imitates that of the child, and expands it. The child's subsequent response attempts to imitate the mother's expansion of the child's previous statement. The mother may help the child by insuring that her expanded imitation of the child's first statement follows as closely as possible to the original structure, so that it will not be too difficult for the child to incorporate the mother's correction in his next response. Mothers may make it clear that their expansions are intended to provide models by starting with the phrase, "Can you say?". In effect, both the modeling and the expansion aspects of the mother's language are simultaneously provided in the same sample of speech. Moerk suggests that mothers become very good at measuring their children's language processing capacities, and consequently they are able to communicate very effectively.

The speech of a mother to her child is very different from her speech to other adults; there are fewer passives, more simple declarative sentences, and fewer subordinate phrases. False starts, hesitations, and errors are much less common in speech to a young child than in communication with another adult (Slobin, 1972). This is found both in middle-class families and in families living in poor urban areas.

There is a striking similarity between Moerk's observations of the mother-child exchanges that lead to the child learning to speak, and observations in the earlier mother-child interactions (see Chapter 5) that form the basis for the child's earliest social learning. Although the two kinds of interactions involve children of markedly different age and level of development, similar patterns of interaction can be discerned. These involve reciprocity, chains of communication in which each partner responds to the other, and careful timing, and sensitive "reading" by the parent of the significance of the child's actions.

Moerk's observations show that, consciously or otherwise, the mother uses a variety of teaching devices to help her child learn to speak. The mother may encourage the child to translate between a picture and the appropriate language label, and she demonstrates encoding by accompanying her own activities and those of the child with verbal descriptions. In addition, the mother may prod her child, through her questions, to encode spontaneously, for instance by saying, "What is that?" or "What are you doing?" (Moerk, 1974). The varied teaching devices to which Moerk draws attention (e.g., imitation through expansion, modeling, asking questions, providing incomplete sentences, question-and-answer games, nursery rhymes, and encouraging the child to look at picture books) all contribute to a child's acquiring a first language in a fairly short period of time.

LANGUAGE ACQUISITION IN PRIMATES

Further evidence about the contribution of learning to language acquisition has been provided by attempts to teach language to animals. Many animals have communication systems, and they can convey information to other members of their species with considerable precision. For instance, honeybees transmit knowledge about the location of local supplies of nectar or pollen to other bees through elaborate dancing movements that have been described by Von Frisch (1927). Ants and many other insect species convey information, typically by their movements or by chemical signals. Moths attract each other by smell, and bats emit auditory signals that make it possible to capture small insects in the dark. Birds use a variety of auditory signals to communicate with each other, and vocalization in mammals has a variety of signaling functions.

Human language is in some respects very different from any system of communication encountered in other species. Greene (1976) lists some important differences. First, although animals have complex signal codes for communicating to other members of their species, they cannot use language to reflect upon internal thoughts, as humans do. Animals do not possess any linguistic code for expressing to others the results of their reasoning processes. The performance of some species, notably primates, at complex tasks such as picking the odd object from each of a succession of three-item sets indicates that they are capable of quite advanced forms of reasoning. Yet they cannot communicate the outcomes of such reasoning to others. Because humans use language both in thought and in communicating with other people, they can pass on their knowledge and experiences, thereby evolving human cultures in which it is not essential, as it is with other animals, for each individual to learn everything from scratch.

Second, people can generate and transmit entirely new messages, whereas animals' communications are limited to a fixed number of signals. The elements of human language can be combined and recombined in a virtually unlimited variety of different ways to express a vast number of separate meanings. Third, the language signals emitted by animals are normally bound to specific stimuli, forming involuntary responses, for instance, the responses to food or to the presence of predators, which the animals cannot choose to make or not make. Greene notes that a gibbon cannot choose not to emit an alarm call when a predator is spotted, even though for the individual it might well be safer to remain quiet. Furthermore, the other gibbons' only response to that call is to run away, and they do so automatically as an involuntary reaction to the signal.

Many people have been interested in the possibility of teaching human language to animals, but until around 1960, attempts met with little success. Talking parrots and Mynah birds have often performed impressively, but even the bird which was trained by the zoo staff to say, "How about the appropriation?" whenever the financial director paid a visit (Carmichael, 1966) was simply demonstrating the power of mimicry; such mimicry has no truly communicative function. In the 1930s a chimpanzee raised by the Kellogg family learned to respond to oral commands at least as accurately as a human child in the first year of life, but the chimpanzee was less successful at responding to new combinations of words, and not able to speak English words at all. Another chimpanzee, raised in the 1940s by Dr. and Mrs. Keith Hayes did learn to express three or four words, but despite the most intensive efforts at language training, it did not develop effective mastery of human language.

Hindsight suggests that the early attempts placed an unnecessary handicap on the chimpanzees by requiring them to actually *speak* in a human language. Chimpanzees are simply not equipped, physiologically, to produce human speech. It is conceivable that if it had not been necessary to perform what for them was an impossible task of producing human speech sounds, they might have made more progress toward gaining language skills. Being able to speak is not, after all, essential for understanding and using a language, and the chimpanzees' failure to learn to speak does not rule out the possibility of their learning to understand and express language by other means.

Sarah and Washoe

In the 1960s one husband-and-wife team, the Premacks (Premack and Premack, 1972) attempted to teach language to a 5-year-old chimpanzee named Sarah, and another couple, the Gardners (Gardner and Gardner, 1969), trained a 1-year-old chimpanzee called Washoe. Washoe was brought up with the human family, while Sarah lived in a cage. The system of communication used for Washoe was a sign language developed for human use. Sarah learned to communicate with plastic shapes of varying shape, size, color, and texture.

In Sarah's training, she was reinforced with food for placing on a board in front of her the plastic chip denoting an appropriate language message. At an early stage she was given a slice of banana and allowed to eat it as her trainer looked on. Later, a pink plastic square was placed close to Sarah and a slice of banana was positioned beyond her reach. When Sarah put the plastic square on the board at the side of her cage, she was given a piece of banana to eat. A similar procedure was followed with apples, represented by a blue plastic shape, and with various other fruits, and Sarah learned a different colored, different shaped plastic "word" for each fruit. By having to choose which of a number of different shapes was the correct one for obtaining, say, a slice of banana, Sarah learned to distinguish between a number of plastic chips, each of which had a distinct meaning. Later on, Sarah also learned the plastic shapes representing transactions involving the objects for which she already had learned the shapes. For instance, she gained the ability to distinguish between "Give apple," "Wash apple," and "Not apple." She also learned to produce three-shape "sentences" in order to receive a reward. For example, she had to make a sentence containing, first, a shape denoting the name of the particular trainer involved (there were several), then the shape representing the required action (e.g., "give") and, finally, the correct object (e.g., "banana").

Sarah learned to produce language sequences that were considerably more advanced than the simple responses to single word messages demonstrated by the earlier investigators, and her language was based on a simple structure, or grammar. She was rewarded only when the sequence of items was correct, as well as the actual words, and she had to pay for her own mistakes. Thus, when she incorrectly produced, "Give apple Gussie" (the name of another chimpanzee), she had to watch while the apple was given to Gussie, much to Sarah's annoyance. To be sure to get what she wanted, Sarah had to provide the correct words in the appropriate sequence (e.g., "Sally give apple Sarah."). Sarah also learned to answer simple questions. She made some mistakes, and was entirely correct on only around 75 percent of occasions. It is possible that her trainers might have sometimes inadvertantly given nonlinguistic cues. Nevertheless, Sarah's accomplishments demonstrate the acquisition of important skills that are basic to the acquisition of human language.

Sarah could learn object-symbol relationships, even in instances when she had never encountered the two items together. For instance, Sarah learned to combine the shapes representing the concepts "name of" and "not name of" with conditional statements. This procedure yielded sentences such as, "If Sarah take apple, Mary (the trainer) give chocolate Sarah," or, "If Sarah take banana Mary no give chocolate Sarah." In this example it is clear that the abilities to reason and to remember are required. Very careful reading of each sentence was necessary if Sarah was to get the reward.

Even more impressive, after learning words representing colors followed by the sentence "Brown color of chocolate," Sarah was able to choose a brown item correctly when she was given the sentence "Take brown" as she confronted four different-colored objects. During the session when Sarah was told "Brown color of chocolate," no actual chocolate had been present. In order to respond correctly to the request "Take brown," Sarah must have attached the language symbol to some internal memory representation of chocolate and its (brown) color. It is clear that Sarah was using language as a vehicle for thinking.

Washoe, a much younger chimpanzee than Sarah, spent much of her time with the Gardner family, and over a period of years she was taught a version of English based on American Sign Language (ASL), which includes hand gestures and signs for words. By 5 years of age, Washoe was able to use 160 different signs in correct sequences of up to five items. Whereas Sarah did not give clear evidence of deliberately producing novel sequences, and did not spontaneously use the plastic shapes unless a trainer initiated communication, Washoe did provide novel sequences that indicated a generative use of language. She would often produce over 150 signs in the course of an evening meal. The way in which Washoe combined her words matched what can be observed in the early speech of human children. Washoe's level of achievement at age 4 was roughly that of a 2-year-old child. Compared with most children, Washoe was at a disadvantage in not having adult models who were highly fluent in the language. A number of deaf children who are fluent in ASL are contributing to further investigations of primate language training.

Experiments such as the ones involving Sarah and Washoe last for several years and are expensive to administer. It remains to be discovered just how far primates can advance toward the acquisition of a human language. However, the demonstration that important language abilities can be learned by chimpanzees, a feat which would have been considered inconceivable 20 years ago, has eliminated a major argument that was advanced in the past to support the view that the ability to acquire language depends on our having a uniquely human innate language acquisition mechanism.

To conclude the present chapter, we have to acknowledge that a complete understanding of the acquisition of human language cannot be achieved solely through research into learning. Nevertheless, mastery of language skills does necessitate considerable learning, and learning mechanisms account for many of the differences between people in the ways they use their capacity for language.

SUMMARY

1. Language cannot be acquired solely through associative forms of learning. The language user has to acquire and use large numbers of rules that govern the form and structure of human language.

2. Since the mental structures that children must possess in order to internalize language rules from the flow of language they experience cannot be acquired through associative learning alone, it has been suggested that an innate mechanism may be necessary.
3. However, developmental psychologists have indicated that the structures needed for language acquisition may be acquired by children in the course of gaining a preverbal understanding of their world. There is considerable continuity between language and prelinguistic knowledge, and abilities such as imitation, imagery, and object recognition depend upon acquired representational mechanisms that are also essential for the subsequent emergence of language.
4. The child's speech is rule governed and structured from the outset, as is indicated by the kinds of errors that young children make.
5. Reinforcement principles contribute to the acquisition of language. Language training procedures that include reinforcement have produced marked improvements in nonverbal autistic and mentally retarded children.
6. Observation contributes to the acquisition of speech. Conversational exchanges with adults, particularly the mother, provide opportunities for corrective feedback and modification of the child's speech.
7. Recent attempts to enable primates to learn human language have had considerable success. The failure of earlier attempts was partly due to the insistence on primates using speech.

Suggestions for Further Reading

Brown, R. (1973) "Development of the first language in the human species." *American Psychologist,* 28:97–106.
Clark, H. H., and Clark, E. V. (1977) *Psychology and Language: An Introduction to Psycholinguistics.* New York: Harcourt Brace Jovanovich.
Edmonds, M. H. (1976) "New directions in theories of language acquisition." *Harvard Educational Review,* 46:175–198.
Inhelder, B. (1971) "The sensory-motor origins of knowledge." In D. N. Walcher and D. L. Peters.(eds.), *Early Childhood: The Development of Self-Regulatory Mechanisms.* New York: Academic Press.

9

Simple Verbal Learning and the Functions of Imagery

OVERVIEW

Having acquired language, people depend on it for many of their learned abilities. The present chapter discusses approaches to verbal learning, and starts by describing attempts to assess the meaningfulness of small verbal units in terms of the ease with which such items evoke other items. A number of ways in which language contributes to human learning are discussed. Relationships between children's speech and behavior are mentioned. Later in the chapter the phenomenon of imagery is introduced. We discuss evidence that the ease of learning verbal items is related to the readiness with which images of them can be formed. Possible reasons for the observed relationships between learning and visual imagery are discussed.

INTRODUCTION

The enormous feat of learning by which almost every human child gains a language is not achieved for nothing. Once it is acquired, we make good use of language, and we continue to do so throughout our lives. It is as crucial to mature thought and communication in humanity as is the air we breathe to our physical well-being.

To behaviorist experimental psychologists of the early twentieth century, language presented something of an embarrassment. It could not be denied that language had a role in much human learning, but it was hard to see how one could take full account of language without introducing a variety of unobservable subjective processes: thinking, imagining, reasoning, and so on. The early behaviorists thought it necessary for psychology to exclude such subjective processes if it was to stay within what they considered to be the rules for pursuing an objective natural science.

One solution, it seemed, was to treat language, or single words to be precise, as items to be combined by simple associative learning. By using words as either stimulus items or response items, and restricting investigations to topics such as the establishment of connections between such elements and measurement of the strength of interword connections, it was possible to study a number of verbal phenomena as associative learning processes. It appeared that the terminology of Pavlov's procedures for establishing connections between stimulus events and motor responses in nonhuman species might be extended without undue strain to forms of human learning in which language was important. A number of theoretical approaches to verbal learning were based to varying extents upon conditioning principles, and some useful contributions were made. Gibson (1940), for example, used the findings of research demonstrating stimulus generalization in animal learning to attempt an explanation of the way people learn to discriminate between verbal items.

Approaches tied to stimulus-response conditioning principles eventually proved to be too self-restricting to sustain effective research into language-based learning. Thinking is crucial in human learning and an approach that sidetracks or ignores it cannot flourish for long. When people encounter verbal materials, they do not merely associate them with other language items. The way in which learners use a word they perceive depends upon what that word means to them. Words are processed in a manner that depends upon the characteristics and circumstances of the individual, not just upon the form of the word. People may process or code a word in any of a variety of possible ways, depending upon their own knowledge and on the nature of the task as they perceive it. For instance, the word may be grouped with other words on the basis of shared semantic attributes or joined with others to make a sentence. Typically, the learner will provide some "effort after meaning," making it easier for the new word item to be incorporated within the individual's existing body of knowledge. In brief, whenever people are confronted with a task that involves learning materials in language form, some mental activity or cognition will take place. Learners use the knowledge and skills they possess to deal with the new item in a manner that is meaningful to them and through which the item can be incorporated with in the cognitive structure which the individuals already possess.

MEASURES OF ITEM MEANINGFULNESS

The fact that an associative approach to verbal learning has limitations does not render it valueless. Following the pioneer investigations of Ebbinghaus, outlined in Chapter 2, research into verbal learning made some further progress. A major problem was to come to terms with the undeniable phenomenon of meaning in language while avoiding becoming involved with the mental processes responsible for thought, which would introduce an unacceptable element of subjectivity.

One approach to meaning was initiated in 1928 by J. A. Glaze. He calculated what he termed the *association value* (AV) of a number of nonsense syllables. Ebbinghaus had known that although the nonsense syllables he used in experiments on learning and memory were partly free of the preestablished associations that he recognized as contributing to the difficulty of using prose materials for experimental investigations of memory, nonsense syllables are not all entirely meaningless. Some three-letter syllables form words (for example, *pig, dog*), and many are easily pronounced (for example, *fid*), or use familiar combinations of initials (for example, *fbi, ibm*). For reasons of this kind, Ebbinghaus and other psychologists who made use of nonsense syllables in experimental research were careful to avoid certain items. Association values are based on a measure of the number of people who indicated that a particular syllable held some meaning for them. Glaze asked 15 students to respond to each of 2000 consonant-vowel-consonant (CVC) syllables. Their responses were taken to form AVs which varied from zero (when no subject indicated that the syllable meant anything to him) to 100 (when all subjects responded that the syllable meant something). In Glaze's data, syllables such as *col, wis, wam, liz, pow* and *fid* yielded AVs of 60 or more, *wyx, yib* and *joq* had values of around 20, and *goo, xuw* and *xyj* received scores of zero.

If associative principles enter into verbal learning, one would predict that syllables with high AVs would be learned more easily than syllables with low AVs, and this appears to be the case. For instance, McGeoch (1930) formed ten-item lists from syllables with low, medium, or high AVs. After studying the list for a period determined by the experimenter, each participant was asked to recall as many items as the person could remember. It was found that the higher the AV of the syllable, then the greater the number of items recalled. When the time allowed for studying lists was around one minute, less than 7 out of the 10 zero AV list items were recalled, on average, compared with around 9 of the 100 AV items. Intermediate levels of performance were found with lists of intermediate AV.

Since the publication of association values by Glaze, a number of investigators have produced further lists of syllables rated for meaningfulness. Most of the later ratings have drawn upon substantially more people than the 15 participants in Glaze's study, and thus provided scores that are more reliable. For instance, Archer (1960) analyzed the responses of over 200 subjects to Glaze's syllables plus the 460 CVC syllables that make meaningful words. On presentation of each syllable, subjects had to ask themselves whether the item was a word, or sounded like a word, or brought any word to mind. They were told to make a positive response to any syllable for which they could give an affirmative answer to any of these questions. The Archer AV score for each syllable was based on the percentage of subjects who made a positive response to that item.

The association values collected by Glaze and by Archer provided an indication of the degree of meaningfulness of different syllables. Noble (1952a) drew up a list involving *word* items, rated for their effectiveness in eliciting associated words by participants who were allowed 60 seconds to write down any word item that came to mind. As one might expect, the word ratings obtained by Noble's method are related to pronounceability (pronounceability ratings having a correlation of $+.78$ with Noble's scores for meaningfulness) and familiarity (the correlation with meaningfulness in nonsense syllables being $+.92$) (Noble, 1953). A large scale study by Underwood and Schulz. (1960) demonstrated close relationships between the meaningfulness of CVC syllables, their pronounceability, and their frequency of occurrence. Underwood and Schultz claimed that the latter is the most fundamental of their attributes, a view that coincides with Thorndike's belief in the centrality of the Law of Exercise.

Item Meaningfulness and Learning

How important in real human experience is the aspect of meaningfulness assessed in these studies? If language learning largely depends upon associations being formed between word items, ratings of the meaningfulness or associability of items would be highly correlated with the ease of learning them. We would also predict that learning word pairs in which the items already form associates to each other (for example, *bat* and *ball*) would proceed far more quickly than learning that involves forming new connections between random words. The findings of empirical studies have shown that, up to a point, learning is indeed related to measures of word meaningfulness. Paivio, Yuille, and Rogers (1969), for instance, found that highly meaningful items were consistently recalled more accurately in a word recall task than items low in meaningfulness. But contrary to what we would expect if verbal association was the fundamental process underlying the learning of linguistic materials, the effects of an entirely different word attribute, the ease with which items evoke visual images, had a considerably larger effect upon recall levels than word meaningfulness.

The results of a number of other studies have demonstrated positive correlations between learning and measures of meaningfulness. A. W. Melton (Hall, 1971) found that serial learning of CVC syllables was related to their association value, as measured by Glaze. McGeoch (1930) observed that after studying ten-item lists of syllables for two minutes, the average number recalled was 7.4 for items with a Glaze association value of 100 percent, 6.4 for 53 percent association value syllables, and 5.1 for zero association value syllables. In an experiment by Noble (1952*b*), subjects who learned lists comprised of items scaled by Noble's ratings of meaningfulness performed consistently better on items rated high in meaningfulness than on less meaningful items.

Degree of meaningfulness is also related to performance at *paired associate* tasks, in which participants have to learn lists made up of pairs of items. For example, Noble, Stockwell, and Pryor (1957) presented syllable pairs, using a memory drum, that differed in meaningfulness. By the tenth trial the correct response rate varied from under 10 percent for the least meaningful items to around 60 percent for the most meaningful syllable pairs. Other researchers have compared the effects of stimulus and response item meaningfulness on learning. Predictably, pairs in which each syllable item is highly meaningful are learned most quickly, and pairs in which both items are low in meaningfulness are most slowly learned. However, those pairs in which the stimulus item is highly meaningful and the response item is rated low in meaningfulness are learned more quickly than pairs in which the rated meaningfulness of the response item is high and that of the stimulus item is low. (Cieutat, Stockwell, and Noble, 1958). Most researchers who have undertaken studies of this kind make a distinction between two apparently separate stages in paired-associate learning, "stimulus learning," and "response learning." Investigators account in these terms for the different effects of stimulus and response item meaningfulness.

The experimental findings make it clear that ratings of the association value (Glaze) and the meaningfulness (Noble, Underwood, and Schulz) of syllable items are related to a number of measures of learning. Associative factors would appear to have an important role in human learning, at least when it involves the somewhat artificial syllable materials used in the experimental research. In the case of words, however, which are more directly relevant to forms of language-based learning regularly undertaken by humans, the relationships between measures of learning and the meaningfulness of single items are smaller and less clear-cut. This is despite the fact that the degree of variability in word frequency between the items used in experimental studies is artificially large, often of the order of 100 to one. Hall (1954) constructed 20-word lists in which the items varied in frequency of occurrence in written English from one per million to over 50 per million, according to the word count by Thorndike and Lorge (1944). Each list was presented five times, and on each presentation every word appeared, alone, for around five seconds, and participants were subsequently required to list all the words they could recall. The findings showed a relationship between word frequency and the number of words recalled, but the recall difference between frequent and infrequent items was relatively small, as shown below:

Word Frequency	Recall
1 per million	12.0
10 per million	13.3
30 per million	15.0
50–100 per million	15.0

Underwood, Ekstrand, and Keppel (1965) also presented word lists on a number of trials, and they subsequently asked subjects to recall the items. They found that frequent words were more likely to be recalled than infrequent words, but the effect of the difference in word frequency was only around 10 percent. These authors also varied the degree of conceptual similarity of the words in the lists. If word-association was the major determinant of verbal learning, similarity would have a large effect upon learning. In fact, as Figure 9.1 shows, the actual influence of conceptual similarity was small, especially in low-frequency word lists.

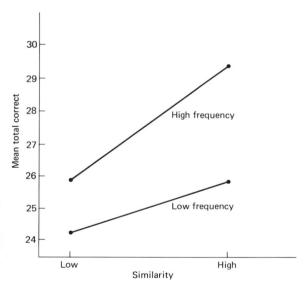

Figure 9.1   Learning as a function of conceptual similarity and word frequency. (Source: Adapted from Underwood, B. J., Ekstrand, B. R., and Keppel, G. "An analysis of intralist similarity in verbal learning with experiments on conceptual similarity." *Journal of Verbal Learning and Verbal Behavior,* 1965, 4:447–462. Reprinted by permission of Academic Press, Inc.)

Word pairs vary in the strength of associations between the items. Strong associations involve words that occur frequently when people are asked to write down what comes to mind when a particular stimulus word is presented. (*Hot*, for example, often evokes the word *cold*.) When the strength of association between word pairs was systematically varied, by selecting the second word in each pair according to its frequency of occurrence as an associate to the first item, it was found that the greater the degree of association between items, the higher the level of recall (Jenkins, Mink and Russell, 1958).

EVIDENCE FOR MEDIATING PROCESSES

The studies described above show that very large differences in word frequency lead to moderate differences in learning. But, as Hall (1971) has emphasised, some experimenters have failed to observe any difference at all in relation to word frequency. Some investigators have even observed either faster learning or more accurate recognition of low-frequency than high-frequency words. The fact that effects of word frequency on learning are so small and unreliable suggests that factors other than stimulus-response associability need to be invoked if we are to provide a satisfactory account for language-based learning. As I indicated earlier, considerable research evidence suggests that learning of verbal and non-verbal materials must involve inner processing that goes beyond the formation of associations between words or between stimulus items and a learner's responses. Some further mental processes must intervene between input and output.

Consider, for instance, a form of human learning that ostensibly resembles animal classical conditioning. In a procedure known as *semantic conditioning* (Mahoney, 1974), it is found that if presentation of a particular word is regularly followed by a painful electric shock, on future sessions the word becomes a conditioned stimulus for autonomic arousal, which can be assessed by measures of pulse or respiration. A finding that is hard to explain in terms of stimulus-response accounts of learning is that if a person is conditioned in this way to respond to one word, for example, *horse*, there is considerable generalization to words that are conceptually similar, such as *donkey* or *cow*. Presenting these words produces greater arousal than words that are phonemically similar to the original word, for example, *house* or *hearse*. It is not possible to explain this generalization effect unless it is assumed that some inner processing takes place in the learner to mediate between the new stimulus (*cow*, for example) and the autonomic response. Such mediational processing must involve the learner's own knowledge, in which an association or semantic relationship exists between *horse* and *cow*. The generalization effect might be produced by associative links between the items, but such links would need to be internal and unobservable mental activities, involving processes that mediate between the observed stimulus items and the observed responses. Any adequate explanation requires what from a behaviorist point of view is an alarming degree of reliance on unobservable mental processing.

Consider also an experiment by Maltzman (1968), who investigated the relationship between degree of semantic generalization (from a conditioned word to another word) to the strength of association between the two words. The purpose of Maltzman's experiment was to discover whether the amount of semantic generalization is greater to words that are frequently produced as associates to the conditioned item than to infrequently reported word associates. The conditioning procedure involved pairing the stimulus word *light* with an unpleasantly loud noise. Subjects' galvanic skin responses were used for the response measures. Subsequently, the subjects were presented with a number of associates to *light*, ranging from frequent, strong associates such as *dark* to infrequent and weak associates, such as *square*. Provided that the interval between the conditioned stimulus (*light*) and the unconditioned stimulus (the noise) during the conditioning trials was small (0.5 seconds) the degree of semantic generalization to a new word stimulus was found to be related to the strength of the association between the conditioned word and the new item. The stronger the association between the conditioned word and the new word, the greater was the galvanic skin response when the new word was presented. This finding demonstrates that the level of semantic generalization is related to the individual's existing knowledge about the particular words involved. Internal mediating processes are necessary. The mediation is probably based upon semantic attributes, or "meanings," of word items, and not simply upon the capacity for words to evoke associated items.

Two other illustrations give further proof of the inadequacy of attempts to account for verbal learning phenomena in terms of relationships between observed stimuli and observed responses. N. E. Miller (Mahoney, 1974) presented a random sequence of the symbols *T* and *4*, and subjects were told to pronounce the symbols aloud. Whenever a *T* was pronounced it was followed by a painful electric shock. Miller subsequently presented a new series of items, in the form of a sequence of identical dots. He asked subjects to "think *T*" on presentation of the first dot, "think *4*" to the second dot, *T* to the third dot, *4* to the fourth dot, and so on, alternating between *T*'s and *4*'s as the dot series progressed. During this session he recorded subjects' galvanic skin responses, as a measure of their arousal. The skin responses demonstrated that thoughts of T produced large increases in autonomic arousal but the "think 4" instruction had no such effect. Hence, although the observed stimuli (the dots) were all identical, the responses to them were very different. The different responses cannot be explained by any objective quality of the stimuli. To explain the observed pattern of skin responses, it is essential to take into account the processing of the perceived stimuli carried out by the participating subjects.

The effects of reinforcers as well as those of stimulus events depend upon the way individual people mentally process them. Participants in an experiment by Dulany (1968) attempted a verbal learning task while seated in an uncomfortably hot room. Each trial of the task was followed by a blast of hot air or cold air. Some subjects were told that an air blast signified a correct response and others were informed that a blast indicated a wrong response. In a number of different conditions cool blasts, hot blasts, and no blasts were alternatively used as positive reinforcers, punishment, and as neutral events. As Mahoney (1974) points out, any nonmediational theory of learning would lead us to predict that the physical properties of the events would determine their influence on subjects' performance at the task. However, Dulany found that the effects of the air blasts were more closely related to what they signified for the learner than to their physical properties, despite the large differences in reward value for over-heated young adults between cold air blasts and hot blasts.

MENTAL PROCESSES IN VERBAL LEARNING

The findings of the above three experiments demonstrate the importance of mental processes in verbal learning. An important goal in modern experimental psychology is to add to our understanding of the nature of these processes. The fact that mental activities cannot be observed directly makes it necessary for psychologists to rely on making inferences from the evidence that can be obtained by observing how people perform at various tasks. One point of view has been that the mental processes underlying learning take the form of associative links between word items. The links were thought to mirror the associations that are apparent when a person is asked to state words which come to mind while reading through a list of word items. However, forming internal word associations is not the only function of mental processing. The experimental evidence to be described shortly indicates that people have at their disposal a variety of processes and strategies that are used in learning.

It is important to remember that because mental processes cannot be observed directly, it is very difficult, if not impossible, to prove conclusively that a theory concerning their precise form is correct or incorrect. As I have said, the inferences we make about mental activities are essentially guesses concerning the inner processes that could account for the way in which people perform certain tasks. Experimental psychologists aim to design studies that enable us to chose which of a number of plausible descriptions of the processes underlying subjects' performance at a task is most likely to be the correct one. An experimental psychologist may design a number of experiments, using considerable ingenuity in the choice of tasks and the choice of the materials to be learned. To throw light on the mental processes underlying performance, possible explanations are systematically tested, with the experimenter eliminating those that cannot account for the obtained experimental results. When there exists a body of data comprising the findings of a number of relevant experiments, it may be possible to decide that one kind of process is more likely to be involved in the brain's mental operations than an alternative hypothesized process.

Conscious Experience and Mental Activity

Modern research into cognitive processing, in which investigators try to describe how the brain codes and transmits information in order for people to learn, represents a return to the concern with "mental life" that occupied Wundt and many other students of psychology around the end of the last century. However, there is an important difference between the new and the old approaches to mental activity. The earlier psychologists leaned toward the view that description and analysis of *conscious experience* would make a large contribution to our understanding of mental activity. This view is now considered to be incorrect. We are now aware that the relationship between conscious thought processes and the mental activities that underlie cognition is not at all simple. Therefore, analyzing the contents of conscious experience will not provide much guidance about the cognitive processes that underlie human thinking. The processing that occurs when we do what is described as "thinking" or "reasoning" does not necessarily use information in any form that is recognizably similar to the items that are consciously experienced. We are aware of words and language units, and we communicate with other people through language, but it is by no means inevitable that information processed in our mental systems remains recognizably verbal.

A system for processing information first encodes or translates it into a form (or "language") that matches the operations of the system. The information may now be in a form that is very different from that in which it was first received. For example, television system conveys all kinds of events that we can experience, but if we look at the workings of a television set and examine its electronic operation to find how it works, we cannot discover anything that corresponds at all directly to what we experience when we watch television. The information that is being processed by a television receiver has been encoded into forms in which it is not identifiable as the phenomena that are being represented.

Television systems are not closely analogous to the human brain, their role being restricted to conveying and transforming information, whereas people have to do things with the information they receive. Computers, however, have more in common with human minds, since computers are required to retain information and to use it in order to solve problems. In computer processing the data first has to be translated into a language that the machine can accept, and after the processing task has been completed, it may be decoded back into the original form. Consequently, the information that is processed within a computer takes a form very different from that in which it existed before being fed into the computer. The computer's task might be to solve a mathematical equation, but examination of the processing that takes place as it solves the problem will reveal nothing that a mathematician would recognize as corresponding to parameters of the equation.

Because communication *between* people involves words and language, we tend to assume that the mental acitvity underlying communication *within* a person must be based upon language as we consciously experience it, mental activity taking the form of the manipulation of linguistic elements. However, evidence from research into visual imagery suggests that our thought processes often involve coded versions of visual images of things, rather than coded forms of verbal descriptions. When people are asked to form visual images of items in a list of words they often retain the information more effectively than when they try to remember the words. As Pylyshyn (1973) points out, this does not mean that the mental processing of events we experience as visual images involves "mental pictures" as such, any more than the processing of verbal items is based directly upon words. In short, the information we experience as either imaged items or verbalized materials is coded into very different forms before being processed.

CONTRIBUTIONS OF LANGUAGE TO HUMAN LEARNING

Although verbal materials may be coded into a new form prior to the mental processing that leads to human learning, linguistic factors have a large influence. This is not so paradoxical as it may appear to be. Imagine human language as being a "program language" that the human brain can accept, that is, a language that can be "read in" to the brain. Problems that are presented in this form can be accepted and processed by the brain's processing system. A good computer program is constructed in a form that will make use of the computer's facilities as effectively as possible, and the way in which the program has been designed will affect the manner in which the computer's facilities are engaged in order to solve the problem. Similarly, the way in which a human task is expressed and articulated before being conveyed to the computing facilities of the human brain has a large effect on whether or not a person will be able to solve it. One person may be better than another individual at solving mathematical problems because of a superior ability to transform problems into forms suitable for the available mental processing capabilities. School children who solve a problem in algebra are, in a sense, "programming" the data they receive so that the data can be processed by the computing facilities they possess.

Simple Language Strategies

Many differences between individuals in ability to learn are essentially differences in the ability to transform material into forms in which it can most easily be acquired. An experiment by Jensen and Rohwer (1963) illustrates this point. Their subjects were mentally retarded adults who performed a learning task requiring them to retain lists containing eight pairs of words. In one condition, the subjects were simply instructed to learn the paired-associate lists, and in another condition they were given sentences, in which the two words of each word pair formed subject and object. For example, if the word pair was *donkey-chair*, an appropriate sentence might be "The *donkey* kicked the *chair*." In the condition that provided mediating sentences, subjects required 13 minutes on average to learn the list of items, which was only half the time required by subjects in a control condition. There was an even larger difference in the number of errors made, the average being 15 in the mediating sentence condition, 73 in the control condition.

How do we account for this large difference in rate of learning? A possible explanation is that the sentence condition transformed the materials into a form which the human learner is better equipped to process. In the present experiment, the sentence transformation had the effect of changing the list materials from pairs of unrelated single word items into meaningful word sequences that obeyed the rules and constraints of language and could be linked to linguistically organized knowledge. As it happens, people's performance at a variety of intellectual tasks has been found to depend to some extent upon the degree to which the learner is able to transform the materials into a form in which they can be processed most effectively by the computing processes of the human brain. As we shall see in the following pages, the strategies that individuals adopt for transforming or for rearranging materials to be learned into forms that facilitate acquisition and retention strongly influence learners' performance at many tasks, and make a large contribution to individual differences in learning.

Let us return to the experiment by Jensen and Rohwer in which learning increased when sentences were provided. We might ask, if such a small change in the circumstances produced such a large increase in the rate of learning, might not any learners faced with a task of this kind construct sentences for themselves, thereby improving their rate of success? In fact, many adults customarily do so. Given a task like the one confronting subjects in the control condition of Jensen and Rohwer's experiment, many people would either construct for themselves verbal connections between the word pairs or supply some other mediating link. For this reason, if we repeated Jensen and Rohwer's experiment with normal adult subjects rather than the mentally retarded people who participated in the study, it is unlikely that performance would differ quite so dramatically between the experimental and control conditions. Many individuals in the control condition of the new experiment would spontaneously follow a strategy that transformed the task from one of arbitrarily associating single word items to one more like that encountered by the subjects in Jensen and Rohwer's experimental condition.

The findings of a further study by Jensen and Rohwer (1965) support this suggestion. The experiment was very similar to the previous one, but the subjects were children of normal intelligence, varying from 5 to 17 years of age. It was found that young children aged up to 11 years (except for the 5-year-olds, who were too young to understand the procedure) performed better in an experimental condition similar to that of the previous study than in a control condition, but there was no difference between conditions in the learning scores of the older children. A probable explanation is that older learners adopted transforming and encoding strategies on their own initiative when faced with an ostensibly unstructured or meaningless verbal learning task. As a result, when placed in the control condition of the experiment, their level of performance was raised to that of younger subjects who were carefully instructed to use a mediating strategy. Younger and less able people cannot produce such strategies spontaneously, and therefore they learn less when they are alloted to a control condition than when they are in an experimental condition, in which they receive special instructions to use a mediating strategy.

Although intelligent adults are more likely than less capable individuals to use effective strategies, even the most successful learners do not spontaneously adopt an optimally effective learning strategy in every situation. An experiment by Bower and Clark (1969) showed that college students may benefit considerably from receiving instructions to follow a procedure not unlike the one which aided retarded individuals in the experiment by Jensen and Rohwer (1963). Bower and Clark's undergraduate subjects learned 12 lists, each of which contained ten concrete nouns. Twelve of the 24 undergraduates formed an experimental group and they were told to link together the words in each list by making up a narrative story which connected them. A typical subject was given the words *vegetable, instrument, college, carrot, nail, basin, merchant, queen, scale, goat* and produced the following narrative:

> a *vegetable* can be a useful *instrument* for a *college* student. A *carrot* can be a *nail* for your fence or *basin*. But a *merchant* of the *Queen* would *scale* the fence and feed the carrot to a *goat*.

Every subject made a new narrative for each list, starting with the first word and adding the other items to the story in the order they appeared in the list. The times taken by individual subjects to construct their narratives varied from 40 seconds to 199 seconds, the average being 104 seconds. For each subject in the experimental group there was a "yoked" subject in a control group. This subject received an equivalent amount of time to learn each list and attempted to learn the words without getting advice to form narratives or any other special instructions. After the period for studying each list, there followed an immediate recall test. At this stage, it was found that the performance of subjects in the experimental and control groups was very similar, with participants in each group recalling almost all the items correctly. But when the students were tested at the end of the session on all the 12 lists together, there was a vast difference in favor of the subjects who had been instructed to form narrative sentences.

As Figure 9.2 shows, these individuals recalled, on average, more than 90 percent of the word items, in the correct list and the correct position. Subjects in the control group recalled less than 20 percent of the items. This result demonstrates that, in this task at least, instructing intelligent people to use a simple strategy leads to a remarkable improvement in learning.

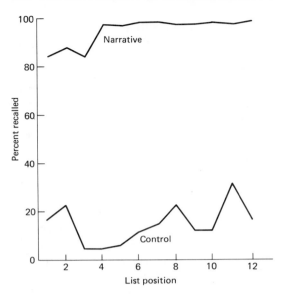

Figure 9.2   Median percentages of words recalled in their correct list and correct position. (Source: Bower, G. H., and Clark, M. L. "Narrative stories as mediators for serial learning." *Psychonomic Science,* 1969, 14:181–182. Reprinted by permission.)

Cross-modal Transfer

Some mediational processes take place in young children even before they are old enough to give clear evidence of possessing representational abilities. Evidence for this assertion is provided by studies in which an item is presented to children via one sensory modality, say vision, and they are later tested for recognition of the object when it is presented via a different modality, say touch. In order for the children to have recognized the equivalence, they must have retained some representation of the object or of its defining attributes. Furthermore, cross-modal recognition is only possible if the representation is not just a literal copy of the item, but is at a coded and more abstract level at which the equivalence of identity is apparent. Bryant, Jones, Claxton, and Perkins (1972) found that infants as young as 8 months of age, before they had acquired any language ability at all, performed at a significantly better than chance level on a cross-modal task requiring them to recognize eliptical shapes when they were alternately presented via vision and touch.

Cross-modal transfer procedures are valuable for investigating the development of mental processes that mediate thought in children who are too young to give reliable verbal reports. Zaporozhets (1965) undertook an experiment in which children aged between 3 and 6 years were encouraged to explore objects in one of four ways involving different sensory modes. Some children explored the objects visually, others tactually, and a third group combined visual and tactile exploration. A fourth group of children handled the objects and manipulated them into holes in a wooden board. Following the session in which the children explored the objects, all the children were tested for visual recognition. In each condition it was found that performance improved markedly with age. At all ages, those children who had the opportunity to see and to touch the objects at the same time remembered more items than children who had only seen the objects or only touched them. Zaporozhets found that up to the age of 4 years, children's ability to recognize the visual forms of objects that had previously been experienced in the tactile mode alone was severely limited, but this ability increased considerably between the ages of 4 and 5 years.

Experiments on cross-modal recognition have also been employed to shed light upon young children's coding and retention of information about objects. For instance, Pick, Pick, and Thomas (1966) designed an experiment to determine whether young children's object recognition depends upon them remembering an image of each object as a whole, or whether they rely on retaining information about particular details of objects. Children perceived a number of letterlike forms either visually or by touch. The recognition tasks required them to judge if each of a number of items was the same or different than a standard object.

Those recognition test items which were not identical to the standard objects could differ from them in any of a number of ways. The test items were produced by transformations in the size, orientation, or linearity of the objects. Determining which transformations children most readily identify helps us to understand how objects are represented in children's memories. In the experiment by Pick, Pick, and Thomas, training was followed by a session in which either the correct object in a recognition test was the same as the original one but the transformations used to produce incorrect objects were different from those to which the subject had been exposed in the training session, or in which a different item was involved, but the other items were produced by familiar transformations. The authors noted that if young children's recognition depends on them retaining a mental image of the whole object, there would be greater transfer from the first to the second session in circumstances where the same standard object (but presented via different modes) was used in both sessions. In fact, there was no cross-modal transfer in that condition but there was transfer in the condition involving similar transformations but different standard objects. This result was interpreted by the researchers as indicating that children do not retain images of whole items. Their ability to recognize objects appears to depend upon them retaining information about specific features.

Labeling Functions of Language

The apparently simple activity of naming a perceived object can have a marked effect upon learning. Adults often do this automatically, and for that reason advising adult subjects to supply the names of common objects may have little or no effect, just as instructions to use mediating sentences that link word pairs may not aid adults, because they form mediating links spontaneously.

Because we adults perform labeling and naming activities automatically and with little or no awareness of our doing so, it is difficult to appreciate that so simple a strategy as providing a word name as they look at an object may considerably aid child learners. Children do benefit from being instructed to do this, just as they (and retarded adults) benefit from instructions to use mediating sentences. For adults, the naming process may be so automatic that we fail to appreciate its value. For young children, instructions to name objects provide an effective albeit simple mediating strategy. Jensen (1971) reported that up to the age of 5 years, children who were told to name objects they were shown could remember more of the items than children who were not instructed to name the objects. Children aged 6 and above do not remember more items when they are told to name them, probably because by this age they have already acquired the habit of providing names spontaneously. Jensen noted differences in spontaneous naming of objects between middle-class and culturally impoverished children, and between normal and retarded individuals. An effect of giving instructions to name items is to reduce the differences between children in the amount they learn.

Further evidence of the value of naming objects is provided by the findings of an experiment by Norcross and Spiker (1957). Preschool children were shown drawings of faces that differed in the shape of the eyes, mouth, and hair. Each child was assigned at random to one of three training groups, and learned names for the drawings of girls' faces (*Peg* and *Jean*) or for the drawings of boys' faces, or they received training in distinguishing between the different faces. Afterwards, all three groups were given a task in which they had to recognize female faces, and the children were rewarded for correct choices. Those children whose training had included learning names for the drawings of girls' faces made correct choices on 22 out of 30 trials, on average, a higher level of performance than that of subjects in the other groups. The children who learned names for the female faces were better at discriminating between such faces in the task than the others despite the fact that children in the other groups were trained to discriminate between faces that were similar to the ones used in the final task. Having to learn the names of particular items appears to be especially valuable. This result was repeated in a second experiment that was carefully designed to insure that all children received the same amount of training. In a further study (Norcross, 1958) it was found that when distinctive names were used (*Wag* and *Kos*) children performed better than when the two names were similar (*Zim* and *Zam*).

Variations in the age at which individuals gain the habit of using strategies that increase learning—labeling and sentence mediation being just two potentially useful learning strategies—are at the heart of the differences between "good learners" and people whose efforts to learn are less successful. The successful learner is likely to be a person who has acquired a repertoire of procedures and strategies that facilitate learning. Faced with a new task, such individuals are more successful than others, not because of any fundamental superiority in the physiological processes underlying learning, but because they have a number of useful strategies at their disposal and they have acquired the habit of regularly using them. Many of the learner activities that are encountered in the present chapter and the succeeding one may be regarded as strategies that individuals use when learning is necessary.

SPEECH AND BEHAVIOR

Relationships between language and behavior are not so readily apparent in young children as in adults, but language first begins to influence the child at a time when an observer's first impression would be that language has no part in the child's experience (Blank, 1974). As the young child learns to speak, language exerts some control over behavior, and the control becomes increasingly precise as the child gets older. Research originating in the USSR has been concerned with the importance of spoken language. Vygotskii (1962) stressed the distinction between language as "inner speech" for conveying a person's thoughts, and language as "external speech," by which a person communicates with others. Luria (1961) has reported a number of Russian investigations showing that verbal control over children's actions increases as they get older. A young child may understand the meaning of a verbal command, but this does not insure that the command will automatically initiate the appropriate behavior. In a typical experiment, a child aged 18 months was told to squeeze a rubber ball he was holding. The child was able to comply with this instruction, but if he was then told "don't squeeze," he would go on squeezing even more vigorously. At this stage, the power of verbal signals to control the child's behavior is incomplete, and the child cannot immediately respond discriminatively according to whether the command "squeeze" occurs on its own or is preceded by "don't". Also, verbal signals that are adequate for initiating the child's response may not be effective for inhibiting or delaying actions. A young child cannot respond correctly to the instruction "When the light comes on, squeeze the bulb." The modification involved in requesting a delayed response instead of an immediate one may appear to adults to be a minor change from the simple command to press the bulb, which the child obeys with no difficulty, but the young child cannot easily make the necessary alteration.

As age increases, the regulating function of speech over behavior becomes more precise. Three-year-old children can follow instructions to press a bulb, and they can also obey the instruction not to press or to delay pressing until a signal occurs. But even at this age, control remains incomplete, and although positive instructions are followed accurately, negative commands continue to give difficulty. For the 3-year-old, saying, "I must not press" does not effectively inhibit a child from doing so. On the whole, the more direct the relationship between the language signal and the designated behavior, the more likely it is that language will exert precise control over the child's actions. For example, children at age 3 who are given the instruction "When the lamp comes on, press twice" tend to perseverate with the action, pressing again and again. However, if they are instructed to say "one, two" as they press, there is a higher probability of effective control.

Beiswenger (1971) designed a number of tasks in which American children aged 3 and 4 years were asked to make conditional responses. For example, a child might be told "Every time the blue light comes on, get a blue marble and put it in the dish." Beiswenger found that children had much more difficulty in following this kind of instruction than an unconditional one such as "Get a yellow marble and put it in the dish," and he agrees with Luria that a lengthy and complex process is necessary for young children to become able to gain verbal control over the organizing and sequencing of their behavior. Children have to acquire the abilities underlying language comprehension and coordinate them with learned mechanisms controlling their motor activities. However, the results of American replications of the experiments reported by Luria do not all agree with Russian findings. Miller, Shelton, and Flavell (1970), for example, observed that the responses of children in a bulb-squeezing experiment varied considerably, and were not always consistent with the findings of the earlier research.

A discussion of language in relation to thoughts and actions inevitably involves an element of speculation. Developmental psychologists in the tradition established by Piaget emphasize the young child's limited abilities for logical thinking. Their explanation of the child's difficulty with obeying conditional instructions would give emphasis to the problem for a young child of having to think of two things at once. The child first has to establish whether or not the circumstances are ones in which the bulb should be pressed, and then either presses or does not press it. The conditional task requires more complex mental operations on the part of the child than are necessary for obeying an unconditional instruction.

IMAGERY AND LEARNING

Around the time of World War II, a suggestion that mental images might contribute to any human learning, let alone forms of learning that involve language and verbal materials, would have struck most psychologists as downright ridiculous. The influence of behaviorism in excluding from consideration phenomenon so unobservable and subjective as visual imagery insured that imagery received little attention. There had been a time, toward the end of the nineteenth century, when imagery had attracted considerable interest. Sir Francis Galton sent a questionnaire to 100 educated people, asking them about the images they experienced in everyday life. He found that individuals varied considerably in the extent to which they experienced imagery, but that most people did have some images, visual ones being the most common. At the time imagery was deliberately being ignored by psychologists within the early behaviorist sphere of influence, evidence did exist to show that imagery made a marked contribution to learning. However, the findings did not receive serious consideration at the time because they came from sources that were not considered to be acceptably scientific.

Mnemonic Systems

Throughout the past two centuries, people have given stage performances of learning and memory feats that demonstrate exceptional success at remembering. Some of the feats memory take the form of recalling the names of large numbers of people, and others involve lengthy lists of items. The means by which such tasks are performed have been described in a number of published books, some with sensational titles, such as, *Give Yourself a Super-Power Memory*. Books of this kind have disappointed some readers, who were led by advertizements to expect that their mental abilities would be transformed. Nevertheless, the methods and techniques that are described can produce considerable improvements at tasks in which lists of unrelated items have to be learned or remembered. In one book, for example, *How to Develop A Super-power Memory*, author Harry Lorayne (1958) tells his readers that when they have studied the systems described in the book they will be able to remember a 50-digit number after examining it just once, a shopping list of 50 items, or the order of a pack of cards. Surprisingly perhaps, such claims are essentially correct. The only major problem with the systems are that the methods for memorizing are complicated, and acquiring them can be difficult and time consuming. Equally important, an ability to memorize long lists is not, for most of us, particularly useful. Acquiring techniques that improve our ability to memorize lists does not solve many of the problems we experience in our everyday lives.

Nevertheless, a method that facilitates any kind of learning deserves to be taken seriously, and investigating how it works may increase our understanding of processes that underlie human learning. The techniques that have been devised to improve memorization are collectively called *mnemonics*. The mnemonic methods that have been introduced for helping people to remember things take various forms. Most adults will have encountered a number of mnemonics, perhaps in the form of rhymes (for instance, "Thirty days hath September . . .") or "first-letter" mnemonics (for example, "Richard of York Gave Battle in Vain", which gives the first letter of each color in the rainbow, in the right order). First-letter mnemonics are commonly used by students at universities (Gruneberg, 1973). A number of mnemonic systems rely on the use of visual imagery, and I shall describe two visual systems that have been widely used, and then consider the role of visual imagery from a broader perspective.

One well-known mnemonic system is based upon visual imagery and a simple rhyme, which has to be learned by heart. The rhyme goes:

One is a *bun*
Two is a shoe
Three is a *tree*
Four is a *door* . . .

and so on, up to ten. Once the rhyme has been carefully learned it can be used to help remember word lists. Learners are instructed to form a clear visual image of each noun in the rhyme, so that each takes on a concrete visual form. They make, for example, a clear image of a particular bun, representing *one*, and another visual image of a particular shoe, for *two*. To memorize a list of new words, learners make a strong visual image for each item, comprising a picture of whatever the word denotes, linked with the image of the object that corresponds to the number representing the word's position in the list. For example, if word number one is *sugar*, the individual learner might form a visual image of a large soft currant bun (*"One* is a *bun"*) covered by a heap of glistening white sugar. The procedure is continued until the list of words is complete.

The method appears to be rather cumbersome, and it necessitates the individual taking some time to learn the rhyme in the first place and to form appropriate images. Furthermore, the rate of presentation must be no faster than around one item every five seconds, otherwise the learner may not have sufficient time to form clear visual images. Nevertheless, the system does work, and it can produce very marked improvements in the learning of ordered lists of word items. To test the method's effectiveness, Hunter (1964) instructed some subjects to use it for learning a word list, while another group of subjects learned the same word list in their own way. Only two out of the 30 subjects who were not instructed to use the mnemonic system could reproduce all the items in a ten-word list after one presentation, but 17 out of 35 individuals who followed the system recalled all the words correctly, and most of the others made only one or two errors.

I have repeated this experiment informally several times, and the findings have been similar to those obtained by Hunter. The need to allow sufficient time for each visual image to be formed is demonstrated by the findings of an experiment by Bugelski, Kidd, and Segmen (1968). They used a visual imagery mnemonic based on the *"One* is a *bun"* rhyme. Figure 9.3 shows the outcome of varying the presentation rate of list items. When the words were presented at a rate of one item per two seconds, subjects using the mnemonic recalled no more words than subjects in a control condition. However, at a slower rate of presentation, one item every four seconds, the mnemonic did improve performance, and there was an even larger improvement when eight seconds were allowed for each word item.

Another system that uses visual imagery to help people learn lists of items is known as the *place method*. A form of it has been used for over 2000 years. Cicero thought it was invented by a Greek

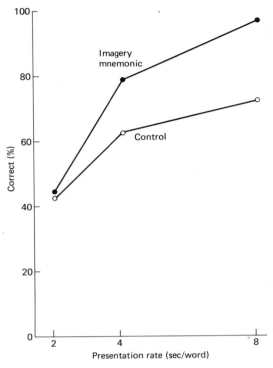

Figure 9.3 Percentage of items recalled in imagery and control conditions of the experiment by Bugelski, Kidd, and Segmen (1968).

poet named Simonides. It is said that after Simonides had recited one of his poems at a large feast he was called away from the banquet hall by a messenger of Castor and Pollux, two gods who were praised in the poem. While Simonides was standing outside, the roof of the building collapsed, and everyone in the hall was killed. The bodies were so mangled that they could not be recognized, but since Simonides knew where each person at the banquet had been sitting, he was able to identify each body by its location. Simonides' method forms the basis of a memory system in which information is retained by forming images of the items to be remembered and pairing each image with a particular location that is familiar to the learner. When the learner wants to recall the words, the individual simply evokes an image of the familiar scene, to which are attached images of the items in the different positions.

In essence, that is the place method. Learners are told to choose a place or building already well-known to them, which contain a number of distinct and easily identifiable locations. They might decide to form an image of a large house they know well, with its various rooms and familiar parts, or they might decide to image the shops in a local high street. Imagine that someone wants to learn the items in a shopping list: eggs, cheese, butter, etc. The person might start by forming an image of eggs attached to the front door, followed by cheese lying on the hall carpet, butter on a sofa in the living room, and bread in the fireplace. It is important that the particular locations are not only well-known to the individual but are chosen in advance, so that the different places can be recalled in the correct order. If the locations are easily retrieved and strong visual images have been formed to connect an item to each location, remembering will present little difficulty.

In one test of the place system, Ross and Lawrence (1968) asked students to use 40 locations around a university campus. The experimenter presented lists of 40 words at the rate of 12 items per minute. In tests given immediately afterwards, subjects were able to recall about 38 of the items, on average, in their correct order, and even after a 24 hour delay recall they averaged about 36 items out of the possible 40. This level of performance is appreciably higher than is normally encountered in research into verbal learning, and when Groninger (1971) compared learning by students who used similar method with learning by control group subjects who were not instructed to use verbal imagery, he found that the imagery group remembered twice as many items.

Compared with the *"One is a bun"* system, the place method has the advantage of drawing upon the learner's existing knowledge. It is not necessary to start by learning an unfamiliar rhyme. Systems based upon the place method vary somewhat in their details, and nineteenth-century writers such as Gregor von Feinagle (Morris, 1977) devised a variety of complicated place methods for retaining lengthy lists of words. However, most of us do not have to learn lists of unrelated items sufficiently often to justify our taking the trouble to learn the more complicated systems.

FUNCTIONS OF VISUAL IMAGERY

Confronted by claims about the effectiveness of mnemonic systems based on visual imagery, experimental psychologists eventually began to design experiments to test these claims, and they proceeded to undertake further research into the function of imagery in human learning. A number of studies were undertaken by Alan Paivio (1969). Paivio notes that to suggest non-verbal imagery is involved in human learning and retention is not to deny that verbal mechanisms are also important. We might expect imagery to be most important in circumstances where the material being learned involves concrete objects and events. Imagery and verbal processes might form two alternative coding systems, or alternative modes of symbolically representing knowledge. For Paivio, the extent to which imagery is involved in a particular instance of learning depends upon the degree of concreteness of the words to be acquired.

Paivio's research into the function of visual imagery in learning has used word items that vary in degree of concreteness, which Paivio has found to be related to the ease with which learners form an image. Most people find it much easier to make images for concrete items such as *bishop* or *altar* than for an abstract word such as *religion*. Lists of word pairs in which the items are concrete and easily imaged are easier to learn than lists of abstract words. Therefore, Paivio (1965) reasoned, if imagery serves a mediating function that contributes to learning, concrete words will be learned more easily than abstract words. He conducted an experiment in which abstract words and concrete words served as the stimulus and response items of a paired-associate learning task. The greatest amount of learning took place when both the stimulus items and the response items forming the pairs were concrete words. The least learning was observed with the abstract-abstract pairs. Intermediate levels of learning occurred with the mixed pairs; subjects performed better with the concrete-abstract word pairs than with the abstract-concrete pairs.

These findings strongly suggest that imagery or some other factor related to the concreteness of words has important effects upon learning. Among many studies measuring the influence of imagery, a number of experiments have been designed to compare the potency of word concreteness with that of other variables known to influence verbal learning. In particular, some investigations have compared the effects of the measured ease with which a word evokes an image with the effects of different values of Noble's measure of meaningfulness. Of course, the degree of concreteness of words may be related to their meaningfulness or associative strength. If word concreteness and meaningfulness are related, it is conceivable that the apparent effect of imagery indicated by the better recall of concrete words might really be due to their high degree of meaningfulness.

To investigate this possibility, Paivio conducted some experiments designed to compare the separate effects of word concreteness and meaningfulness. In one study (Paivio, 1967) he found a correlation of +.54 between the learning of word paired-associate lists and the ease of forming an image to the first (stimulus) item in each pair. The correlation between learning and the imageability of the second (response) word in each pair was +.31. These correlations were higher than the corresponding ones between learning and the meaningfulness of the stimulus and response items, these being +.37 and +.21 respectively. However, in calculating these correlations, the two variables, imageability and meaningfulness, are not completely separated because each is correlated with the other, the correlation between them being +.69. In order to make a separation between imageability and meaningfulness, thus making it possible to estimate what the effects of each variable would have been had it not been correlated with the other one, one computes what are known as "partial correlations." This provides a way of calculating the correlation between learning and each of the variables on its own, with the influence of the other correlated variable "partialled out" to avoid its confounding influence. Paivio found that when meaningfulness was partialled out in this way, the learning scores for word paired-associates correlated +.47 with the imagery of the stimulus item and +.25 with that of the response item. Thus, extracting the contribution of meaningfulness had relatively little effect on the relationship between learning and imageability. However partialling out the effects of imagery on the correlation between learning and meaningfulness has a much more dramatic effect, reducing to zero the correlations between learning and both stimulus word and response word meaningfulness. Clearly then, imageability on its own is closely related to learning; item meaningfulness is not. This finding raises the possibility that some of the observed correlations between learning and degree of meaningfulness (or associative strength) mentioned earlier in the present chapter, may have been inflated by uncontrolled effects of imageability. It is interesting to note that the possibility that imageability of words might influence learning was not considered at all at the time when the earlier research was undertaken.

Paivio, Smythe, and Yuille (1968) carried out a further investigation into the separate effects of word imagery and meaningfulness on learning. They used two lists of 32 noun paired-associates. In one list the words were all similar in degree of meaningfulness, but 16 of them were of high imagery value and 16 were low in imageability. The second list contained 32 words which were similar in imagery value, but in which 16 of them had high meaningfulness scores and the other 16 were low in meaningfulness. The word frequencies of items within each list were carefully controlled.

The composition of the two lists made it possible to compare learning of paired-associate word lists in which either the ease of forming images or the word meaningfulness was varied, with the other factor held constant. Figure 9.4 shows the effects the two variables on subjects' recall of the lists. First, it can be seen that varying the imagery values of the words had a much larger effect on performance than varying the meaningfulness. This agrees with the other findings by Paivio (1967). In the case of the lists that varied in word imagery the effect of overall differences in imagery values (HH lists compared with LL lists) was quite large. An interesting comparison is between the HL and the LH lists. One might have expected to find roughly equivalent levels of learning, since the average imagery value of words in the HL lists and the LH lists was the same. But as Figure 9.4 shows, subjects recalled considerably more items from the HL lists than from the LH lists, showing that it is better to have the high imagery items in the first (stimulus) position than in the response position of the word pairs.

Why should this be so? A possible explanation is that when people form images of a pair of words, the first word image acts as a

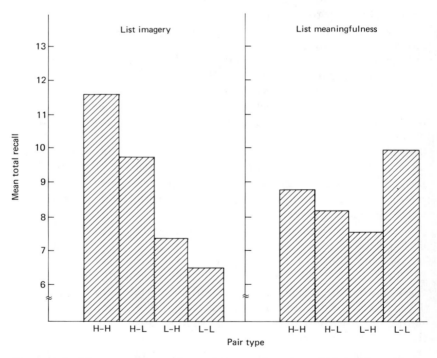

Figure 9.4   Mean recall over four trials as a function of high (H) and low (L) values of the stimulus and response items in paired-associate lists. (Source: Adapted from Paivio, A., Smythe, P. C., and Yuille, J. C. "Imagery versus meaningfulness of nouns in paired-associate learning." *Canadian Journal of Psychology,* 1968, 22:427–441.)

kind of anchor, to which the second image is subsequently attached. Paivio (1969) has suggested that an imaged stimulus item forms a "conceptual peg" that provides a cue serving to reconstitute a compound image involving stimulus and response words. This makes it possible to retrieve the imaged information and to recode it into the appropriate word. As a result of the stimulus word having the anchoring function, when the response item has a low imagery value, retention of only that particular word suffers. When the stimulus word does not readily evoke an image, both items in the pair are adversely affected.

The effects of word imagery on learning are not restricted to paired-associate tasks. Imageability also affects performance in a variety of tasks that require individuals to retain verbal materials. In an experiment by Paivio, Yuille, and Rogers (1969) there were two lists, one in which imagery values were held constant and meaningfulness varied, and one in which meaningfulness was constant and words differed in imagery value. Each list contained 12 nouns, and learning was tested after each presentation. As in Paivio, Smythe and Yuille's (1968) paired-associate learning study, when meaningfulness was held constant, high imagery nouns were recalled more accurately than low imagery nouns, on each of four trials. When imageability was held constant, lists of highly meaningful nouns were learned more quickly than lists of less meaningful words. The effect of varying the meaningfulness of the items was considerably less than that of varying the imagery of list words (Figure 9.5).

Practical Uses of Imagery

The fact that learning of words has been shown to be related to the ease with which images are formed encourages us to look for practical applications of strategies that use imagery, in addition to their application in the mnemonic systems I have already described.

Morris (1977) notes that despite the apparent value of mnemonic systems, most people make little use of them. He gives two possible reasons. The first is that some effort is involved in learning the systems. Second, they are only effective for certain kinds of materials, such as word items. However, present research has shown that imagery does make important contributions to a number of learned abilities, including reading (Jorm, 1977), sentence retention (André and Sola, 1976), and remembering objects in real scenes (Dirks and Neisser, 1977).

A kind of learning for which strategies that involve using visual

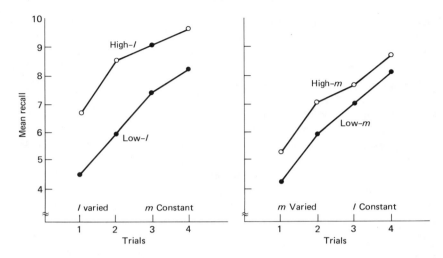

Figure 9.5   Mean free-recall scores for items of high and low imageability (*l*) and meaningfulness (*m*). (Source: Adapted from Paivio, A., Yuille, J. C., and Rogers, T. B. "Noun imagery and meaningfulness in free serial recall." *Journal of Experimental Psychology*, 1969, 79:509–514. © 1969 American Psychological Association. Reprinted by permission.)

images can be especially helpful is second-language acquisition. Some findings reported by Atkinson (1975; Raugh and Atkinson, 1975) show that systematic use of an ingenious learning procedure that requires the learner to form visual images leads to marked improvements in the vocabulary-learning aspect of acquiring a foreign language. The method involves a number of steps. First, there is an "acoustic link" stage of learning, in which each spoken English word is associated to an English "key word" that is chosen because it is similar in sound to part of the foreign word equivalent that is being learned. For example, the English word *pot* provided the key word for the Spanish word for *duck* (*pato*), which is roughly pronounced *pot-o*. Next, there follows a second stage of learning in which a link based on imagery is formed. The learner has to make a mental image of the key word object interacting with the English word. For instance, in the case of *pot* and *duck* the learner might form a vivid mental image of a duck trying to hide under an overturned flower pot. In this manner, the English word comes to evoke the Spanish word and vice versa, via the visual image.

The key word method may appear cumbersome, but a series of experiments have shown it to be highly effective in practice. It has enabled students to gain substantially higher learning scores than others who follow a conventional rote learning approach. This method, which strongly depends upon visual imagery, provides a practical way to facilitate the arduous and time-consuming vocabulary learning that is essential for acquiring any foreign language.

Imagery and Visual Processes

The fact that learning is related to the imagery values of words does not provide certain proof that the activity of forming images makes a direct contribution to learning. However, the research findings strongly suggest that verbal processes cannot account for all forms of learning. The assumption that all higher mental processes are based upon coding of language, a view expressed in its most literal form by J. B. Watson's statement that thinking is a kind of inner speech, appears to be wrong. There are additional forms of evidence to support the view that some higher mental processes depend upon encoding information nonverbally. This not only so in Pylyshyn's (1973) sense that the processes underlying thought are not verbal, but also in the sense that not all mental processing even starts with information in verbal form.

Consider some findings obtained by Posner and Keele (1967). They asked subjects to look at a visual display containing two letters of the alphabet, displayed side by side. The subjects had to make a choice response according to whether the two stimuli represented the same letter or different letters. The materials in the experiment were either upper-case letters (for example, A) or lower-case letters (for example, a). When the two items represented the same letter, subjects had to respond "same" as quickly as possible. It was found that the average time to react (the "reaction time") was about 70 milliseconds slower when two items representing the same letter were dissimilar in physical structure (for example, A and a) than when they were physically identical (for example, A and A). This result indicates that at some stage in the task, subjects were processing information in a nonverbal form, otherwise identical reaction times would be expected.

There is considerable further evidence from a variety of tasks that human learning and thinking utilize forms of representing information in which verbal processes are absent or unimportant, except at the stage of receiving or transmitting the data. A number of experiments have shown that people are capable of recognizing literally hundreds of briefly inspected pictures with great accuracy (Shepard, 1967; Howe, 1967b). This ability cannot be explained in terms of verbal encoding processes. When people look at lengthy series of monochrome photographs depicting similar objects (such as a sequence of 60 pictures of trains inspected by subjects in

Howe's investigation), it is most unlikely that they provide a distinctive verbal description for every single different item. It is much more probable that some kind of visual coding is involved.

A study by Shepard and Metzler (1971) provides further data which would be extremely difficult to explain if the mental processing of the items was restricted to verbal representations. The subjects looked at pictures of two 3-dimensional models, and they had to decide if by rotating one picture it could be made to match the other one. The time taken by subjects to answer the question was found to be related to the angular displacement between the two models and to the amount of rotation that is necessary to mentally rearrange them in coinciding positions, permitting the subject to match them. To perform this task by purely verbal processing would be virtually impossible. In brief, the experimental findings strongly indicate that some kinds of mental processing start with visual rather than purely verbal representations of the information.

How does imagery contribute to learning? The findings of a number of studies suggest that we can make a distinction between imagery processes that contribute to learning, on the one hand, and verbal processing, on the other hand. Visual imagery processes have something in common with visual perception and share some of the same mechanisms. One of the first investigations to produce results supporting this statement was an experiment by Brooks (1968). He used a measure of the extent to which performing one task interfered with another as an indication of whether they depended on related mental processes. Subjects looked at a large block capital letter F, which was later removed. The subjects were asked to imagine they were progressing around the block F in a clockwise direction, starting at the bottom left hand corner. The task was to specify whether each corner they encountered was an open angle or not. They responded by saying "yes" or "no" according to the kind of angle that was encountered at each of the corners, or by pointing to a visual display on which the letters Y and N represented "yes" and "no", or by tapping with the left hand for "yes" and with the right hand for "no." Thus the response could be either verbal (saying "yes" or "no") or nonverbal (pointing and tapping). If the task of following the outline of the F was accomplished by verbal coding, one would predict that the verbal mode of responding (by speaking) would interfere with task performance to a greater extent than nonverbal responding (by pointing or tapping). However, if the task was accomplished by nonverbal imagery that involved spatial coding of the letter F, one would expect that having to respond by speech would interfere less than pointing and tapping. It was found that the average time to complete the task was appreciably less when subjects responded verbally, by saying yes" or "no" (11.3 seconds), than in either the tapping condition (14.1 seconds) or the pointing condition (28.2 seconds). The fact that the pointing form of response generated the greatest amount of interference with performance of the tracking task supports the view that the subjects performing the task undertake mental functions that are based upon some kind of spatial representation. The finding that verbal responses produced the least interference indicates that verbal processes were not crucial in the tracking task.

Brooks also provided a situation in which the main task was a verbal problem, in place of the spatial tracking task. Subjects were required to remember a sentence, and they had to classify each word according to whether it was a noun or not a noun. Again, the form of the response was either to say "yes" or "no", or to point to "yes" or "no" on a visual display, or to tap appropriately. In the new situation, the requirement to respond verbally did not reduce the amount of time needed to perform the task. It resulted in considerably more time being taken (13.8 seconds) than in either of the pointing (9.8 seconds) or the tapping (7.8 seconds) conditions. In short, when the task was a verbal one, having to respond verbally produced the greatest amount of interference. It is reasonable to infer that since verbal responding produced the least amount of interference with the task that involved tracking the letter F, the subjects performed the tracking task on the basis of nonverbal representation of the data.

Further evidence for separate mental processing of imaged and vocalized information is provided by some findings of an investigation by G. Atwood, reported by Bower (1970). College students learned associated words that were linked by sentences and the words were either concrete and easily imaged (for instance, "A *pistol* hanging from a *chain*") or abstract and not readily represented by an image (for example, "The *theory* is *nonsense*"). They listened to lists of sentences, read at the rate of one per five seconds. After each sentence, some of the participants had to react to a brief distracting signal, either auditory or visual, consisting of the digit *1* or *2*. The subjects had to respond by saying the alternative digit, that is, *2* or *1*. For some subjects the distracting task was presented visually, for others it was auditory, and some people received no distraction at all. All of the subjects were given sentences of each kind, that is, ones that contained concrete items and readily evoked images, and ones that were highly abstract. Subjects in the group that had no distracting task recalled more of the words than people in either of the other groups, with their recall of concrete items being more accurate (82 percent correctly recalled) than that of abstract items

(70 percent). Comparing the other subjects, it was found that with abstract sentences those people who had an auditory distracting task (hearing *1* or *2*) suffered more in their recall of the words (by 26 percent from the 70 percent level of the control group, to 44 percent) than subjects who had a visual distracting task (seeing *1* or *2*) among whom the drop in recall averaged only 10 percent, from 70 percent to 60 percent.

The fact that the auditory task interfered more than the visual task suggests that there was more sharing of processing capacities between the abstract materials and the auditory task than between the abstract materials and the visual task. The reverse occurred with the concrete words, which readily evoked representation in image form. Here, the visual auditory task reduced recall by 24 percent, from 82 percent (by subjects in the control group) to 58 percent. The auditory distracting task had a much smaller effect on the recall of the concrete items, reducing percentage recall by a mere 6 percent, from 82 percent to 76 percent. It seems that in the case of the concrete items, in sharp contrast with the abstract items, a visual distracting task interfered with recall much more than a verbal task. This finding supports the suggestion that processing of concrete items involves mechanisms or encoding facilities that are shared with those required for visual perception.

Some investigators who have repeated Atwood's experiments have not obtained identical results (Baddeley, 1976), and it is probable that visual tasks interfere with the processing of concrete materials only if the learner is actively involved in forming visual images (Baddeley, 1976). As Baddeley points out, presenting concrete items does not automatically result in subjects forming visual images. Baddeley, Grant, Wight, and Thomson (1974) found that in the absence of specific instructions to form images, the distracting effect of a visual tracking task was no greater on concrete noun-adjective word pairs (for example, *strawberry-ripe*) than on abstract pairs (for example, *gratitude-infinite*).

The results of an ingenious experiment by Bower (1972) provide further evidence that abstract verbal materials and readily imaged concrete items may be processed separately. Bower's subjects learned word pairs by one of two methods. Subjects following a visual imagery strategy were told to visualize scenes in which two objects were related, and other subjects followed a rote repetition method. At the same time as learning the word pairs, subjects had to engage in either of two distracting tasks. One distracting task was largely visual, and the other was tactile. The visual distracting task required subjects to track with their finger a wavy line that appeared in a display slot, 1 inch high and 12 inches wide. The line moved erratically from one side of the slot to the other. This distracting task demanded close visual attention, and if the imagery strategy depended on mental processes that were shared by the processing underlying visual perception, this distraction would markedly interfere with learning. The other distracting task did not involve vision, and subjects were told to close their eyes as they tracked with their fingers a raised length of string that was exposed in the horizontal slot, glued to the paper, and, like the line in the visual task, moved in each direction. Thus the tracking tasks were essentially the same except that the tactile condition used touch rather than visual information. If visual imagery involves processes that are shared with visual perception, we would expect to find that the tactile tracking task would produce less interference than the visual tasks.

The results confirmed the expectations. Bower observed, in line with the findings of Atwood and most other investigators, that learning was considerably better with the imagery strategy than with rote repetition. The average percentage of words correctly recalled was, respectively, 60 percent and 28 percent in the two conditions. With the imagery strategy, the visual distracting task produced a lower level of recall (55 percent) than the tactile task (66 percent), but with the rote learning task, there was no difference in recall levels with the two interfering tasks. The percentage of items correctly recalled was 28 percent in each of the two conditions. These additional findings are consistent with the view that visual perception and visual imagery have some processing capacity in common. This conclusion would lead one to expect that nonvisual forms of imagery would also be subject to interference by tasks that involved the same perceptual modality. In fact, Segal and Fusella (1969) found that in a detection task faint lights were unlikely to be detected if the subject was simultaneously imagining a visual scene. They also observed that detection of auditory tones was reduced if the subject was required to evoke an auditory image, for example the sound of a telephone ringing.

EIDETIC IMAGERY

Over the years there have been many popular accounts of individuals said to possess a "photographic memory" enabling them, for instance, to remember all the words on a page after inspecting it. Careful investigations have revealed that around 8 percent of children (Haber and Haber, 1964) possess what is termed *eidetic imagery*. This provides a child with very accurate records of a perceived visual stimulus, often sufficiently clear and detailed to enable a child to "read off" the content without any deliberate retrieval or recall strategy being involved. Eidetic imagery relies upon a fairly literal record of the visual stimulus, and children may recall the letters forming a long word in the visual display although they are unable to spell it.

Eidetic images are distinct from the ordinary visual images experienced by children and adults. The children designated as eidetic imagers by Haber and Haber (1964) could give detailed verbal descriptions of their images of each of four pictures they had been shown. The images always lasted for at least 40 seconds and were detailed enough for the contents of the pictures to be described with considerable accuracy. When children were describing their eidetic images they always spoke of the pictures as if they were still present, never using the past tense, and they always described the images as being colored. When describing the actual contents of the images the children would make the scanning movements with their eyes that are customarily employed in perceiving real objects, but children who did not experience eidetic images rarely scanned in this manner.

Possessing the ability to form eidetic images might appear to indicate above-average powers of practical memory, but in fact, the contrary appears to be the case. Eidetic imagers are unable to make use of their apparently valuable images in any useful way. Their imagery appears to make no contribution to learning. Indeed, findings obtained by Siipola and Hayden (1965) indicate that eidetic imagery may be related to mental retardation, and the incidence of eidetic imagery among retarded children is a least four times as high as it is among normal children. Although eidetic imagery may at first appear to be an impressive ability, it may really be a primitive recording mechanism that is only functional early in life, if at all. In most children it is soon outgrown and superseded by representational abilities that are less literal, and the children retain information that has been more extensively coded by them and is meaningful to them. Eidetic imagery may have a function of recording data in raw and unprocessed form. Such a function could be useful at an early stage of development.

EXCEPTIONAL ABILITY TO REMEMBER

Distinct from the substantial numbers of children who can form eidetic images are some rare cases of individuals who possess exceptional ability to remember. In some instances, such abilities depend on abnormal imagery. Stromeyer and Psotka (1970) used a technique in which two visual displays were presented, containing thousands of filled or empty cells. These formed a meaningful display when a person saw them both at the same time, but they were entirely meaningless when each was presented on its own. Stromeyer and Psotka were able to find just one subject who could detect the pattern if one of the displays was first presented to one eye, and, after it had disappeared, the second display was exposed to the other eye. Since nonvisual retention of the information in the meaningless single display would not be possible, it follows that the subject retained some kind of visual image. She could retain this information for an inter-stimulus interval as long as 24 hours.

Among other rare instances of supernormal ability to form visual images is the case of a person described by Coltheart and Glick (1974). She could form strong visual images of each of the letters in sentences of as long as six words, and she used the images to spell out the letters backwards at great speed. In addition, the remarkable memorizing power of the Russian mnemonist "S," whose feats are reported in a book by A. R. Luria (1968), depended to a large extent upon an extraordinary ability to form and retain visual images. This man remembered almost everything he experienced; the capacity of his memory and the durability of retained materials appeared to be practically unlimited. For instance, Luria asked "S" to memorize a display of 50 numbers, arranged in four columns and 13 rows. After "S" had spent three minutes examining the table, he reproduced all the items perfectly, in any order that Luria requested, column by column, diagonally, or as a single 50-digit number. Several months later, Luria asked "S" to reproduce the table once more, and again he was able to do so, without error. Some of the tests designed to measure the retention of "S" were given, with no advance warning, as long as 15 or 16 years after the session on which the material had originally been presented. A number of further experiments involving letters and other materials produced striking results. It was clear from his answers to Luria's questions that when "S" reported the retained material he did so, as did the eidetic imagers described above, by "reading" from a visual image. "S" reported that he could *see* whatever he was asked to recall, and for that reason the order in which he was asked to reproduce information made no difference to him. To remember something perceived on a previous occasion, "S" found it necessary to bring back to mind the total occasion in which the items had originally occurred. He took some time to do this, but once the necessary images had been evoked, "S" simply read off the items that were needed.

Although most of us would like to possess his ability to remember vast quantities of information, "S" does not seem to have been a person to be envied. He reported often being frustrated by finding himself unable to forget things. It was very difficult for him to erase images that had outlived their usefulness, and he found that imagery often blocked his understanding of the meaning of written descriptions. This made abstract reasoning very difficult.

Even without the evidence we possess from case studies of individuals possessing extraordinary abilities to form visual images, the findings of experiments on visual imagery show that our mental processes use kinds of representation that involve visual encodings of verbally presented knowledge.

SUMMARY

1. Early research into verbal learning placed stress on the measurement of item meaningfulness, defined in terms of the tendency of the item to evoke other items and to be evoked as associations to other verbal materials. However, such measures of meaningfulness are only weakly related to learning. This finding is consistent with the view that purely associative explanations of verbal learning processes are inadequate.
2. The results of a number of experiments demonstrate that considerable mental processing mediates between presentation of verbal material to people and the subsequent responses or performance that indicate they have learned the material.
3. Learning may be increased by instructing individuals to use any of a variety of strategies, in which language performs elaborative, labeling, or other mediating functions.
4. The control of speech over behavior becomes increasingly precise as children become older, indicating closer integration between language and a person's activities.
5. Findings of experimental research show that concrete word items that can readily be imaged are more easily learned than abstract items.
6. Research investigating the relationship between imagery and verbal learning demonstrates that the capacity to form visual images involves some of the mental processes underlying visual perception.
7. Some children can form extremely clear and durable visual images, called eidetic images, but these do not appear to make a useful contribution to human learning, and are more common in retarded than in normal children. Unusual ability to form images has been encountered in the cases of a number of people having exceptional ability to remember.

Suggestions for Further Reading

Bower, G. H. (1972) "Mental imagery and associative learning." In L. W. Gregg (ed.), *Cognition in Learning and Memory*. New York: Wiley.
Crowder, R. G. (1976) *Principles of Learning and Memory*. Hillsdale, New Jersey: Lawrence Erlbaum.

Kausler, D. H. (1974) *Psychology of Verbal Learning and Memory.* New York: Academic Press.

Morris, P. (1977) "Practical strategies for human learning and remembering." In M. J. A. Howe (ed.), *Adult Learning: Psychological Research and Applications.* London: Wiley.

Paivio, A. (1971) *Imagery and Verbal Processes.* New York: Holt, Rinehart and Winston.

Learning
and Human Memory

OVERVIEW

Chapter 10 concentrates on the retention rather than the acquisition of materials in language form. Research into human memory has demonstrated that it is necessary not only to make provision for storing information, but also to insure that it can be retrieved readily. This is only possible when the items in long-term memory are carefully organized. The present chapter discusses some of the ways that are available for organizing items retained for long periods in human memory.

LEARNING AND REMEMBERING

The word "memory" has occurred from time to time in previous chapters. What is the relationship between learning and memory? It would be an exaggeration to say that the two words are interchangeable in psychology, but their meanings in contemporary research undoubtedly overlap, both in respect to the kinds of performance that are regarded as providing evidence of learning and memory and in respect to the mental processes that are thought to underlie performance at learning and memory tasks. The term "memory" in psychology usually denotes an interest in the retention of knowledge, and it may imply an interest in processes of input, retrieval, and other activities that contribute to information being remembered. The use of the term "learning" in psychology normally implies some concern with change in people's behavior, or in their knowledge. The various phenomena denoted by the two words do not form entirely separate classes: no new ability can be acquired without the learner retaining information, and people's activities are frequently influenced by knowledge or skills retained in memory.

The mental processes required for a person to perform a typical learning task are not separate from or independent of the processes that underlie performance at memory tasks. In general, acquistion phenomena are emphasized in research into learning, and retention processes are studied in research into memory. However, any actual task of either learning or memory depends upon the individual also performing a number of additional activities, such as perceiving and transforming information from the environment, attending, and retrieving knowledge that has been retained in memory.

The ability to retain information in memory also contributes to a person's competence at tasks of comprehension, reasoning, and thinking. The difficulty of tasks that necessitate these functions is often related to the weight of the memory demands imposed. Furthermore, individual differences in people's performance at such tasks are related to differences between people in their capacity to retain information. A practical implication of these observations is that if children and adults can be helped to retain information more effectively, considerable gains may follow in learning and in the other skills mentioned above.

How does a person's ability to remember contribute to performance at tasks that are not ostensibly ones of memory? Consider first the role of remembering in computation. Compare the following two mental arithmetic problems:

1. Multiply 22 × 22
2. Multiply 222 × 222

The second problem is a much harder exercise in mental arithmetic than the first, but the actual computational operations that are involved in the two problems are remarkably similar. Both 1 and 2 require the ability to multiply two times two, and both require digits to be added. The second problem does demand a greater number of digits to be multiplied, and doing so produces larger numbers. However, these sub-tasks are not very demanding, and they do not satisfactorily account for the greatly increased difficulty of 2 compared with 1. The real cause of difficulty with the second problem is that it is necessary to retain various combinations of numbers in temporary or "working" memory. People have a very limited capacity to keep quantities of items in mind. That this is a major limitation in performing the task is apparent when we ask how we might make the task of multiplying 222 × 222 easier. The answer, of course, is to find a way of easing the memory load, perhaps by using paper and pencil, to store externally the information which we find so difficult to retain in our heads while we are undertaking the necessary multiplication and addition operations.

Consider another task in which the memory requirement is central, although it may not be immediately apparent that this is the case. Trabasso (1977) introduces the following problem:

1. Edith is fairer than Suzanne.
2. Edith is darker than Lili.
3. Who is the darkest?

Trabasso notes that problems of this kind are generally considered to demand logical reasoning abilities, in particular the capacity to make inferences. However, it is equally possible to describe the task requirements in terms of the necessity to code and retain information. Trabasso notes that solution of the above problem depends upon the premises being represented mentally, in the form of some kind of ordered list. Doing so necessitates encoding, ordering, matching, and retrieval processes. Analysis of the task in terms of components such as these memory functions is probably the most fruitful means available at present for understanding the way in which humans actually perform a problem of this kind.

Once we start to consider what detailed functions need to be performed in these and in many other instances of learning and thinking, it becomes clear that the operations of memory are essential. Even the simplest kinds of comprehension depend upon effective retention of items in memory. "The man kicked the dog" would be a meaningless word sequence to a reader who was unable to retain information about the first words until he reached the final ones. The demands upon memory that are involved in comprehending a lengthy and complex sentence are considerable. Similarly, the operations of memory are crucial to learning, and an understanding of memory is necessary for an understanding of learning processes in humans.

The difficulty of placing "learning" and "memory" in clear perspective is increased by the fact that in psychological research the two terms are associated with different experimental traditions. As I have explained earlier, soon after Ebbinghaus' time the study of learning came to be dominated by the definitions, theories, methods, and assumptions of early behaviorist approaches to animal learning. As I have said earlier, it is now apparent that what appeared around 1920 to be the most promising approach to the study of animal learning and the best way to form an acceptably scientific discipline does not now seem to provide the most effective way to build a science of human learning. However, present-day approaches to learning in experimental psychology have not entirely shed the influences of the older tradition, which emphasized behavior and its acquisition. It was partly for this reason that when, in the 1950s and onwards, a number of psychologists became interested in certain aspects of learning, particularly in the retention and retrieval of knowledge and the manner in which it is represented in a learner's cognitive system, they regarded their efforts as being within the research field of human memory rather than learning.

If there can be said to exist a tradition of human memory research, it is one in which, starting with Bartlett's investigations, individual scientists have been encouraged to make inferences about possible mechanisms underlying human performance at the experimental tasks. In most research into memory there is an implicit conceptualization of human learners as individuals who encode, process, and make active use of information rather than simply acquiring it. It is also accepted that the knowledge a person generates or retains makes at least as large a contribution to learning and cognition as does the information that the person is currently receiving from the external environment via the sensory receptors.

ATTRIBUTES OF HUMAN MEMORY

In this chapter we shall describe some memory research that helps us to understand how the human learner is able to retain large amounts of highly organized knowledge.

During the years following World War II, a large number of ideas and methods generated by research in diverse areas, including information theory, computer processing, and what has become known as "artificial intelligence"; have been taken up by psychologists, resulting in considerable advances in our understanding of human cognition.

In the 1950s and 1960s the separate traditions of research into learning and memory produced a curious situation in which investigators studying "memory" and reseachers investigating "verbal learning" separately designed experiments that used similar materials to solve what in many respects were similar problems, but they had markedly different terminologies and explanatory theories to describe their aims and to explain the implications of their findings. On the whole, the verbal learning researchers stayed within the behaviorist tradition. They were strongly associationist, and their explanations invoked concepts such as "interference" between responses, "excitation," "inhibition," and "unlearning". These are broadly recognizable to students familar with psychological research into animal behavior. The verbal learning approach, which was also indebted to Ebbinghaus' early efforts to apply experimental methods to the investigation of human abilities, produced some real achievements, including the findings about word associability and meaningfulness that were described in the previous chapter. Memory researchers have been more eclectic, and being less tied to any particular approach or source of inspiration, they have felt free to use ideas arising from developments outside psychology. Memory researchers have introduced hypothetical systems that attempt to explain the information-processing mechanisms of humans.

Since around 1960, the distinctions between the "memory" and the "verbal learning" approaches have become increasingly blurred. So far as the acquisition and retention of human knowledge is concerned, the information-processing accounts encountered in human memory research have tended to dominate the earlier verbal learning tradition.

We shall now consider some of the memory research that has a bearing upon the understanding of human learning. In order to think, to reason, to learn or to remember, or to recognize things as being meaningful or familiar, it is essential to store large quantities of information. To give a simple illustration, young children cannot recognize their mother until they can retain information concerning her attributes. Only then will they be in a position to check that what they perceive matches something in their own memory. It is also necessary to retain certain information temporarily. The brain has stores or "registers" where data can be briefly retained while mental operations are performed on it.

If the sole task of a human memory was to store information, the only limitation upon memory would be in the amount of storage capacity available, just as the number of shirts that can be kept in a drawer is limited only by the size of the drawer. If I want to store more shirts I can get a larger drawer, or increase the number of drawers available. But certain difficulties can arise. What if I were to throw all my belongings into one vast drawer? The items would undoubtedly all be stored there but problems would be encountered when I needed to use a particular item, in which event it might take an unreasonably long time to locate it. A satisfactory storage system is one which does not simply retain the materials in it, but also permits them to be easily located and retrieved whenever they are required (Howe, 1970a). If the store contains a very large number of different items, insuring speedy access to each of them is usually achieved by organizing the items in some manner. This is true irrespective of the particular form of the stored items, be they shirts, files on hospital patients, munitions, items of information in a computer memory, library books, or the goods in a grocery store. Thus, the rate at which items can be removed from a store, that is the "output" of items, may be limited. The rate of retrieval depends not only upon storage capacity but also upon the manner in which the stored items are organized.

However, stored items cannot become organized unless the system possesses some capacity for organization, as any storekeeper, quartermaster, librarian, or computer programmer knows. Libraries, for instance, achieve the necessary organization by a process of cataloguing. Once catalogued, a book can be put into its proper place, according to the rules of the cataloguing system. By referring to the catalogue, a book can be located on demand without borrowers having to look at all the books in the library until they find the one they are searching for. However, the process of cataloguing books takes time, and it places a limit on the number of books that can be absorbed into the library store within a fixed period of time. Human memory is not entirely dissimilar in this respect; the number of items that can be placed in storage in a manner which is appropriately organized to enable quick access to them is by no means unlimited.

It quickly becomes apparent that a retention system having some of the characteristics of a human memory must include careful provision for input and output requirements, and not just storage alone. Comparison with other storage systems suggests further complications. For example, the books in a library are not all organized in exactly the same manner. Fiction is ordered according to the alphabetic position of the author's name, whereas nonfiction books are classified on the basis of their subject matter. There is nothing inevitable about this; fiction might conceivably be organized by subject matter and nonfiction books according to the author's name. The detailed procedures for cataloguing books are chosen so as to be optimally convenient for people who use the library. One characteristic that many libraries share with human memories is that some materials need to be permanently stored in a readily accessible form, but others require only temporary storage. A librarian who has limited cataloguing (input) resources might well decide to forego careful cataloguing of some of those items that do not need to be retained for long, for example, daily newspapers. For these, the librarian might choose to adopt a form of processing that is less costly or time consuming than the full procedure used for separately cataloguing nonfiction books in the library. Human memory might make a similar distinction. Imagine that someone looks up a telephone number and needs to retain it in memory just long enough to be able to dial the number or write it down. Assuming that the memory capacity for organizing new information in a way that makes it permanently available is strictly limited, it might be a wasteful use of the memory system to give information that is required for only a few seconds exactly the same processing as information that requires permanent retention. If would be more economical to have a way of temporarily storing some materials, without necessitating the involvement of extensive processing capacity. In this way, the restricted capacity available for processing new information can be reserved for those materials that definitely require it. Many researchers have found it useful to distinguish between long-term memory and short-term memory. The contents of short-term memory roughly correspond to "what is being remembered" at a given time. They form a kind of "working memory" that stores information while it is being used in a mental task.

Experimental research into human memory has yielded a number of findings in support of this possibility. Considerable evidence indicates that not all information entering memory is retained in precisely the same way. For instance, consider the situation in which subjects listen to lists of letters or digits and then attempt to recall them. What happens if there are more items than the person can remember? One might suppose that, depending on the form taken by the underlying mechanisms, either the items presented toward the end of a list might disrupt retention of the earlier items, squeezing them out of a limited-capacity short-term store, or that the late items might fail to gain access to memory at all because it is already full. Alternatively, squeezing more and more materials into a memory system of fixed capacity might affect each item equally, compressing them all into a system designed to accommodate only a small number of items. In fact, none of these things occurs. Rather than the limitation on memory capacity affecting just the early items, or just the late items, or all the materials equally, it is the items in the middle of the list that suffer. This is shown in Figure 10.1, which illustrates the findings of an experiment by Jahnke (1963), in which the subject tried to recall lists of varying lengths. It is clear that there is an increasing tendency for the middle items of the longer lists to be recalled less accurately than the early and late items.

It is hard to say precisely how one can best explain the curves shown in Figure 10.1. A possible reason for the relatively accurate recall of the early items, compared with the others, is that opportunities for rehearsal might be greater with the early parts of a list, particularly if the chosen rehearsal strategy is one that always starts with the first item. As for the materials at the end of a list, which are also recalled more accurately than the mid-list items, it is possible that the high level of recall is related to the relatively brief amount of time during which they need to be stored, compared with items occurring earlier in the list.

The experimental evidence provides some support for these suggestions. For example, if recall is requested as soon as presentation of a list of items if completed, the items that occur at the beginning of a list are generally found to have become more highly consolidated in memory than the items that occurred later. Memory for the early items in a list is more resistant than that for later items to the disrupting effects of various activities (Howe, 1965). As for the items presented at the end of a list (P3 in Figure 10.2), if they are the ones that have to be recalled first (recall position 1 in Figure 10.2) they

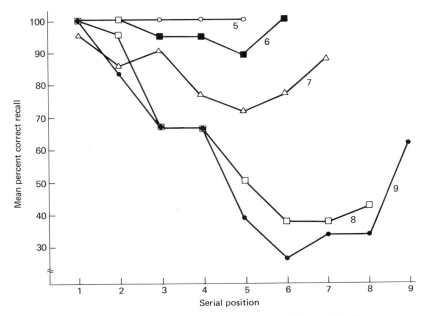

Figure 10.1 Serial position curves for consonant lists. The lines show how accuracy of recall varies as a function of the serial position of the individual consonants within lists. (Source: Adapted from Jahnke, J. C. "Serial position effects in immediate serial recall." *Journal of Verbal Learning and Verbal Behavior,* 1963, 2:284–287. Reprinted by permission of Academic Press, Inc.)

are recalled more accurately than the early list items, but if these late items are the last to be recalled (recall position 3 in Figure 10.2) they are the least accurately recalled. The great vulnerability of the late items in a list to the distraction of having to recall the other items indicates that the late items are initially retained in a form that, although accurate, is less consolidated than the storage of the early items. The conclusion that items occurring earlier in the list have become more consolidated in memory than the later ones is based on the finding that the accuracy with which early items (P1 in Figure 10.2) are recalled is not so greatly affected by whether they are the first (recall position 1) or last items (recall position 3) to be requested. In Figure 10.2. P1, P2, and P3 represent the first, second, and third 3-item groups of letters forming a 9-item list. Each group of 3 letters appeared for 3 seconds, the total time for a 9-item list being 9 seconds.

The results shown in Figure 10.2 indicate that by the time the presentation of a list has been completed, some of the early items

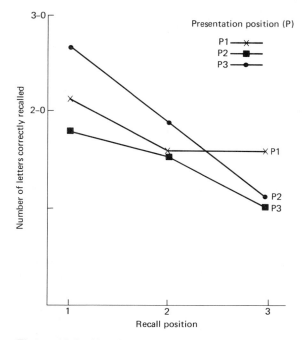

Figure 10.2   Number of letters recalled (out of 3) as a function of recall position, with presentation position as a parameter. (Source: Howe, M. J. A. "Intra-list differences in short-term memory." *Quarterly Journal of Experimental Psychology,* 1965, 17:338–342. Reprinted by permission of Academic Press, Inc.)

(P1) have been forgotten. However, when early items are the last items to be recalled, those of them that are still retained have become appreciably more consolidated in memory than the later items in the list (P3), and are more resistant to the distracting influence of having to recall other parts of the list. (The effects of this are shown by comparing recall of each group of items at recall positions 1 and 3.) The point to note is that whatever the precise explanation, differences do exist between the various items, the early ones being more highly consolidated than the ones in the final positions of a list, even within a list presented over a total period of only 9 seconds. This finding appears to support the view that items in memory are not all stored in precisely the same way.

MULTI-PROCESS MODELS OF MEMORY

Research into human memory has produced a large amount of experimental evidence, encouraging psychologists to advance theories concerning the operation of memory systems. Such theories can be depicted as flow diagrams that indicate how the various components of a memory system might work in combination. Figure 10.3 shows such a theory or "model" of the workings of human memory, in diagram form.

Figure 10.3 suggests that information received via the sensory receptors is first retained, very briefly, in a "peripheral" store that retains items for long enough to enable them to be more fully processed. The information in a peripheral store may be a coded representation of the physical characteristics of the material, not totally unlike magnetic tape storage of auditory information. A limitation of such a store is that one cannot locate its contents via their meaning. However, at the next stage in the model shown in Figure 10.3, the "short-term store," the material is retained in a more extensively processed form. In the terms of the library analogy, some "cataloguing" has occurred, making it easier for particular items to be retrieved from memory on demand. The time span for retention of materials in a peripheral store is under a second, but a short-term store may retain items for periods of up to around half a minute. In the view of some researchers, the time until an item is forgotten from short-term memory depends on the other demands that are placed upon the limited capacity of this subsystem of memory. The requirement to attend to new information may compete with short-term memory for a limited processing capacity that is "shared" to some extent between memory and attention. One difference that is

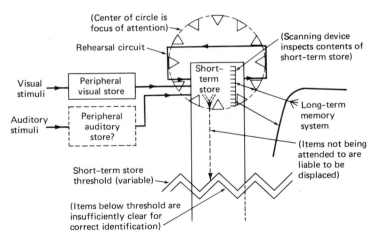

Figure 10.3 A diagrammatic model for retention of verbal materials in human memory. (Source: Howe, M. J. A. *Introduction to Human Memory*, 1970. Reprinted by permission of Harper & Row, Publishers.)

supposed to exist between the short-term memory and retention in the peripheral store is that while retention in the latter is automatic and involuntary, the individual can exert a degree of conscious control over the input of materials to short-term memory. By rehearsal, for example, items can be recirculated, thus delaying forgetting.

After entering the short-term store, information may be transferred to a more permanent memory system. The factors determining whether a particular item will be permanently retained or not in a long-term store have never been specified in detail, but it has been widely assumed that transfer depends upon active (but not necessarily conscious) processing by the individual concerned. Items in the short-term store that match or are related to materials already in long-term memory may be incorporated into a long-term system. The assumption is that materials in the long-term store are retained there on the basis of relatively abstract attributes related to their semantic features (that is, their meaning). This view is consistent with the finding that recall of word items is facilitated by presenting retrieval cues in the form of words that share a meaning with the to-be-recalled word. (For example, presenting the word *cabbage* may help a person retrieve the retained item *cauliflower.*)

Items that are temporarily retained in a short-term store, on the other hand, are not so extensively processed. Recalling them is less likely to be facilitated by providing materials that share the meaning of a to-be-remembered item. It is more likely to be influenced by materials that share their physical attributes. For instance, Conrad and Hull (1964) and Wickelgren (1965) observed that retention of items in short-term memory can be disrupted by presenting other materials that share some of their auditory or acoustic properties (as do *b* and *t, d, e,* or *c*). The discovery that a similar-sounding item can have a disruptive effect on retention of materials in short-term memory supports the view that items may be retained partly on the basis of auditory or acoustic attributes.

The findings of memory research demonstrate that remembering is not just a matter of storing information. Careful provision for input and retrieval of materials is essential, and evidence that items can be stored on the basis of any of a variety of different kinds of attributes, ranging from physical characteristics to semantic features, had made it necessary to postulate multi-process theories of human memory.

Those accounts of memory that take the form of flow diagrams describing the flow of information through a number of component parts, starting with input and ending with a long-term memory store, are not entirely satisfactory as literal descriptions of the operation of human memory. Such models do serve the useful function of making explicit the need for distinct forms of encoding in memory, but they have difficulty in accommodating some of the evidence about how people actually perform in real memory tasks. One source of difficulty lies in the fact that some kinds of data appear to gain immediate access to a permanent store as soon as they are perceived, and from the moment of their presentation they can be retrieved on the basis of meaningful attributes, rather than physical characteristics. Does this mean that such materials bypass both the peripheral store and the short-term system? This is not entirely clear. Another difficulty with models or theories that postulate the transmission of information along a succession of separate subsystems is there would be major problems in gaining access to stored information. For instance, it is not clear if something can be retained in more than one store at the same time.

If it cannot, it is hard to imagine a person knows in which store the item will be found. This and other difficulties have led some researchers to suggest that the notion of entirely separate stores should be abandoned.

Levels of Processing

An alternative account (Craik and Lockhart, 1972) allows for the fact that items can be stored in memory on the basis of different kinds of attributes, ranging from physical characteristics to complex abstractions, but does not consider it necessary for every remembered item to be transmitted through a sequence of different storage processes. Instead of postulating entirely separate stores, Craik and Lockhart prefer to assume only that there are different "levels of processing." Such an approach may not specify the detailed principles according to which a particular item becomes coded in a particular way, but it is accepted that the level of coding of a retained item depends as much upon the way in which the item is perceived and understood by the person involved as upon the structural characteristics or "hardware" of the memory system. As Kintsch (1977) observes, "Memory depends on the nature of the subject's perceptual and cognitive analyses of the stimulus, and the deeper and the more elaborate these analyses are, the better retention" (Kintsch, 1977, p. 229).

The findings of an experiment by Craik and Tulving (1975) illustrate the importance of processing levels. These authors asked their subjects different kinds of questions about words, which were subsequently displayed for one-fifth of a second each. One kind of question asked the subject to say whether or not the word was typed in capital letters. Other questions asked whether the word to be displayed rhymed with a given word. A third type of question asked if the word would fit into a given sentence. To answer this form of question correctly it was necessary to attend to the meaning of the briefly displayed word. After a series of items, recall and recognition tests were given. It was found that the probability of recalling an item for which the prior question had required attending to the meaning was roughly twice as high as the probability of recalling one of the words preceded by a different kind of question. Recognition scores for words that had been preceded by a sentence question (requiring the subject to process the meaning of the word) averaged over 80 percent, compared with only about 15 percent for an equivalent word when it had been preceded by a question asking whether it was in capital letters. Additional research, involving experimental controls for factors such as the time and the effort required in the different circumstances, have confirmed that a strong relationship exists between accuracy of retention and level of coding (Kintsch, 1977).

ORGANIZATION OF RETAINED INFORMATION

The organization of long-term memory is especially relevant to human learning. For the retention of knowledge, organizing and encoding processes are two sides of the same coin. The way in which people organize the items retained in their memory depends to a large extent upon what they know about the items. For example, a learner who knows the different attributes of the items in the following list could organize them in a number of ways.

APPLE
alligator
pear
PUMA

The words may be organized on the basis of:

1. Letter size—*APPLE PUMA* (and) *alligator pear*
2. Initial letter—*APPLE alligator* (and) *PUMA pear*
3. Semantic class—*APPLE pear* (and) *PUMA alligator*

An individual who possesses some but not all of these three kinds of knowledge about the items will be able to organize the words in a corresponding number of ways.

Research into memory has shown that recall of sequences containing unrelated items such as digits and letters can be increased by simply grouping them, without taking any account of the characteristics of the individual items. If a person who is given a list of ten random digits to remember mentally divides them into groups of three or four, recall is significantly enhanced (Oberly, 1928; Wickelgren, 1964). However, the effects of those forms of organization and grouping that do not take individual item attributes into account are strictly limited. The majority of studies of organization in learning and memory do consider the particular items, and typically involve items being grouped on the basis of characteristics they share or perceived relationships between them. An outcome of such grouping is to reduce the number of effectively separate list items that have to be retained in memory. People find it very difficult to retain a large number of entirely separate items. They often try to overcome this limitation by searching for relationships, associations, or shared attributes, on the basis of which the different items can be linked together. When they are attempting to remember something, individuals may follow a strategy of generating items from their long-term memory, checking to discover if any of the generated items match the ones they are trying to remember. Such a strategy may be effective because the individuals are thereby transforming their task from one of *recalling* the words to one of *recognizing* them. Recognition is usually easier than free recall. Thus in the following list:

table
horse
chair
cow
bull

if the items are perceived by the learner as being entirely unrelated, the recall requirement might be to:

1. recall *table*
2. recall *horse*
3. recall *chair*
4. recall *cow*
5. recall *bull*

However, if learners discern the shared relationships between some of the words, their recall strategy might be something like:

1. recall *table*
2. generate (from existing knowledge) items in same class: "chest," "sideboard," "chair"
3. recognize *chair*
4. recall *horse*
5. generate: "goat," "sheep," "cow," "bull"

6. recognize *cow*
7. recognize *bull*

In effect, because learners make use of existing knowledge in order to generate items that they subsequently recognize, the list ceases to be one of entirely separate items. Reducing the number of items that have to be separately retrieved makes the memory task considerably easier.

Simple Coding Strategies

Some forms of organization do literally reduce the number of items that have to be remembered. For example, in an experiment by S. Smith (reported by Miller, 1956), the experimenter presented lists of the binary digits *0* and *1*. For most people, the memory span for lists containing random orderings of these symbols is around nine items, only slightly more than the average memory span for lists that draw upon all nine digits. Smith trained subjects to group the digits in pairs and then recode them, denoting *00* as *0*, *01* as *1*, *10* as *2*, and *11* as *3*. By transforming the items in this manner the 18-digit series *101000100111001110* is reduced to a 9-item sequence, *220213032*, and the latter is considerably easier to remember. Very few people can recall the whole 18-item list following one presentation of it, but if someone quickly encodes the original 18-item sequence into a list of nine items, and when recall is required decodes the remembered 9-item list to obtain the original 18-item list again, the person may be able to reproduce the entire list correctly. Smith's subjects were trained to do just this. Some of them transformed each two-digit sequence in the original list into one item, in the manner described above. Others were trained to use similar but more complex schemes, in which groups of three, four, or even five of the original binary digits were encoded as one item. If sufficient practice was given for coding to be achieved speedily and without difficulty, subjects' recall scores were considerably increased when they followed a strategy of encoding the items in this way. Using himself as a subject, Smith managed to increase his own memory span for lists containing the digits *0* and *1* to as many as 40 items. This was achieved by recoding each group of five digits into a single unit. It thus became unnecessary to retain 40 separate items since the number to be remembered was reduced from 40 to eight, a figure that was within Smith's capacity for remembering items over short periods.

In everyday life people frequently encode materials, thereby reducing the number of separate items to be remembered. In those circumstances in which encoding is highly practiced it may take place automatically, without the individual making a deliberate decision to encode. Faced with the letter sequence M I C E for example, most adults immediately perceive one single word rather than four separate letters. However, a 4-year-old child who can recognize letters but cannot spell words will perceive M I C E as being four letters, and for that child learning the sequence would necessitate retaining four separate items. Older children who are beginning to learn to read may perceive four separate letters at first, but through a deliberate effort to spell the word they may be able to encode all four into a single word item. The point illustrated by the M I C E sequence is that the effective number of separate items contained in a body of information depends not only upon what is presented to the learners, but also upon the encoding and organizing activities that they undertake. Their ability to carry out such activities depends in turn upon the knowledge of the items and the mental skills they possess.

Chunking

Miller (1956) coined the term *chunk* to describe the unit of information that functions as a single item for the individual learner. A chunk is, essentially, one familiar item. In the sequence C M I E each letter forms a familiar item, or chunk. But if we reorder the letters to form M I C E, all four items together constitute a single chunk for anyone who can read English. Miller pointed out that learning and memory are limited by the number of chunks in verbal materials to a greater extent than they are by the actual amount of data that is carried in the materials. If lists containing different types of items, for instance, digits, letters, and words, are each presented at the rate of one item per second, the number of items that are remembered is not greatly affected by the kind of list item. This is despite the fact that each digit, which can be regarded as one of ten possible digits, carries less "information" than each letter, which is one of 26 possible items. That is to say, more is communicated by telling someone which item is present out of a possible 26 items (as with letters) than which one of a possible 10 items (in the case of digits) is present. In turn, a single letter carries much less information than a single word, since the number of possible words is much higher. Despite the large differences in the amount of information that is transmitted by digits, letters, and words, the number of items that can be correctly recalled in a short-term test is relatively constant: around seven or eight of whatever they are.

According to Miller, considerable learning goes into the formation of chunks, or familiar units. The memory span is restricted to a fixed number of chunks, but the amount of information that a person can remember can be increased by his forming larger and larger chunks. In other words, although we cannot increase the actual number of chunks remembered, we can increase their capacity. We do so by using our ability to encode and reorganize the materials presented to us, either deliberately, as in the experiments conducted by S. Smith, or automatically, when the materials are already well learned, as in the case in which four letters make the single word M I C E.

The process of learning to form increasingly large chunks is illustrated by Miller's description of what happens when a person learns the telegraphic Morse code. Initially, every *dit* and every *dah* forms a separate chunk. After some time, the learner gains the ability to organize groups of sounds into letters, and this makes it possible to deal with the sequence forming each letter as being a single chunk, thereby increasing the learner's capacity to remember and transmit the coded information. After further extended practice it becomes possible to organize the letter sequences as words and, later still, whole phrases begin to be perceived as single units. Thus, successively higher levels of organization are achieved and the individual is eventually able to encode and process the material in chunks that are much larger than the simple *dit* and *dah* units which initially functioned as chunks. It thus becomes possible to increase very considerably the length of the messages that can be remembered.

Organization into Categories

If a person is unable to combine a number of separate units into one unit, the individual may be able to increase retention by making use of any relationships, connections, or associations he can detect in the material. The earlier illustration, in which following recall of *horse* from a list of words, the individual was able to generate and recognize the associated items *cow* and *bull*, gives an indication of one way in which a learners might be able to use what they already know in order to help remember a number of items that share attributes or are associated to each other. Experimental findings show that people can undertake organizational functions that facilitate retention and retrieval of related word items. For example, Jenkins and Russell (1952) presented in random order a list of 28 words that had been taken from 24 pairs of highly associated words (for example, *table - chair*). After requesting subjects to recall the words, the experimenter examined the precise sequence in which items were recalled, and it emerged that the two words forming each of the original pairs were frequently recalled together, despite the random ordering of presentation. Jenkins, Mink and Russell (1958) observed that the greater the strength of the relationship between items in an associated word pair, the higher the number of words recalled when they were presented in random order, and not as pairs. In a similar experiment by Deese (1959), the author constructed word lists in which each item was an associate of a number of the other items in the list. He calculated the average frequency with which the different list items occurred as associates to other list items, and constructed 18 different lists, each containing 15 words, varying in the average inter-item associative strength. He then presented the lists to 48 subjects who had not participated in the previous stage of the experiment. He measured the number of words they recalled and calculated the correlation between the average number of words recalled from a particular list and the inter-item associative strength of that list. Deese found that there was a high positive correlation (r = + 0.88) between recall and associative strength. The accuracy of recall of a list was positively related to the extent that the different word items in a list tend to elicit each other.

These findings indicate that when people learn verbal materials, they use their existing knowledge about interword associations or relationships in order to organize the items. Experimental results indicate that the organization which people achieve is not based solely upon associations between single words, and can also involve groupings that are made on the basis of category membership or shared meanings. Bousfield (1953) presented to his subjects a list of 60 words, constructed from 15 words in each of four categories, *"animals" "names," "professions,"* and *"vegetables,"* but in random order. When the subjects were required to write down all the items they could recall, the recall sequences were found to contain clusters in which the items from each of the four categories appeared together. Words that frequently occur as a response to their category heading produced more clustering, and they were more likely to be recalled than words which occur more rarely as responses (Bousfield, Cohen, and Whitmarsh, 1958).

The above results indicate that, at some stage in the task, people use their knowledge of categories in order to organize verbal materials they are trying to learn. However, it is conceivable that the findings could have been produced by subjects' associations between single words. Since items in the same category tend to occur as associates of each other, it is not always easy to decide whether or not interword associations can be ruled out as an explanation of observed clustering of words into categories. A study by

Cofer (1965) was designed to separate the effects of word association and organization according to categories. Cofer presented lists that differed in both the frequency with which the word items occurred as associates to other items and in the extent to which items shared conceptual categories. For example, *bed* and *chair* are associatively related to one another and they also share membership in the same category, "furniture," whereas *bed* and *dream* are associatively related but do not share category membership. Cofer found that when the frequency of association between the items in different lists was equivalent, lists in which the items formed categories yielded more clustering by subjects than lists in which the items did not form categories. In short, categorization per se had an effect on clustering over and above the effects of word association. On the whole, categorization had a larger influence on clustering in those lists in which there was little associative overlap between the words than in lists in which the words occurred frequently as associates of each other.

INDIVIDUAL SCHEMES OF ORGANIZATION

The investigations described above demonstrate that when a verbal sequence contains words from a number of separate categories, people cluster the recalled words into the categories, and the more they cluster the items, the more they remember. Mandler (1968) has noted that in experiments of this kind it is only possible to detect those forms of organization that are provided by the experimenter. In real life, different people organize and process identical materials in highly idiosyncratic ways, although there is some correspondence between individuals, particularly when organization takes the form of grouping items into well-known categories. Mandler illustrates the importance of individual differences in organizing by describing an imaginary person who forms a list of the names of some people he knows. His own organization of the list rests on a division of the names into blood relations, professional acquaintances, and social acquaintances. If he is asked to recall the list he will probably cluster the names according to these three categories. However, if he were to show the same list to a stranger, and then ask him to recall the names, the new person would not cluster the items into the original three categories. The absence of such clustering would not necessarily indicate a lack of any organization. Another person might classify the items in a similar but not identical manner. This might happen, for instance, if the first person's wife was asked to inspect the list.

Mandler and Pearlstone (1966) conducted a study that demonstrates the importance of individual patterns of organization. Half of the subjects received a pile of 52 cards, on each of which there was a single noun. They were told to sort the nouns into categories, on the basis of any system of grouping they liked. The only restriction was that the 52 words had to be divided into at least two groups and not more than seven groups. After sorting the cards in this manner, the subjects returned them and they were then given another set of the identical word cards, but in a different random order. The subjects were told to group these as well, using the identical categories they had chosen for the first pack, so far as these could be remembered. This procedure was repeated for a number of sortings of the cards, until each person achieved two identical groupings of the 52 words into the same categories on two successive trials. Next, each of the other subjects was given the cards as categorized by one of the subjects in the first group. The task was identical; to sort the packs of word cards on successive trials until they had achieved identical categorizations with two successive sets of cards. The only difference between the two groups of subjects was that subjects in the second group started with the words as categorized by another person while subjects in the first group commenced by organizing the cards according to their own choice. The effect of this difference was considerable; subjects who started by choosing their own organization of the cards achieved the criterion performance of two identical orderings on successive trials in half as many trials as subjects in the second group. Furthermore, the subjects who were able to organize the cards in the manner they preferred achieved the same levels of retention, as measured by recall scores, after considerably less exposure to the words.

Number of Categories

Up to a point, people will recall more items if they are encouraged to group the items into a large number of categories. Mandler (1968) found that when people organized word lists into between two and seven categories, there was a very high correlation ($r = +0.95$) between accuracy of recall and the number of categories chosen. Thus, for up to seven categories, the higher the number, the greater the amount of information that is remembered. However, when unlimited numbers of categories were allowed, Mandler observed no substantial improvement if the number of categories exceeded seven.

Memory for categorized words depends not only on the number of categories but also upon the number of items per category. Mandler found that recall declined when the number of items in each category exceeded about five. He suggested that retention of lengthy categorized lists could be improved by further dividing the categories into subcategories, thus forming a multi-level, hierarchical pattern of organization. Some support for his suggestion is given by the findings of a study by Cohen and Bousfield (1956) in which lists containing four categories of words, each further divided into two subcategories of five items each, were recalled more accurately than lists containing either four categories with ten items per category or eight categories containing five words each. Research by Bower, Clark, Lesgold, and Winzenz (1969) provided further evidence of the value of hierarchical organization of word lists, in which items were categorized at a number of separate levels. They presented words organized into conceptual categories, Figure 10.4 being typical of their hierarchically organized arrays.

All the words in Figure 10.4 are minerals, either metals or stones, and they are further subdivided into rare, common, and alloy metals, and precious and masonry stones. In a number of experiments Bower and his colleagues found that presenting items in this way led to higher levels of retention than presenting the same words for an equivalent amount of time in random order or organized into simple categories. In one of their experiments, recall following one presentation of 112 words averaged 73 words for items in hierarchical arrangements, compared with 21 words recalled, on average, when the items were in a random order. By the second trial, most of the subjects for whom the words were hierarchically organized could remember all 112 of the words, but at a corresponding stage in the experiment subjects given random ar-

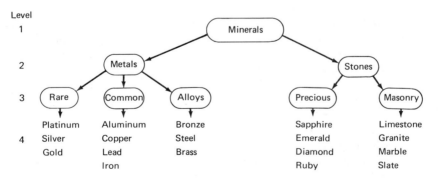

Figure 10.4   A conceptual hierarchy for mineral words. (Source: Bower, G. H., Clark M. C., Lesgold A. M., and Winzenz D., "Hierarchical schemes in recall of categorized word lists." *Journal of Verbal Learning and Verbal Behavior,* 1969, 8:323–343. Reprinted by permission of Academic Press, Inc.)

rangements of the same words remembered less than 40 percent of them. Bower, Clark, Lesgold, and Winzenz suggested that the main value of hierarchical organization is to give people rules that can be used for a retrieval plan, enabling learners to gain access to the correct items when recall is requested.

SUBJECTIVE ORGANIZATION

Most of the research into organization that has been described in the previous section involved word items that were carefully selected by the experimenter, even if the subject was allowed to decide how to organize them. In everyday life learners often organize verbal materials in circumstances in which no provision at all has been made for grouping or categorization. An approach developed by Tulving (1962) makes it possible to observe and measure the manner in which individual learners impose their own kinds of organization upon word materials that have been selected at random. Tulving's procedure was to present a list of 16 words, which the subject attempted to recall. Then the words were presented again, in an entirely different random order, and once more each subject attempted recall. This procedure was repeated on a number of separate trials, and subsequently the experimenter examined each subject's successive recall attempts, noting in particular the order in which different items occurred. Tulving noticed that although the order in which the 16 words were presented changed completely from each trial to the next, the order in which the items were *recalled* was relatively constant. Items that were reported by a subject in adjacent positions on one recall trial tended to be adjacent to each other in the same subject's next attempt at recall on the following trial. The subjects were clearly imposing some consistency on the order of the recall of the items, despite the constantly changing order of presentation. Tulving applied the term *subjective organization* to denote the process underlying the observed consistency of recall order. The fact that items are recalled together on successive recall attempts suggests that the items have been related together by the subject in some kind of organizational scheme. They are processed and retrieved in relation to each other, forming something like a single unit or chunk.

Tulving's trial-by-trial analysis demonstrates that through a process of subjective organization, items are clustered together by human learners in a manner that is similar to that observed by Bousfield (1953), even without any organizational system or categorization being provided. Tulving found that people differ in the degree to which they subjectively organize word lists. Subjective organization (SO) was measured by calculating the number of adjacent items in one of a subject's attempts at recall that were also adjacent on the next recall attempt. Tulving noted that for each person, as recall increased from trial to trial, so did the degree of subjective organization, and accuracy of recall and degree of SO were highly correlated. In addition, Earhard (1967a) observed that fast learners subjectively organize materials more than slow learners.

What is the Function of Subjective Organization?

Tulving's demonstration that degree of SO is related to the accuracy of recall suggests that organization is an actual cause of increased learning, but it does not prove that is so. It appears likely that SO makes a contribution to the increased accuracy of recall, possibly by reducing the number of effectively separate items to be retained. However, it is also conceivable that SO is simply a side-effect, which just happens to accompany improved performance, and is not a cause of improvement. Further experiments were designed to discover the exact functions of SO in human learning and memory.

A possible cause of the observed relationship between recall accuracy and SO is that both increasing SO and increasingly accurate recall are outcomes of repeated presentations of the materials, repetition being the important causal factor. This possibility can be tested by performing an experiment in which repetition is not accompanied by increasing SO. If repetition is the key factor, it would lead to increased learning, irrespective of the amount of SO. In an experiment by Tulving (1966), the effects of repetition were tested under conditions that minimized the occurrence of SO. The task for each subject was to learn a list of 22 words. The list was presented 12 times, and following each presentation subjects attempted to remember the list items. As one might expect, recall improved from trial to trial. Prior to this part of the study, half of the subjects had been exposed to the same 22 words on six additional trials. These subjects received, in total, 18 presentations of the words, compared with the 12 presentations for the other subjects. However, on the first six presentations of the words to the subjects who saw them 18 times in all, each word had been presented as part of a word-letter pair, which the subjects had to pronounce aloud. Because of the different structuring of the word lists in the first six presentations, any organization that was undertaken by subjects during these trials was incompatible with the SO that occurred during the subsequent 12 trials.

If repetition was the dominant cause of learning, one would

expect that the subjects who received 18 presentations would learn more words than the other subjects, who had only 12 trials. However, the people who had the extra presentations were not able to undertake a greater amount of task-appropriate SO than the other subjects. Therefore, if SO is a cause of learning, and not just a side-effect of repetition, the performance of those people who received 18 presentations would be little or no better than that of subjects who had only 12 presentations. The result of the experiment was that the two groups of subjects did not differ significantly in amount of learning, despite the difference in number of presentations. This finding clearly supports the view that SO does have an influence on learning. Repetition is normally associated with increased learning, partly because it provides opportunities for increased organization by learners, but repetition in circumstances where appropriate SO is prevented appears to have little effect. This conclusion receives further support from the findings of an additional experiment by Tulving. On this occasion, subjects first learned a list of nine words, and they were then required to learn another list consisting of either 18 new words or nine new words and nine of the same word items that had previously been learned. As Figure 10.5 indicates, on the first attempts to learn the 18-item lists those people who had already learned nine of the words recalled more items than the other subjects. However, in the long run, the subjects who received 18 new words learned them more quickly. Tulving claims that this finding shows that the form of SO imposed by subjects as they learned the original list was not appropriate for learning the items in the context of the longer lists that followed.

Further evidence that is consistent with the view that organization imposed by individual learners leads to improved performance in learning tasks is provided by studies which have compared the size and number of ungrouped items in materials recalled by subjects. Tulving found that from one trial to the next, the number of items processed separately (as indicated by measures of the consistency of word order in recall attempts) stays fairly constant, but that the size of such items (which Tulving calls "S-units" and are similar to Miller's "chunks") increases.

However, the view that SO is a major cause of learning has not gone unchallenged. Some writers have suggested that the relatively poor performance of subjects who learn some items and then have to transfer what they have acquired to a different task may be due to causes other than the inappropriateness of the SO that occurs in the first stage. Factors that might cause difficulty in such "part-to-whole

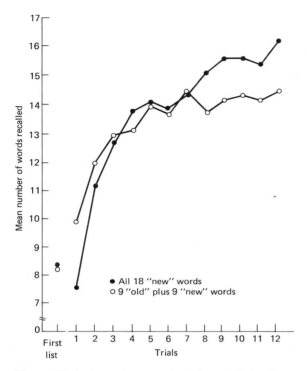

Figure 10.5   Learning rate for 18-word lists. (Source: Tulving, E. "Subjective organization and effects of repetition in multitrial free-recall learning." *Journal of Verbal Learning and Verbal Behavior,* 1966, 5:193–197. Reprinted by permission of Academic Press, Inc.)

transfer" situations include the tendency of subjects to devote a disproportionate amount of time to the new items in the final task (Roberts, 1969) and their suspicion that items recognized from the original list are intrusions rather than items which also form part of the new list (Slamecka, Moore, and Carey, 1972). Also, findings by Wood and Clark (1969) and Novinski (1972) indicate that when subjects are told in advance that the words learned in the first stage of the task are to be used again on the second stage, the gap between their performance and that of individuals who can use the same pattern of SO throughout both stages is reduced or eliminated. Nevertheless while these findings open the possibility that repetition *per se* may be more effective than Tulving's findings appear to indicate, there is little doubt that SO makes a contribution to human learning.

RETRIEVAL

Having established that verbal materials on which the learner has been able to impose some organization (with or without the aid of the experimenter) are more easily learned than unstructured materials, a number of investigators have speculated about the exact point within tasks of learning and memory at which organization makes an impact. Organization might contribute to the storage and retention of items or it might facilitate retrieval of the items at the time they are recalled. These alternatives are not entirely distinct, since retention and retrieval are closely intertwined. To return to our library analogy, an inevitable outcome of reorganizing the books stored would be to affect the way in which a library user has to proceed in order to locate them. The situation in human memory is not entirely different. As any librarian knows, there are a number of ways of organizing knowledge, and the organizing of information within human mental structures involves various kinds of organization which differ appreciably between individuals. There are also large cultural differences, and a search for any one way in which the human brain organizes information is a lost cause.

The organization that is necessary for efficient learning of verbal materials cannot take place in the absence of appropriate forms of encoding. Learners retain the meaningful attributes of verbal materials (Bellezza, Richards and Geiselman, 1976), and draw upon semantic knowledge (that is, knowledge about meanings) in order to encode items (Waters and Waters, 1976). Young children may be hindered by their lack of knowledge about the semantic attributes of word materials (Perlmutter and Myers, 1976).

When people try to remember information, they may follow a retrieval plan. Broadly speaking, retrieval plans are ways of generating cues that will help the individual to gain access to items that are currently stored in memory. The common finding that when list items are remembered, the order of recall shows clustering of the items into categories indicates that some kind of retrieval scheme exists. Each word that is recalled provides a cue for retrieving other words in the same group or category. Recall schemes typically depend upon the learner being able to remember items that serve as cues for locating other words to be remembered. Effective cues may be provided by the first word or the first letter of a sequence, and anyone who has had to learn poetry by rote will appreciate that if the first word in a line can be recalled, the battle is half won. M. Earhard (1967b) found that one effective learning strategy was to organize word lists alphabetically, so that each successive letter served as a retrieval cue for the word it began.

Most forms of organization require the learner to be able (on the basis of existing knowledge) to discern connections or relationships between items. Word associations provide one kind of connection, and if associated words are being retained, an effective retrieval strategy may be to emit the associates of a word that can be recalled and recognize those of them that match items in memory. Alternatively, a retrieval strategy might be conducted by searching through items linked by their possessing a shared meaning, or semantic attributes. Word items may be located in an individual's permanent store of knowledge according to their semantic attributes. For example, a *cow* has attributes of

> being an animal
> being a mammal
> being domesticated
> having four legs
> producing milk,
> and so on.

Similarly, a *lion*

> is an animal
> is a mammal
> has four legs
> is fierce,
> and so on.

The knowledge that is possessed about the different semantic attributes of a particular item depends on the individual. In general, an adult will possess a fuller list than a young child of the semantic attributes that define, say, *cow*.

THE REPRESENTATION OF KNOWLEDGE IN SEMANTIC MEMORY

If word concepts are located in memory on the basis of their semantic attributes, any two items that share a number of semantic attributes (as do *horse* and *donkey*, for example) will be in some respect "closer" to each other in the individual's knowledge structure than two items that share no meaningful attributes (for example, *table* and *donkey*). Assuming that the "closeness" of items as they are represented in a person's memory influences the ease of progressing from one to the other during retrieval, a plan that starts with a one-word item and searches for other items linked to it will be an effective one.

Developmental Changes in Semantic Memory

The details of any account of the manner in which items are related to one another within a person's body of knowledge must be highly speculative at this stage. However, it is clear that organization of material in long-term memory makes use of their semantic properties. The findings of an investigation by Ceci showed that when children are taught about previously unfamiliar attributes of words, they make use of the newly learned attributes in order to group words that are presented in a list of items. As a result, these children recall the words more accurately than other subjects who have spent an equal amount of time becoming familiar with the same words, but have not been taught about their semantic attributes.

Stephen Ceci (Howe, 1976) showed pictures of animals to children aged 3 and 4 years, and he explained to them that the birth of each animal occurred in one of three different ways. The characteristics of the three different natal classes (placental, monotreme, and marsupial) were carefully explained to the children, using a set of drawings. Other children of similar age, who formed a control group, spent an equal amount of time with the experimenter, looking at pictures of the same animals and discussing them, but the experimenter did not describe to them the semantic attribute of means of birth in each animal. In a later session the children were shown nine of the original pictures again, and after a ten-minute period during which there was a distracting task, they were asked to recall the animals they had recently seen. At this stage it was found that the children to whom the semantic attribute of natal class had been explained remembered substantially more items than the other children. Furthermore, when the order of the words recalled was examined, it was found that children in the first group showed almost total clustering into groups defined by the different natal classes. No equivalent semantic grouping was observed in the recall sequences produced by the other children. In short, the children who had learned about semantic features of words spontaneously categorized the items on the basis of this knowledge, without needing any instructions to do so, and categorizing items in this way increased the accuracy of recall.

Experiments that have been designed to compare the effects of different retrieval activities provide information about the ways in which a person uses existing knowledge to help remember lists of words. Research by Tulving and others (Tulving and Pearlstone, 1966; Tulving and Osler, 1968; Tulving and Thomson, 1973; Tulving, 1974) has shown that if a word is presented to a subject together with an associated word, and a new word that is also an associate of the original word is presented at the time of recall, the new word will not always facilitate recall of the original item. This is despite the fact that the new word would appear to provide a cue for retrieving the original item. Instead, there is a degree of what Tulving terms *encoding specificity*. The specific encoding operations that take place when the item to be remembered is first presented determine whether a particular cue that is provided at the time of recall will be effective or not. Only if the meaning that is coded when the original word and the accompanying item are presented is the same as a meaning of the new word that is provided as a retrieval cue, will the latter help a subject to recall the correct item. Thus, if the original word to be remembered, *BALL* was accompanied by *dance*, subsequent presentation of the *bat* as a retrieval cue would be ineffective. Although *bat* is semantically related to *BALL* it does not elicit the particular meaning inherent in the *dance-BALL* pair that was originally presented.

The encoding of word pairs is sufficiently specific to prevent many words that are meaningfully related to an item that is being retained in memory from functioning as effective retrieval cues. However, a word presented at the time of recall may aid recall even though it is not the same word as the one paired with the to-be-remembered item at the time of presentation, so long as the same meaning is evoked. A word will be effective as a retrieval cue if it shares a meaning with that contained in the memory trace that was initially stored. In the above instance, words such as *dress* or *music*, which are not only semantically related in meaning to *BALL* but also semantically linked to the meaning of the *dance BALL* input pair, would be more likely to facilitate retrieval of the correct item. Light and Carter-Sobell (1970) presented lists containing adjective-noun pairs, such as *strawberry-JAM*. If a different adjective was subsequently provided that suggested the same meaning or interpretation of the noun (for example, *cherry*), recognition was appreciably more accurate than when an adjective related to *JAM* but indicating a different meaning of it (for example, *traffic*) was used. At it happens, not only do many words have a number of possible meanings, but word pairs often have more than one alternative semantic interpretation (Baddeley, 1976). Barclay, Bransford, Franks, McCarrell, and Nitsch (1974) have shown that whether or not a given stimulus word will facilitate recall of a particular item in memory depends not so much on the cue word and the to-be-remembered item having identical dictionary definitions as on their sharing the semantic interpretation placed upon them by the particular learner. It is how the individual codes and interprets the items that is important.

One way to assess the effectiveness of a retrieval plan is to measure the time taken to retrieve an item. Meyer and Schvaneveldt (1975) used reaction time measures in a study requiring subjects to judge whether letter sequences were actual words or not. After seeing two related words, a third item had to be judged. On some occasions the third item was a word that had a meaning which coincided with an interpretation of the pair comprising the first two words, as in the two sequences below:

save   bank   money
day   date   time

In other sequences the first and second words were meaningfully related, and the third word was related to the second word. However, the meanings of the pairs formed by words one and two and words two and three were different, as in the following sequences:

river   bank   money
fig   date   money

When the third word was related to the second word but linked to it via a meaning that was different to the one implicit in the pair comprising words one and two, not only was the average reaction time (558 milliseconds) longer than when the meanings of the two pairs were compatible (505 milliseconds), but it was longer than when the third word was quite unrelated to the other two (551 milliseconds). This finding indicates that in inappropriate word retrieval strategy elicited by the first two words actually makes identification of the third word more difficult than it would have been in the absence of the prior words.

The encoding specificity effect observed by Tulving can be used as the basis of a technique for providing information about relationships between people's knowledge and their ability to remember things. Remembering is often regarded as being independent of existing knowledge, but the findings of recent research indicate that remembering and knowing are highly dependent upon each other. Two experiments by Ceci and Howe (1978a) were undertaken to discover whether differences in the knowledge possessed by children of different ages contribute to the developmental differences in memory test performance that are demonstrated by the superior recall of older than younger children at a variety of memory tasks. If young children semantically encode word items they perceive, one would expect that they would be as susceptible as adults to the compatibility of meanings evoked by the input pair comprising a word to be remembered and a related word item on the one hand, and between the word provided as a recall cue and the to-be-remembered word, on the other hand. If the input pair is

money   BANK

and the output cue is

saving

the latter word evokes a meaning that is compatible to that of the previous pair.

Therefore, it will serve as an effective retrieval cue for the correct word, *BANK*. However, if the input pair is

pay   BILL

and the output cue is

bird

⋅the word *bird* does not evoke any meaning that is compatible with that of the original pair, and therefore the probability of *BILL* being recalled is low.

If a young child knows the semantic relationship between a to-be-remembered word and its input cue, and encodes the to-be-remembered item on the basis of this knowledge, recall in the presence of an incompatible output cue will be lower than when a compatible cue is supplied, as is the case with adults. But in some instances, a young child will not know about the meaningful relationship (for adults) between a particular to-be-remembered word and its input cue. For example, Ceci and Howe's child subjects did not possess knowledge of the shared meaning in pairs such as *ankle-CALF, man-RAKE* and *quick-RASH*. With input pairs like these, where the child lacks knowledge about their semantic relationships, retrieval cues that are incompatible with the meanings of the original input cues would not be expected to depress recall. Thus, although the word *cow* elicits a meaning that is incompatible with any meaning retained by adults who were given the input pair *ankle-CALF*, it does not actually function as an incompatible cue for the young child. Hence the children's very absence of knowledge, which prevents them from discerning that input and output cue pairings are not compatible, may lead to them recalling *more* items than adults on some occasions.

The main findings of the investigation by Ceci and Howe (1978*a*) are shown in Figure 10.6. As can be seen in the upper curve, the young children recalled just as many items as the older children when they possessed the semantic knowledge (+ KN) necessary for encoding word pairs in terms of their shared meanings, and when the meanings of the pairs containing the to-be-

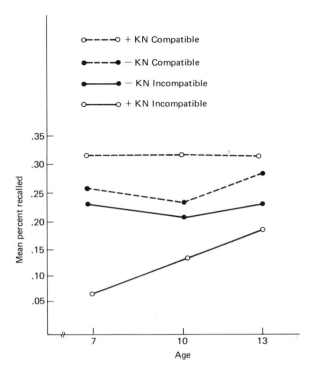

Figure 10.6   Recall as a function of compatibility (compatible, incompatible) of input and output encodings, and subjects' knowledge (*KN*) of them. (Source: Ceci, S. J., and Howe, M. J. A. "Semantic knowledge as a determinant of developmental differences in recall." *Journal of Experimental Child Psychology,* 1978, 26:230–245. Reprinted by permission of Academic Press, Inc.)

remembered word, and the accompanying word, and the retrieval cue and the to-be-remembered word, were similar or compatible. Similar findings have been obtained by Geis and Hall (1976). Thus, when young children possess appropriate knowledge to enable them to encode items semantically, they may retain as many items as older children. Some age-related differences in children's ability to remember are largely due to the greater amounts of appropriate knowledge possessed by older people. When care is taken to insure that even the youngest subjects do possess the knowledge that is essential for the test item to be meaningfully encoded, age differences disappear, although younger children may require more time than older people to encode word items and to recognize them. (Chi, 1977).

Chi (1978) found that 10-year-old children who were keen chess players could recall the positions of chess pieces more accurately than adults who had limited knowledge of the game. The sheer degree of knowledge about chess had a large influence upon recall. Brown (1975) draws attention to the fact that skilled adult chess players can remember the locations of about 24 pieces (in legitimate positions), whereas unskilled amateur players can only remember around ten positions. The value of having extensive knowledge about items one is trying to remember is further demonstrated in Hunter's (1962; 1977) descriptions of a mathematician, Professor A. Aitken, who possessed a remarkable ability to remember numerical symbols. He could perform a variety of calculating feats, for instance, recalling the value of *pi* to one thousand decimal places. His success at such feats was largely due to his extensive knowledge about the items he was remembering, which reduced effort necessary for calculation. Thus, on hearing the sequence *1961*, Aitken immediately recognized it as being the product of 34×53, and the sum of either $42^2 + 5^2$ or $40^2 + 19^2$, rather than a random sequence of unconnected digits.

Flexibility of Retrieval Plans

In the study by Ceci and Howe (1978a), the only condition in which older children performed appreciably better than younger children was the one (+KN Incompatible in Figure 10.6) in which (a) all children did possess the semantic knowledge necessary for meaningfully processing the word pairs, but (b) the input and output cues evoked incompatible meanings, as in the instance in which input (presentation) and output (retrieval) pairs were, respectively, *pay-BILL* and *BILL-bird*. A possible explanation of the age difference in this condition is that when faced with a situation in which an incompatible output cue initiates a search process that fails to locate the to-be-remembered word (*BILL*), older children demonstrate greater resourcefulness and flexibility in redirecting their search for the correct word. Worden (1976) has shown that older subjects are often more successful than younger children at searching for and retrieving items they have retained in memory. Ceci and Howe (1978b) performed a further experiment to investigate age differences in the manner in which subjects retrieve information stored in memory. Consider the following words:

stagecoach
buffalo
cowboy

rickshaw
ox
mandarin
land-rover
camel
belly-dancer

Inspection of the list reveals that the words can be categorized in either of two ways. First they form a number of separate taxonomic classes: "travel" (*stagecoach, rickshaw, land-rover*), "animals" (*buffalo, ox, camel*), and "people" (*cowboy, mandarin, belly-dancer*). Alternatively the words can be categorized according to a number of different themes: "the Wild West" (*stagecoach, buffalo, cowboy*); "the Orient" (*rickshaw, ox, mandarin*); and "the Desert" (*land-rover, camel, belly-dancer*). Suppose that some people have attempted to learn word lists of this kind and they understand both the taxonomic and thematic forms of classification. When they try to recall a list of such items from memory, they might adopt a strategy of relying exclusively on just one of the two alternative forms of classification, to provide cues to facilitate retrieval of the words. Thus, they might think of the category "people," and remember all the items in that category, and then "animals" and "travel," without switching from the taxonomic mode of classification to the thematic classification. Others might rely exclusively on the thematic organization of the words, using the thematic category headings as retrieval cues.

Alternatively, people might be willing to switch between the two bases of categorization whenever they found that they could not recall any more words from a particular thematic or taxonomic category. Having exhausted the words they can recall from the categories "travel," "animals," and "people," they might try using the thematic groups ("the Wild West," etc.) as a basis for cuing retrieval of further words that they have retained in memory but have not yet been able to recall. It would be reasonable to expect that this more flexible strategy, involving switching between the two alternative bases of classification as well as between the different groups of words, would yield higher levels of recall. It provides the learner with additional retrieval cues to help recall items when no more words can be elicited by one classificatory system. We might also expect that older children will be more flexible than younger children. This follows partly as a result of greater knowledgeability and partly, perhaps, because of the difficulties which (as Piaget and others have noticed) young children experience in attending to more than one task dimension at the same time.

Ceci and Howe suggested that if children of different ages were given lists like the one shown above, older subjects would adopt more flexible retrieval strategies, and their recall protocols would demonstrate a greater amount of switching between the two bases of classification. They also predicted that subjects who switch between classifications in retrieval would recall more words than subjects who do not make switches. The results confirmed both of these predictions. When subjects retrieved the words at the time of recall, 10-year-olds switched between the two modes more than twice as often as 7-year-olds, and four times as often as 4-year-olds. Among the 10-year-olds, in every 60 instances in which two words recalled successively came from different groups of items, 38 of the instances involved a shift from the thematic to the taxonomic mode of classification, or vice versa. But in the 4-year-olds, only nine out of 60 instances when successive words recalled were from different groups involved a switch between thematic and taxonomic modes. Furthermore, at each age there was a significant positive correlation between the number of words remembered and the proportion of intermodal switches.

It is conceivable that the higher levels of recall in the older children were not actually caused by greater retrieval flexibility, since the observed relationship between retrieval flexibility and accuracy of recall could have been due to a third factor. Older children might simply have been more likely to *retain* information about both of the modes. In that case they would have more opportunities for switching between the modes and they would also be able to draw upon a larger number of retained items. To check on this possibility, Ceci and Howe used the "reduction method" devised by Tulving and Watkins (1975) to assess the extent to which people retained information, irrespective of their ability to recall it. The technique uses the fact that when several retrieval cues are provided, test performance demonstrates that people have *retained* more items than are normally *recalled* in a free recall test. Using the results of a cued recall test as an indication of the traces actually retained, Ceci and Howe established that children of different ages possessed similar proportions of traces containing each of the two modes of information. This finding indicates that the low level of recall by the 4-year-olds was not due to a failure to retain information in each of the modes. The difference in switching between thematic and taxonomic grouping was a genuine retrieval phenomenon, and not just the outcome of age differences in items retained. The more flexible retrieval strategies of the older children contributed to their superior performance at the memory task.

REHEARSAL

The degree to which a retrieval strategy is effective depends to a marked extent upon the manner in which the learner has processed information as it is perceived. Locating materials in memory is partly determined by the processing of them at the time of input, just as the manner in which library books are located depends upon how they were originally catalogued and organized. The mental processing that occurs as each new item is perceived cannot be directly observed, but it is possible to gain some control over input processing by varying the time available for learners to rehearse items, or by requiring subjects to adopt particular rehearsal strategies. Subjects might be asked to rehearse one item at a time, in which case opportunities for grouping items in memory would be very limited. Alternatively, they might be encouraged to rehearse the items in groups.

Some experiments on rehearsal were undertaken in an attempt to explain the apparently curious finding, described earlier in this chapter, that after listening to lists of letters or digits, people can sometimes remember a larger proportion of the items if they are asked to recall them in reverse order, starting with the items at the end of the list, than if they recall them in the order of presentation (Howe, 1965; 1966; Posner, 1964). The detailed findings of these experiments indicate that if recall is required immediately after presentation, the items at the end of lists are more vulnerable than the early items to the interfering effects produced by the activity of having to recall the other items, or by the time taken in doing so. Retention of the items at the beginning of lists is less sensitive to this interference.

Why are the items at the beginning of lists less vulnerable to the effects of time and interfering activities than the items at the end of a list? Why do the early items become more highly consolidated in memory? It is not simply a matter of forgetting being greatest in the first seconds following presentation, since the accuracy with which later items are recalled does not simply decline to the level of the early items but goes appreciably below that level. A possible explanation is that while the list is being presented, early items are more extensively rehearsed than the items at the end of a list. A rehearsal strategy that many people adopt as they listen to a list presented at a rate of around one item per second is to repeatedly rehearse those items already presented, always starting with the first item in the list. For example, if the list is:

B X A G C D L N

what people might actually rehearse to themselves as the list is presented might be something like the following:

$$B \quad B \quad B \quad BX \quad BX \quad BXA \quad BXA \quad BXAG \quad BXAGC$$

With a rehearsal strategy that is something like the above one, early items will be favored, at the expense of items occuring toward the end of a list. The greater vulnerability of the items toward the end of a list may be due to these items receiving less rehearsal than the earlier ones.

One way to test this explanation is to devise a situation in which rehearsal is rigidly controlled, so that every item receives exactly the same opportunities for being rehearsed. Under such circumstances, if it is true that the high vulnerability of later items in the above experiments was due to rehearsal differences, we would expect all items to be equally consolidated and equally resistant to distracting activities. An experiment by Howe (1967a) included a condition in which the items in nine-consonant lists were presented three at a time. Subjects were instructed to rehearse each three-item group aloud, repeating it until the next three letters appeared. In another condition, items were presented in the same manner, but subjects would rehearse in whatever manner they chose. When each list ended, subjects in both conditions either performed a distracting task for three seconds and then attempted recall or they immediately tried to recall one of the three-letter sequences from the list.

If rehearsal is the cause of differences in resistance to forgeting between the early and late items, we would expect to find that, in the condition in which subjects rehearsed according to their own choice, the effects of a distracting task would differ between early and late list items. This would not be the case, however, in the condition in which all items were equally rehearsed. This is precisely what was observed. When rehearsal was strictly controlled, the effect of having to do a distracting task immediately after the list had been presented was to reduce the number of letters recalled from each three-item group by around 0.70 items, irrespective of the position of the letters within a list. But in the condition in which subjects followed their preferred rehearsal strategy, the interference task reduced recall of the three items at the beginning of lists by 0.64, on average, whereas the average reduction in the final three items was 1.42, well over twice as much. The suggestion that differences in consolidation are largely due to the extent to which different items are rehearsed receives strong support from these findings.

Rehearsal is most effective when it facilitates meaningful processing of the material. Simply repeating the single items in word lists does not improve recall (Craik and Watkins, 1973). Increasing the time available for rehearsal is most likely to aid learning if the person is encouraged to encode and process the items according to their meaningful attributes (Craik and Tulving, 1975). The fact that older children and adults more often rehearse materials spontaneously than young children may contribute to age-related differences in performance at a variety of learning tasks (Flavell, Beach and Chinsky, 1966). However, as Naus, Ornstein and Aivano (1977) report, it is not simply the amount of rehearsal that is important. The quality of rehearsal, and the extent to which it contributes to meaningful encoding and organization is equally important. Thus Kingsley and Hagen (1969) found that children who rehearsed the names of pictured objects cumulatively, rehearsing the complete set, up to the most recently presented item, recalled more of them than children who simply rehearsed each item as it was presented, one at a time. Children do not gain the habits of spontaneously naming and rehearsing items until sometime after reaching an age when they can profit from doing so. They have to learn how to time rehearsals appropriately, taking full advantage of intervals between presentation of the different items (Hagen, Hargrave, and Ross, 1973). Of course, the extent to which items can be effectively grouped for rehearsal depends upon the individual's degree of knowledge about the meanings of the items being rehearsed (Chi, 1976; Huttenlocher and Burke, 1976).

Compared with young children, older children and adults simply know more about how to remember things. In the youngest children, even the idea of intentionality to learn is absent and has to be acquired. With increasing age, there is greater use of various strategies that reflect a clear intention to learn (Brown 1975a; Flavell and Wellman, 1977). Although learning often occurs in the absence of an intention to learn, the activities associated with trying to remember make a large contribution to developmental improvements in performance (Wellman, 1977).

SUMMARY

1. In order for language materials to be remembered, it is essential for a learner to possess a memory system that includes provision for gaining quick access to large quantities of stored information.
2. Information in memory may be retained on the basis of any of a number of characteristics. Encoding processes determine whether items are retained on the basis of their physical attributes or abstracted qualities of them.
3. Gaining access to particular items when large numbers of them are retained, as in human memory, is possible only if stored items are or-

ganized in a manner that enables them to be readily located when they are required. A variety of organizational schemes contribute to the retention and retrieval of human knowledge. Grouping and organizing verbal items into semantic categories may improve remembering, whether or not the experimenter makes provision for such categorization in designing the materials to be retained.

4. The ease of retrieving items from memory depends upon their organization. Research investigating the effectiveness of various items as cues to facilitate retrieval has provided evidence about the manner in which items in memory are stored and organized.

5. The way in which materials are retained in a person's long-term memory are related to the person's knowledge about their semantic attributes.

6. Various control procedures, including conscious rehearsal, contribute to materials being retained in memory.

Suggestions for Further Reading

Baddeley, A. D. (1976) *The Psychology of Memory*. New York: Harper & Row.

Brown, A. L. (1975) "The development of memory: Knowing, knowing about knowing, and knowing how to know." In H. W. Reese (ed.), *Advances in Child Development and Behavior*, Vol. X. New York: Academic Press.

Kintsch, W. (1977) *Memory and Cognition*. New York: Wiley.

Norman, D. A. (1976) *Memory and Attention: an Introduction to Human Information Processing*. New York: Wiley.

Learning from Prose

OVERVIEW

Most of the research described in the previous two chapters used single words as the unit for analysis, and there were good reasons for doing so. However, when we learn from materials in language form, the meaning is usually expressed by word sequences that obey linguistic constraints. The meaning of a sentence is not just the sum of the meanings of the individual words. The present chapter surveys investigations of learning from language sequences in the form of meaningful prose materials. We find that people often retain the meaning of such passages, but not their literal form. Understanding and retaining information presented in the form of language may involve the learner in actively seeking for meaning in the materials by relating their content to existing knowledge. The chapter also describes experiments investigating the ways in which language-based information may be represented within the structure of knowledge possessed by a learner.

KNOWLEDGE IN LANGUAGE FORM

Experimental investigations in which people are required to learn lists of words have made a real contribution to our understanding of the acquisition and retention of knowledge. In particular, the findings of research described in the previous chapter make it clear that learning is strongly influenced by the activities and strategies that each individual adopts, and by the individual's existing knowledge. However, in real life the learning of materials in language form usually involves organized sequences that contain considerably more words than one, and in speech and written language the which word sequences have a meaning over and above the individual meanings of the separate words. The effective units of meaning are sentences or phrases rather than single words. A number of studies have investigated the learning that takes place when a person reads a passage in the form of written prose. Until about 1950 little research was undertaken into the learning of meaningful knowledge in language form, but such research has increased remarkably in recent years, and some of the most promising developments will be surveyed in the present chapter.

In research that examines learning and remembering of single words, it is customary for the experimenter to assess recall or recognition of particular items. In prose learning research, the experimenter is usually more interested in the extent to which a person can retain the *meaning* of the information presented, rather than its literal form. People can remember the meaningful content of prose materials long after they have forgotten the precise wording, possibly because prose materials are extensively (or "deeply") coded by the learner.

Measuring a person's success at acquiring knowledge that is in the prose form introduces practical difficulties that are not encountered when lists of single words are learned. For instance, to measure how accurately someone has retained the meaningful content of a passage, it is necessary to make decisions about what the meaningful content involves. Thus it is hard to decide, whether or not someone who has been exposed to the statement that there are numerous mountains in Switzerland should be judged as having retained this information if the person simply recalls that Switzerland has many hills. In judging whether particular meaningful content has been correctly recalled or not there may be an element of arbitrariness. It is possible to find out if one's measurements of meaningful learning are adequately reliable, however, by comparing the scores given by the different judges (Howe, 1970b). It is also possible to minimize differences between scorers by providing guidelines that specify what is acceptable. Alternatively, learning of meaningful materials can be assessed by asking subjects to *recognize* which parts of a passage have been changed when it is presented on a second occasion (Carver, 1973). Requiring subjects to recognize changes, instead of asking for active recall of the passage, enables the measurement of meaningful learning to be relatively objective. However, any attempt to assess meaningful learning has a degree of subjectivity. Even if an "objective" test in constructed, such as a multiple-choice test battery, subjectivity is still involved, although, in this case, it is at the stage of test construction rather than in the scoring of test responses.

Language can be regarded as a way of structuring information in a way that enables a person who knows that language to process it and extract the meaning. Any sequence of words that follows the structure of English grammar may initially seem to be meaningful, even if it is not. As William James remarked in *Principles of Psychology,*

> If words (do) belong to the same vocabulary, and if the grammatical structure is correct, sentences with absolutely no meaning may be uttered in good faith and pass unchallenged. Discourses at prayer-meetings, reshuffling the same collection of cant phrases, and the whole genus of penny-a-line-isms, and newspaper reporters' flourishes give illustration of this. "The birds filled the tree-tops with their morning song, making the air moist, cool and pleasant," is a sentence I remember reading once in a report of some athletic exercises in

Jerome Park. It was probably written unconsciously by the hurried reporter, and read uncritically by many readers . . . Nonsense in a grammatical form sounds half rational; sense with grammatical form upset sounds nonsensical (James, 1890, p. 263–264).

APPROXIMATIONS TO ENGLISH

Miller and Selfridge (1950) carried out an experiment in which they deliberately varied the extent to which word sequences obeyed the constraints of the English language. Using a technique that was similar to ones developed by C. E. Shannon (1951) for measuring the degree of sequential organization in a language, Miller and Selfridge were able to construct a number of word sequences which formed what they called *approximations to English*. The approximation to English method is illustrated by an outline of the manner in which tests were constructed. To obtain a "second-order approximation" sequence, Miller and Selfridge would present one common word to a participant, who would be instructed to use that word in a sentence. A record would then be made of the word the person provided directly following the one given, and that new word would be given to a second participant. This participant, too, would be asked to use the word in a sentence, and the third participant would be asked to form a sentence which included the word that the second participant had written down following the one that had been given to him. The words provided by all participants were then put together to form a sequence.

An example of a second-order approximation to English sequence formed in this manner is shown below:

have to take a part of their house is to make that here is nothing is close to 22 three blind man and then he

The second-order sequence is not quite an arbitrary list of words, since each item has to make sense in the context of the preceding word. Thus, if a given word was *horse*, the next item might be *was, goes, gallops, on, which,* or *next,* but it could hardly be *tree, menu* or *bulldozer.*

To obtain a higher-order sequence, the same procedure is followed, but the participant adds words to a structured language sequence of more than one word. Thus, for a third-order sequence each participant would be shown the two-word sequence comprising the second of two words shown to the previous participant, plus the word which he had added. A typical list formed in this way is

family was large dark animal come roaring down
the middle of my friends love books passionately
every kiss is fine

Lists of the fourth and fifth orders of approximation were also prepared. In each case, each participant would contribute a word to a language sequence of n minus 1 word items to form a nth order list. Thus the higher the order of approximation, the greater the extent to which lists followed the constraints of structured English.

The approximation to English measure enables the construction of sequences having varying degrees of similarity to the structure of English language. It has been used in numerous investigations. Miller and Selfridge made word lists at all orders of approximation between zero and seven, and they performed a simple recall experiment. At each order there were four lists, varying in length from ten to 50 words, and there were also four extracts containing actual prose. Subjects were asked to listen to each list and afterwards write down what they could remember, in as near as possible to the correct order. In scoring, the number of correct words were counted, irrespective of order. The main results are shown in Figure 11.1.

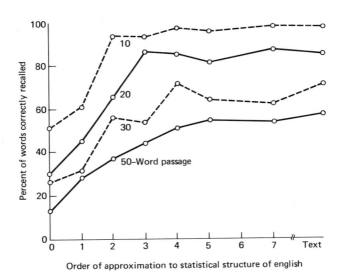

Figure 11.1 Percentage of words from lists of different lengths that were correctly recalled at various orders of approximation to English. (Source: Miller, G. A., and Selfridge, J. A. "Verbal context and the recall of meaningful content." *American Journal of Psychology,* 1950, 63:176–185. © 1950 The University of Illinois Press.)

As Figure 11.1 indicates, the higher the order of approximation to English, the larger the number of words recalled, at least up to about the fifth order, from which point further constraints had little or no effect. With the shortest passages, perfect recall was achieved at around the second order of approximation, producing a ceiling effect that left no room for improvement. The effects are seen more clearly with the longer word sequences.

A number of further experimental reports confirmed the main findings of the study by Miller and Selfridge. Marks and Jack (1952) and Coleman (1963) found that when recall scores took into account not only the number of words remembered but also their order, the improvement at the higher orders of approximation was greater than Miller and Selfridge had observed. Other researchers found that performance was directly related to the degree of approximation to English in a variety of different tasks involving learning and memory (for example, Lloyd and Johnston, 1963; Sharp, 1958; Tulving and Patkau, 1962; Postman and Adams, 1960; Simpson, 1965), and order of approximation has been found to affect the ease of reproducing prose passages (Sumby and Pollack, 1954), copying (Hogan, 1961), reading aloud (Lawson, 1961; Pierce and Karlin, 1967), comprehending speech under poor sound conditions (Miller, Heise and Lichten, 1951), perceiving whether speech sequences delivered to different ears are identical (Treisman, 1964), reporting back such sequences (Moray and Taylor, 1958), and translating between different languages (Treisman, 1965).

The approximation to English method is by no means a perfect way to measure similarity to language. One of the problems of using it to investigate prose learning is that matters of syntax (relating to the grammatical rules contributing to language structure) and semantics (relating to the meaning of the passage) are inevitably confounded. Psychologists investigating language have undertaken extensive research into the effects of syntatic and semantic factors. Some interesting findings were obtained by Marks and Miller (1964), who performed an experiment in which people had to remember sentences constructed in one of four different ways. Some of the sentences were grammatical and meaningful, for example:

Noisy parties wake sleeping neighbors.
Accidents kill motorists on the highways.

Other sentences were grammatical but not meaningful, and were constructed by combining the appropriate parts of speech from a number of different sentences. Examples are:

Noisy flushes emit careful floods.
Trains steal elephants around the highways.

The third and fourth conditions both involved words presented in random order, for example:

Between gadgets highway passengers the steal.
Neighbors sleeping noisy wake parties.

After listening to a number of sentences, the subject attempted to recall them. It was found that sequences that were grammatical but not meaningful were not so accurately recalled as normal sentences. However, former sequences were easier than ungrammatical sequences formed either by presenting the words comprising a normal sentence in random order or by randomly ordering the meaningless but grammatical sequences. Marks and Miller reported that both semantic and syntatic factors make a contribution to learning. The influence of syntax was also demonstrated by Epstein (1961; 1962) who presented sequences of either nonword syllables or actual words with appropriate cues that provided a kind of grammatical structure, as in the following examples.

The Yigs wur vulmy rixing hum.
Cruel tables sang falling circles to empty bitter pencils.

Epstein found that sequences like these were easier to remember than lists in which the same items were ordered randomly, if the items forming a sequence were all shown at the same time. When the sequences were presented by ear, grammatical tags improved performance if the sequences were read with appropriate intonation, but not if they were recited in a monotone (O'Connell, Turner, and Onuska, 1968).

THE REPRESENTATION OF STRUCTURED KNOWLEDGE IN MEMORY

When information is expressed in language form, the syntactic and semantic aspects of communication are partly inseparable, each depending upon the other. However, to investigate learning of language-based materials it is customary to consider each aspect on its own. A study by Collins and Quillian (1969) has helped to generate research into the semantic aspects of language. Collins and Quillian have been interested in the manner in which knowledge is represented in a learner's memory. As I remarked in the previous chapter, for the individual to be able to retain and to retrieve large amounts of knowledge, the stored information must be appropriately coded and effectively organized. The research by Collins and Quillian takes into account the fact that an individual's knowledge consists not only of collections of words, but also of statements and

propositions expressing the properties of items and their relationships. Consider the following sentences:

A canary has gills.
An ostrich can move around.
Salmon is edible.
A shark has wings.
A fish can swim.

Some of these statements are true, the others are not. How does
a person decide whether propositions of this kind are true or false?
Can people decide about the truth of some of these propositions
more quickly than others? Collins and Quillian produced a diagram
which indicates a way in which the information required to answer
these questions might be represented in a person's long-term memory. This is shown in Figure 11.2.

Note that the diagram is heirarchically organized, and contains
statements at three separate levels. At the top are propositions about
the properties of a superordinate class, *animal*. Beneath this are two
subclasses, *bird* and *fish*, with appropriate properties specified, and
on a still lower level there are particular members of each subclass,
namely *canary, ostrich* (*birds*) and *shark, salmon* (*fishes*).

Note that the organization of propositions shown in Figure 11.2
is only a *theory* about how this knowledge is actually represented in
the cognitive structure of a human learner. It appears to be a plausible account, providing an apparently sensible and economical way

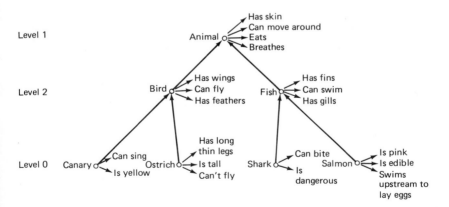

Figure 11.2   Hierarchical model of semantic memory. Basic elements of
model are semantic entries, relational markers, and property lists.
(Source: Collins, A. M., and Quillian, M. R. "Retrieval time from semantic
memory," *Journal of Verbal Learning and Verbal Behavior,* 1969,
8:240–247. Reprinted by permission of Academic Press, Inc.)

of representing knowledge. It is conceivable, however, that it may be completely erroneous as an account of the way in which human brains actually organize and retain the information shown in the diagram. Fortunately, there are ways of testing the model, to assess how closely it corresponds to the actual organization of knowledge in human memory. Consider the following two statements:

A canary is yellow.
A canary has skin.

Imagine that a learner is asked to verify each of these propositions. If Figure 11.2 provides a reasonably accurate guide to the manner in which the knowledge is represented in memory, verifying the truth of one of the sentences will necessitate considerably more processing than the other. The information needed to establish that "A canary is yellow" is all retained at the same location in the hierarchy, and it is not necessary to combine information from different levels. Deciding whether it is true that "A canary has skin" is a much more complex matter. Information has to be retrieved from different levels, and data must be transferred through a number of steps.

It should be possible to gain some idea of the amount of processing needed to judge the truth of a statement by measuring the length of time that is taken to make a judgement. Let us assume that the time required depends upon the number of steps or levels through which it is necessary to move in order to locate required information. In that case, we can start to assess the validity of Figure 11.2 by discovering whether actual time taken to make judgments about different statements is related to the number of steps involved, according to the diagram. This is roughly what Collins and Quillian attempted to do.

Subjects were presented with a number of sentences, one at a time, and the experimenter measured the time taken to decide about the truth of the statement. Collins and Quillian predicted that, in general, the time ("reaction time") to make a decision about a statement involving two entries in the hierarchy (for example, "A canary is an animal," or "An ostrich is a bird") would be directly related to the number of levels that have to be traversed in order for the decision to be made. If it was also necessary to compare a word entry (e.g., "A canary") with a property (e.g., "can sing"), the time taken would be longer by a constant amount than a judgment that involved the same number of levels, but did not involve matching an item and a property.

As Figure 11.3 indicates, the original results obtained by Collins and Quillian, based upon performance by subjects on items that

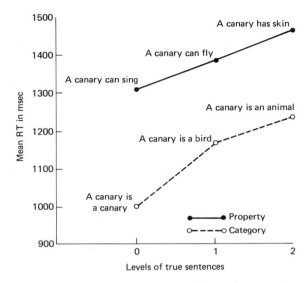

Figure 11.3   Semantic search times for false sentences, comparison of properties, or classification, for plausible or implausible relations. (Source: Collins, A. M. and Quillian, M. R. "Experiments in Semantic Memory." In *Cognition in Learning and Memory*, L. W. Gregg (ed.), 1972. Reprinted by permission of John Wiley & Sons, Inc.)

were represented in a number of organized hierarchies, were broadly in line with the predictions. The bottom line of Figure 11.3 indicates that the time required to decide if an item fell in a particular category was directly related to the number of intervening levels involved. Furthermore, when an item and its property had to be matched (the top line in Figure 11.3) the reaction time increased. As predicted, the additional amount of time required to match an item with a property was constant, and was independent of the number of levels separating the two entries. Another prediction was that if two successive sentences required a subject to traverse the same path in the hierarchy, the priming of the common path by the first sentence would increase the speed of the decision making in the second sentence. This was found to be so. For example,

A canary can fly.
A canary has a beak.

However, some additional findings do not agree with Collins and Quillian's predictions. Conrad (1972) suggested that the relationship between reaction times and the number of intervening levels between items could have been caused by the fact that the number of intervening levels between two words tends to be inversely related to the strength of association between them. She observed that when the sentences were presented in a different form to that of Collins and Quillian, the reaction times were altered. One would not expect this to happen, if knowledge is organized in the manner shown in Figure 11.2. In their original study, Collins and Quillian retained the subject of different sentences and varied the predicate, as in:

A canary is yellow.
A canary can fly.
A canary has skin.

Conrad presented sentences differently, as follows:

An animal has skin.
A bird has skin.
A canary has skin.

If the representation of propositions depicted in Figure 11.2 is correct, we would predict that reaction times to decide on the truth of sentences like these last three should follow the same pattern as those for the former three, and be directly related to the number of levels involved. But Conrad found that when the subject of a sentence varied and the predicate statement remained constant, there was no consistent increase in reaction time as a function of the number of levels involved. In discussing the divergence between this result and the earlier findings of Collins and Quillian, Conrad suggested that differences in associative strengths might have contributed to the earlier results. Conrad's findings suggest that the diagramatic models provided by Collins and Quillian do not provide entirely satisfactory accounts of the representation of knowledge. There are other discordant results, for example, the finding that the reaction times for untrue statements do not closely parallel those for true statements, and the observation that additional factors such as the plausibility of statements can influence reaction time.

It now seems that an entirely adequate representation of organized knowledge would need to be more detailed and complicated than the diagrams originally proposed by Collins and Quillian. However, their work has demonstrated that it is possible to propose and test theories about the mental representation of meaningful knowledge. It has created interest in the important and difficult task of discovering how knowledge in the language form is actually retained in the minds of human learners. Among complicating factors that influence performance, in addition to those already mentioned, are the size of the category (Landauer and Meyer, 1972), the salience of an item as a category member, and the familiarity of the concept (Rips, Shoben, and Smith, 1973). Thus, it is more quickly decided that a *ramier* is not an edible vegetable than it is not an animal (category size); that a *robin* is a bird is more quickly decided than that a *chicken* is (salience of category membership); and that *lions* are mammals is more quickly decided than that they are animals (familiarity of class). In addition, true statements can usually be judged more quickly than false statements, and decisions about the truth of positive statements are made more quickly than are decisions about negative statements (Trabasso, 1972).

It will not be easy to discover exactly how all knowledge is represented in the minds of human learners. The fact that the complex rules which govern language are involved both in representing knowledge in memory and in communicating knowledge adds to the difficulty of the challenge. However, there have been some notable recent achievements in this area by researchers who have introduced concepts from psycholinguistics and artificial intelligence in addition to the findings of information processing approaches to psychology. Monographs by Winograd (1972), Kintsch (1974), Anderson and Bower (1973), and Anderson (1976) have contributed to a growing understanding of how human knowledge is acquired and used in mental processing.

THE INFLUENCE OF BARTLETT

Some earlier research into learning from prose was initiated by studies described in a book called *Remembering* published in 1932 by Sir Frederick Bartlett. Bartlett's research placed special emphasis upon the active role of the individual learner. He stressed that what is learned is not acquired through passive assimilation, but is strongly influenced by interpretative processes. New information is perceived in the context formed by the learner's existing body of knowledge. The existing knowledge people have, together with their feelings and their attitudes, predispose them to retain some things accurately, to forget others, and to distort some newly perceived information to enable it to be assimilated within an existing knowledge structure.

It has long been known that individuals selectively remember or forget things according to their own prejudices, attitudes, hopes, and expectations, and studies measuring the recall of events that people have witnessed confirm that systematic memory distortions are common. Bartlett (1932) argued that such distortions are the rule rather than the exception. They occur not only when material being learned has some importance to the individual but even when the content is quite neutral. Bartlett introduced the phrase "effort after meaning" to describe what he considered to be an important learner function. Like researchers within the modern cognitive tradition, Bartlett noted that in order to retain new information, individuals seek ways of integrating the data into their existing body of structured knowledge, which is formed by past learning experiences.

When we say that something is meaningful to us we mean that it can be related to things we already know; we possess a frame of reference that gives significance to the new information. One of Bartlett's procedures required students to listen to stories that described events taking place within an unfamiliar culture. The stories contained elements that were strange and relatively devoid of meaning within the context of the learner's own cultural background. For example, part of one of the narratives read:

> And the warriors went on up the river to a town on the other side of Kalama. The people came down to the water and they began to fight, and many were killed. But presently the young man heard one of the warriors say, "Quick, let us go home; that Indian has been hit." How he thought, "Oh, they are ghosts." He did not feel sick, but they said he had been shot.
>
> So the canoes went back to Egulac, and the young man went ashore to his house, and made a fire. And he told everybody and said: "Behold, I accompanied the ghost, and we went to fight. Many of our fellows were killed, and many of those who attacked us were killed. They said I was hit, and I did not feel sick."
>
> He told it all, and then he became quiet. When the sun rose he fell down. Something black came out of his mouth. His face became contorted. The people jumped up and cried. He was dead. (Bartlett, 1932, p. 65.)

Bartlett found that when British students tried to remember stories of this kind, the reproduced versions were much more conventional in relation to the learner's cultural background than the original version. Content that could not easily be understood or interpreted within the framework of the listener's cultural experience tended to be forgotten or to become distorted in the direction of greater conventionality. In some of the experiments, a story was read by one student who then reproduced it and then passed on this account to another student. This student would read that version and pass it on, and in this way the story would be transmitted along a chain of seven or eight people. When the different versions were compared, it was apparent that the successive accounts were progressively more conventional, retaining only those characteristics that were readily assimilated into the shared past experience of the individuals in the chain. For instance, the fourth reproduction of the above extract took the following form:

> And they went to Kamama, and the strife waxed fierce between them and the foe. And the young man fell, pierced through the heart by an arrow. And he said to the warrior: "Take me back to Malagua, for that is my home". So the warrior brought him back, and the young man said: "I am wounded, but I am not sick, and feel no pain".
>
> And he lived that night, and the next day, but at sunset his soul fled black from his mouth, and he grew stark and stiff. And when they came to lift him they could not, for he was dead (Bartlett, 1932, p. 122).

By the eighth reproduction of the passage it had become:

> In the course of the fight further on, the Indian was mortally wounded, and his spirit fled. "Take me to my home", he said, "at Momapan, for I am going to die." "No, you will not die", said a warrior. In spite of this, however, he died, and before he could be carried back to the boat, his spirit had left this world (Bartlett, 1932, p. 124).

The story clearly becomes shorter and more conventional, shedding aspects that are hard for British students to assimilate. Bartlett observed similar changes when, instead of obtaining successive reproductions by different individuals, he required a particular person to make repeated attempts to reproduce the story after intervals of time. Bartlett noticed that in addition to any random forgeting, various systematic changes occurred. Details were omitted, as were parts of the passage that were out of line with the learner's expectations, and when parts of a passage were apparently incongruous or hard to understand, items were introduced to make the content more easily explicable. For example, the passage "something black came out of his mouth," which most participants found rather strange, often became "foamed at the mouth." Words were changed to more familiar synonyms, for instance, *canoes* to *boats,* and the order of events was sometimes altered.

In subsequent research, many of Bartlett's statements about things that happen when someone tries to remember unfamiliar materials have been substantiated by further evidence, often in the form of results that are more precise and more clearly quantifiable than Bartlett's own.

Bias Toward the Familiar

The tendency toward recalled prose information being more conventional than the original passage is illustrated by experiments observing the biases that occur when sentences are reconstructed from memory. Turner and Rommetveit (1968) asked school children to study a number of sentences, each of which was paired with a picture. Subsequently they were shown the pictures again, and asked to recall the sentence. Half the sentences were of active form and half were passive. Although the pictures did not induce a bias in either direction, the children produced active sentences much more often than passive ones, displaying a bias to recall what is normal or common.

Similarly, Clark and Clark (1968) found that when students were asked to recall sentences, their reproductions displayed similar biases, for instance, toward moving the subject of the sentence toward the beginning. Coleman (1962) observed a related effect in an experiment that required subjects to recall word sequences made by presenting the words from a prose passage in scrambled order. A typical sequence was:

> About was good-looking way and treating made of that a him the quiet youngster nice he manner and them girls will go with.

The subjects' recall attempts provide instances of the "effort after meaning" phenomenon, to which Bartlett drew attention. Although participants were carefully requested to recall the words in the exact order of presentation, after passing through a chain of people, each of whom studied it and attempted to reproduce it, the reproduced passage provided by the sixteenth person was:

> He was a youngster nice quiet with manners, good-looking and a way of treating them that made the girls go wild about him.

EFFECTS OF CONTEXT

The importance of having an adequate frame of reference is illustrated by a result of a study by Bransford and Johnson (1973). The participants listened to the following passage, and they were first told that the title of the passage was "Watching a Peace March from the Fortieth Floor."

> The view was breathtaking. From the window one could see the crowd below. Everything looked extremely small from such a distance, but the colorful costumes could still be seen. Everyone seemed to be moving in one direction in an orderly fashion and there seemed to be little children as well as adults. The landing was gentle and luckily the atmosphere was such that no special suits had to be worn. At first there was a great deal of activity. Later, when the speeches started, the crowd quieted down. The man with the television camera took many shots of the setting and the crowd. Everyone was very friendly and seemed glad when the music started (Bransford and Johnson, 1973, p. 412).

When tested for recall of this passage, most subjects were able to reproduce it quite accurately, but the sentence about the landing was not usually recalled. It did not seem to fit into the structure of the passage, and subjects lacked an appropriate frame of reference by which to connect it to their own knowledge. A second group of subjects heard the same passage, but it was preceded by an entirely different title, "A Space Trip to an Inhabited Planet." With the latter title, the sentence had a definite place within the passage as a whole, and it was accurately recalled by most participants.

An even more striking instance of the effect of providing an appropriate context has been described by Dooling and Lachman (1971). Read the following passage carefully.

> With hocked gems financing him/our hero bravely defied all scornful laughter/that tried to prevent his scheme/your eyes deceive/he had said/an egg/not a table/correctly typifies this unexplored planet/now three sturdy sisters sought proof/forging along sometimes through calm vastness/yet more often over turbulent peaks and valleys/days became weeks/as many doubters spread fearful rumors about the edge/at last/from nowhere/welcome winged creatures appeared/ signifying momentous success (Dooling and Lachman, 1971, p. 217).

Some of the subjects in the study by Dooling and Lachman read the above passage without any title, but for other subjects it was preceded by the heading "Christopher Colombus Discovering America." Their performance was considerably better than that of the others.

Sometimes a picture can provide a context for a verbal description more effectively than a title in words. Bransford and Johnson (1972) asked some students to read the following passage:

> If the balloons popped the sound wouldn't be able to carry since everything would be too far away from the correct floor. A closed window would also prevent the sound from carrying, since most buildings tend to be well insulated. Since the whole operation depends on a steady flow of electricity, a break in the middle of the wire would also cause problems. Of course, the fellow could shout, but the human voice is not loud enough to carry that far. An additional problem is that a string could break on the instrument. Then there could be no accompaniment to the message. It is clear that the best situation would involve less distance. Then there would be fewer potential problems. With face-to-face contact, the least number of things could go wrong (Bransford and Johnson, 1972, p. 719.)

Some of the students had previously seen the picture in Figure 11.4 overleaf, and they recalled twice as many ideas from the passage as did students who did not see the picture.

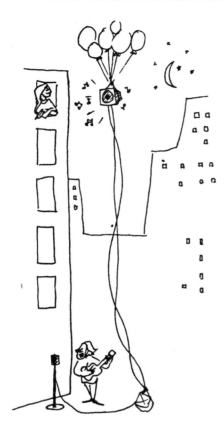

Figure 11.4   The picture used by Bransford and Johnson to provide a context for their *balloon* passage. (Source: Bransford, J. D., and Johnson, M. K. "Contextual prerequisites for understanding: some investigations of comprehensive and recall." *Journal of Verbal Learning and Verbal Behavior*, 1972, 11:717–726. Reprinted by permission of Academic Press, Inc.)

These findings demonstrate that even the shortest title or a simple picture cue can influence how a passage is interpreted. A title can function to direct learners toward those parts of their own structured knowledge that provide a context which gives meaning to the new information. The studies remind us that meaning is not simply a property inherent in the material presented, but is a product of the interpretive activities that individuals perform on information transmitted to them.

Comparisons Between New Learning and Existing Knowledge

When people receive information that is similar to something they already know, and therefore they do possess a relevant frame of reference for the new material, it may become so firmly connected in their mind to older knowledge that they are soon unable to distinguish between the new information they have just received and their previous knowledge. Kintsch (1975) asked people to read passages about topics with which they were already familiar, an instance being the biblical account of Joseph and his brothers. If subjects were asked to recall a text of this kind 24 hours after they had read it, they were almost completely unable to distinguish between what had been stated in the particular passage and their background knowledge of the biblical events. No such confusion occurred if recall was requested immediately after the passage had been read.

Rumors

Some ill effects of the circumstances in which people lack an adequate frame of reference with which to assess and retain important information were observed in an investigation of war-time rumors reported in 1947 by Allport and Postman. In the *Psychology of Rumor,* Allport and Postman pointed out that the "effort after meaning" noted by Bartlett, in which people transform their perceptions of new information into versions that are meaningful or "make sense" to each individual, is particularly intense in war-time conditions in which there is considerable ambiguity and uncertainty about knowledge that is of great importance to many people. In such circumstances rumors are likely to occur, and they thrive on the lack of reliable information. Bartlett's findings suggest that the accuracy with which people retain and communicate information depends upon the adequacy of their own existing knowledge as a frame of reference. In the absence of relevant previous experience, the individual will be unable to interpret the new material and to retain it in an integrated fashion. What happens then depends upon how important the information is perceived to be. If it is regarded as unimportant, individuals may not sustain their attention for long to parts of the material that cannot be readily assimilated. However, if individuals do regard the information as being important, but lack the background of knowledge and experience necessary to interpret it or retain it accurately, they may retain the material in a distorted form.

The circumstances in which rumors arise differ from those of Bartlett's experiments in that the lack of a frame of reference is accompanied by a much higher degree of interest in the informational content. Allport and Postman found that rumors frequently arose and quickly spread in war situations because information, especially concerning relatives and loved ones, was both very scarce and extremely important. In those circumstances, distortions and alteration led to a variety of wild rumors.

Bartlett's findings suggest, and those of the research into semantic memory surveyed in Chapter 10 also indicate, that when people attend to new information, the version they retain and reproduce is one that has been subjected to a fair amount of encoding and interpretation. In the case of a lengthy prose passage, in which literal or verbatim retention of the passage's exact wording is impossible, people do not normally even try to retain an exact copy. Individuals make inferences and build interpretations around what they see and hear. Their retention of a message may involve storage of some fragments of the literal message together with those inferences and interpretations that are made on the basis of existing knowledge. Clark and Clark (1977) point out that verbatim memory for precise wording is not often necessary in everyday life. Tasks such as those in which an actor memorized the lines of *Hamlet* or a student "learns" a long poem, require different skills from those necessary in the usual circumstances in which we remember information.

REPEATED PRESENTATION AND RECALL OF PROSE PASSAGES

It would be valuable to have an assessment of the size of the effects of those learners' active encoding and interpreting processes that Bartlett remarked upon. To what extent is recall influenced by what learners contribute rather than by the form of the material as it is presented to them? An experiment by Kay (1955) provided some data on this matter. Adult students listened to a prose passage and afterwards they were asked to write down what they could remember of it. A week later they were asked to recall it again, and then the correct passage was read to them once more. On the following week the students were again asked to recall the passage and subsequently they listened to the correct version. The experiment continued in this way for five weeks in all. Thus, in the course of the study there were a number of repeated presentations, and the subjects were repeatedly asked to reproduce what they could remember from the passage.

To study the effects of repeated representation and repeated recall attempts, Kay examined the different reproductions that each student produced on successive weeks. The improvements from one week to the next were very small, which is surprising when one considers that the repeated presentations of the correct passage might appear to have provided excellent opportunities for subjects to modify and correct the versions they retained in memory. The most striking finding was that the contents of each attempt at recall were influenced less by the repeated correct presentation than by the student's own previous reproductions. Stated briefly, on any given week the contents of each individual's attempt to reproduce the passage closely matched the person's own previous attempt at recall. If an item had appeared in one of a student's attempts at reproduction, it was likely to reappear in the following reproduction. This was not only true for correct items, but also for incorrect ones, despite the fact that the repeated presentation of the correct passage appeared to have given excellent opportunities for the students to modify the contents of their own memories. The content of each attempt at recall was influenced more by the students' own past reproductions than by the information presented to them.

These findings were substantially repeated in a later experiment by Howe (1970b). On the first of four sessions, each one week apart, American university students listened to a prose passage, and two minutes after it was finished they were told to write down what they could remember. The subjects were told to concentrate on reproducing the meaningful content as accurately as possible. Afterwards they heard a second presentation of the original passage. In a second session, one week later, they again listened to the original version, and on the following two weeks there were two more sessions. The prose passage, an extract from Saul Bellow's novel *Henderson the Rain King*, was 160 words in length, and it was read to the students at a rate of 120 per minute. It was chosen because although not difficult to understand, the content is sufficiently unfamiliar to prevent subjects from making correct guesses about the contents of the passage on the basis of a few items that are remembered.

In order to score retention of the meaningful content, irrespective of recall of the precise word sequence, guidelines for scoring were provided in which the important content of each of 20 segments of the passage was reduced to a phrase of two or three words. Items were judged correct if the original phrases or synonyms of them were recalled, and examples of acceptable and unacceptable attempts were given in the guidelines. Two judges scored the attempts at recall, and the product-moment correlation of 0.89 between their scores indicated that the method of measuring recall of the meaning was reliable.

The average recall scores rose gradually but steadily from around eight correct items out of 20 in the first session to around 12 items in the final session. Comparisons of the detailed contents of each individual's successive recall attempts in the different sessions strongly confirmed Kay's observation that from one week to the next the materials a person reproduces are remarkably similar. In both experiments, subjects were not able to profit as much as they expected to from the opportunities for modifying the contents of memory. Some students spontaneously voiced their frustration at being unable to produce the improvements they had anticipated making. It appears that the retained version that people draw upon as they attempt to reproduce the information is particularly stable in their memory and highly resistant to any changes, either in the direction of increased accuracy or toward further forgeting.

If the meaning of an item was reproduced correctly on the first recall trial, there was a 0.7 probability, on average, of it being recalled again on the succeeding trial. When a particular item was recalled on all the first three attempts, the probability of it being correctly recalled again on the final test was as high as 0.98. But if an item was not recalled on the first trial, the average probability of it being recalled at the following attempt was only 0.2. Even in the final session, by which time the passage had been presented on three separate occasions, if an item had not previously been reproduced the average probability of it being recalled correctly was only 0.2.

There was a similar pattern of results when verbatim recall was measured. Verbatim scoring makes it possible to judge memory for those items that are provided by subjects in their attempts at recall that were not in the correct version. If such an incorrect addition occurred on both of the first two recall trials, the probability of it being reproduced again on the third trial was 0.6. Thus, incorrectly added items were by no means easily lost, despite their absence from the correct version. If a word item had been presented as many as four times in the correct passage, but had not yet been recalled, the probability of it being reproduced on the fourth trial was only 0.1. However, an incorrect addition which had been introduced by a subject on just one occasion in a recall test was twice as likely to be repeated on the next test, the probability being 0.2.

Precisely why the materials retained by individuals in this experiment were so strongly influenced by the person's own reproductions is not entirely clear. It appears, however, that the encoding, interpreting, and processing that the individual undertakes with meaningful verbal materials had the effect of giving the coded materials considerable stability within the individual's body of knowledge. The possibility that what people remember is closely related to what they themselves have reproduced simply because of the fact that they have been highly active is not supported by the evidence. Some further results (Howe, 1972) indicate that the actual encoding that takes place is at least equally influential. If activity per se was the crucial factor, we would expect to find that when retention was assessed in a way that did not involve the information being actively reproduced, future retention would be unaffected. However, if multiple-choice tests (which do not require the learner to actively reproduce the materials) are used to assess retention, the degree of similarity of content between one attempt and the next is similar to that which is found when active recall is required. Howe (1972, 1977a) observed that correct choices were repeated from one test to the next and that the probability of incorrect choices being repeated was also high, around 0.7 compared with the chance probability of 0.33. Howe, Ormond, and Singer (1974) observed that the activity of recalling information did have some effect. Learners who repeatedly listened to the correct prose passages and also responded in an active manner by making copies of passages or summaries repeated fewer errors and made greater improvements from one session to the next one.

RETROACTIVE INTERFERENCE IN PROSE LEARNING

The findings obtained by Bartlett and subsequent investigators have a bearing on the phenomenon of *retroactive interference*. Learning may decrease if materials that are similar to those being learned are inserted between the original presentation of the items and subsequent tests measuring retention. However, the findings of some experiments suggest that this phenomenon only occurs when verbatim learning of the precise sequence of words is demanded, and that no retroactive interference is encountered when only the meaning, and not the exact form, has to be retained.

The matter has practical importance, since if retroactive interference does take place whenever learning tasks that involve similar kinds of knowledge occur in close succession, it would be wise to advise teachers and learners to take the precaution of separating the sessions. But if the phenomenon is only encountered with forms of verbal learning that demand verbatim retention, there is less reason for concern about it. Except in acquiring foreign languages, verbatim forms of learning are not often essential in most people's lives. Bartlett's findings would lead us to expect that if retroactive interference does influence meaningful learning, it would have an effect in those circumstances in which people perceive materials similar to ones being learned and they are also required to recall the similar items. The majority of studies in which no retroactive interference has been observed have not required subjects to recall or actively reproduce the items that are similar to the material being learned. Howe and Cavicchio (1971) carried out an experiment to investigate the possibility that retroactive interference is encountered when materials that are highly similar to meaningful information being learned do have to be reproduced by the learners. Participants learned about similar life-saving methods that can be used to induce breathing. No evidence of retroactive interference emerged in the findings. However, a later experiment that involved learning a number of structurally similar fictional biographies did yield evidence of a retroactive interference effect (Howe and Colley, 1976a). This was small in magnitude despite the materials being highly similar. Retroactive interference with meaningful learning has also been detected by some other investigators (Anderson and Myrow, 1971; Bower, 1974; Crouse, 1971; Myrow and Anderson, 1974).

It is possible that although retroactive interference effects can be discerned, they may be too weak to be of much practical importance for learning in the circumstances of daily living. However, it is equally possible that those effects that have been observed in the necessarily short learning sessions used in experimental research might underestimate the influence of retroactive interference in the lengthier and more drawn-out circumstances of learning in everyday human life.

LEARNERS' ACTIVITIES IN ACQUIRING KNOWLEDGE

The research by Bartlett and his successors demonstrates that prose learning is accomplished by the active processing on the part of the individual learner, just as the acquisition of lists of words is. A number of investigators have studied effects of various kinds of learner activities on forms of learning that have educational importance.

The Effects of Questions

Requiring students to answer questions as they attempt to learn from prose passages may be desirable on a number of counts. Learners are encouraged to be active in their approach, their attention is maintained, they are given some indication of what is considered important, and they are told whether or not their answers are correct; thus they gain useful feedback knowledge about their progress. It is not surprising that the provision of frequent questions is considered to be one of the advantageous aspects of "teaching machine" and "programmed learning" methods of instruction. The effectiveness of asking questions is demonstrated by an experiment (Rothkopf, 1966) in which undergraduate students read passages from Rachel Carson's book *The Sea Around Us*. A 5000 word chapter was divided into seven sections, and two short-answer questions were prepared for each section. In one condition, students received two questions before reading each section and the answer was provided immediately after the student had attempted it. Another condition was identical to the previous one but provided no solutions. In a third condition, all the questions and answers for the whole of the 5000 word passage were given before the students started reading. A fourth condition included the two questions on each section just after the student had read the section, and not before, and a fifth condition was identical to the previous one except that no answers were given. Finally, there were three control conditions. In one of them there were no questions at all. The second control condition was identical to this, except that the students were told that the chapter contained a good amount of detailed information, and they were encouraged to read it slowly and carefully. Students in the final control condition did not read the chapter at all, but simply studied the questions and the correct solutions.

When the students in each of the different groups had completed the whole chapter, they received a test consisting of 25 questions that were different from any of the questions encountered previously. The effect of having to answer questions during presentation of the passage was found to depend upon their positioning. Inserting questions before the subjects read each section did not improve learning, but having questions after each section led to an improvement in performance on the 25-item test. In addition, students in a control group who were instructed to pay attention to the detailed information performed better than another control group which received no special instructions. The direct effect of having the same questions administered at the end of the chapter was considerable, as one might expect. After reading the chapter, students who had previously seen the questions correctly answered around 40 percent more of them than control group subjects who were encountering the questions for the first time.

The questions in Rothkopf's study may have been beneficial in helping learners attend to the detailed contents of a passage. In this case, we would predict that if all the questions concerned a particular aspect of the content, attention would be focused on that aspect of the passage. To investigate this possibility, Rothkopf and Bisbicos (1971) required students to read the passage used in the previous experiment, divided into the same seven sections, with two questions for each section. For some students each question required an answer in the form of a proper name or a measured quantity, such as a date or a measurement. The questions given to other subjects required word answers, typically a technical term. The experimenters found that providing questions about a particular aspect of the material facilitated performance on the questions in a subsequent test that concerned the same aspects. As in the previous study, performance at answering questions that were different from the ones accompanying the chapter was improved if the questions during the chapter occurred after each relevant section but not if the questions preceded the part of the passage that included material answering them.

Mathemagenic Activities

It has been argued by Rothkopf (1970) that the character of questioning tends to shape the character of the knowledge that is acquired. Therefore, the pattern set by the instructional materials which a student encounters may determine the manner in which students gain knowledge. Varying the kinds of questions that are posed and their positioning provides one way of directing the activities involved in a student's gaining knowledge. Rothkopf uses the term *mathemagenic activities* to refer to the activities of the student in the learning situation. He states that they are too numerous to be exhaustively enumerated, but include reading, asking questions, and inspecting objects. Mathemagenic activities also include ones that do not make a direct contribution to learning, such as yawning, looking out of the window, and sleeping. Rothkopf's concern is to emphasize that the activities of the learner are particularly important. Although the contents of instruction and instructional methods are not without significance, if is ultimately what the students themselves do that determines what they learn. It follows that to increase the amount a student learns in an instructional setting, it is necessary to influence the learner's own activities.

The above conclusion, which Rothkopf arrived at on the basis of his research into instructional methods, is identical to the one suggested by other investigations into the learning of prose and verbal materials. Learning is something that learners do, and it cannot be done for them. As Rothkopf acknowledges, the questions that are asked prior to the presentation of a passage form one of many possible influences upon the mathemagenic activities determining what a student actually learns. Watts and Anderson (1971) observed that students who had been required to apply the principles described in a prose passage to new situations retained more information than individuals who had simply been required to reproduce examples in the text. Howe and Colley (1976b) found that when university student learners were given successive prose passages to learn, followed by similar sets of questions, a definite "set" of expectancy was induced. When students were given further passages of similar form, they concentrated their attention on those aspects of the new passage that corresponded to the parts of the early passages on which they had been questioned. The students read 20-sentence passages which contained geographical and historical information about a fictitious country. Individuals who were given questions following a third passage that were different in form from the questions encountered in two previous passages gave a substantially lower number of correct answers than students who received similar questions on all three tests. Conscious expectations were not necessarily involved; subjects who subsequently stated that they had expected the questions following the third passage to be similar in form to the other questions performed no worse than people who had no such expectations.

The findings of the different kinds of research appear to support the view that learners should be encouraged to be as active as possible (Howe, 1977a). It would appear prudent to instruct a learner to undertake the activity of summarizing or recording information to be learned, rather than taking a more passive role. However, the findings of an investigation conducted to test this particular suggestion indicate that reliable improvements in prose learning are not quite so easily achieved.

Learners' Activities and Presentation Variables

Howe and Singer (1975) decided to examine the effects of some learner activities on learning from prose material. Learning took place under circumstances which, while adequately controlled for experimental purposes, were also fairly like those in which students normally acquire knowledge. The first prediction was that the amount of learning that took place would be related to the extent to which people had to process the information in an active manner. Eighty-six undergraduate students were told to read a prose extract, approximately 300 words in length, describing the use of cloud-seeding procedures designed to control the weather. It was thought that this choice of materials resembled, in difficulty and degree of abstraction, the learning matter to which university students are normally exposed, but the content was unfamiliar, minimizing differences between students in background knowledge. Some of the subjects were told to spend ten minutes reading the material, giving any surplus time to rereading. Subjects in a second group were told to use the ten-minute period for copying the passage, word for word. The third group of subjects received the same amount of time, but they were told to make a summary of each paragraph in the passage.

It was predicted that those students who were required to make summaries would remember the passage most accurately since they were required to undertake the greatest amount of active processing. Of the other groups, it was expected that the copiers would do better than the passive readers since the former students were required to be active, even though copying appears to necessitate less extensive processing than is necessary to make summaries. The results that had been obtained in an early study by Gates (1917) encouraged the authors to predict that the students in the conditions demanding greater amounts of activity would learn more than the others. Gates had found that children retained more information if they were required to recite aloud the information they were reading. The greater the proportion of study time spent in recitation, the more accurately the material was recalled by Gates's subjects.

As it happened, the predictions were entirely wrong. The students who simply read the passage and were expected to learn the least, learned more, on average, than subjects in either of the other groups. People who made the summaries did retain more items than those who simply copied the passage. The average numbers of meaningful segments correctly recalled (out of a possible 25) were 16.3 for the students who just read the passage, 13.4 for students who made summaries, and only 10.3 for those who copied the passages. A test of long-term retention yielded a similar pattern of findings.

With hindsight, it is easy to give reasons for students who summarized or copied prose information failing to learn as much as the individuals who only had to read the passage. The condition in which students simply read the passage was the one which allowed them the greatest degree of freedom to pace learning activities to suit themselves, taking extra time over anything that seemed difficult, skipping what appeared obvious or unimportant, and generally dividing time and attention to fit individual preferences. Subjects in the other conditions were considerably more constrained by the requirements of the task. Since university undergraduates form an able population, insofar as acquiring knowledge from printed materials is concerned, they might be expected to have some expertise in pacing learning effectively and in adopting effective procedures and strategies. In the present study, those individuals who were simply told to read the passage could control and organize their own activities in accordance with their understanding of the nature of the task. This situation was more appropriate for them than the somewhat inflexible regimen of activities prescribed in the alternative conditions.

Another potentially important factor that was neglected in designing the above experiment was the manner in which the information was presented. Many investigations into learning prose materials have concentrated on presentation variables, such as rate, mode, and instructional format. As we have seen, an outcome of recent research has been to show that differences in learner activities and strategies have a greater influence on the acquisition of knowledge than differences in the way the material is actually presented. But the fact that learner activities have been shown to be influential should not lead us to neglect presentation variables entirely. It is conceivable that the effects of presentation variables and learner activities interact with one another, with the outcome of particular student activities depending upon the manner in which the information has been made available, and vice versa.

A further experiment investigated the effects of varying both the form of presentation and the activities followed by the subject. The experimental design was influenced by the observation that the results of Howe and Singer's (1975) first experiment differed strongly from some findings of an earlier study by Howe, Ormond and Singer (1974), which measured learning under what appeared to be very similar circumstances. One difference between the two experiments was that the earlier one used auditory presentation, whereas students in Howe and Singer's first experiment read the material. It had previously been assumed that the procedural difference was relatively unimportant, but this now appeared to be untrue. When people listen to a prose passage, the fixed rate of presentation imposes a considerable degree of constraint upon them, and instructions to undertake specific activities are unlikely to make much difference to their already limited freedom of action. But if the materials are presented in written form, the instruction to copy the passage does impose additional restrictions upon the individual students, who would otherwise be free to proceed at their own chosen rate. It follows that the effects of requiring students to undertake a particular activity might differ considerably according to the form of presentation that is being used. In their next experiment, Howe and Singer systematically varied both the mode of presentation and the activities that subjects were required to undertake. Ninety-six university students participated, each of whom was assigned to one of six experimental conditions. The passage on cloud seeding used in the previous study formed the prose material to be learned, and presentation took one of three forms: A, a typed version of a passage which each subject read individually; B, auditory presentation at dictation speed; and C, auditory presentation at normal speaking rate. In condition C, the passage was presented three times. The total time during which the subjects were exposed to the prose passage for 12 minutes in each of the experimental conditions.

There were two forms of student activity, the second independent variable. Subjects either recorded the content of the passage by writing it down or copying it (X), or they made no overt response at all (Y). All subjects were told that they would be required to recall the contents afterwards, and they were asked to pay close attention to the subject matter. Following the presentation period, a verbal reasoning task was administered, lasting seven minutes, to provide sufficient delay between presentation and recall of the main passage to insure that the scores obtained from the recall tests would provide a fairly stable indication of long-term retention and would not just be a measure of immediate recall. The scores (out of 25) indicate the number of meaningful units that were correctly recalled following the different experimental conditions.

AX	read and record	14.7
AY	read	18.5
BX	listen at dictation speed and record	13.3
BY	listen at dictation speed	12.6
CX	listen at normal speaking rate and record	8.7
CY	listen at normal speaking rate	17.6

It can be seen that both the form of presentation and the activities undertaken by subjects strongly influenced learning, and that the effects of the two variables were interdependent. When written presentation was used, students who simply read the passage performed better than those required to make copies. This result essentially repeats the finding of the previous experiment. (It is interesting to note that, in line with the findings of the earlier study, the recall scores of the subjects who read the material and who were not required to make active responses were higher than the scores obtained in any of the five other conditions.) However, with auditory presentation at dictation speed, subjects who simply listened to the passage did not perform better than students who were told to copy the passage. In the two conditions in which subjects listened as the prose passage was read to them at a normal rate of presentation, students who only had to listen recalled considerably more items, in fact twice as many, as students who had to attempt the almost impossible task of writing down all they heard. A difference in learning of this order is quite remarkable when one considers that in the different experimental conditions the identical materials were studied for exactly the same amount of time.

STUDIES OF STUDENT NOTE TAKING

Investigations of student note taking shed further light upon prose learning. If we accept that individual learning depends to a marked extent upon the coding and processing activities formed by each learner, it follows that knowledge about the way in which individuals process materials they are attempting to learn may help us to understand the nature of learning and to predict what knowledge individuals will acquire. Part of the value of note-taking studies resides in the fact that the notes students prepare may give us an indication of the way in which they have encoded or interpreted the material that was presented to them. Schultz and di Vesta (1972) as well as the present author (Howe, 1974) noted that it may be valuable to use notes made by students to investigate relationships between learning and student's coding processes.

Findings of one note-taking study suggest that the more extensive the processing learners perform upon materials they are attempting to acquire, the greater the amount of learning. Howe (1970c) required students to take notes as they listened to a prose passage, and afterwards the students were asked to hand in their notes to the experimenter. One week later all the participants attempted written recall. Subsequently, the notes were assessed and measures were made of both the number of words in each student's notes and the number of meaningful ideas from the passage that were judged to be successfully communicated in the notes. Next, a ratio was calculated for each student by dividing the number of ideas communicated by the number of words used. This ratio indicates a student's degree of success at recording the meaningful content in a small number of words. It partly reflects the extent to which the students have processed the passage into their "own words," departing from the verbatim content of the original. Subsequently, a correlation was calculated between the ratio obtained in the above manner and each individual's score on the recall test. There was a significant positive correlation ($r = +0.53$), suggesting that accuracy of retention was positively related to the extent which the original material had been transformed into a student's own words.

As the findings of the experiments by Howe and Singer (1975) demonstrate, students who take notes when materials to be learned are presented to them do not necessarily learn the materials better than the students who do not take notes. The available evidence about the direct effect of taking notes on learning is contradictory. Many of the numerous studies comparing learning under conditions which do and do not include provision for note taking have yielded no statistically significant differences in learning (Hartley and Marshall, 1974; Howe, 1975b; Howe and Godfrey, 1977; Weener, 1974). Whether or not taking notes will facilitate learning in a particular situation depends upon detailed features of the circumstances involved. Of course, the value of note taking does not rest solely upon the direct effect of notes upon learning. By taking notes, individuals also provide themselves with a version of the information that they need to know, in a form which is easily understandable for them, and the notes that people have prepared themselves may provide a more useful aid for future learning than notes that have been made for them by someone else (Fisher and Harris, 1973).

When students take notes on a prose passage, their retention of the various parts of the passage may be strongly influenced by their note taking. In the experiment by Howe (1970c) it was found that a meaningful item in the prose passage was over six times more likely to be recalled by a particular student if it had been written down as part of that person's own notes than if it had not appeared in the individual's notes. This huge difference occurred despite the fact that the notes the students made were removed from them immediately after they were finished, so the students had no opportunity to inspect them or learn from them, and despite the fact that there was a one-week interval between the original presentation of the passage, at which time the notes were made, and the test for retention of the contents.

ASSESSING THE DIFFICULTY OF PROSE MATERIALS

In order to be able to make confident predictions about learning from a particular prose passage, it is necessary not only to consider the kinds of learner activities that are important, but also to assess the difficulty of the information that has been communicated. We need some way of objectively measuring just how difficult particular materials are. The contents of a passage determine whether an individual can understand it, and the amount of new information in the passage will contribute to the load upon the learner's memory, affecting the accuracy with which the information can be retained. It would be useful to have ways of measuring the degree to which the contents of a passage are potentially relatable to the existing knowledge of an individual student. This desirable goal is not easily reached, but progress has been made toward measuring some aspects of prose knowledge that affect the difficulty of learning it. A system devised by Kintsch (1975) represents the meaning of the test by a number of linked propositions. Consider the following sentence:

Turbulence forms at the edge of a wing and grows in strength over its surface, contributing to the lift of a supersonic aircraft.

Kintsch reformulates the meanings contained in this sentence in the propositions depicted in Figure 11.5.

Note that some of the propositions in Figure 11.5 are connected to each other, each proposition forming a simple statement that involves a word concept. Kintsch claims that the propositions are formed according to rules that are part of a person's knowledge of the world. When a number of propositions are expressed as one continuous sentence, it is assumed that the reader will be able to derive a list of propositions corresponding to the information in the mind of the writer. The larger the number of propositions that are involved, the greater the amount of processing that is necessary.

Kintsch designed an experiment to measure the influence of the number of propositions contained in a passage on the length of time required to read it. Subjects received sentences of around 15 words in length containing between four and nine propositions. Kintsch observed that as the number of propositions increased, so did the reading time, although the number of words remained constant. In another experiment, Kintsch's subjects read prose passages, each 70 words in length and containing 25 propositions. After studying each passage, the participants were tested for recall, and the findings displayed in Figure 11.6 demonstrate the relationships between recall and the length of time spent studying the passage.

Figure 11.6 shows that spending more time in reading the pass-

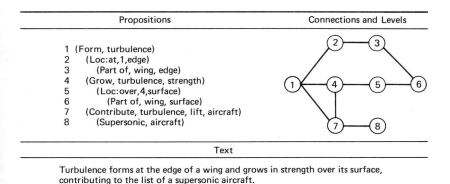

Propositions	Connections and Levels
1 (Form, turbulence) 2 (Loc:at,1,edge) 3 (Part of, wing, edge) 4 (Grow, turbulence, strength) 5 (Loc:over,4,surface) 6 (Part of, wing, surface) 7 (Contribute, turbulence, lift, aircraft) 8 (Supersonic, aircraft)	

Text

Turbulence forms at the edge of a wing and grows in strength over its surface, contributing to the list of a supersonic aircraft.

Figure 11.5 Sample text base and text. (Source: Kintsch, W. "Memory for prose." In *The Structure of Human Memory*, edited by C. N. Cofer. W. H. Freeman and Company. © 1976.

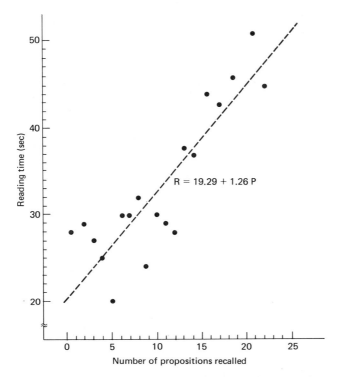

Figure 11.6   Reading time as a function of the number of propositions recalled. (Source: Kintsch, W. "Memory for prose." In *The Structure of Human Memory,* edited by C. N. Cofer. W. H. Freeman and Company. © 1976.)

age led to an increase in the number of propositions recalled, an extra 1.7 seconds of reading time being required, on average, for each additional proposition to be remembered. The findings of both experiments show that readers are sensitive to the amount of information they have to process in prose materials. However, although prose sentences can be reduced to series of propositions, sentences are not simply lists of propositions. As Kintsch recognized by incorporating different levels into his schematization of relationships between propositions (Figure 11.5), some propositions are more basic or important than others. Rumelhart (1975) has shown that highly complex structures may be necessary, in order to provide adequate descriptions of the manner in which the simple meaningful elements in a prose passage contribute to the meaning as a whole.

Kintsch's findings support the common-sense view that success at prose learning is closely related to the ease of understanding the material. Immediate retention of prose is strongly influenced by the syntactic sentence structure (Sachs, 1967, 1974), but the meaning or semantic content of a passage is a much more important determinant of retention over long periods. As stated earlier, learners retain the meaningful content rather than the literal form of a prose passage. In an experiment by Sachs (1967), subjects listened to sentences that were subsequently repeated in identical or similar form. There were four kinds of test sentences: some were identical; some contained a formal change in the precise wording that did not alter the meaning; some involved a change from active to passive sentence structure, but retained the meaning of the sentence, and; in the fourth kind of test sentence, the meaning of the original was changed. Examples are given below:

Original sentence form:
He sent a letter about it to Galileo, the great Italian scientist.

Semantic change:
Galileo the great Italian scientist sent him a letter about it.

Passive:
A letter about it was sent to Galileo, the great Italian scientist.

Formal:
He sent Galileo, the great Italian scientist, a letter about it.

Sachs varied the interval of time between the first presentation of a sentence and repetitions of it in identical or altered form. She found that immediately after people listened to a sentence they could detect any kind of change. About 87 percent of the judgments about the equivalence of a new sentence to the original one were correct, irrespective of the particular form of change involved. However, with a delay between presentation and recall, the pattern of results was very different. If recall was delayed by only the time taken to say another 80 syllables of the continuing prose passage, recognition of changes that did not alter the meaning dropped to about 60 percent. Correct judgments when there was a change of meaning remained above 80 percent, and active-to-passive changes were more often correctly identified than formal changes. In a subsequent experiment, Sachs (1974) found that active-to-passive changes were much more accurately recognized following visual than auditory presentation. It appears that the deeper the level of processing sentences, the more accurately they are retained, as was the case in the list-learning experiments discussed in Chapter 10.

Sachs's technique of testing retention by asking people to judge whether sentences were the same or different to ones previously seen was also used by Carver (1973). He was interested in the relationship between the learners' subjective estimate of the difficulty of understanding a prose passage, and their ability to remember the passage. It would be very useful to know how successful learners are at judging how difficult it will be for them to learn a passage. If their predictions are accurate, such learner judgments can be of considerable value in educational learning circumstances. Carver found that people's subjective measures of understanding were reliable and also sensitive to changes in the speed at which a passage was presented. Carver's method for testing prose learning was similar to that of Sachs, and required subjects to attempt to recognize the parts of a sentence that had been changed. This test was found to be more sensitive than alternative measures of recall and comprehension to changes in the rate at which passages were presented. The test procedure involved dividing prose passages into phrases. Recognition materials consisted of the original passage with about one in five of the phrases changed, but with the changes remaining plausible and meaningful in the context of the whole passage.

Using a test based on Carver's procedures, Howe and Smart (1976) found that the ease of identifying changes in meaning was related to subjective estimates of difficulty. Contrary to Sachs's findings, however, increased time intervals did not affect recognition of changes in wording to a markedly greater extent than they influenced recognition of meaning changes. Semantic changes were recognized most often, followed by passive-to-active, then formal, paralleling Sachs's findings. Increases in syntactic complexity that did not also involve increase in semantic difficulty did not affect recognition, but changes in syntactically complex sentences that were also semantically difficult were especially hard to recognize. These findings, together with Kintsch's results, support the general conclusion that the long-term retention of prose information is influenced more by the semantic complexity of the statements and propositions involved than by the grammatical determinants of sentence complexity.

SUMMARY

1. When people learn from information in language form, they often retain the meaning but not the literal form of the language sequences they are given. Language provides a way of structuring information in a manner that enables it to be processed effectively by individuals who have acquired the ability to use language.
2. Research based on verbal materials which approximate in varying degrees to the structure of English has shown that the ability to process and retain verbal materials is closely related to the similarity of their

structure to English language form. Both semantic and syntactic factors influence the ease of learning sentence-length word sequences.

3. Investigations into the representation of semantic knowledge indicates that it may be possible to assess the validity of theories about how information is represented by measuring how long it takes the individual to verify propositions based on that knowledge.

4. Research by Bartlett and subsequent investigators has shown that comprehension and retention of information involves efforts by learners to find meaning by seeking for relationships between new materials and existing knowledge. The individual may retain a version of the items that is distorted in the direction of the person's existing knowledge. Learning can be strongly influenced by providing contexts that enable people to locate aspects of their own existing knowledge to which the new materials can be readily integrated.

5. People learn materials they produce themselves or actively reproduce more readily than items they merely perceive.

6. The results of studies of student note taking support the view that learners' own activities have important effects upon what is acquired.

7. Presenting similar meaningful materials in close succession can lead to interference effects. However, their influence upon meaningful learning is fairly small.

8. Success at learning from prose passages is related to the ease of understanding the materials. The greater the number of propositions contained in a passage of given length, the greater the amount of time required.

Suggestions for Further Reading

Cofer, C. N. (1977) On the constructive theory of memory. In I. C. Uzgiris and F. Weizmann (eds), *The Structuring of Experience*. New York: Plenum.

Kintsch, W. (1975) Memory for prose. In C. N. Cofer (ed.), *The Structure of Human Memory*. San Francisco: Freeman.

CHAPTER **12**

Individual Differences in Human Learning

OVERVIEW

People differ in their ability to learn, and the present chapter investigates factors contributing to individual differences. Some differences in learned achievements are due to causes such as attention and motivational variables, rather than to variability in learning processes as such. Various causes of individual differences are discussed, much of the evidence having been obtained from three broad categories of research: comparisons between normal and mentally retarded learners, social class comparisons, and cross-cultural studies.

INTRODUCTION

The many factors that contribute to human learning inevitably produce individual differences in ability to learn. Learning has a major influence upon the kind of person each of us becomes, and it determines what we can do, what we know, and what we think about and talk about. In most cultures, individual differences in the ability to learn are an important cause of variability in the lives people lead. We would like to know why some people's efforts to learn are more successful than those of others. This question will be easier to answer when we have an understanding of the ways in which more successful and less successful learners differ from each other. The more we know about the detailed ways in which effective and ineffective learners differ the more successful we will be at helping the less successful to improve their learning.

In the preceding chapters we encountered a large number of influences upon human learning. Some, such as attentional state and motivational factors, are important for many kinds of learning, and others are more specific. Imitative ability and observation are especially crucial for social learning, while learning that involves the use of language is strongly affected by a range of mental activities that underlie strategies such as rehearsal, organization, verbal elaboration, and semantic encoding. It has been shown that developmental changes in such activities make a large contribution to increasing ability to learn. In typical experiments that investigate learning by measuring the effects of a particular variable on performance, there is a tendency to neglect differences between people. In fact, such differences are often very large, even within the relatively homogeneous college student populations that have provided the experimental subjects for much of the experimental research into human learning. Researchers investigating learning may look upon individual differences as something of a nuisance factor since variability between people tends to obscure the effects of the variables under consideration, but in real life, differences between people in ability to learn are far too important to ignore.

LEARNING AND MENTAL ABILITY

Since learning is basic human ability, we might expect that performance at tasks that involve learning would be highly correlated with scores obtained in tests of intellectual powers such as intelligence. Measures of intelligence do give some indication of ability to learn, and there are positive correlations between learning and intelligence, but they tend to be surprisingly low. There are a number of reasons for this, one of them being the fact that an individual who is good at one kind of learning may not be at all successful at learning other things.

We might also expect that research into the measurement of intelligence and mental abilities would make a useful contribution to our understanding of the nature of human learning. However, until very recently the two forms of research have been so different in aims and in methods that neither has had much impact upon the other (Hunt, Frost and Lunneborg, 1973; Hunt and Lansman, 1975). Scores on intelligence tests do not provide much specific information that can help us answer questions concerning how and why individuals differ in their performance at particular learning tasks. Hunt and Lansman point out that nineteenth-century studies of individual differences by Sir Francis Galton were based on the attempt to explain differences in people's abilities by reference to the processes underlying them. However, subsequent developments in the measurement of human abilities have emphasized classifying people in ways that, although useful for practical purposes, have not produced increased understanding of why one individual is more able than another. Explanations of superior test performance tend to be phrased in such terms as "because he has a high IQ" or "because she possessed high verbal ability."

The tests that have been developed within the psychometric approach emphasizing measurement can be highly valuable for classifying pupils and for making predictions about their likelihood of being successful at particular activities. Such tests do not, however, give us any clear insight into what it is about the good learners, or the individuals with "high verbal ability" that make them different from others. Equally important, the psychometric approach gives us very few clues about what people whose attempts to learn are ineffective might do, or what skills they should acquire, in order to bring their own performance up to a level similar to that of the successful individual.

We do not simply need to know how well the different individuals perform, we also want to understand how learning is influenced by individual differences in the skills and processes that underlie performance at a particular learning task. To give a simple illustration, if we were to discover that all the students who performed well at a school task were individuals who carefully attended to certain aspects of the task materials, and that individuals who performed less well tended to attend to different things, we could use this information in order to help the people who failed. Simply knowing that some of the children are of "higher ability" than others at meeting the demands of the task would not be helpful. The test score information yielded by the psychometric approach tends to be restricted to statements of the latter kind. Knowing about individual differences in the detailed mechanisms and processes that underlie people's performance can make it possible to locate real sources of variability in ability to learn.

Genetic Determinants

We cannot discuss individual differences without mentioning the topic of hereditability. There is continuing controversy about the influence of hereditary factors on human achievement. It has been suggested that one should apportion values to the relative effects of environmental and hereditary determinants of learning, but such a view rests on the fallacious belief that these are distinct forces that can be simply added or multiplied together. In fact, the ways in which environmental and genetic influences combine are highly complicated, and for this reason behavior geneticists have noted that,

> It is nonsense to speculate that observed levels of IQ for individuals or groups of individuals are mostly innate because the hereditability of the trait may be high. To support this kind of judgment, every possible genotype would have to be raised in every possible environment and each with sufficient replication to permit the assessing of the reliability of such data. Then and only then could we make definitive statements about the relative effects of environment and hereditability (McGuire and Hirsch, 1977, p. 68).

The matter is a complicated one, particularly since it is not only desirable to be able to measure the magnitude of the hereditary contribution, but it is also necessary to specify the precise manner in which genetically transmitted factors influence human learning. Although there has been considerable research into hereditary determinants of achievement, the limited knowledge we do possess is almost solely about the first of the above two problems. Concerning the more difficult but equally important aim to specify the precise ways in which hereditary factors make their contribution, we remain largely ignorant. Genetic causation is rarely a simple matter, even in the case of specific physical characteristics. The ways in which genetic factors influence the multiply-determined phenomena that underlie human learning are complex, and involve lengthy chains of interacting processes. Furthermore, as Hunt and Lansman (1975) point out, most of the existing evidence concerning relationships between human abilities and hereditary phenomena takes the form of observed correlations. Just knowing that ability and genetic constitution are related leaves us in the dark about *how* genetic factors influence performance, and the demonstration that a relationship exists does not provide proof that any cause-and-effect link is involved. Even if we knew for certain that genetic determinants contribute to individual differences in achievement at learning, we would remain ignorant about which of the numerous ways in which genetic factors might conceivably influence performance are actually used. However, it has been suggested that abilities underlying some skills, such as the ability to perform spatial tasks, might be influenced by genetic links that are less complex and require fewer genes than are necessary for other mental abilities. Future research will certainly expand our present knowledge.

At this stage we do not have to be greatly concerned with hereditary influences. There is no doubt that such factors are important, and it would be valuable to possess greater detailed knowledge than is now available concerning the manner in which hereditary factors may contribute to learning. But nothing that is discovered in the future about genetic influences will alter the fact that acquired knowledge and skills do have to be learned. Learning cannot be bypassed. There may be hereditary reasons for one person finding it easier than another to acquire a particular learned ability, but the fact remains that both people have to learn substantially the same things. Hereditary variations may indeed be among the causes of individual differences in human learning, but verifying this possibility would not tell us much about the nature and form of learning differences. It is important to know about the latter, if we are to be in a position to raise the performance levels of people who do not learn easily toward the standards achieved by good learners.

INDIVIDUAL DIFFERENCES IN THE FIRST MONTHS OF LIFE

Very early in the lives of infants, it is possible to discern individual differences in a number of attributes that influence ability to learn.

Korner (1971) describes a variety of differences between infants that can have implications for later experience and development. Some of the differences affect children's activities directly and others concern ways in which children perceive and experience events that occur in their presence. At birth, some infants cry considerably more than others. Since crying serves to bring about social contact with the mother, it follows that differences between babies in crying may contribute to differences in patterns of caretaking and social interactions, and thus affect early social learning. In addition, Korner found that the babies she observed differed appreciably in how readily they were soothed by being picked up when crying, and in the time they remained comforted. Such differences may influence the mother's behavior toward her child. Especially if she is inexperienced in child care, her feelings of competence may be affected by the child's reaction to her efforts at soothing. Her feelings, in turn, may influence her own actions in a number of the situations involving mother-infant interactions that are important for the child's early social learning.

Young infants also vary in cuddliness, and this leads to differences in the way they are handled (Schaffer and Emerson, 1964). Some infants protest and actively resist when their mothers attempt to embrace or hug them. The "noncuddlers" are generally more restless than other children and dislike physical constraints. As a result, they receive less physical contact than infants who are more cuddly. Although the development of attachments is not necessarily impaired in noncuddlers, the nature of interaction between mother and infant is inevitably affected. Schaffer and Emerson observed faster motor development in the noncuddlers, possibly as a direct outcome of their active and restless behavior.

In Korner's investigation, she found a number of additional early differences that might affect social interactions and social learning. For example, some infants engaged more frequently than others in spontaneous oral activities such as sucking and mouthing, and young infants varied considerably in the amount of persistence at self-comforting activities of finger sucking or placing the hand in the mouth. As Korner remarks, these differences can influence the extent to which the infant needs to make demands upon the mother in order to reduce tension, and at a later stage they may affect the progress of weaning. Some of the early differences I have mentioned may contribute to children's perception of themselves as being helpless and dependent or relatively independent.

Young infants also vary considerably in their sensory receptivity, and this affects how they perceive and experience the environment that forms their everyday world. Some infants like, and appear to need, a large amount of sensory stimulation. They are said to have a "high visual threshold." Other infants have lower visual thresh-olds, and are sensitive, easily overwhelmed, and made anxious by too much stimulation. The effects of differences in early social ac-tivities and differences in early sensitivity to stimulation may be augmented when the two factors are combined. For example, Korner notes that infants who cry often in the earliest months tend to be picked up. Apart from the effect of this on their social behavior, when infants are picked up they usually become visually attentive, and thus gain some visual stimulation. It would seem that infants who have a high visual threshold and benefit from extra stimulation will gain more from the experience of being picked up than infants with a low visual threshold. The latter infants already receive all the stimulation they require and are upset by over-stimulation. It fol-lows that the effects of maternal neglect, in which the mother does not regularly pick up and play with her child, will be more severe in the case of infants with a high visual threshold than in infants with a lower threshold. The latter do not gain the same benefit from the extra visual stimulation that results from being picked up.

Investigations in which children have been assessed in early infancy and reexamined several years later (Escalona, 1973) confirm that it is possible to make accurate predictions about learned achievements on the basis of some early characteristics. For in-stance, it was correctly predicted that infants with a high level of activity, which tends to impede the learning of verbal symbols and early concept acquisition, would become 5-year-olds with higher scores on motor performance than on verbal achievement items. Similarly, highly sensitive infants became 5-year-olds who were capable of highly differentiated expressive behavior and were able to state meanings and states of feeling with accuracy and subtlety. Escalona emphasizes that the child's experience cannot be inferred simply from a knowledge of the objective properties of the envi-ronment. She points out that having a home full ot toys does not guarantee that the child is experiencing rich stimulation. She notes,

> "It is what the child does or does not do, how he behaves in the context of whatever the environment provides, that defines and describes his actual life experience" (Escalona, 1971, p. 149).

DIFFERENCES IN PROCESSING INFORMATION

The cognitive processes that underlie learning and memory per-form a number of functions. Although existing knowledge of the information-processing mechanisms that regulate human learning is far from complete, some of their activities can be specified with some certainty. For example, as we remarked in Chapter 9, information needs to be transformed or encoded at certain stages. In addition, if data has to be retained for short and longer periods, there must be provision for gaining quick access to stored information, and data must be transmitted between different parts of the system. In any system that contains a number of processes, a bottleneck may occur if any one part cannot easily cope with the demands placed upon it; the efficiency of the whole system is dependent upon the effectiveness of its weakest or slowest part. Thus, if a storage component of the brain's information-processing system is too small to keep up with the demands, or if the mechanism for retrieving information is too slow, or if an important route through which information is transmitted has insufficient processing capacity, the performance of the whole system will suffer.

It is conceivable that individual differences in any of a number of mental mechanisms involved in human learning could make important contributions to individual differences in ability to learn. Information must be retained at various points in the cognitive processes underlying learning. The peripheral memory store investigated by Sperling (1960) retains visual materials for very brief periods, typically less than one second, thereby maintaining information over sufficient time for initial scanning or encoding functions to be undertaken. Since this initial storage system may determine the amount of newly received information that can be processed, particularly high or particularly low levels of efficiency at this stage of memory may lead to differences in the effectiveness of a range of cognitive functions, including human learning.

Hunt and Lansman (1975) draw attention to the large individual differences in performance at the task used by Sperling (1960) to assess the characteristics of the visual memory store. Sperling reported the performance of four subjects at a task that assessed how long information was maintained. Afte 150 milliseconds, one subject still retained 85 percent of the original input, whereas the poorest subject had only 60 percent still available. If the amount of information processing that can take place is directly related to the length of time that information is held in this store, the individual differences revealed in this task could be of considerable significance.

A number of further instances of individual differences in processing capacity are described by Hunt and Lansman. Normal individuals differ by a factor of two to one in their ability to identify the loudness and the quality of auditory tones (Moore and Massaro, 1973). There are large differences between people in the performance of tasks that require subjects to identify whether two letters are the same or different, on the basis of either their physical characteristics (AA, BB—same; BA, AB—different), or their name code

(*Aa, Bb*—same; *Ab, Ba*—different) (Posner and Keele, 1967). Subjects who obtain high scores in tests of verbal intelligence perform the above task approximately a third faster than subjects whose verbal intelligence test scores are in the bottom 25 percent (Hunt, Frost, and Lunneborg, 1973). Furthermore, some people are considerably better than others at being able to switch channels when different auditory messages are presented to the two ears. This ability appears to be related to control skills, and the performance levels of truck drivers at a task of this kind have been found to be correlated with their safety records. Research by Das, Kirby, and Jarman (1975) indicates that individual differences in the kinds of processing that predominate are associated with distinct patterns of intellectual abilities.

It is largely as a result of learning that people acquire the strategies and procedures that enable them to learn efficiently. Mature individuals can draw upon mental skills they possess and upon existing knowledge, thereby increasing their effectiveness as learners. Because learning is cumulative, abilities acquired in the past can be used to facilitate learning in the present. The repertoire of skills at the disposal of mature learners, together with the knowledge they possess, provide a number of short cuts to learning that are not available to immature learners and mentally retarded individuals. They have no alternative but to approach many tasks of learning by rote repetition, leading to the gradual formation of new associations. The successful adult can introduce a variety of elaborative and organizational activities, for example, providing sentences that join two to-be-learned word items in order to reduce the number of effectively separate units and lighten the burden that is placed upon memory.

Differences between good and poor learners do not, on the whole, lie in the successful learners possessing any one particular mental skill or using a particular strategy that is not possessed by others. The good learner is simply in a position to call upon a wider range of appropriate procedures. The successful learner will have acquired a repertoire of intellectual skills, varying in function and complexity. When faced with a new task that necessitates learning, such a person will most probably have appropriate mental tools available for the task, in the form of an effective learning strategy or procedure. To speak of "good" and "poor" learners is an oversimplification, of course. People differ in their patterns of abilities, and the fact that someone displays expertise in learning to play the piano is no guarantee that the same individual will find it easy to acquire the ability to speak a foreign language.

Rehearsal and Scanning Activities

Differences in the way people rehearse provide another cause of variability in learning. As we found in Chapter 10, both the quantity and the quality of rehearsal may influence performance. Brown, Campione, and Murphy, (1974) observed that training subjects to use a rehearsal strategy led to improvements in learning by mentally retarded people but it did not help college students. The implication is that the students were rehearsing spontaneously, and therefore instructions to do so did not greatly alter their activities. In support of this conclusion there is the additional finding that the introduction of procedures to prevent rehearsal led to a decrease in the amount of learning by college students but not by the mentally retarded subjects.

People differ in the speed at which they can process information. Hunt and Lansman (1975) draw attention to the large differences between people's levels of achievement at a task devised by Sternberg (1966). The subjects perceived a group of items and had to state as quickly as possible whether a single "probe" item they subsequently saw was the same as one of the items in memory, or not. Reaction times were plotted as a function of the number of items retained, the slope of the resulting line providing an indication of the rate at which retained information was scanned by the subject. The activity of scanning items that are held in memory is an important one for human cognitive functioning, and differences between people in their speed of such scanning may lead to individual variability in many forms of human learning. Hunt and Lansman point out that there are large individual differences in scanning speed. They note that the differences are so large that it was necessary for Sternberg to report data from individual cases, rather than group averages. Hunt and Lansman found that individuals who obtain high verbal intelligence test scores scanned more rapidly, on average, than other subjects. The correlations with verbal intelligence scores were relatively low, however, and did not account for all of the considerable intersubject variability in speed of scanning.

Individual Differences in Encoding

Encoding is one kind of function that we have shown to be necessary for learning. This has the effect of translating data into forms in which they can be effectively processed by the human brain. We would expect that differences between people in encoding skills would have a marked effect upon learning. The following study of encoding makes use of an effect known as *release from proactive inhibition*. This can occur when the physical qualities of information presented, for example the sound and length of words, remains constant but the meaning changes. Proactive inhibition is said to build up when repeated trials include similar stimulus items. The first item is remembered easily, but subsequent items may be forgotten, because, it is claimed, there is a build-up of inhibition. Following a number of trials involving similar stimuli, if a different type of stimulus event is then presented it will be clearly remembered. Superficially, the phenomenon resembles the effect of "dishabituation" (see Chapter 3), in which presentation of a novel item after habituation has occurred to a repeated stimulus produces a large "dishabituated" response.

Our present interest in the release from proactive inhibition effect lies in the fact that knowing which kinds of changes produce release gives an indication of how a person has been encoding the items. For example, if we find that presenting a stimulus that means the same as a previous item but is physically different (for example, *car* following *automobile*) produces release, it would appear that the items have been stored in memory on the basis of physical characteristics. However, if items that are physically different from a previous item but of similar meaning do *not* produce release from proactive inhibition, but items that are physically similar but different in meaning (for example, *male, mail*) do cause release, the pattern of results would suggest that items are being encoded by the learner on the basis of their meanings. The release from proactive inhibition effect can thus provide an indication of how people have encoded the materials that are shown to them. In one experiment, Hunt, Frost, and Lunneborg (1973) presented word lists that started with names of vegetables. The stimulus category was switched to occupations, and it was found that the category change produced a release from proactive inhibition. The magnitude of the release effect was greatest in those subjects who obtained the highest scores in tests of verbal ability. Differences associated with verbal ability were especially large when words were scored correct only if they were recalled in the right order. The findings indicate that the most able subjects were more inclined than the others to encode the word items on the basis of their meanings.

The Contribution of Individual Differences to Memory Task Performance

One of the investigations by Hunt, Frost, and Lunneborg (1973) shows how performance may be influenced by the combined effects of various differences between people. They used a task in which subjects were required to remember information for a short time, and the analysis of the task into its components was based upon Atkinson and Shiffrin's (1968) model of memory. The model assumes that the capacity of the short-term memory system (STM) is restricted to r separate items, r being around seven. When STM capacity is full, subsequent presentation of further items may result in existing items being lost from STM, but items can be maintained there by active rehearsal. Items may also gain access to a long-term memory (LTM) that has unlimited capacity, but items in LTM can become inaccessible or be lost for other reasons.

On the assumption that the above description corresponds, at least roughly, with the operations of human memory, Hunt, Frost, and Lunneborg made predictions about differences in people's performance at the various component processes underlying remembering. In the above description, the following events are said to occur when a subject receives new information:

1. Information is entered into STM with probability α. It is assumed that α is under the control of the subject, and may vary according to the kind of stimuli involved.
2. The effect of entering a new item into STM upon existing stored items depends upon the subject's rehearsal strategy and the size of STM in terms of the number of items (r) it can contain.
3. Information about an item in STM is transferred to LTM at rate θ. The proportion of the information about an item that enters LTM is a function of θ and of the time the item is retained in STM.
4. Information in LTM becomes unavailable by a negative exponential function, with decay parameter τ.

Atkinson and Shiffrin compared the predictions based on this model, with the parameters α, r, θ, and τ, to actual performance by subjects on a task involving memory for continuous paired-associate sequences of pairs made up of a letter and a two-digit number, for example,

A—12
B— 42
C—16
and so on.

After testing recall, by providing a stimulus item, for example B, and eliciting the correct answer (42), a new to-be-associated number would be provided. The probability of a correct response was measured as a function of the number of items between presentation of the pair and the request for recall of the digit item. Atkinson and Shiffrin matched the data from subjects' actual task performance with the predictions of the model, and then decided on values of the parameters which best fitted the data. They could then predict the effects of making various changes in the experimental conditions. Their forecasts were reasonably successful. Hunt, Frost, and Lunneborg (1973) made certain predictions on the basis of knowledge about individual differences. Comparing the performance data obtained from students with low and high scores on tests of verbal comprehension, they found differences between people in some of the above parameters, namely on α (the probability of information entering STM) and r (STM capacity). This indicates that students with the high verbal ability had appreciably higher capacities than others for these components of verbal tasks. In addition, they may have used their existing capacities more effectively. As Hunt and Lansman point out, this kind of approach can take us beyond the simple statement that some people have better memories than others, and gives insight into the differences between individuals in the way their memory systems are used.

Demonstrating that individual differences exist in some of the particular forms of information processing that lead to human cognition and learning helps to pinpoint some of the specific factors contributing to individual differences. Further examinations of the ways in which people differ in performance of the tasks devised to investigate cognitive processes will yield evidence about the precise forms and locations of the information-processing differences that underlie human variability in learned achievements.

EVIDENCE FROM COMPARISONS BETWEEN NORMAL AND MENTALLY RETARDED PEOPLE

Research that has been undertaken in order to extend our understanding of the differences between normal people and mentally retarded individuals provides a useful source of evidence about individual differences in learning. Mentally retarded people tend to be very poor learners, and comparisons between normal and mentally retarded individuals can contribute knowledge about some of the ways in which people differ in the way they learn. This knowledge can be valuable for helping retarded individuals to acquire methods of learning that are more effective than their existing habits.

We might expect to find some fundamental differences in basic mental processes between normal and mentally retarded learners.

For example, there might be differences in the rate at which signals are transmitted along and between neurons, since physical activity is fundamental to human information processing. However, it has not yet proved possible to discover individual differences in physical brain activity that are clearly related to psychological performance. Identifying the physical correlates of learning has turned out to be much more difficult than early investigators expected it to be. Thorndike (1931) suggested that learning capacity is related to the number of neuronal connections available for the formation of new associations. Other attempts at explanation have stressed the speed at which signals can be transmitted along neuronal networks as being a possible limiting factor, by which good and poor learners may be distinguished. But there is no clear evidence to support any single explanation of this kind, and it is now clear that the goal of understanding the neuronal mechanisms of human learning and memory will not easily be achieved (Thompson, 1976). Furthermore, in the light of current knowledge it seems unlikely that when the physiological correlates of learning are known they will be found to be related to measures of learning in any simple or straightforward way.

One apparently promising strategy for increasing our understanding of differences in learning between normal and mentally retarded people is to compare their performance at the very simplest forms of learning. Individual differences in performance are largely due to the use of strategies and procedures that use acquired mental skills and habits, and to motivation, attention, and the involvement of existing knowledge. It would be interesting to compare people at forms of learning in which these broader influences are excluded or largely absent. If it was possible to devise a learning situation from which these factors have been removed, we could examine associative kinds of learning in a relatively pure form, uncontaminated by the additional influences that contribute to human learning in everyday circumstances.

Such a possibility is less easy to achieve in practice than in theory, and it is virtually impossible to devise actual instances of "pure" learning from which the broader influences are entirely absent. Classical conditioning is the form of learning that comes closest to this. When appropriate control procedures are provided, a classical conditioning procedure might appear to provide researchers with a reasonably clear glimpse at the formation of new associations. Some experiments have been undertaken in the USSR and in the West to compare the progress of classical conditioning in normal and mentally retarded individuals. In these studies, age was held constant and the learning of normal and mentally retarded individuals was compared. Summarizing the evidence from studies of this kind, Estes (1970) concluded that the most striking finding running through the conditioning studies was the absence of conspicuous differences in rates of acquisition between normal and retarded subjects, or between retarded individuals differing in mental ability. The findings give no support at all to the view that differences in a basic associative ability underlying all forms of learning are at the heart of individual differences in ability to learn. Although such a possibility has not been completely disproved, it appears to be more profitable to look elsewhere for the causes of variability in learning.

We must avoid hasty generalizations about the specific learning deficits in mentally retarded individuals. They, like other people, vary enormously. Some individuals who are diagnosed as being retarded suffer from pathological functioning of physically identifiable brain processes. However many of the observed differences between normal and retarded learners are due to the combined effects of various broader influences upon learning. Some of the differences are due to the factors that produce variability in learning by ordinary individuals. A variety of causes, including deficits in attention, motivational abnormalities resulting from unusual patterns of reinforcement, failure to learn appropriate mediating and elaborative skills, lack of encoding abilities, poor rehearsal practices, and retrieval and organizational deficits, can all reduce a person's ability to learn and justify describing the individual as retarded, even in the absence of specific organic impairment.

Skills of Attending

Experiments in which normal and retarded subjects were compared in learning to make discriminations have provided one source of evidence concerning factors contributing to individual differences in learning. In a typical experimental session, the subjects are individually shown a number of pairs of objects, and their task is to choose which item from each pair is the "correct" one. In order to be able to respond correctly, the learner has to discover which of a number of stimulus dimensions (for example, shape, color, or size) is the crucial one, and which are irrelevant. Over a number of trials, performance usually improves until the probability of making a correct response on the first presentation of each new pair of items approaches 100 percent.

Inspection of the average task scores of a group of subjects shows a steadily rising curve, suggesting gradual learning. But if the performance of each individual is plotted separately on a graph, a different state of affairs is revealed. There is a first stage in which there is hardly any change in performance from one trial to the next, shown by a nearly horizontal slope in the part of the graph corresponding to the early trials. Next, there is a steep slope, indicating a stage of rapid learning. The flat early part appears to represent the period in which the learners are discovering for themselves which are the relevant task dimensions to which they should attend. The subsequent steep rise represents the associative learning stage, in which the individual is acquiring a learned connection between the appropriate dimension and the correct response. Comparison between different people on tasks of this kind reveal marked individual differences. A high level of performance may be depicted either by an unusually short first stage (showing how long the learner takes to discover the appropriate dimension), or by an unusually steep final rise (representing the subsequent associative learning stage), or by both. When we examine the individual graphs of the best and the poorest performers, we find that the differences do not lie in the steepness of the slope representing the final associative learning stage, but in the length of the early stage. The efficient learners gain by requiring less time to discern which of the available dimensions is the crucial one. It is in the effectiveness of their attentional skills rather than an associative learning process that they stand out from the people who perform less well.

The findings of a number of experiments described by Estes (1970) support this conclusion. Differences between normal and retarded children in degree of success at discrimination learning tasks tended to disappear when care was paid to insuring that all subjects did actually attend to the appropriate task cues. Furthermore, research by Zeaman and House (1967) has demonstrated that individual differences at discrimination learning are much reduced if one compares learners at only those parts of the tasks in which variability in attentional skills is not crucial.

The individual differences in attention that are significant for human learning lie not in people's total capacity to attend but in the way they selectively direct attention toward appropriate aspects of the task at hand. Any person is usually attending to something, but the effective learner has also acquired habits that involve giving attention to those cues that are most relevant for success. As I remarked in Chapter 3, children at school who can maintain attention to the printed word or to the teacher's voice are more likely to succeed than children who customarily direct their attention to whatever is happening outside the classroom window.

Impulsivity and Inhibitory Processes

Research into mental retardation has shown that the extreme impulsivity of some children can hinder learning. In many instances of learning it is necessary for the individual to slow down at certain points in order to make a decision before proceeding to make a response. When the learner has to make a choice or discrimination, it is often important to inspect a number of task elements before an actual response is made. It is sometimes possible to make covert responses, by which individuals are able to consider the effects of various possible actions, through "vicarious trial and error" (or VTE), before committing themselves to one particular course of action. Individuals who are unusually impulsive or easily distracted may not be able to avoid making premature responses, or they may be distracted by irrelevant information. Such individuals will clearly be at a disadvantage compared with others. Most young children tend to be impulsive, but normal children become less so as they get older, and they gain the ability to delay their actions when it is appropriate to do so (Kagan, 1965). Excessive impulsiveness, which may sometimes be due to a child simply failing to learn effective scanning skills, can hinder a child from acquiring important basic activities. For instance, it has been found that among children in their first year at school those individuals who are more impulsive than others make an unusually large number of errors in recognizing words, and they are thereby handicapped in learning to read.

Slow learning in some retarded people may be caused by an absence of certain inhibitory processes that are present in normal learners. It is found, for instance, that when learning occurs in massed blocks of trials, performance is normally positively related to the duration of rest intervals between trials. A possible explanation (Ellis, 1970) is that during the massed trials there is a build-up of inhibition. The greater the amount of inhibition that is produced, the more a learner will profit from having a relatively long interval between blocks of trials, since rest intervals enable inhibition to dissipate. Ellis found that the gains mentally retarded subjects showed from increased intervals between blocks of trials did not come close to those of normal subjects. This may have been because less inhibition built up in the mentally retarded subjects and hence there was less to dissipate. The above explanation is somewhat speculative, however, since the precise form and function of the hypothesized inhibitory processes have never been specified with a satisfactory degree of precision.

Rehearsal

Research into mental retardation has also yielded a number of suggestions about the possible effects of deficiencies in storage and retrieval mechanisms that are required for human learning. It has been suggested that mentally retarded people have poor rehearsal strategies, and evidence mentioned in Chapter 10 supports this suggestion. Ellis (1970) notes that while variations in the presentation rate of word lists produce large differences in the recall accuracy of normal subjects, especially in the case of early items, in mentally retarded learners performance is not greatly improved by slower presentation. Since a reduced rate of presentation provides increased opportunities for early items to be rehearsed, it is possible that the difference in the effect of slower presentation is due to the failure of retarded people to take advantage of the slower rate to rehearse items in the way normal learners do. The performance of mentally retarded subjects who were given careful training in the use of rehearsal operations improved dramatically (Butterfield, Wambold, and Belmont, 1973). Mentally retarded children were observed by Brown (1975b) to be as good as normal subjects at a picture recognition task, but when they also had to keep track of items in different categories the retarded individuals performed very poorly. Good performance at the tracking task depended on the items being rehearsed, and when retarded subjects were specially trained to rehearse as they attempted the task, their recall increased to a level close to that of the normal subjects. Another possible cause of poor memory in retardates is that they suffer from a reduced "stimulus trace." The latter is described by Ellis (1970) as a reverberatory mechanism persisting only for a few seconds. However, there is little firm evidence for this suggestion.

Transfer

A further way in which some mentally retarded subjects differ from competent learners lies in the degree to which skills and actions can be transferred to circumstances that are similar but not identical to those in which the original learning took place. In one investigation it was found that retarded subjects who had been trained to respond to an auditory tone were less likely than normals to respond in the same way if a similar but not identical tone was subsequently presented (O'Connor and Hermelin, 1963). Comparison studies involving normal and retarded learners are often difficult to interpret with any certainty. A possible explanation of this finding is that since the

retarded subjects needed a larger number of trials to achieve criterion, they were more often reinforced for responding to the particular original tone. However, the conclusion that the retarded learners
were demonstrating reduced generalization is at least equally likely
to be correct. Careful training can produce marked increases in the
amount of transfer that takes place (Campione and Brown, 1974).

It should not be forgotten that motivational factors, which can
exert a considerable influence on learning, as we discovered in
Chapter 3, may be among the determinants of the low levels of
learning ability in retarded people. There are a variety of ways in
which motivation can contribute to an individual's poor performance. For example, in early childhood a person's exploratory activities may have been highly restricted, perhaps due to chronic
illness or too much anxiety on the part of a parent, or possibly because of the physical restrictions of a home environment where
adequate care is lacking. As a result, the child may fail to obtain
valuable experience that is normally acquired through exploring
activities. Or perhaps a child might have unusually punitive parents
who severely restrict his activities. If children lack opportunities to
learn about the natural consequences of their actions, they may fail
to acquire knowledge that is essential as a basis for further learning.
Repeated failure in early childhood may be another motivational
barrier. As an outcome of failing repeatedly in those situations in
which it is necessary to learn new abilities, children may come to
avoid such situations. Consequently, they not only reduce their
chances of failing, as was their intention, but also deprive themselves of opportunities to acquire skills and knowledge that are
required for normal living.

EVIDENCE FROM SOCIAL CLASS RESEARCH

Research into differences associated with social class phenomena
has provided a further source of evidence about individual variability in learning. Social class is not a unitary causal factor. Identifying
an individual's class background gives a rough indication about the
probable life circumstances of a person, but it does not provide any
precise or detailed knowledge about the individual's environment,
let alone the person's capabilities. Describing the social class of
people makes it possible to identify, in a very broad and approximate manner, the kinds of social and economic contexts they have
experienced, and this information may form a useful starting point
for more detailed analysis of the effects of environmental forces.
(Measures of social class have often been used in ways that indicate
an erroneous belief that they do provide accurate indices of the

environment, and it is necessary to emphasize the fact that they do not. In studies designed to compare the relative contributions of inherited and environmental determinants of intelligence, it has been customary to use social class data for the ratings of the quality of the child's environment. Such measures give only the roughest indications of the actual quality of the environment experienced by individual children, and may lead to the relative influence of environmental causes being underestimated.)

It is possible to obtain relatively direct measures of the actual environmental forces operating upon a child. These measures are considerably more useful as predictors of a child's achievements than are measures of social class or related factors such as parental occupation and educational standards. Marjoribanks (1972) found that whereas the correlations between dimensions of a child's intellectual ability and the parents' status were typically around + 0.3, correlations between intellectual ability and the environmental forces a child actually encountered were appreciably higher, around + 0.6 in the case of numerical and verbal abilities.

Social class and learning are related, and they will continue to be so long as class differences exist in life styles. Some class-related differences in learned achievements are apparent quite early in life. For instance, a number of researchers have observed early differences in the way language is used. Kagan (1970) reported that 2-year-old middle-class children played with toys for longer periods than children from lower-class families, and were more likely to complete their play activities. Findings concerning the effects of different styles of mother-infant interaction on children's early social behavior, such as those by Mary Ainsworth described in Chapter 5, might lead us to expect that any class-related differences in patterns of interaction would produce corresponding differences in children's ability. This does appear to be the case.

Caution is essential in interpreting the findings of research into child-rearing practices, especially since they may change from one decade to the next, but some class differences appear to be fairly stable. On the whole, American middle-class mothers are likely to be more tolerant of impulsive actions in their young children than lower-class parents, middle-class parents are less likely to punish lapses in self-control, and they tend to discipline their children by disapproval and withdrawal of affection, whereas lower-class parents more frequently apply physical punishments (Hess, 1970). The children of middle-class parents are expected to show greater independence in certain everyday skills, such as feeding and dressing. There is a tendency for working-class parents to place more stress upon neatness, cleanliness, and obedience, and for middle-class parents to attach greater importance to curiosity, independence, and consideration for others. As we might expect, middle-class parents tend to place greater stress on the importance of independent achievement. However, in reporting these findings it is important to note that they are based upon averages, and that there are large overlaps between social classes in all the various measures. The fact that a particular child comes from one social class background does not necessarily mean that one can predict with a high probability of being correct the reactions of the child's parents on any of the above variables. We can make fairly confident predictions about the average parental values of large numbers of people, and we can predict the average behavior and patterns of interaction of large groups of children grouped according to social class. But we cannot make confident exact statements about the family circumstances of individual children.

Class Differences in Interaction with Children

A number of investigations have found class-related differences in early verbal communications between mother and child. On the whole, middle-class mothers are more prone than working-class mothers to talk to their children, to give specific instructions, to expect their children to respond to them in words rather than simply complying physically, to make systematic use of rewards, and to provide their children with information that is helpful either for carrying out present activities successfully or for improving competence in the future (Hess, 1970). Middle-class mothers were observed by some investigators to be considerably more responsive than lower-class mothers to their children's requests, and less likely to give orders that are not accompanied by an explanation. Zunich (1961) observed a greater amount of physical contact between middle-class mothers and their children, and noted that the middle-class mothers were more likely to become involved in helping and directing their children's activities, to watch their children and interact with them at play, and to sometimes interfere with their activities. Children of middle-class parents have been observed to seek the attention of their mothers more frequently than children from lower-class backgrounds. It is difficult to specify cause-and-effect relationships with any certainty, but the latter finding may be a result of the more responsive middle-class mothers being more likely to reinforce attention-seeking behavior.

In general, the results of observational studies point to the conclusion that middle-class mothers tend to become more aware of their children's needs and feelings as a consequence of being responsive and attentive, communicating frequently with their children, and showing interest in their activities. The fact that middle-class parents are more likely than lower-class parents to explain the reason for a request being made and less likely to use punishment as a control technique may contribute to parent and child becoming more aware of each other's individual characteristics.

Cultural differences associated with national and racial backgrounds complicate any analysis of social class phenomena. A further difficulty is introduced by the fact that in large countries such as the United States the members of cultural and racial minorities may cluster at one part, typically the lower end, of social class scales. However, similar patterns of differences between social class may be found in separate nations. Investigations carried out in Britain reveal class-related differences that are very similar to the ones observed in North America. Newson and Newson (1968) observed more interactions between middle-class British parents and their children, more story telling, and more encouragement to talk at mealtimes. They less frequently used punishments or threats that were based on distortion of the truth (for example, "Don't do that or the policemen will come and take you away") than working-class mothers, and they were more likely to tell their children the reasons for parental actions or demands.

It is difficult to specify the precise causes of the class-related differences in parental behavior. Differences in wealth affect some activities, and the educational factors that determine a parent's knowledge and abilities for self-expression are also important. The social-class differences that can be observed generally reflect the needs of all parents to function effectively in the differing social circumstances of their lives, and to adapt their behavior to everyday requirements. There is no evidence of any unwillingness on the part of lower-class mothers to function adequately as parents, nor any indication of class differences in the degree of love and concern for children. Nor is there any conscious preference on the part of working-class parents for punishment as a means of control. The possibility that differences in the manner in which parents control their children are due to variations in the parents' intelligence is not supported by the evidence. The particular forms of middle-class behavior toward children that differ from the behavior of working-class parents are not ones for which the latter possess insufficient mental ability.

In general, class differences in the way parents interact with children are due not to any specific single causes, or to the working-class parents being deficient in necessary skills, but to broader variations in cultural styles and conditions of life. Hess

(1970) argues that the behavior of parents toward their children reflects the manner in which the parents themselves have learned to cope with life. The reactions and attitudes of lower-class people toward authority tend to be different from those of middle-class parents. Hess has noted that orientation which people acquire toward people in authority and toward using authority and discipline "transmits and reinforces the orientation of adults towards the economic and social system of which they are a part."

The differences in parental behavior toward their children probably contribute to the class-related differences observed in the children themselves. Hess and his colleagues have noticed that the performance of young children at intelligence tests and at tests of conceptual development is related to the behavior of the mother toward her child. They found that the children's achievements were positively correlated with the degree to which mothers successfully anticipated the children's needs, provided them with necessary information and appropriate feedback, and adopted methods of control that involved explaining a situation and taking the child's feelings into account. Similarly, evidence from studies of early mother-infant social interaction showed that the children of mothers who were sensitive and responsive tended to be compliant and cooperative and to develop skills for communicating their needs to adults. In addition, there is some evidence of early class-related differences in attentional skills. At 1 year of age middle-class children sustained their attention to visual patterns for longer periods, displaying an ability which is crucially important for learning (Kagan, 1970).

The available evidence points to the conclusion that differences in early environment and in the experiences associated with daily living in different social-class settings are a major cause of class-related differences in performance. However, the fact that hereditary factors may exert an influence complicates the situation.

Class Differences in Social Effectiveness

In addition to the possible outcomes of social class factors upon a child's learned skills and abilities, social class membership may have a further kind of influence that is equally crucial. The way in which people regard themselves, particularly in respect of their feelings of independence and of either being personally effective in achieving their own goals, or of being powerless, on the other hand, may depend to a marked effect upon their social-class background. There are several reasons for this. First, the extent to which a person is actually able to exercise power in society is undeniably related to social class, mainly through wealth, access to information, experience in expressing oneself publicly, and possession of communicative skills. An objectively founded belief among working-class parents that they have little power to change the circumstances of their lives may have a number of implications for their children's learning. A symptom of this is the reluctance of some working-class parents to contact a child's teacher and to insure that their views are considered by school authorities and that they are kept informed about the child's detailed progress at school. Lower-class people suffer as consumers of services, including education, through having less information on which to base their choices and through lacking knowledge and skills that contribute to the effectiveness of complaints or demands for one's rights. Hess argues that the capacity for effective self-assertive activities is hindered by the working-class individual's awareness of being relatively powerless, for the reasons we have just discussed. Consequently, class differences in achievements tend to be maintained from one generation to the next.

Various sources of evidence point to the conclusion that working-class mothers feel themselves to be less independent, less autonomous and less able to control events in their lives than middle-class individuals. Kagan and Tulkin (1971), who found that during the infants' first year, middle-class mothers spoke to their children more often than lower-class mothers, noted that it was not unusual for the mother who did not frequently talk to her young child to express the view that doing so had no useful effect until the age at which the child was beginning to talk. These mothers thought that only after the child began to talk did it become important for the mother to speak back. The mother whose communications with her child are influenced by such a view may be depriving the child of opportunities for imitation and observational learning. As I remarked in Chapter 8, these are important for early language development. Reluctance to stimulate a child's early vocalization may be one indication of a general belief by the mother that she has little power to influence her child's development. Such an attitude may be linked to the broader fatalism and feelings of oneself as being relatively powerless that we noted to be especially common, for good reason, in people with little education.

A mother's feeling that she is powerless to influence her child can have other adverse effects. For example, those attempts at compensatory education that involve assisting the mother to become an effective teacher of her child can only be really effective if the mother does come to believe that what she does will have some effect. It may be more necessary than is commonly realized to convince the mother that her activities will actually be influential before she will be willing to cooperate wholeheartedly and to make important changes in the ways in which she interacts with her child. If the mother reluctantly allows an intervention program to be imposed upon her, while privately doubting that it will have much success, the interventions will most probably be ineffective.

Social Class and Learning Strategies

A series of experiments by Bresnahan and Shapiro (1972) has yeilded evidence of class-related differences in strategies of learning. Lower-class children were observed to be more likely to persevere in any incorrect responses they made in a learning task. This could be because, in their experience, rewards were related to their own behavior in a way that was more random and less systematic than it was for middle-class children. This hypothesis is supported by the finding that reinforcing middle-class children on a completely random basis led to them behaving in the same manner as the lower-class subjects, and learning just as little. The authors state that class-related differences in the extent to which rewards are experienced as being dependent upon the individual's own behavior affect children's strategies when confronted by a new learning task. They state, "A person is most able to conform to those contingencies with which he has had the most recent experience or the most extensive experience. People who have overlearned one contingency do not readily shift their behavior when the contingency or the nature of the task is shifted" (Bresnahan and Shapiro, 1972, p. 75).

Bresnahan and Shapiro's results indicate that the distinction between internal and external controls of behavior is related to a class-related difference in approaches to learning. For Rotter (1966), external control is characterized by the circumstances in which a reinforcing event that follows some action is perceived by the individual as being the result of luck, chance or fate, or of the activities of other people, and hence unpredictable and not contingent upon the individual's own actions. Internal control is present when people perceive an event to be contingent upon their own behavior. Differences in perception of the direction of control have clear implications for learning, and the influence people's estimates of the probability of their attempts to learn being successful.

Jensen (1973) has claimed that it is possible to discern class-related differences in learning styles, with working-class children performing well at associative tasks but being relatively poor at abstract reasoning. Some evidence for this distinction exists, but there is no firm support for Jensen's view that such a difference is related to innate, hereditarily transmitted factors.

Social Class Differences in Language

Some class-related individual differences that are especially crucial for human learning are produced by the way people use language. The many educational programs that have been devised at one time or another to help provide compensatory education or "enrichment" in order to ameliorate the effects of impoverished cultural backgrounds associated with conditions of poor housing, low educational status, and parental absence or negligence, have almost all given major emphasis to language and communication skills. Some programs, such as that of Bereiter and Engelmann (1966), have been almost exclusively concerned with language abilities. Bereiter and Engelmann claimed that cultural deprivation is practically synonymous with language deprivation. They consider that most of the deficits in achievements that are associated with differences in cultural background are due to language deficiencies and to a lack of the kinds of learning that are transmitted through language.

Language problems are most extreme in the case of distinct cultural minority groups, rather than in lower-class families in general, but there is considerable evidence to support the view that marked class-related differences exist in ability to use language for communicating meanings. In regard to particular minorities, it has been remarked that some of the findings that have been cited as evidence of language impoverishment might be more accurately regarded as language differences. The fact that an urban ghetto dweller's language is not identical to the speech of a middle-class person does not necessarily mean that the former's language is impoverished. However, when people are tested at tasks that make use of the language forms of the majority culture, differences tend to be interpreted as being deficiencies, and when instruction at school is provided only in the language spoken by the majority, individuals who speak in a minority dialect are at a definite disadvantage, and their language differences may lead to real deficits in learning (Baratz, 1969; Labov, 1970). Language differences generally function as deficiencies when individuals have to function in a language at which they are less than fully adept.

As we have seen, early class-related differences in language have been found in a number of investigations. Hess and Shipman (1968) found that the way in which a mother speaks to her children has a strong influence upon their own language-based behavior. Mothers and their 4-year-old children were observed together as the children performed a number of tasks that demanded interaction between mother and child. The children's performance scores were highly correlated with the preciseness of the mothers' verbal instructions. There was a negative correlation between a child's performance and the extent to which the mother made negative statements or comments. Another indication that a mother's speech was especially important lay in the fact that the measures of the mother's language were more highly correlated with the children's achievements than was a combined index of social class and the mother's IQ. A year later, the same children were given a test of word vocabulary. Correlations were calculated between the scores on the test and a number of measures of maternal factors that had been assessed in the previous year. The authors found that among the various measures, the one that proved the most effective single predictor of a child's performance in the vocabulary test administered a year later was the mother's original vocabulary test score. Some further results suggest that middle-class mothers are more effective at varying their speech, making it more or less simple and redundant to match the child's growing ability to understand (Snow, 1972).

Bernstein's Views

The view that spoken language is a factor leading to class-related differences in learning and educational achievement has been developed by a British sociologist, Basil Bernstein (1961). Bernstein considers that individuals from all social classes are equally effective at communicating to each other within groups of familiar people, for instance in the family or at work, but that middle-class people are more successful at communicating with others who are unfamiliar or who do not share a similar social background or pattern of experience. Bernstein argues that since the circumstances of school and educational institutions, which involve unfamiliar people, are ones in which relatively impersonal and public kinds of communication are necessary, working-class individuals are placed at a disadvantage.

The way in which people communicate in any situation is influenced by the social relationships that exist between the people involved. When children are in a group of other children, they use language that is different in both content and structure from the language they use when they are talking to adults. In particular, Bernstein notes, when two people share an interest in, and knowledge about, a topic they are discussing, a great deal of meaning can be conveyed without the words and the verbal descriptions being as detailed and as explicit as they would have to be for an outsider to understand the discussion. When background knowledge, feelings, assumptions, and values are all shared, and can be taken for granted, it may be possible to convey meanings by small gestures or by a slight variation in pitch. Speech can be abbreviated without loss of meaning to the participants, who communicate with each other "against a background of closely shared identifications and effective empathy which removes the need for elaborate verbal expression" (Bernstein, 1961). To a person who does not possess the background knowledge shared by the participants, the messages exchanged may appear incomprehensible, illogical and incomplete, effective communication of this informal kind being restricted to a small number of people.

It is claimed by Bernstein that lower-class people tend to be restricted to this informal use of language, in which individuals communicate against a background of common knowledge. Bernstein considers that children who are brought up in lower-class families become able to use language effectively as a form of communication only in those circumstances where complex, precise, and fully explicit forms of language are unnecessary. If children do not gain experience in interacting with people who do not share their background and their life experience, they may fail to acquire some of the skills necessary for doing so.

It is not easy to verify or disprove Bernstein's many statements about the nature and causes of class-related language differences. Concerning the ideas summarized above, it is true that lower-class boys when conversing have a tendency to complete their remarks with phrases like "Didn't I?" "Wouldn't it?" and "You know what I mean," all of which assume the listener's agreement, and discourage any discussion that does not tacitly imply acceptance of the speaker's viewpoint. Communication thus tends to be restricted to the area of agreement and shared assumptions between the talkers. Bernstein found that middle-class children were more likely to use expressions such as "I think," that allow greater freedom for respondents to develop the conversation along their own lines, and to express disagreement without disrupting the flow of conversation. In general, whether or not the class-related differences in communication are quite so marked or as consistent as Bernstein implies, the evidence shows that considerable differences do exist in the way in which children from different social classes learn to use language. These language differences appear to exert marked influences on individual patterns of learned achievements.

CULTURAL DIFFERENCES IN LEARNING

People who have been brought up in the same country, speaking the same language, experiencing similar mass media, and subject to common laws and customs, tend to be like one another in many respects. Some of the questions that have been asked, concerning whether particular human characteristics are acquired through learning or whether they indicate the presence of innate "wired in" human characteristics, are easier to answer if we have access to groups of people who share less of our early experiences than people living in our own countries. For example, we might wish to know if the useful strategy of grouping word items to be remembered into meaningful categories is a universal human characteristic, or not. If it is, we might be justified in assuming that grouping largely depends upon mental processes that do not have to be acquired by particular forms of learning. We can obtain useful evidence concerning this matter from developmental studies, but cross-cultural investigations can provide a valuable further source of pertinent data. Comparisons between groups of people whose upbringing and experiences are widely different can help us to discover the extent to which each of us depends upon what we have learned.

In many circumstances it is found that educated individuals learn more effectively than nonliterate people, even when the learning task does not require reading or writing skills. Some cross-cultural investigations have aimed to explain the differences in performance. It was observed by Cole, Gay, Glick, and Sharp (1971) that groups of Liberian students who had attended school performed much better at a multi-trial free-recall test than subjects from an adjacent rural village where no one had been to school. The experimenter presented a list of 20 words, made up of randomly ordered items from each of four categories: *clothing, food, tools,* and *utensils.* The high school students recalled, on average, about ten words on the first trial. Over successive trials, they steadily improved until, by the fifteenth trial, around 17 words were recalled. Those subjects who lacked schooling recalled an average of ten words on the first trial, like the other participants, but although this increased to about 12 words by the third trial, there was no further increase in performance over the remaining 12 trials.

What caused this difference? One clue is provided by considering the data showing the extent to which, at recall, the items in particular categories were clustered together. There was a very large difference between the two groups. The school-educated subjects clustered the items very markedly, according to semantic categories, with the degree of clustering increasing considerably as the trials progressed, whereas the noneducated individuals hardly clustered the items at all. This finding suggests that some aspect of organization or grouping may have contributed to the difference in the number of items recalled. The subjects who had attended school may have been more successful in retaining the items because they grouped them into categories, or possibly because they used grouping schemes to retrieve items from memory.

A possible explanation of the nonliterate subjects' poor performance is that their learning was based upon rote memorization, by which they attempted to retain a literal copy of the materials in an order precisely matching that of presentation. If this were so, one would expect the order of recall in the noneducated subjects to be especially highly correlated with the order of presentation. In fact there was no significant correlation, indicating the rote memorization suggestion is not a correct explanation. It is also conceivable that the items or the categories were unfamiliar to the uneducated people. However, Cole's data indicate that the items were perfectly familiar, and considerable care had been given to choosing them. Could the method of grouping words have been unsuitable for uneducated subjects? Perhaps a thematic grouping like that used by Ceci and Howe (1978a) (see Chapter 10) might be more satisfactory. It has been found that young American children are more likely to group items according to themes (for example, Western, Oriental, Desert in the study by Ceci and Howe) than by categories (for example, buildings, animals, etc.) (Denney and Ziobrowski, 1972). The illiterate young people in Cole's study might have shared such a preference. However, constructing lists of thematically rather than categorically or taxonomically related items produced findings identical to the original ones, with no reduction in the difference between the two groups of participants (Medin and Cole, 1975). Could it be that unschooled individuals have particular problems with verbal items? This possibility was tested by devising a situation in which actual objects were used, instead of words. Once more, however, the pattern of findings was unaffected. Is it possible that the difference in performance was due to motivational factors? (Certainly, the task must have seemed somewhat pointless to the villagers.) To test this suggestion, incentives were provided, enabling participants to earn the equivalent of more than a day's pay for performing well. Again, however, the innovation failed to influence the results, and the individuals who had received schooling continued to perform much better than the others.

The one important underlying difference that did emerge lay in the extent to which people have effective retrieval strategies. In a new test, the items were presented in categories, and participants were required to recall all the items in one category at a time. Subjects would first be told, "Tell me all the clothes you remember," and afterwards they would be asked for the items in a second category, and so on through all the different groups. This procedure was effective in raising the performance levels of the unschooled villagers. It appeared that they were not good at retrieving information, unaided, at the time of recall. It is interesting to note that the difficulty the nonliterate subjects experienced with retrieving word items was similar to that experienced by younger children in the investigation of retrieval flexibility by Ceci and Howe (1978b). In the latter study, the younger subjects' difficulty appeared to lie in switching from a taxonomic (semantic category) grouping to a thematic grouping, or vice versa.

A number of explorers and anthropologists have suggested the possibility that nonliterate people may be especially good at memorizing things verbatim, by rote. Bartlett (1932) claimed that primitive people are well equipped for tasks of literal memorization, and he considered that high achievement at this kind of learning is associated with a restricted mental life, in which the individual has few interests, all of which are somewhat concrete. Bartlett suggested that the social organization of primitive cultures reflected restricted mental activity and organization, and that this was compatible with very accurate and detailed literal memory.

Cole, Gay, Glick, and Sharp (1971) compared the abilities of literate and nonliterate children at a rote learning task. They followed a simple procedure in which the subjects were shown a number of objects, one at a time, and they were then tested for recall. At the ages of 6 and 10 years nonliterate children from the Kpelle people in Liberia in North Africa performed roughly as well as American children of similar age on the early trials of the task. But when repeated trials were given, the performance of the Kpelle children did not improve so much as that of the American children, paralleling the findings with older nonliterate subjects described earlier. Those Kpelle children who had received a certain amount of formal education performed better than those with no education. In general, the results obtained by Cole and his colleagues give no support at all to the view that nonliterate people are better at rote learning than educated individuals. It is conceivable, however, that the subjects living in a primitive culture might have been handicapped to some extent by the fact that the circumstances of the test must have been completely unfamiliar to them.

Primitive Thought

The combined findings of a number of experiments by Cole, Gay, Glick, and Sharp indicate that American children are more likely than rural Kpelle children to impose various kinds of organization upon the materials they are required to learn. As a result, performance improves to a greater extent following practice. When they are learning verbal materials, American children more frequently make use of strategies that involve mediational and elaborative skills. As a partial result, the amount of transfer of learning from one task to similar tasks is greater among American child subjects than in Kpelle children. Lack of verbal mediating processes probably contributed to the poorer performance of Kpelle children at those kinds of discrimination tasks in which performing well depends on verbal coding and processing of the relevant information. In a task that required subjects to discriminate between objects on the basis of color, unschooled Kpelle children showed less transfer, in the form of "learning to learn," than did children who had attended school.

At one time it was widely believed that primitive people bore a relation to the members of civilized societies that was similar to the relationship of children to adults. Human society was seen as evolving in a developmental continuum from the primitive to the civilized. It was also considered that each individual organism repeats the anatomical history of the species in embryological development. Such a view was summarized by Haeckel's statement that "Ontogeny recapitulates phylogeny." Combining these views led to a number of nineteenth-century assumptions. It was suggested by Darwin that the evolution of culture permits us to make inferences about the evolution of the individual intellect. It was also considered that primitive adults can be regarded as early forms of adults in advanced societies. Since the European child is an early form of the European adult, the primitive adult was thought to be in some respects equivalent to the civilized child. Franz Boas and other anthropologists subsequently demonstrated that these ideas rest on a fallacious belief that observed similarities in thought, for example between European children and adult people in primitive societies, imply close similarities in culture, and vice versa. Although culture and thought are undoubtedly related, the connections between them are neither straightforward nor invariable.

Some of the cultural factors that are found to influence children brought up in different societies are similar to the factors that account for social class differences. For instance, Cole, Gay, Glick, and Sharp (1971) mention that the strict and directive upbringing of children associated with certain cultures leads to forms of intellectual functioning that are imprecise and undifferentiated, lacking explicit analysis and articulation. Bernstein (1961), writing about social class differences, predicts a similar outcome of restrictions in early environment. However, he also emphasizes the contributing effects of the mother having (largely as a result of restrictions in *her* early experience of life) an imprecise conception of herself as an individual person, and as having a limited ability for precise articulation of personal feelings and wishes. Whorf (1956) has emphasized the importance of the languages used by different cultures in giving form and direction to human thought. Whorf stressed that language functions as a shaper of ideas, and guides the mental activity of the individual. It is not simply a reproducing instrument for communicating thoughts that are already fully formed. From a crosscultural perspective, Whorf echoes the thoughts of a researcher such as Bernstein who has studied social class differences. It is hardly surprising that similar ideas emerge, since social classes can be regarded as forming subcultures within a broader society.

The thought processes of individuals in nonliterate societies may not be quite so different nor so much simpler than those of people in advanced societies as at first appears to be the case. In *The Savage Mind*, Levi-Strauss (1966) has asserted that differences between modern thought and so-called primitive thought are relatively superficial. He notes that all human groups form categorizations or taxonomies of those items in their environments that they perceive as having significance, in order to discover or impose some order in the world experienced. Differences in the way people think can be found in the detailed forms of their categorical systems, but these differences are relatively minor. Primitive tribes form taxonomies on the basis of how objects appear, or what their function is. Categorization in Western cultures may be based on abstracted information about items, or abstractions of their properties, as is demanded by the kinds of knowledge structures that we call "science." The basis of categorization may not be at all apparent to a person who lacks knowledge of the scientific system, but the principles underlying the use of a different taxonomy or a system of categorization are substantially the same.

Levi-Strauss has drawn attention to some extremely elaborate taxonomic schemes for organizing knowledge that have been devised and adopted by people who lack technology and live an ostensibly very simple existence. One primitive tribe is described as having as many as 5000 terms to describe varied species of flora and fauna. By no means all of these items have any practical or utilitarian function for the people who name and categorize them in such detail; the naming and categorization of the different items by these people represents an interest that can be termed "academic" in form. Levi-Strauss also mentions a number of highly complex and sophisticated forms of reasoning, detached from pragmatic considerations of apparent survival value, in societies whose level of technological and material development might tempt us to assume that mental activity is correspondingly simple and restricted. Some Australian aborigine tribes are cited as instances of people who combine extreme primitiveness in material life with impressive intellectual complexity and sophistication in connection with social customs, systems of belief, and fashions of bodily decoration.

CONCLUSION

The evidence from research into culturally related differences in learning points to the importance of certain basic skills, in particular ones underlying the organization of verbal materials and the retrieval of information retained in memory. On the whole, the various kinds of evidence which we have examined for information about the nature of individual differences in learning point to remarkably similar conclusions. Investigations of individual differences from the perspective of human development, learning in normal people, mental retardation, social class comparisons, or cross-cultural studies, all reveal differences in mental habits, skills, and strategies underlying learning. Motivation is especially important, as is the effectiveness of the learners' skills of selectively attending. Processes of encoding, elaborating, and organizing, which involve use of the knowledge an individual already possesses, are found to be crucial for a wide range of tasks. It is also essential for a person to have effective retrieval strategies and control processes such as rehearsal, which contribute to the acquisition and retention of knowledge. Individual differences in performance at tasks that depend upon the ability to learn are usually found to be related to differences in one or more of these underlying factors, each of which makes an important contribution.

SUMMARY

1. It is argued that knowledge about the specific ways in which successful and unsuccessful learners differ in their abilities can be valuable for helping the less successful to learn more effectively.
2. Performance in tests of learning is not closely correlated with general measures of ability. Evidence concerning genetic determinants does not help us to understand the nature of the differences in *how* individuals learn.
3. Individual differences in abilities that influence learning are evident from the earliest months of life.
4. Considerable individual variability is encountered in a number of the cognitive processes that underlie human learning and retention.
5. Individual differences in attentional skills and in motivation make important contributions to learned achievement.
6. Research into mental retardation has suggested a number of ways in

which learning by mentally retarded individuals differs from that of normal learners. Mentally retarded people are less likely to make use of mediational strategies and rehearsal. Partly as a result, there is less transfer of training in retarded than in normal learners. Mentally retarded learners may be more impulsive and appear to lack certain inhibitory processes contributing to normal learning.

7. Research into social class differences that influence learning indicates the importance of a number of factors related to different lifestyles and patterns of interaction between children and adults. Language skills appear to be a particularly important factor in class-related differences.

8. Cross-cultural research supports the view that differences in strategies for learning, particularly ones involving the organization of items to be retained, have large effects on learning.

Suggestions for Further Reading

Belmont, J. M. (1978) "Individual differences in memory: the cases of normal and retarded development." In M. M. Gruneberg and P. Morris (eds.), *Aspects of Memory*. London: Methuen.

Cole, M., Gay, J., Glick, J. A., and Sharp, D. W. (1971) *The Cultural Context of Learning and Thinking*. New York: Basic Books.

Estes, W. K. (1970) *Learning Theory and Mental Development*. New York: Academic Press.

Hunt, E., and Lansman, M. (1975) Cognitive theory applied to individual differences. In W. K. Estes (ed.), *Handbook of Learning and Cognitive Processes, Vol. I: Introduction to Concepts and Issues*. Hillsdale, New Jersey: Lawrence Erlbaum Associates.

13

Some Concluding Remarks

OVERVIEW

The book concludes with some general remarks about the nature of human learning. There are a number of reasons for the lack of comprehensive theories of human learning. It is suggested that a good approach to help people learn is to encourage them to acquire and use strategies and procedures that can be applied in a variety of situations. The chapter also mentions compensatory education, suggesting that the failure of some attempts reflects an underestimation of the difficulty of establishing permanent gains. I point out that what a person learns is not solely determined by qualities of the objective environment.

LEARNING AND THEORIES OF LEARNING

The many instances of learning that we have encountered in the preceding chapters are too diverse and too varied for it to be possible to summarize all the findings of research in a few simple conclusions. An awareness of the sheer diversity of learning is one reason for the absence in contemporary psychology of broad theories that apply to all forms of learning. Another reason lies in the fact that the learning processes that contribute to a person's learned capabilities do not form a distinct system that can be detached from the other causes of human ability. A general theory of learning which presupposes that a clear distinction can be made between learning processes, on the one hand, and other contributing influences—such as perception, remembering, attention, and motivational factors—on the other hand, is not feasible. The fact that all the instances to which we think it fitting to apply the word "learning" share some common elements does not permit us to infer that all learning is caused by mental processes that are distinct from the processes underlying other psychological phenomena.

Difficulties such as these, rather than any aversion to theorizing, account for the absence of any contemporary learning theory that is both broad enough and detailed enough to be comparable to the mid-twentieth-century accounts of learning theorists such as Hull. As we have seen, most psychologists studying human learning, except perhaps for those working in the Skinnerian tradition, are guided by theories of some kind, using the word "theory" to refer to scientific attempts to explain and understand the underlying causes of phenomena. But such theories are typically narrower than the earlier theories of learning. They are designed to apply only to the acquisition of particular forms of behavior, particular skills, or particular kinds of knowledge. Yet in one respect the recent theories are broader: they refer to mental activities that enter into other psychological activities in addition to processes of acquisition. For instance, theoretical views about the learning of semantic knowledge have implications for an understanding of retention and retrieval as well as for the acquisition of knowledge. Theories about learned social behavior are intended to contribute to our understanding of the maintenance as well as the acquisition of human activities.

Considering learning in the broadest sense, it is a truism to say that many factors can exert an influence. Some influences contribute to diverse forms of learning. For instance, most kinds of learning are affected by motivational factors, and success at many kinds of learning is influenced by the availability of appropriate attentional skills. However, in investigations of social learning it is common to find considerable emphasis on the motivational influences which form reinforcing events. In investigations of the acquisition of knowledge, on the other hand, it is rare for motivation to be explicitly mentioned. This is not because motivational factors do not influence verbal learning; most researchers in this area would agree that adequate motivation is crucial for acquiring knowledge. But the ways in which motivational factors exert an impact in social and verbal forms of learning are different. In social learning research it is usually possible to distinguish between learned behavior and the motivational (reinforcing) factors involved, whereas the motivational influences on acquiring knowledge may be bound to, or inherent in, what is learned, as is implied when we speak of information as being relevant, interesting, or useful. Another difference lies in the fact that while in social learning learned behavior may be directly reinforced, in instances of learning that take the form of acquiring knowledge, the primary function of motivational factors is to direct attention to the material rather than to influence learning directly. In research into verbal learning it is customary for the experimenter to devise conditions in which it can be assumed that a degree of attention will be maintained by the subjects. If it were not comparatively easy to insure this, we might expect to find greater emphasis on attentional factors and motivation in research into the acquisition of verbal knowledge. As it happens, verbal learning researchers do emphasize attentional and motivational influences in those situations where it cannot be taken for granted that all subjects participating in an experiment will pay sustained attention. A case in point is the research on mentally retarded learners, as described in the previous chapter. It is not inevitable that motivational influences should receive greater emphasis in social learning research than in research investigating verbal learning.

An additional cause of the confusing variability in the ways in which different kinds of learning are investigated lies, as we have seen, in the different traditions of experimental research into alternative forms of learning. Modern research into social forms of learning has evolved from earlier studies in a fairly continuous line of development, and today's experiments display the influence of early research. In recent investigations of the acquisition of verbal knowledge, we discern sharper breaks with earlier research traditions. Contemporary approaches, such as information-processing analyses, display less continuity with earlier approaches and a stronger impact of modern influences from outside psychology.

HELPING THE LEARNER

How do we help people learn? In what ways can we put into practice the considerable knowledge about human learning that now exists? We can help, up to a point, simply by consistently following a number of principles that are readily derived from investigations of human learning. We know, for example, that attention to the relevant environmental events is vital, so we would be wise to insure that instructional procedures make provision for gaining and maintaining learners' attention. We know that giving encouragement is often reinforcing, and that providing informative feedback in the form of knowledge of results about an individual's progress may help the person to make necessary adjustments in behavior. We also know that if learners can be helped to approach learning tasks in a fairly active manner their attention will be maintained and they may encode and process the material at a more abstract level than if they perceive the task to be one of absorbing information passively.

We know that certain mental skills, which are themselves acquired through learning, can greatly facilitate the acquisition of new knowledge. Mental processes that function to transmit information and encode it, to mediate between unconnected items, and to integrate new information with existing knowledge, form the basis of a variety of procedures or strategies that form the "tools of the trade" for learning. The good learner is an individual who has acquired a large repertoire of such tools, and has gained habits and skills of applying them effectively. The strategies and procedures that form the tools for learning are diverse in their detailed forms, but they all share the function of enabling individuals to introduce their own previously acquired knowledge and previously acquired skills in new situations. They thereby give form and structure to the new materials and reduce the amount of effectively unfamiliar and unstructured information that has to be acquired.

Findings surveyed in earlier chapters have shown that instructions to follow strategies involving imagery, rehearsal, or organization, or to adopt effective retrieval plans, can often lead to increased learning and remembering. In general, strategies produce improvements when they give the learner a planned sequence of activities that is appropriate to the task and is based upon an understanding of the mental capacities available to the learner. A good illustration is provided by Butterfield, Wambold and Belmont's (1973) attempt to improve the performance of mentally retarded adolescents at a short-term memory task. Following presentation of a six-letter list each subject was shown one of the items on its own, and had to indicate its position in the original list. The subjects learned a plan for performing the task correctly by using their existing capabilities in a coordinated and organized fashion. The adolescents were taught first to form a group from the first three letters in each list, and then to rehearse these as a single group. The aim of this procedure was to insure that the early items would be retained in memory.

The subjects were then trained to attend to the three final items in each list, so that these could be very briefly held in short-term memory. At the final stage in the task when the probe item was presented, the adolescents were taught to check whether it matched any of the three later items. If it did, the subject responded immediately by indicating its position. If the probe item was not among the three final letters the subject was to search the early items. Since these items had been rehearsed as a group, retention of them was not greatly affected by the delay and interference caused by presentation of the final items and the requirement to search for them upon presentation of the probe.

This procedure was highly successful, and approximately doubled the number of items correctly identified. The reasons for success were that it made use of memory processes that the retarded adolescent subjects already possessed, for instance short-term memory capacity and the ability to rehearse (which the experimenters had established were not impaired) and it contributed an important element that they lacked, coordination between memory processes. The experimenters did not try to alter basic processes, but introduced plans for directing the capacities that subjects already possessed in an effectively coordinated manner.

The effectiveness of such plans does not depend upon the individual deliberately following a strategy, or being aware of following a plan, or even having a deliberate intention to remember. In a study by Turnure, Buium and Thurlow (1976) five-year-old children were asked "What?" and "Why?" questions about common items dipected in pictures, for example, "What is the soap doing under the jacket?". This procedure led to them recalling about ten times as many items as were recalled by children who simply provided word labels for the items and four times as many items as children who either provided conventional sentences linking the objects or had sentences provided for them. The children had been given no indication that their retention of the items would be tested; the requirement to engage in some activity that involved them in processing the items in a meaningful way seems to have been more important.

In the present author's view, some of the most promising future developments toward greater understanding of human learning will be a consequence of increased interest in the activities of individual learners, and the mental processes underlying such activities. In education, there will be greater recognition of the need to specify the most effective basic skills and strategies for learning and remembering, and there will be further attempts to help learners to acquire such skills, which are widely applicable. The emphasis throughout the present book (and particularly in Chapters 9 and 10) on learners' methods, procedures, and strategies, reflects a belief in the centrality and practical importance of these processes.

LEARNING AIDS AND DEVICES

Instructional devices developed by educators in recent years have incorporated some of the principles outlined in the above paragraphs. The use of programmed learning formats, presented in book form or via teaching machines, was strongly advocated in the 1950s and early 1960s. They provided short sequences (or "frames") of information, followed by a question that required an active response on the part of the student, followed in turn by the provision of the appropriate answer or some similar kind of feedback. The innovations had a fair measure of success, even if the programmed learning movement never really amounted to the revolution that some of its adherents insisted it was. Many students undoubtedly enjoyed the novelty of machine presentation. However, although such techniques were reasonably successful in teaching various kinds of knowledge, ranging from mathematical statistics to the appreciation of poetry, programmed learning is not nearly so extensively used today as people once predicted that it would be. One reason for the relative absence of a long-term impact of these techniques lies in the fact that programmed learning uses somewhat inflexible formats of presentation. One cannot move backwards and forwards through the information presented in programmed form with the freedom that is possible with an ordinary book. Another fact that became increasingly apparent is that, so far as learning is concerned, it is the quality of the instructional material that matters most, including the way the materials are written and organized. This is the case whatever format of instruction is used. If the material is poorly written and inadequately organized it will be ineffective for teaching purposes, however attractive the method of presentation. Ultimately, the particular form in which information is made available may not be very important.

The introduction of computers in education has made it possible to devise instructional procedures that are similar to ones used in simple forms of programmed learning but are considerably more flexible and more responsive to the requirements of each individual learner. One advantage of computer-assisted instruction is that in selecting the rate and the sequence of instruction for a particular student, it is not only possible to take into account that person's most recent responses, as is done in conventional programmed instruction, but it is also possible to use information about the individual's previous progress and any additional relevant information that is available about the person's abilities, knowledge, attitudes, and earlier progress. This advantage, together with the more extensive facilities for machine-student communications that advanced technological facilities provide, results in the interaction between computer and the individual student approaching much more closely to that ideal situation in which one teacher is instructing one student. The sequence of instruction can be constantly restructured and adjusted in the light of information about the student's progress. When the material to be presented via computer-assisted instruction is designed with care and imagination, the method can be very effective, although it is generally expensive to use.

COMPENSATORY LEARNING

People sometimes have unrealistic expectations about the outcomes of educational innovations and changes that have been designed to help children learn. "Compensatory education has been tried, and apparently it has failed," concluded Arthur Jensen in 1969, and many people accepted this authoritative-sounding conclusion. But there have been numerous instances in which compensatory efforts have been very successful. Many of the less successful attempts to improve the levels of children's abilities were very brief in duration, poorly designed, and staffed by untrained personnel. No one but the most naively optimistic observer should have expected them to bring about permanent gains. In many situations in which gains were produced by short compensatory programs, critics were quick to note that the effects were not permanent, citing this observation as evidence that compensatory education was bound to fail. In fact, there have never been any reasonable grounds for expecting that permanent positive educational changes can be induced by a brief "shot in the arm" procedure. It would be wrong to assume that improvements in intelligence and basic abilities cannot be achieved at all, simply because they are not gained quickly or easily. The successes of carefully designed long-term compensatory programs demonstrate that, given the necessary resources, compensatory education can be highly effective.

THE INDIVIDUAL AND THE ENVIRONMENT

Few researchers investigating human learning today accept the extreme environmentalist positions of Watson, Skinner, and other behaviorist writers, but there remains a tendency to believe that improvements in learning can be achieved by straightforward changes in the direction of making a child's world more interesting or "stimulating." Developmental investigators, following a tradition rooted in the work of Rousseau and developed as an empirical science by Piaget, view children as highly active beings who explore and experiment with their environment. As a result they "construct" the knowledge they require through interaction with the world. Children's experience is the outcome of their own mental activities *and* the environment in which they are placed, and not of *one* or the other. As Merleau-Ponty (1962) has written, "We choose our world and the world chooses us."

Some of the implications of this viewpoint were encountered in the previous chapter, in connection with the research of Korner (1971) and Escalona (1973). Recall that environmental conditions vary in impact as a function of the differing abilities and patterns of reaction and response that can be observed in very young infants. Differences exist prior to the time at which they can be produced by learning. On the basis of the available evidence, Escalona concludes that if we are to understand how children are affected by the environment and to make predictions about the outcome of environmental influences upon individual children, we need to know what children actually experience. She insists that we cannot infer this from simply knowing the properties of the child's objective world. We may recall her statement that a home full of toys does not mean that the child is necessarily receiving much stimulation. She points out that the actual life experience of a child which most strongly influences what he will actually learn is determined by how the child acts in the context of whatever stimulation the environment may provide.

Biographical accounts of the early lives of real people direct us to a similar conclusion. When we read descriptions of the early lives of people who have excelled in one way or another at abilities and skills that demand unusual amounts of learning, we find that indications of environmental stimulation in the earliest years do little to help us predict which of a number of people will be the one to achieve eminence. On the whole, the childhoods of eminent individuals are more likely than not to have included what we regard as a "good" home environment, that is, one abounding in books and conversation, with attentive parents who are able and willing to contribute directly to their child's education. But this generalization is by no means universally true, otherwise the world would never have experienced the genius of Balzac, Newton, H. G. Wells and scores of other outstanding people. In those circumstances where the desirable environmental conditions summarized above are definitely present, there is little basis for distinguishing between the particular home backgrounds of the few people who have excelled in life and the many who have not.

In some cases the early background of an eminent person does appear to have been an ideal one for producing the individual who emerged from it. Charles Darwin, for instance, received his early upbringing at the hands of warm and attentive parents who were educated, valued books, were interested in biological studies, and encouraged curiosity and the spirit of enquiry. His immediate family included a number of distinguished people, including his grandfather, Erasmus Darwin. But in general we will make little progress toward understanding how certain people became eminent unless we are prepared to look at the way in which the particular individuals made use of the pattern of environmental events forming their world. When we do consider at the same time both the qualities of young people and the nature of their early environment, we are much more likely to gain insight into the experience and the progress of the people concerned. Consider, for instance, the case of Sir Richard Burton. Burton was an amazing man who was famous for many things. He was outstanding as an explorer, an anthropologist, a linguist, a translator, and as a swordsman. He wrote over 40 books about his explorations and studies, two books on swords and swordsmanship, two volumes of poetry, over a hundred articles on various subjects, and he translated 16 volumes of the *Arabian Nights*, plus another ten volumes of folklore, Portuguese literature, and Latin poetry. Most of Burton's prodigious accomplishments depended in one way or another on his mastery of foreign languages. He learned about 40 separate languages. Without his linguistic abilities he would not only have been unable to achieve success as a translator, he would never have been able to acquire his enormous understanding of different cultures, and he would not have learned so much as he did from his many travels and explorations.

It would be useful to know how Burton came to specialize in learning foreign languages, and knowing about Burton's early life and the kinds of environments he encountered does help us to understand something of how his extraordinary linguistic achievements were acquired. Burton's parents spent much of their adult lives in different parts of the European continent, and for the Burton children to be able to communicate with others of their own age it was essential to acquire appropriate language skills. Thus the outgoing and energetic young Richard Burton was repeatedly placed in the position in which attempts to learn new languages were rewarded by the acquisition of communicative skills that had a ready use. By the time Burton reached adulthood he must have gained some confidence in his own language-learning abilities, and he would have acquired skills and habits that could be applied for learning yet more languages. For most of us, acquiring a new language is difficult, arduous and time consuming. Lacking the motivation provided by being able to put our newly acquired skill to immediate use, few people have the perserverance to persist for long with a new foreign language. For Burton, things were very different, not because the intellectual task of learning a language was necessarily any easier for him, but because he had gained the experience of having his persistence regularly rewarded. By the time Burton was a young man he knew that he could succeed, and he had proved to himself that the outcome of his efforts was sufficiently rewarding to justify the long hours of drudgery involved. From Burton's own account of the way in which he went about learning each new language, it is clear that the methods he used were not particularly unusual, and that he did not find the process of learning to be at all easy. What set Burton apart was his sheer determination, and the willingness to submit himself to lengthy periods of practice and repetitive work, much of which he found extremely tedious. Knowing something about the unusual value for him of learning languages in childhood gives us a clue to his persistence and to his resulting achievements.

Everyone is influenced by the circumstances of early life, but the ways in which environmental factors determine what an individual learns are more varied and more complex than could ever be expressed by the concept of a unidimensional environmental force, varying in quality from "deprived" to "enriched," that impinges upon an essentially passive learner. We certainly depend upon the surrounding world, but we are not slaves of our environments. The active nature of the learning processes, by which each of us constructs a world of experience that is always a little different from the world our neighbors experience, insures that there remains some room for choice in how we, as learners, harvest the ocean of information that surrounds us all.

SUMMARY

1. Although different forms of learning share some common elements, it is not inevitable that all kinds of learning are caused by identical mental processes or by mechanisms that are entirely distinct from the ones contributing to other psychological capacities. These considerations contribute to the difficulty of deriving comprehensive theories of human learning as such.
2. Evidence from a number of different sources supports the view that people can be helped to learn by receiving instruction in the use or general strategies and procedures for learning that can be applied in a variety of situations. Teaching-machine methods of instruction can be effective if they make provision for learner activities associated with effective performance, but they tend to lack flexibility.
3. Efforts at compensatory education can only be effective if they are carefully planned, effectively communicated, and of reasonably long duration. In the past, over-optimism about the outcomes of inadequate programs has led to disappointment.
4. What is learned by any person depends upon the qualities of the environment as experienced by the particular individual. The objective attributes of the environment cannot provide a complete guide to what people learn. We also need to know about individual factors determining how people actually experiences their world.

References

Ainsworth, M. D. S., and Bell, S. M. (1969) "Some contemporary patterns of mother-infant interaction in the feeding situation." In A. Ambrose (ed.), *Stimulation in Early Infancy*. New York: Academic Press.

Ainsworth, M. D. S., Bell, S. M., and Stayton, D. J. (1974) "Infant-mother attachment and social development: socialization as a product of reciprocal responsiveness to signals." In M. P. M. Richards (ed.), *The Integration of a Child into a Social World*. London: Cambridge University Press.

Allport, G. W., and Postman, L. (1947) *The Psychology of Rumor*. New York: Holt, Rinehart and Winston.

Allyon, T., and Michael, J. (1959) "The psychiatric nurse as a behavioral engineer." *Journal of the Experimental Analysis of Behavior*, 2:323–334.

Anderson, J. R. (1976) *Language, Meaning and Thought*. Hillsdale, New Jersey: Erlbaum.

Anderson, J. R., and Bower, G. H. (1973) "Recognition and retrieval processes in free recall." *Psychological Review*, 79:97–123.

Anderson, R. C., and Myrow, D. L. (1971) "Retroactive inhibition of meaningful discourse." *Journal of Educational Psychology*, 62:81–94.

André, T., and Sola, J. (1976) "Imagery, verbatim and paraphrased sentences, and retention of meaningful sentences." *Journal of Educational Psychology*, 68:661–669.

Archer, E. J. (1960) "A re-evaluation of the meaningfulness of all possible CVC trigrams." *Psychological Monographs*, 74 No. 10 (Whole No. 497).

Ardrey, R. (1966) *The Territorial Imperative*. London: Dell.

Ashton, R. (1973) "The state variable in neonatal research." *Merrill-Palmer Quarterly*, 19:3–20.

Atkinson, R. C. (1975) "Mnemotechnics in second-language learning." *American Psychologist*, 30:821–828.

Atkinson, R. C., and Shiffrin, R. M. (1968) "Human memory: a proposed system and its control processes." In K. Spence and J. T. Spence (eds.), *The Psychology of Learning and Motivation*, Vol. II. New York: Academic Press.

Ausubel, D. P. (1968) *Educational Psychology: A Cognitive View.* New York: Holt, Rinehart and Winston.

Azrin, N. H. (1977). "A strategy for applied research." *American Psychologist,* 32:140–149.

Bachrach, A. J., Erwin, W. J., and Mohr, J. P. (1965) "The control of eating behavior in an anorexic by operant conditioning techniques." In L. P. Ullman and L. Krasner (eds.), *Case Studies in Behavior Modification.* New York: Holt, Rinehart and Winston.

Baddeley, A. D. (1976) *The Psychology of Memory.* New York: Harper & Row.

Baddeley, A. D., Grant, S., Wight, E., and Thomson, N. (1974) "Imagery and visual working memory." In P. M. A. Rabbitt and S. Dornic (eds.), *Attention and Performance,* Vol. V. London: Academic Press.

Bandura, A. (1969) *Principles of Behavior Modification.* New York: Holt, Rinehart and Winston.

Bandura, A. (1973) *Aggression: A Social Learning Analysis.* Englewood Cliffs, New Jersey: Prentice-Hall.

Bandura, A. (1977) *Social Learning Theory.* Englewood Cliffs, New Jersey: Prentice-Hall.

Bandura, A., Grusec, J. E., and Menlove, F. L. (1966) "Observational learning as a function of symbolization and incentive set." *Child Development,* 37:499–506.

Bandura, A., and Harris, M. B. (1966) "Modification of syntactic style." *Journal of Experimental Child Psychology,* 4:341–352.

Bandura, A., Ross, D., and Ross, S. A. (1963a) "Imitation of film-mediated aggressive models." *Journal of Abnormal and Social Psychology,* 66:3–11.

Bandura, A., Ross, D., and Ross, S. A. (1963b) "Vicarious reinforcement and imitative learning." *Journal of Abnormal and Social Psychology,* 67:601–607.

Bandura, A., and Walters, R. H. (1959) *Adolescent Aggression.* New York: Ronald Press.

Bandura, A., and Walters, R. H. (1963) *Social Learning and Personality Development.* New York: Holt, Rinehart and Winston.

Baratz, J. C. (1969) "A bi-dialectical task for determining language proficiency in economically disadvantaged Negro children." *Child Development,* 40:889–901.

Barclay, J. R., Bransford, J. D., Franks, J. J., McCarrell, N. S., and Nitsch, K. (1974) "Comprehension and semantic flexibility." *Journal of Verbal Learning and Verbal Behavior,* 13:471–481.

Bartlett, F. C. (1932) *Remembering.* Cambridge, England: Cambridge University Press.

Becker, W. C., Madsen, C. H. Jr., Arnold, R., and Thomas, D. R., (1967) "The contingent use of teacher attention and praise in reducing classroom behavior problems." *Journal of Special Education,* 1:287–307.

Beiswenger, H. (1971) "Linguistic and psychological factors in the speech regulation of behavior in young children." *Journal of Experimental Child Psychology,* 11:63–75.

Bell, S. M., and Ainsworth, M. D. S. (1972) "Infant crying and maternal responsiveness." *Child Development*, 43:1171–1190.

Bellezza, F. S., Richards, D. L., and Geiselman, R. E. (1976) "Semantic processing and organization in free recall." *Memory and Cognition* 4:415–421.

Belmont, J. M. (1978) "Individual differences in memory: the case of normal and retarded development." In M. M. Gruneberg and P. Morris (eds.), *Aspects of Memory*. London: Methuen.

Bennett, A. (1910) *Clayhanger*. (Modern ed., Harmondsworth, England: Penguin Books).

Bereiter, C., and Engelmann, S. (1966) *Teaching Disadvantaged Children in the Preschool*. Englewood Cliffs, New Jersey: Prentice-Hall.

Bernstein, B. (1961) "Social structure, language and learning." *Educational Research*, 3:163–176.

Bijou, S. W. (1957) "Patterns of reinforcement and resistance to extinction in young children." Child Development, 28:47–54.

Bitterman, M. E. (1965) "Phyletic differences in learning." *American Psychologist*, 20:396–410.

Blank, M. (1974) "Cognitive functions of language in the preschool years." *Developmental Psychology*, 10:229–245.

Bloom, K. (1975) "Social elicitation of infant vocal behavior." *Journal of Experimental Child Psychology*, 20:51–58.

Bloom, K., and Esposito, A. (1975) "Social conditioning and its proper control procedures." *Journal of Experimental Child Psychology*, 20:51–58.

Bloom, M. (1973) *One Word at a Time*. The Hague: Mouton.

Boakes, R. A., and Halliday, M. S. (1970) "The Skinnerian analysis of behavior." In R. Borger and F. Cioffi (eds.), *Explanation in the Behavioral Sciences*. Cambridge, England: Cambridge University Press.

Boring, E. G. (1950) *A History of Experimental Psychology*, Second edition. New York: Prentice-Hall.

Bousfield, W. A. (1953) "The occurrence of clustering in the recall of randomly arranged associates." *Journal of General Psychology*, 49:229–240.

Bousfield, W. A., Cohen, B. H., and Whitmarsh, G. A. (1958) "Associative clustering in the recall of words of different taxonomic frequencies of occurrence." *Psychological Reports*, 4:39–44.

Bower, G. H. (1970) "Analysis of a mnemonic device." *American Scientist*, 58:496–510.

Bower, G. H. (1972) "Mental imagery and associative learning." In L. W. Gregg (ed.), *Cognition in Learning and Memory*. New York: Wiley.

Bower, G. H. (1974) "Selective facilitation and interference in retention of prose." *Journal of Educational Psychology*, 66:1–8.

Bower, G. H., and Clark, M. C. (1969) "Narrative stories as mediators for serial learning." *Psychonomic Science*, 14:181–182.

Bower, G. H., Clark, M. C., Lesgold, A. M., and Winzenz, D. (1969) "Hierarchical retrieval schemes in recall of categorized word lists." *Journal of Verbal Learning and Verbal Behavior*, 8:323–343.

Bower, T. G. R. (1967) "Phenomenal identity and form perception in an infant." *Perception and Psychophysics*, 2:74–76.

Bowlby, J. (1951) *Maternal Care and Mental Health.* London: World Health Organization.

Bowlby, J. (1969) *Attachment: Attachment and Loss, Vol. I.* London: Hogarth Press.

Brackbill, Y. (1958) "Extinction of the smiling response in infants as a function of reinforcement schedule." *Child Development,* 29:115–124.

Bransford, J. D., and Johnson, M. K. (1972) "Contextual prerequisites for understanding: some investigations of comprehension and recall." *Journal of Verbal Learning and Verbal Behavior":* 717–726.

Bransford, J. D. and Johnson, M. K. (1973) "Considerations of some problems of comprehension. "In W. G. Chase (ed.), *Visual Information Processing.* New York: Academic Press.

Breland, K., and Breland, M. (1966) *Animal Behavior.* New York: Macmillan.

Bresnahan, J. L., and Shapiro, M. M. (1972) "Learning strategies in children from different socioeconomic levels." In H. W. Reese (ed.), *Advances in Child Development and Behavior,* Vol. VII. New York: Academic Press.

Bridger, W. H. (1961) "Sensory habituation and discrimination in the human neonate." *American Journal of Psychiatry,* 117:991–996.

Broadbent, D. E. (1958) *Perception and Communication.* Oxford: Pergamon Press.

Bronfenbrenner, U. (1960) "Freudian theories of identification and their derivatives." *Child Development,* 31:15–40.

Brooks, L. R. (1968) "Spatial and verbal components of the act of recall." *Canadian Journal of Psychology,* 22:349–368.

Brown, A. L. (1975a) "The development of memory: Knowing, knowing about knowing, and knowing how to know." In H. W. Resse (ed.), *Advances in Child Development and Behavior.* Vol. X. New York: Academic Press.

Brown, A. L. (1975b) "The role of strategic behavior in retardate memory." In N. R. Ellis (ed.), *International Review of Research into Mental Retardation,* Vol. VII. New York: Academic Press.

Brown, A., Campione, J. C., and Murphy, M. (1974) "Keeping track of changing variables: long-term retention of a trained rehearsal strategy by retarded adolescents." *American Journal of Mental Deficiency,* 78:446–453.

Brown, P., and Jenkins, H. (1968) "Autoshaping of the pigeon's key-peck." *Journal of the Experimental Analysis of Behavior,* 11:1–8.

Brown, R. (1973) "Development of the first language in the human species." *American Psychologist,* 28:97–106.

Brown, R., and Bellugi, U. (1964) "Three processes in the child's acquisition of syntax." *Harvard Educational Review,* 34:133–151.

Brown, R., Cazden, C., and Bellugi, U. (1970 "The child's grammar from one to three." In J. P. Hill (ed.), *Minnesota Symposium on Child Psychology,* Vol. II. Minneapolis: University of Minnesota Press.

Brown, R., and Herrnstein, R. J. (1975) *Psychology.* London: Methuen.

Bruner, J. S. (1965) "The growth of mind." *American Psychologist,* 20:1007–1017.

Bruner, J. S. (1966) *Toward a Theory of Instruction.* Cambridge, Massachusetts: Harvard University Press.

Bruner, J. S. (1970) "The growth and structure of skill." In K. Connolly (ed.), *Mechanisms of Motor Skill Development.* New York: Academic Press.

Bruner, J. S. (1975) "The ontogenesis of speech activities." *Journal of Child Language,* 2:1–19.

Bryan, W. L., and Harter, N. (1897) "Studies on the telegraphic language: The acquisition of a hierarchy of habits." *Psychological Review,* 6:345–375.

Bryant, P. R., Jones, P., Claxton, V., and Perkins, G. M. (1972) "Recognition of shapes across modalities by infants." *Nature,* 240:303–304.

Bucher, B., and Lovaas, O. I. (1967) "Use of aversive stimulation in behavior modification." In M. R. Jones (ed.), *Miami Symposium on the Prediction of Behavior: Aversive Stimulation.* Coral Gables, Florida: University of Miami Press.

Bugelski, B. R., Kidd, E., and Segmen, J. (1968) "Image as a mediator in one-trial paired-associate learning." *Journal of Experimental Psychology,* 76:69–73.

Butterfield, E. C., Wambold, D. C., and Belmont, J. M. (1973) "On the theory and practice of improving short-term memory." *American Journal of Mental Deficiency,* 77:654–669.

Campione, J. C., and Beaton, V. L. (1972) "Transfer of training: some boundary conditions and initial theory." *Journal of Experimental Child Psychology,* 13:94–114.

Campione, J. C., and Brown, A. L. (1974) "The effects of contextual changes and degree of component mastery on transfer of training." In H. W. Reese (ed.), *Advances in Child Development and Behavior,* Vol. IX. New York: Academic Press.

Cannon, W. B. (1932) *The Wisdom of the Body.* New York: Norton.

Cantor, J. H., and Cantor, G. N. (1964) "Children's observing behavior as related to amount and recency of stimulus familiarization." *Journal of Experimental Child Psychology,* 1:241–247.

Cantor, G. N., and Cantor, J. H. (1965) "Discriminative reaction time performance in preschool children as related to stimulus familiarization." *Journal of Experimental Child Psychology,* 2:1–9.

Carmichael, L. (1966) "The early growth of language capacity in the individual." In E. H. Lenneberg (ed.), *New Directions in the Study of Language.* Cambridge, Massachusetts: M. I. T. Press.

Carver, R. P. (1973) "Understanding information processing, and learning from prose materials." *Journal of Educational Psychology,* 64:76–84.

Ceci, S. J., and Howe, M. J. A. (1978a) "Semantic knowledge as a determinant of developmental differences in recall." *Journal of Experimental Child Psychology,* 26:230–245.

Ceci, S. J., and Howe, M. J. A. (1978b) "Age-related differences in free recall as a function of retrieval flexibility." *Journal of Experimental Child Psychology,* 26:432–442.

Chi, M. T. H. (1976) "Short-term memory limitations in children: capacity on processing deficits." *Memory and Cognition,* 4:559–572.

Chi, M. T. H. (1978) "Knowledge structures and memory development." In R. Siegler (ed.), *Children's Thinking: What Develops?* Hillsdale, New Jersey: Erlbaum.

Chi, M. T. H. (1977) Age differences in memory span. *Journal of Experimental Child Psychology,* 23:266–281.

Chomsky, N. (1959) "Review of B. F. Skinner, 'Verbal Learning'." *Language,* Vol. 35.

Chomsky, N. (1971) "Implications for language teaching." In J. P. B. Allen and P. van Buren (eds.), *Chomsky: Selected Readings,* pp. 26–58. London: Oxford University Press.

Chomsky, N. (1972) "Psychology and ideology." *Cognition,* 1:11–46.

Cieutat, V. J., Stockwell, F. E., and Noble, C. E. (1958) "The interaction of ability and amount of practice with stimulus and response meaningfulness (*m, m'*) in paired-associate learning." *Journal of Experimental Psychology,* 56:193–202.

Clark, H. H., and Clark, E. V. (1968) "Semantic distinctions and memory for complex sentences." *Quarterly Journal of Experimental Psychology,* 20:129–138.

Clark, H. H., and Clark, E. V. (1977) *Psychology and Language: An Introduction to Psycholinguistics.* New York: Harcourt Brace Jovanovich.

Clifton, R., Siqueland, E. R., and Lipsitt, L. P. (1972) "Conditioned head turning in human newborns as a function of conditioned response requirements and states of wakefulness." *Journal of Experimental Child Psychology,* 13:43–57.

Cofer, C. N. (1965) "On some factors in the organizational characteristics of free recall." *American Psychologist,* 20:261–272.

Cofer, C. N. (1975) Ed., *The Structure of Human Memory:* San Francisco: Freeman.

Cohen, B. H., and Bousfield, W. A. (1956) "The effects of a dual-level stimulus-word list on the occurrence of clustering in recall." *Journal of General Psychology,* 55:51–58.

Cohen, S. (1971) "The development of aggression." *Review of Educational Research,* 41:71–85.

Cole, M., Gay, J., Glick, J. A., and Sharp, D. W. (1971) *The Cultural Context of Learning and Thinking.* New York: Basic Books.

Coleman, E. B. (1962) "Sequential interferences demonstrated by serial reconstructions." *Journal of Experimental Psychology,* 64:46–51.

Coleman, E. B. (1963) "Approximations to English: some comments on the method." *American Journal of Psychology,* 76:239–247.

Collins, A. M., and Quillian, M. R. (1969) "Retrieval time from semantic memory." *Journal of Verbal Learning and Verbal Behavior,* 8:240–247.

Collins, A. M., and Quillian, M. R. (1972) "Experiments on semantic memory and language comprehension." In L. W. Gregg (ed.), *Cognition in Learning and Memory.* New York: Wiley.

Coltheart, M., and Glick, M. J. (1974) "Visual imagery: a case study." *Quarterly Journal of Experimental Psychology,* 24:55–65.

Connolly, K., and Stratton, P. (1969) "An exploration of some parameters affecting classical conditioning in the neonate." *Child Development,* 40:431–441.

Conrad, C. (1972) "Cognitive economy in semantic memory." *Journal of Experimental Psychology*, 92:149–154.

Conrad, R., and Hull, A. J. (1964) "Information, acoustic confusion and memory span." *British Journal of Psychology*, 55:429–432.

Corter, C. M., Rheingold, H. L., and Eckerman, L. O. (1972) "Toys delay the infant's following of his mother." *Developmental Psychology*, 6:138–145.

Craik, F. I. M., and Lockhart, R. S. (1972) "Levels of processing: a framework for memory research." *Journal of Verbal Learning and Verbal Behavior*, 11:671–684.

Craik, F. I. M., and Tulving, E. (1975) "Depth of processing and the retention of words in episodic memory." *Journal of Experimental Psychology: General*, 104:268–294.

Craik, F. I. M., and Watkins, M. J. (1973) "The role of rehearsal in short-term memory." *Journal of Verbal Learning and Verbal Behavior*, 12:599–607.

Crouse, J. H. (1971) "Retroactive interference in reading prose materials." *Journal of Educational Psychology*, 62:39–44.

Crovitz, H. F. (1970) *Galton's Walk: Methods for the Analysis of Thinking, Intelligence, and Creativity.* New York: Harper & Row.

Crowder, R. G. (1976) *Principles of Learning and Memory.* Hillsdale, New Jersey: Erlbaum.

Cunningham, M. (1972) *Intelligence: Its Organization and Development.* New York: Academic Press.

Das, J. P., Kirby, J., and Jarman, R. F. (1975) "Simultaneous and successive syntheses: an alternative model for cognitive abilities." *Psychological Bulletin*, 82:87–103.

David, M., and Appell, G. (1969) "Mother-child interaction and its impact upon the child." In A. Ambrose (ed.), *Stimulation in Early Infancy.* New York: Academic Press.

Davison, G. C. (1968) "Systematic desensitization as a counterconditioning process." *Journal of Abnormal Psychology*, 73:91–99.

Deese, J. (1959) "Influence of inter-item associative strength upon immediate free recall." *Psychological Reports*, 5:305–312.

DeNike, L. D. (1964) "The temporal relationship between awareness and performance in verbal conditioning." *Journal of Experimental Psychology*, 68:521–529.

Denney, N. W., and Ziobrowski, M. (1972) "Developmental changes in clustering criteria." *Journal of Experimental Child Psychology*, 13:275–282.

Dennis, W. (1960) "Causes of retardation among institutional children: Iran." *Journal of Genetic Psychology*, 47, 96–106.

Dirks, J., and Neisser, U. (1977) "Memory for objects in real sciences: the development of recognition and recall." *Journal of Experimental Child Psychology*, 23:315–328.

Dodd, B. J. (1972) "Effects of social and vocal stimulation on infant babbling." *Developmental Psychology*, 7:80–83.

Dooling, D. J., and Lachman, R. (1971) "Effects of comprehension on retention of prose." *Journal of Experimental Psychology*, 88:216–222.

Drabman, R. S., and Thomas, M. H. (1974) "Does media violence increase children's tolerance of real-life aggressiveness?" *Developmental Psychology*, 10:418–421.

Dulany, D. E. (1968) "Awareness, rules and propositional control: a confrontation with S-R behavior theory." In T. R. Dixon and D. L. Horton (eds.), *Verbal Behavior and General Behavior Theory*. Englewood Cliffs, New Jersey: Prentice-Hall.

Earhard, M. (1967a) "Subjective organization and list organization as determinants of free recall and serial recall memorization." *Journal of Verbal Learning and Verbal Behavior*, 6:501–507.

Earhard, M. (1967b) "The facilitation of memorization by alphabetic instructions." *Canadian Journal of Psychology*, 76:584–595.

Ebbinghaus, H. (1964) *Memory: A Contribution to Experimental Psychology*. New York: Dover.

Edmonds, M. H. (1976) "New directions in theories of language acquisition." *Harvard Educational Review*, 46:175–198.

Eisenberg, L. (1972) "The *human* nature of human nature." *Science*, 176, No. 4031:123–128.

Ellis, N. R. (1970) "Memory processes in retardates and normals: theoretical and empirical considerations." In N. R. Ellis (ed.), *International Review of Research into Mental Retardation*, Vol. IV. New York: Academic Press.

Emde, R. N., and Harrison, R. J. (1972) "Endogenous and exogenous smiling systems in early infancy." *Journal of Child Psychiatry*, 11:177–200.

Engen, T., Lipsitt, L. P., and Kaye, H. (1963) "Olfactory responses and adaptation in the human neonate." *Journal of Comparative and Physiological Psychology*, 56:73–77.

Epstein, W. (1961) "The influence of syntactical structure of learning." *American Journal of Psychology*, 74:80–85.

Epstein, W. (1962) "A further study of the influence of syntactical structure on learning." *American Journal of Psychology*, 75:121–126.

Escalona, S. K. (1973) "The differential impact of environmental conditions as a function of different reaction patterns in infancy." In J. C. Westman (ed.), *Individual Differences in Children*. New York: Wiley.

Estes, W. K. (1969) "Reinforcement in Human Learning." In J. Tapp (ed.), *Reinforcement and Behavior*. New York: Academic Press.

Estes, W. K. (1970) *Learning Theory and Mental Development*. New York: Academic Press.

Estes, W. K. (1978) Learning theory and cognitive psychology. In W. K. Estes (ed.), *Handbook of Learning and Cognitive Processes*, Vol. VI. Hillsdale, New Jersey: Erlbaum.

Etzel, B. C., and Gewirtz, J. L. (1967) "Experimental modification of caretaker-maintained high-rate operant crying in a 6- and a 20-week-old infant (Infant tyrannotearus): extinction of crying with reinforcement of eye contact and smiling." *Journal of Experimental Child Psychology*, 5:303–317.

Fantz, R. L. (1964) "Visual experience in infants: decreased attention to familiar patterns relative to novel ones." *Science*, 146:668–670.

Fantz, R. L. (1967) "Visual perception and experience in early infancy: a look at the hidden side of behavior development." In H. W. Stevenson, E. H. Hess, and H. L. Rheingold (eds.), *Early Behavior: Comparative and Developmental Approaches.* New York: Wiley.

Feshbach, S. (1970) "Aggression." In P. H. Mussen (ed.), *Carmichael's Manual of Child Psychology,* 3rd ed., Vol. II. New York: Wiley.

Fisher, J. L., and Harris, M. B. (1973) "Effect of note-taking and review on recall." *Journal of Educational Psychology,* 65:321–325.

Fitts, P. M., and Posner, M. I. (1967) *Human Performance.* Belmont, California: Brooks/Cole.

Fitzgerald, H. E., and Brackbill, T. (1976) "Classical conditioning in infancy: development and constraints." *Psychological Bulletin,* 83:353–376.

Flavell, J. H., Beach, D. R., and Chinsky, J. M. (1966) "Spontaneous verbal rehearsal in a memory task as a function of age." *Child Development,* 37:283–299.

Flavell, J. H., and Wellman, H. M. (1977) "Metamemory." In R. V. Kail and J. W. Hagen (eds.), *Perspectives on the Development of Memory and Cognition.* Hillsdale, New Jersey: Erlbaum.

Fuller, P. R. (1949) "Operant conditioning of a vegetative human organism." *American Journal of Psychology,* 62:587–590.

Furth, H. (1969) *Piaget and Knowledge.* Englewood Cliffs, New Jersey: Prentice-Hall.

Fygetakis, L., and Gray, B. B. (1970) "Programed conditioning of linguistic competence." *Behavior Research and Therapy,* 8:153–163.

Gagné, R. M. (1970) *The Conditions of Learning,* 2nd ed. New York: Holt, Rinehart and Winston.

Garcia, J., and Koelling, R. (1966) "Relation of cue to consequence in avoidance learning." *Psychonomic Science,* 4:123–124.

Gardner, R. A., and Gardner, B. T. (1969) "Teaching sign language to a chimpanzee." *Science,* 165:664–672.

Gates, A. I. (1917) "Recitation as a factor in memorizing." *Archives of Psychology,* 6, No. 40.

Geis, M. F., and Hall, D. (1976) "Encoding and incidental memory in children." *Journal of Experimental Child Psychology,* 22:58–66.

Gerst, M. S. (1971) "Symbolic coding processes in observational learning." *Journal of Personality and Social Psychology,* 19:7–17.

Gewirtz, J. L. (1969) "Mechanisms of social learning: some roles of stimulation and behavior in early development." In D. S. Goslin (ed.), *Handbook of Socialization Theory and Research.* Chicago: Rand McNally.

Gibson, E. J. (1940) "A systematic application of the concepts of generalization and differentiation to verbal learning." *Psychological Review,* 47:196–229.

Gibson, E. J. (1969) *Principles of Perceptual Learning and Development.* New York: Prentice-Hall.

Gibson, J. J., and Gibson, E. J. (1965) "Perceptual learning: Differentiation or enrichment?" *Psychological Review,* 62:32–41.

Gibson, E. J., Gibson, J. J., Pick, A. D., and Osser, H. A. (1962) "A developmental study of the discrimination of letter-like forms." *Journal of Comparative and Psychological Psychology,* 55:897–906.

Glaze, J. A. (1928) "The association value of nonsense syllables." *Journal of Genetic Psychology,* 35:255–269.

Gottlieb, G., and Simner, M. L. (1966) "Relationship between cardiac rate and non-nutritive sucking in human infants." *Journal of Comparative and Physiological Psychology,* 46:128–131.

Greene, J. (1976) *Language.* (Social Psychology, Block Three). Milton Keynes, England: Open University Press.

Groninger, L. D. (1971) "Mnemonic imagery and forgetting." *Psychonomic Science,* 23:161–162.

Gruneberg, M. (1973) "The role of memorization techniques in finals examination preparation." *Education Research,* 15:134–139.

Guess, D. (1969) "A functional analysis of receptive language and productive speech: acquisition of the plural phoneme." *Journal of Applied Behavior Analysis,* 2:55–64.

Guess, D., and Baer, D. M. (1973) "An analysis of individual differences in generalization between receptive and productive language in retarded children." *Journal of Applied Behavior Analysis,* 6:311–329.

Guess, D., Sailor, W., Rutherford, G., and Baer, D. M. (1968) "An experimental analysis of linguistic development: the productive use of the plural morpheme." *Journal of Applied Behavior Analysis,* 1:297–306.

Haber, R. N., and Haber, R. B. (1964) "Eidetic imagery: 1. Frequency." *Perceptual and Motor Skills,* 19:131–138.

Hagen, J. W. Hargrave, S., and Ross, W. (1973) "Prompting and rehearsal in short-term memory." *Child Development,* 44:201–204.

Haith, M. M., and Campos, J. J. (1977) "Human Infancy." *Annual Review of Psychology,* 28:251–293.

Hall, J. F. (1954) "Learning as a function of word frequency." *American Journal of Psychology,* 67:138–140.

Hall, J. F. (1971) *Verbal Learning and Retention.* Philadelphia: Lippincott.

Hall, R. V., Lund, D., and Jackson, D. (1968) "Effects of teacher attention on study behavior." *Journal of Applied Behavior Analysis,* 1:1–12.

Hallstein, J. R. (1965) "Adolescent *anorexia nervosa* treated by desensitization." *Behavior Research and Therapy,* 3:87–91.

Hamlyn, D. W. (1970) "Conditioning and behavior." In R. Borger and F. Cioffi (eds.) *Explanation in the Behavioral Sciences.* Cambridge, England: Cambridge University Press.

Harlow, H. F. (1949) "The formation of learning sets." *Psychological Review,* 56:51–65.

Harlow, H. F. (1958) "The nature of love." *American Psychologist,* 13:673–685.

Harris, F. R., Wolf, M. M., and Baer, D. M. (1964) "Effects of adult social reinforcement on child behavior." *Young Children,* 20:8–17.

Harris, M. B., and Hassemer, W. G. (1972) "Some factors affecting the complexity of childrens' sentences: the effects of modeling, age, sex and bilingualism." *Journal of Experimental Child Psychology,* 13:447–455.

Hartley, J., and Marshall, S. (1974) "On notes and note-taking." *Universities Quarterly*, 28:225–235.

Hein, A., Held, R., and Gower, E. C. (1970) "Development and segmentation of visually controlled movement by selective exposure during rearing." *Journal of Comparative and Physiological Psychology*, 73:181–187.

Held, R., and Hein, A. (1963) "Movement-produced stimulation in the development of visually guided behavior." *Journal of Comparative and Physiological Psychology*, 56:872–876.

Hess, E. H. (1970) "Ethology and developmental psychology." In P. H. Mussen (ed.), *Carmichael's Manual of Child Psychology*, 3rd ed., Vol. I. New York: Wiley.

Hess, R. D., and Shipman, V. C. (1968) "Maternal attitudes towards the school and the role of the pupil: some social class comparisons." In A. H. Passow (ed.), *Developing Programs for the Educationally Disadvantaged*. New York: Teachers College Press.

Hogan, J. A. (1961) "Copying redundant messages." *Journal of Experimental Psychology*, 62:153–157.

Holding, D. H., and Macrae, A. W. (1966) "Rate and force of guidance in perceptual-motor tasks with reversed or random spatial correspondence." *Ergonomics*, 9:289–296.

Howe, M. J. A. (1965) "Intra-list differences in short-term memory." *Quarterly Journal of Experimental Psychology*, 17:338–342.

Howe, M. J. A. (1966) "A note on order of recall in short-term memory." *British Journal of Psychology*, 57:435–436.

Howe, M. J. A. (1967a) "Consolidation in short-term memory as a function of rehearsal." *Psychonomic Science*, 7:355–356.

Howe, M. J. A. (1967b) "Recognition memory for photographs in homogeneous sequences." *Perceptual and Motor Skills*, 24:1181–1182.

Howe, M. J. A. (1970a) *Introduction to Human Memory: a Psychological Approach*. New York: Harper & Row.

Howe, M. J. A. (1970b) "Repeated presentation and recall of meaningful prose." *Journal of Educational Psychology*, 61:214–219.

Howe, M. J. A. (1970c) "Using students' notes to examine the role of the individual learner in acquiring meaningful subject matter." *Journal of Educational Research*, 64:61–63.

Howe, M. J. A. (1972) *Understanding School Learning: A New Look at Educational Psychology*. New York: Harper & Row.

Howe, M. J. A. (1974) "The utility of taking notes as an aid to learning." *Educational Research*, 16:222–227.

Howe, M. J. A. (1975a) *Learning in Infants and Young Children*. London: Macmillan.

Howe, M. J. A. (1975b) "Taking notes and human learning." *Bulletin of the British Psychological Society*, 28:158–161.

Howe, M. J. A. (1976) "Good learners and poor learners." *Bulletin of the British Psychological Society*, 29:16–19.

Howe, M. J. A. (1977a) "Learning and the acquisition of knowledge by students: some experimental investigations." In M. J. A. Howe (ed.), *Adult Learning: Psychological Research and Applications.* London: Wiley.

Howe, M. J. A. (1977b) *Television and Children.* London: New University Education.

Howe, M. J. A., and Cavicchio, P. M. (1971) "The possibility of retroactive interference in a meaningful learning task." *Alberta Journal of Educational Research,* 17:49–53.

Howe, M. J. A., and Colley, L. (1976a) "Retroactive interference in meaningful learning." *British Journal of Educational Psychology,* 46:26–30.

Howe, M. J. A., and Colley, L. (1976b) "The influence of questions encountered earlier on learning from prose." *British Journal of Educational Psychology,* 46:149–154.

Howe, M. J. A., and Godfrey, J. (1977) *Student Note-Taking as an Aid to Learning.* Exeter, England: Exeter University Teaching Services.

Howe, M. J. A., Ormond, V., and Singer, L. (1974) "Recording activities and recall of information." *Perceptual and Motor Skills,* 39:309–310.

Howe, M. J. A., and Singer, L. (1975) "Presentation variables and students' activities in meaningful learning." *British Journal of Educational Psychology,* 45:52–61.

Howe, M. J. A., and Smart, H. (1976) "The role of the individual human learner in acquiring verbal knowledge." Unpublished Final Report to Social Science Research Council, University of Exeter.

Hull, C. L. (1943) *Principles of Behavior.* New York: Prentice-Hall.

Hull, C. L. (1952) *A Behavior System.* New Haven: Yale University Press.

Hunt, E., Frost, N., and Lunneborg, C. (1973) "Individual differences in cognition: a new approach to intelligence." In G. H. Bower (ed.), *The Psychology of Learning and Motivation,* Vol. VII. New York: Academic Press.

Hunt, E., and Lansman, M. (1975) "Cognitive theory applied to individual differences." In W. K. Estes (ed.), *Handbook of Learning and Cognitive Processes,* Vol. I. Hillsdale, New Jersey: Erlbaum.

Hunter, I. M. L. (1962) "An exceptional talent for calculative thinking." *British Journal of Psychology,* 53:243–258.

Hunter, I. M. L. (1964) *Memory: Facts and Fallacies,* 2nd ed. Harmondsworth, England: Penguin Books.

Hunter, I. M. L. (1977) "An exceptional memory." *British Journal of Psychology,* 68:155–164.

Huttenlocher, J., and Burke, D. (1976) "Why does memory span increase with age?" *Cognitive Psychology,* 8:1–31.

Inhelder, B. (1971) "The sensory-motor origins of knowledge." In D. N. Walcher and D. L. Peters (eds.), *Early Childhood: The Development of Self-Regulatory Mechanisms.* New York: Academic Press.

Jaffe, J., Stern, D. N., and Peery, J. S. (1973) " 'Conversational' complexity of gaze behavior in prelinguistic human development." *Journal of Psycholinguistic Research,* 2:321–330.

Jahnke, J. C. (1963) "Serial position effects in immediate serial recall." *Journal of Verbal Learning and Verbal Behavior,* 2:284–287.

James, W. (1890) *The Principles of Psychology*. New York: Holt, Rinehart and Winston.

James, W. (1903) *Talks to Teachers*. New York: Longmans.

Jenkins, J. J., Mink, W. D., and Russell, W. A. (1958) "Associative clustering as a function of verbal association strength." *Psychological Reports*, 4:127–136.

Jenkins, J. J., and Russell, W. A. (1952) "Associative clustering during recall." *Journal of Abnormal and Social Psychology*, 47:818–821.

Jensen, A. R. (1971) "The role of verbal mediation in mental development." *Journal of Genetic Psychology*, 18:39–70.

Jensen, A. R. (1973) *Educability and Group Differences*. New York: Harper & Row.

Jensen, A. R., and Rohwer, W. D. (1963) "Verbal mediation in paired-associate and serial learning." *Journal of Verbal Behavior*, 1:346–351.

Jensen, A. R. and Rohwer, W. D. (1965) "Syntactical mediation of serial and paired-associate learning as a function of age." *Child Development*, 36:601–608.

Jorm, A. F. (1977) "Effect of word imagery on reading performance as a function of reader ability." *Journal of Educational Psychology*, 69:46–54.

Kagan, J. (1965) "Reflection-impulsivity: the generality and dynamics of conceptual tempo." In J. D. Krumboltz (ed.), *Learning and the Educational Process*. Chicago: Rand McNally.

Kagan, J. (1970) "On class differences in early development." In V. H. Denenberg (ed.), *Education of the Infant and Young Child*. New York: Academic Press.

Kagan, J. (1972) "Do infants think?" *Scientific American*, 74:76–82.

Kagan, J., and Tulkin, R. R. (1971) "Social class differences in child rearing during the first year." In H. R. Schaffer (ed.), *The Origin of Human Social Relations*. New York: Academic Press.

Kausler, D. H. (1974) *Psychology of Verbal Learning and Memory*. New York: Academic Press.

Kay, H. (1955) "Learning and retaining verbal material." *British Journal of Psychology*, 42:34–41.

Kay, H. (1969) "The development of motor skills from birth to adolescence." In E. A. Bilodeau and I. M. Bilodeau (eds.), *Principles of Skill Acquisition*. New York: Academic Press.

Kay, H. (1977) "Learning and society." In M. J. A. Howe (ed.), *Adult Learning: Psychological Research and Applications*. London: Wiley.

Kaye, H. (1965) "The conditioned Babkin reflex in human newborns." *Psychonomic Science*, 2:287–288.

Kaye, H. (1967) "Infant sucking behavior and its modification." In L. P. Lipsitt and C. C. Spiker (eds.), *Advances in Child Development and Behavior*, Vol. III. New York: Academic Press.

Kaye, K. (1977) "Towards the origin of dialogue." In H. R. Schaffer (ed.), *Studies in Mother-Infant Interaction*. London: Academic Press.

Kazdin, A. E. (1975) *Behavior Modification in Applied Settings*. Homewood, Illinois: Dorsey Press.

Kelly, E. L. (1967) "Transfer of training: an analytic study." In B. P.

Komisar and C. B. M. Macmillan (eds.), *Psychological Concepts in Education*. Chicago: Rand McNally.

Kessen, W., Haith, M. M., and Salapatek, P. H. (1970) "Human infancy: a bibliography and guide." In P. H. Mussen (ed.), *Carmichael's Manual of Child Psychology*, 3rd ed., Vol. I. New York: Wiley.

Kessen, W., and Mandler, G. (1961) "Anxiety, pain and the inhibition of distress." *Psychological Review*, 68:396–404.

Kingsley, P. R., and Hagen, J. W. (1970) "Induced versus spontaneous rehearsal in short-term memory in nursery school children." *Developmental Psychology*, 1:40–46.

Kintsch, W. (1974) *The Representation of Meaning in Memory*. Hillsdale, New Jersey: Erlbaum.

Kintsch, W. (1975) "Memory for prose." In C. N. Cofer (ed.), *The Structure of Human Memory*. San Francisco: Freeman.

Kintsch, W. (1977) *Memory and Cognition*. New York: Wiley.

Kondas, O. (1967) "Reduction of examination anxiety and "stage-fright" by group desensitization and relaxation." *Behavior Research and Therapy*, 5:275–281.

Konorski, J. (1967) *Integrative Activity of the Brain*. University of Chicago Press.

Korner, A. F. (1971) "Individual differences at birth: implications for early experience and later development." *American Journal of Orthopsychiatry*, 41:608–619.

Kuhn, T. S. (1962) *The Structure of Scientific Revolutions*. University of Chicago Press.

Kushner, M. (1968) "The operant control of intractable sneezing." In C. D. Spielberger, R. Fox, and B. Masterson (eds.), *Contributions to General Psychology*. New York: Ronald Press.

Labov, W. (1970) *The Study of Nonstandard English*. Urbana, Illinois: National Council of Teachers of English.

Landauer, T. K. and Meyer, D. E. (1972) "Category size and semantic-memory retrieval." *Journal of Verbal Learning and Verbal Behavior*, 11:539–549.

Lang, P. J., and Lazovick, A. J. (1963) "Experimental desensitization of a phobia." *Journal of Abnormal and Social Psychology*, 66:519–525.

Lawson, E. A. (1961) "A note on the influence of different orders of approximation to the English language upon eye-voice span." *Quarterly Journal of Experimental Psychology*, 13:53–55.

Lazarus, A. A. (1961) "Group therapy of phobic disorders by systematic desensitization." *Journal of Abnormal and Social Psychology*, 63:504–510.

Lazarus, A. A., Davison G. C., and Polefka, D. A. (1965) "Classical and operant factors in the treatment of a school phobia." *Journal of Abnormal Psychology*, 70:225–229.

Lenneberg, E. H. (1966) "A biological perspective of language." In E. H. Lennegerg (ed.), *New Directions in the Study of Language*. Cambridge, Massachusetts: M. I. T. Press.

Leonard, G. B. (1968) *Education and Ecstasy*. New York: Delacorte Press.

Levinson, B., and Reese, H. W. (1967) "Patterns of discrimination learning set in preschool children, fifth-graders, college freshmen, and the aged." *Monographs of the Society for Research in Child Development*, 32:No. 115.

Levi-Strauss, C. (1966) *The Savage Mind*. Chicago University Press.

Light, L. L., and Carter-Sobell, L. (1970) "Effects of changed semantic context on recognition memory." *Journal of Verbal Learning and Verbal Memory*, 9:1–11.

Lintz, L. M., and Fitzgerald, H. E. (1966) "Apparatus for eyeblink conditioning in infants." *Journal of Experimental Child Psychology*, 4:276–279.

Lipsitt, L. P. (1963) "Learning in the first year of life." In L. P. Lipsitt and C. C. Spiker (eds.), *Advances in Child Development and Behavior*, Vol. I. New York: Academic Press.

Lipsitt, L. P., and Kaye, H. (1964) "Conditioned sucking in the human newborn." *Psychonomic Science*, 1:29–30.

Lloyd, K. E., and Johnston, W. A. (1963) "Short-term memory as a function of contextual constraint." *Journal of Experimental Psychology*, 65:460–467.

Lovaas, O. I. Berberich, J. P., Perloff, B. F. F., and Schaeffer, B. (1966) "Acquisition of imitative speech by schizophrenic children." *Science*, 151:705–707.

Lorayne, H. (1958) *How to Develop a Super-power Memory*. Preston, England: Thomas.

Lorenz, K. (1966) *On Aggression*. New York: Harcourt, Brace Jovanvich.

Luria, A. R. (1961) *The Role of Speech in the Regulation of Normal and Abnormal Behavior*. New York: Liveright.

Luria, A. R. (1968) *The Mind of a Mnemonist*. New York: Basic Books.

Lynn, R. (1966) *Attention, Arousal and the Orientation Reaction*. Oxford: Pergamon Press.

McGeoch, J. A. (1930) "The influence of associative value upon the difficulty of nonsense syllable lists." *Journal of Genetic Psychology*, 37:421–426.

McGeoch, J. A., and Irion, A. L. (1952) *The Psychology of Human Learning*. New York: Longmans.

McGuire, T. R., and Hirsch, J. (1977) "General intelligence (g) and heritability (H^2, h^2)." In I. C. Uzgiris and F. Weizmann (eds.), *The Structuring of Experience*. New York: Plenum Press.

Mackay, D. (1975) *Clinical Psychology: Theory and Therapy* London: Methuen.

McKenzie, B., and Day, R. H. (1971) "Operant learning of visual pattern discrimination in young infants." *Journal of Experimental Child Psychology*, 11:45–53.

McLaughlin, B. (1971) *Learning and Social Behavior*. New York: Free Press.

Macnamara, J. (1972) "Cognitive basis of language learning in infants." *Psychological Review*, 79:1–13.

McNulty, J. A. (1966) "The measurement of "adopted chunks" in free recall learning." *Psychonomic Science*, 4:71–72.

Madsen, C. H. Jr., Becker, W. C., and Thomas, D. R. (1968) "Rules, praise, and ignoring: elements of elementary classroom control." *Journal of Applied Behavior Analysis*, 1:139–150.

Mahoney, M. J. (1974) *Cognition and Behavior Modification.* Cambridge, Massachusetts: Ballinger.

Mahoney, M. J., Moura, N. G., and Wade, T. C. (1973) "Relative efficiency of self-reward, self-punishment and self-moitoring techniques for weight loss." *Journal of Consulting and Clinical Psychology*, 40:404–407.

Maltzman, I. (1968) "Theoretical conceptions of semantic conditioning and generalization." In T. R. Dixon and D. L. Horton (eds.), *Verbal Behavior and General Behavior Theory.* Englewood Cliffs, New Jersey: Prentice-Hall.

Mandler, G. (1968) "Organization and memory." In K. W. Spence and J. T. Spence (eds.), *The Psychology of Learning and Motivation*, Vol. II. New York: Academic Press.

Mandler, G., and Pearlstone, Z. (1966) "Free and constrained concept learning and subsequent recall." *Journal of Verbal Learning and Verbal Behavior*, 5:126–131.

Marjoribanks, K. (1972) "Environment, social class, and mental abilities." *Journal of Educational Psychology*, 43, 103–109.

Marks, L. E., and Miller, G. A. (1964) "The role of semantic and syntactic constraints in the memorization of English sentence." *Journal of Verbal Learning and Verbal Behavior*, 3:1–5.

Marks, M. R., and Jack, O. (1952) "Verbal context and memory span for meaningful material." *American Journal of Psychology*, 65:298–300.

Marquis, D. P. (1931) "Can conditioned responses be established in the newborn infant?" *Journal of Genetic Psychology*, 39:479–492.

Medin, D., and Cole, M. (1975) "Comparative psychology and human cognition." In W. K. Estes (ed.), *Handbook of Learning and Cognitive Processes*, Vol. I. Hillsdale, New Jersey: Erlbaum.

Merleau-Ponty, M. (1962) *Phenomenology of Perception.* London: Routledge and Kegan Paul.

Metz, J. R. (1965) "Conditioning generalized imitation in autistic children." *Journal of Experimental Child Psychology*, 2:389–399.

Meyer, D. E., and Schvaneveldt, R. W. (1975) "Meaning, memory structure, and mental processes." In C. M. Cofer (ed.), *The Structure of Human Memory.* San Francisco: Freeman.

Millar, W. S. (1976) "Operant acquisition of social behaviors in infancy: basic problems and constraints." In H. W. Reese (ed.), *Advances in Child Development and Behavior*, Vol. XI. New York: Academic Press.

Miller, G. A. (1956) "The magical number seven, plus or minus two: some limits on our capacity for processing information." *Psychological Review*, 63:81–97.

Miller, G. A., Galanter, E., and Pribram, K. H. (1960) *Plans and the Structure of Behavior.* New York: Holt, Rinehart and Winston.

Miller, G. A., Heise, G. A. and Lichten, W. (1951) "The intelligibility of speech as a function of the context of the text materials." *Journal of Experimental Psychology*, 41:329–335.

Miller, G. A., and Selfridge, J. A. (1950) "Verbal context and the recall of meaningful material." *American Journal of Psychology*, 63:176–185.

Miller, N. E., and Dollard, J. (1941) *Social Learning and Imitation*. New Haven, Connecticut: Yale University Press.

Miller, S., Shelton, L. J., and Flavell, J. H. (1970) "A test of Luria's hypothesis concerning the development of verbal self-regulation." *Child Development*, 41:651–655.

Mischel, W. (1970) "Sex-typing and socialization." In P. H. Mussen (ed.), *Carmichael's Manual of Child Psychology*, 3rd ed., Vol. II. New York: Wiley.

Moerk, E. (1972) "Principles of interaction of language learning." *Merrill-Palmer Quarterly*, 18:229–257.

Moerk, E. (1974) "Changes in verbal child-mother interactions with increasing language skills of the child." *Journal of Psycholinquistic Research*, 3:101–116.

Montagu, A. (1976) *The Nature of Human Aggression*. New York: Oxford University Press.

Moore, J., and Massaro, D. (1973) "Attention and processing capacity in auditory recognition." *Journal of Experimental Psychology*, 99:49–54.

Moray, N., and Taylor, A. M. (1958) "Statistical approximations to English and French." *Language and Speech*, 1:102–109.

Morris, D. (1967). *The Naked Ape*. New York: McGraw–Hill.

Morris, P. (1977) "Practical strategies for human learning and remembering." In M. J. A. Howe (ed.), *Adult Learning: Psychological Research and Applications*. London: Wiley.

Murphy G., and Kovach, J. K. (1972) *A Historical Introduction to Modern Psychology*. New York: Harcourt Brace Jovanovich.

Myrow, D. L., and Anderson, R. C. (1974) "Retroactive inhibition of press as a function of the type of test." *Journal of Educational Psychology*, 68:303–308.

Naus, M. J., Ornstein, P. A., and Aivano, S. (1977) "Developmental changes in memory: the effects of processing time and rehearsal instructions." *Journal of Experimental Child Psychology*, 23:237–251.

Newell, A. (1967) "Thoughts on the concept of process." In J. F. Voss (ed.), *Approaches to Thought*. Pittsburgh University Press.

Newson, J., and Newson, E. (1968) "Some social differences in the process of childrearing." In J. Gould (ed.), *Penguin Social Sciences Survey 1968*. Harmondsworth, England: Penguin Books.

Noble, C. E. (1952a) "An analysis of meaning." *Psychological Review*, 59:421–430.

Noble, C. E. (1952b) "The role of stimulus meaning (*m*) in serial verbal learning." *Journal of Experimental Psychology*, 43:437–446.

Noble, C. E. (1953) "The meaning-familiarity relationship." *Psychological Review*, 60:89–98.

Noble, C. E., Stockwell, F. E., and Pryor, M. W. (1957) "Meaningfulness (*m'*) and association value (a) in paired-assocate syllable learning." *Psychological Reports*, 3:441–452.

Norcross, K. J. (1958) "Effects on discrimination performance of similarity of previously acquired stimulus names." *Journal of Experimental Psychology,* 56:305–309.

Norcross, K. J. and Spiker, C. C. (1957) "The effects of type of stimulus pretraining on discrimination performance in preschool children." *Child Development,* 28:79–84.

Nordquist, V. M., and Bradley, B. (1973) "Speech acquisition in a nonverbal isolate child." *Journal of Experimental Child Psychology,* 15:149–160.

Norman, D. A. (1976) *Memory and Attention: An Introduction to Human Information Processing,* 2nd ed. New York: Wiley.

Novinski, L. S. (1972) "A re-examination of the part-whole effect in free recall." *Journal of Verbal Learning and Verbal Behavior,* 11:228–233.

Oberly, H. S. (1928) "A comparison of the spans of attention and memory." *American Journal of Psychology,* 40:295–302.

O'Connell, D. C., Turner, E. A. and Onuska, L. A. (1978) "Intonation, grammatical structure and contextual association in immediate recall." *Journal of Verbal Behavior,* 7:110–116.

O'Connor, N., and Hermelin, B. (1963) *Speech and Thought in Severe Subnormality.* Oxford: Pergamon.

Orme, M. E. J., and Purnell, R. F. (1968) "Behavior modification and transfer in an out-of-control classroom." Paper delivered at the American Educational Research Association Convention, Chicago.

Osborne, J. G. (1969) "Free time as a reinforcer in the management of classroom behavior." *Journal of Applied Behavior Analysis,* 2:113–118.

Osgood, C. E. (1953) *"Method and Theory in Experimental Psychology."* New York: Oxford University Press.

Paivio, A. (1965) "Abstractness, imagery, and meaningfulness in paired-associate learning." *Journal of Verbal Learning and Verbal Behavior,* 4:32–38.

Paivio, A. (1967) "Paired-associate learning and free recall of nouns as a function of concreteness specificity, imagery, and meaningfulness." *Psychological Reports,* 20:239–245.

Paivio, A. (1969) "Mental imagery in associative learning and memory." *Psychological Review,* 76:241–263.

Paivio, A. (1971) *Imagery and Verbal Processes.* New York: Holt, Rinehart and Winston.

Paivio, A., Smythe, P. C., and Yuille, J. C. (1968) "Imagery versus meaningfulness of nouns in paired-associate learning." *Canadian Journal of Psychology,* 22:427–411.

Paivio, A., Yuille, J. C., and Rogers, T. B. (1969) "Noun imagery and meaningfulness in free and serial recall." *Journal of Experimental Psychology,* 79:509–514.

Papousek, H. (1967a) "Conditioning during postnatal development." In Y. Brackbill and G. C. Thompson (eds.), *Behavior in Infancy and Early Childhood.* New York: Free Press.

Papousek, H. (1967b) "Experimental studies of appetitional behavior in human newborns." In H. W. Stevenson, E. H. Hess, and H. L. Rheingold (eds.), *Early Behavior: Comparative and Developmental Approaches.* New York: Wiley.

Papousek, H., and Bernstein, P. (1969) "The functions of conditioning and stimulation in human neonates and infants." In J. A. Ambrose (ed.), *Stimulation in Early Infancy*. New York: Academic Press.

Parry, N. H. (1972) "Infants' responses to novelty in familiar and unfamiliar settings." *Child Development*, 43:233–237.

Parton, D. A. (1976) "Learning to imitate in infancy." *Child Development*, 47:14–31.

Patterson, G. R., Littman, R. A., and Bricker, W. (1967) "Assertive behavior in children: a step toward a theory of aggression." *Monographs of the Society for Research in Child Development*, Vol. 32.

Perlmutter, J., and Myers, N. A. (1976) "A developmental study of semantic effects on recognition memory." *Journal of Experimental Child Psychology*, 22:438–453.

Peterson, D. R., and London, P. (1965) "A role for cognition in the behavioral treatment of a child's eliminative disturbances." In L. P. Ullman, and L. Krasner (eds.), *Case Studies in Behavior Modification*. New York: Holt, Rinehart and Winston.

Peterson, R. F., and Peterson, L. R. (1968) "The use of positive reinforcement in the control of self-destructive behavior in a retarded boy." *Journal of Experimental Child Psychology*, 6:351–360.

Piaget, J. (1970) "Piaget's theory." In P. H. Mussen (ed.), *Carmichael's Manual of Child Psychology*, 3rd ed., Vol. I. New York: Wiley.

Pick, H. L., and Pick, A. D. (1970) "Sensory and perceptual development." In P. H. Mussen (ed.), *Carmichael's Manual of Child Psychology*, 3rd ed., Vol. I, New York: Wiley.

Pick, H. L., Pick, A. D., and Klein, R. E. (1967) "Perceptual integration in children." In L. P. Lipsitt and C. C. Spiker (eds.), *Advances in Child Development and Behavior*, Vol. III. New York: Academic Press.

Pick, A. D., Pick, H. L. and Thomas, M. L. (1966) "Cross-model transfer and improvement of form discrimination." *Journal of Experimental Child Psychology*, 3:279–288.

Pierce, J. R., and Karlin, J. E. (1957) "Reading rates and the information rate of a human channel." *Bell System Technical Journal*, 36:497–516.

Posner, M. I. (1964) "Rate of presentation and order of recall in immediate memory." *British Journal of Psychology*, 55:303–306.

Posner, M. I., and Keele, S. W. (1967) "Decay of visual information from a single letter." *Science*, 158:137–139.

Postman, L., and Adams, P. A. (1960) "Studies of incidental learning: VIII: the effects of contextual determination." *Journal of Experimental Psychology*, 59:153–164.

Prechtl, H. F. R. (1969) "Brain and behavioral mechanisms in the human newborn infant." In R. J. Robinson (ed.), *Brain and Early Behavior: Development in the Fetus and Infant*. New York: Academic Press.

Premack, A. J., and Premack, D. (1972) "Teaching language to an ape." *Scientific American*, 227, No. 4:92–99.

Pylyshyn, Z. W. (1973) "What the mind's eye tells the mind's brain: a critique of mental imagery." *Psychological Bulletin*, 80:1–24.

Ramey, C. T., and Ourth, R. L. (1971) "Delayed reinforcement and vocalization rates of infants." *Child Development*, 42:291–297.

Raugh, M. R., and Atkinson, R. C. (1975) "A mnemonic method for learning a second language vocabulary." *Journal of Educational Psychology,* 67:1–16.

Reason, J. T. (1977) "Skill and error in everyday life." In M. J. A. Howe (ed.), *Adult Learning: Psychological Research and Applications.* London: Wiley.

Reese, H. W., and Lipsitt, L. P. (1970) *Experimental Child Psychology.* New York: Academic Press.

Rescorla, R. A. (1968) "Probability of shock in the presence and absence of CS in fear conditioning." *Journal of Comparative Physiological Psychology* 46:105.

Rheingold, H., Gewirtz, J. L., and Ross, H. W. (1959) "Social conditioning of vocalizations in the infant." *Journal of Comparative and Physiological Psychology,* 52:68–73.

Rheingold, H. L., Stanley, W. C. and Doyle, G. A. (1964) "Visual and auditory reinforcement of a manipulatory response in the young child." *Journal of Experimental Child Psychology,* 1:316–326.

Rips, L. J., Shoben, E. J., and Smith, E. E. (1973) "Semantic distance and the verification of semantic relations." *Journal of Verbal Learning and Verbal Behavior,* 12:1–20.

Risley, T. R. (1968) "The effects and side effects of punishing the autistic behaviors of a deviant child." *Journal of Applied Behavior Analysis,* 1:21–34.

Ritter, B. (1968) "The group desensitization of children's snake phobias using vicarious and contact desensitization procedures." *Behavior Research and Therapy,* 6:1–6.

Roberts, W. A. (1969) "The priority of recall of new items in transfer from part-list learning to whole-list learning." *Journal of Verbal Learning and Verbal Behavior,* 8:645–652.

Rock, I. (1966) *The Nature of Perceptual Adaptation.* New York: Basic Books.

Ross, H. S., Rheingold, H. L., and Eckerman, I. O. (1972) "Approach and exploration of a novel alternative by twelve-month-old infants." *Journal of Experimental Child Psychology,* 13:85–93.

Ross, J., and Lawrence, K. A. (1968) "Some observations on memory artifice." *Psychonomic Science,* 13:107–108.

Rothkopf, E. Z. (1966) "Learning from written instructive materials: an exploration of the control of inspection behavior by test-like events." *American Educational Research Journal,* 3:241–249.

Rothkopf, E. Z. (1970) "The concept of mathamegenic activities." *Review of Educational Research,* 40:325–336.

Rothkopf, E. Z., and Bisbicos, E. E. (1971) "Selective facilitative effects of interspersed questions on learning from written materials." *Journal of Educational Psychology,* 58:56–61.

Rotter, J. B. (1966) "Generalized expectancies for internal versus external control of reinforcement." *Psychological Monographs,* 80:No. 609.

Routh, D. K. (1969) "Conditioning of vocal response differentiation in infants." *Developmental Psychology,* 1:219–226.

Rovee, C. K., and Rovee, D. (1969) "Conjugate reinforcement of infant exploratory behavior." *Journal of Experimental Child Psychology,* 8:33–39.

Rumelhart, D. E. (1975) "Notes on a scheme for stories." In D. G. Bowbrow and A. Collins (eds.), *Representation and Understanding.* New York: Academic Press.

Rutter, M. (1972) *Maternal Deprivation Reassessed.* Harmondsworth, England: Penguin Books.

Sachs, J. S. (1967) "Recognition memory for syntactic and semantic aspects of connected discourse." *Perception and Psychophysics,* 2:437–442.

Sachs, J. S. (1974) "Memory in reading and listening to discourse." *Memory and Cognition,* 2:95–100.

Sameroff, A. J. (1971) "Can conditioned responses be established in the newborn infant?" *Developmental Psychology,* 5:1–12.

Sameroff, A. J. (1972) "Learning and adaptation in infancy: a comparison of models." In H. W. Reese (ed.), *Advances in Child Development and Behavior,* Vol. VII. New York: Academic Press.

Schaffer, H. R. (1971) *The Growth of Sociability.* Harmondsworth, England: Penguin Books.

Schaffer, H. R. (1977) *Mothering.* London: Fontana/Open Books.

Schaffer, H. R., and Emerson, P. E. (1964) "The development of social attachments in infancy." *Monographs of the Society for Research in Child Development,* 29: No. 94.

Schultz, C. B., and di Vesta, F. J. (1972) "Effects of passage organization and note-taking on the selection of clustering strategies and on recall of textual materials." *Journal of Educational Psychology,* 63:244–252.

Sears, R. R., Rau, L., and Alpert, R. (1965) *Identification and Child Rearing.* Stanford University Press.

Segal, S. J., and Fusella, V. (1969) "Effects of imaging on signal-to-noise ratio with varying signal conditions." *British Journal of Psychology,* 60:459–464.

Seligman, M. E. P. (1970) "On the generality of the laws of learning." *Psychological Review,* 77:406–418.

Seligman, M. E. P. (1975) *Helplessness: On Depression, Development, and Death.* San Francisco: Freeman.

Shannon, C. E. (1951) "Prediction and entropy of printed English." *Bell System Technical Journal,* 30:50–64.

Sharp, H. C. (1958) "Effect of contextual constraint upon recall of verbal passages." *American Journal of Psychology,* 71:568–572.

Shepard, R. N. (1967) "Recognition memory for words, sentences and pictures." *Journal of Verbal Learning and Verbal Behavior,* 6:156–163.

Shepard, R. N., and Metzler, J. (1971) "Mental rotation of three-dimensional objects." *Science,* 171:701–703.

Sheppard, W. C. (1969) "Operant control of infant vocal and motor behavior." *Journal of Experimental Psychology,* 7:36–51.

Sheppard, W. C., and Willoughby, R. H. (1975) *Child Behavior: Learning and Development.* Chicago: Rand McNally.

Sherman, J. A. (1971) "Imitation and language development." In H. W.

Reese (ed.), *Advances in Child Development and Behavior*, Vol. VI. New York: Academic Press.

Siegel, A. (1971) "The effects of media violence on social learning." In W. Schramm and D. F. Roberts (eds.), *The Process and Effects of Mass Communication*, Rev. ed. Urbana, Illinois: University of Chicago Press.

Siipola, E. M., and Hayden, S. D. (1965) "Exploring eidetic imagery among the retarded." *Perceptual and Motor Skills*, 21:275–286.

Simpson, W. E. (1965) "Effects of approximation to sentence word-order and grammatical class upon the series of word lists." *Journal of Verbal Learning and Verbal Behavior*, 4:510–514.

Sinclair-de-Zwart, H. (1969) "Developmental psycholinguistics." In D. Elkind and J. H. Flavell (eds.), *Studies in Cognitive Development: Essays in Honor of Jean Piaget*. New York: Oxford University Press.

Siqueland, E. R., and Lipsitt, L. P. (1966) "Conditioned headturning in human newborns." *Journal of Experimental Child Psychology*, 3:356–376.

Skinner, B. F. (1938) *The Behavior of Organisms: An Experimental Analysis*. New York: Prentice-Hall.

Skinner, B. F. (1957) *Verbal Behavior*. New York: Prentic-Hall.

Slamecka, N. J., Moore, T., and Carey, S. (1972) "Part-to-whole transfer and its relation to organization theory." *Journal of Verbal Learning and Verbal Behavior*, 11:73–82.

Slobin, D. I. (1968) "Imitation and grammatical development in children." In L. R. Boulder and H. Osser (eds.), *Contemporary Issues in Developmental Psychology*. New York: Holt, Rinehart and Winston.

Slobin, D. I. (1972) "Seven questions about language development." In P. C. Dodwell (ed.), *New Horizons in Psychology, Vol. II*. Harmondsworth, England: Penguin Books.

Snow, C. E. (1972) "Mothers' speech to children learning language." *Child Development*, 43:549–563.

Sostek, A. M., Sameroff, A. J., and Sostek, A. J. (1972) "Evidence for the unconditionability of the Babkin reflex in newborns." *Child Development*, 43:509–519.

Sperling, G. (1960) "The information available in brief visual presentations." *Psychological Monographs*, 74: No. 498.

Spielberger, C. D., and De Nike, L. D. (1966) "Descriptive behaviorism versus cognitive theory in verbal operant conditioning." *Psychological Review*, 73:306–326.

Staats, A. W. (1968) *Learning, Language, and Cognition*. New York: Holt, Rinehart and Winston.

Staats, A. W. (1971) *Child Learning, Intelligence, and Personality*. New York: Harper & Row.

Stayton, D. J., Hogan, R. T., and Ainsworth, M. D. S. (1971) "Infant obedience and maternal behavior: the origins of socialization reconsidered." *Child Development*, 42:1057–1069.

Stern, D. M. (1974) "Mother and infant at play; the dyadic interaction involving facial, vocal and gaze behaviors." In M. Lewis and L. A.

Rosenblum (eds.), *The Effects of the Infant on its Caregiver.* New York: Wiley.

Sternberg, S. (1966) "High speed scanning in human memory." *Science,* 153:652–654.

Stratton, G. M. (1897) "Vision without inversion of the retinal image." *Psychological Review,* 4:341–360.

Stromeyer, C. F., and Psotka, J. (1970) "The detailed texture of eidetic images." *Nature,* 225:346–349.

Sumby, W. H., and Pollack, I. (1954) "Visual contribution to speech intelligibility." *Journal of the Acoustical Society of America,* 26:212–215.

Thomas, D. R., Becker, W. C., and Armstrong, M. (1968) "Production and elimination of disruptive classroom behavior by systematically varying teacher's behavior." *Journal of Applied Behavior Analysis,* 1:35–45.

Thompson, R. F. (1976). "The search for the engram." *American Psychologist,* 31:209–227.

Thorndike, E. L. (1931) *Human Learning.* New York: Prentice-Hall.

Thorndike, E. L., and Lorge, I. (1944) *The Teacher's Word Book of 30,000 Words.* New York: Teachers College Press.

Thorpe, W. H. (1956) *Learning and Instinct in Animals.* London: Methuen.

Thorpe, W. H. (1974) *Animal Nature and Human Nature.* London: Methuen.

Tinbergen, N. (1951) *The Study of Instinct.* Oxford: Oxford University Press (Clarendon Press).

Tolman, E. C. (1932) *Purposive Behavior in Animals and Men.* New York: Prentice-Hall.

Trabasso, T. (1972) "Mental operations in language comprehension." In R. O. Freedle and J. B. Carroll (eds.), *Language Comprehension and the Acquisition of Knowledge.* Washington, D. C.: Holt, Rinehart and Winston.

Trabasso, T. (1977) "The role of memory as a system in making transitive inferences. In R. V. Kail, and J. W. Hagen (eds.) *Perspectives on the Development of Memory and Cognition.* Hillsdale, New Jersey: Erlbaum.

Treisman, A. M. (1964) "Monitoring and storage of irrelevant messages in selective attention." *Journal of Verbal Learning and Verbal Behavior,* 3:449–459.

Treisman, A. M. (1965) "The effects of redundancy and familiarity on translating and repeating back a foreign and a native language." *British Journal of Psychology,* 56:369–379.

Tulving, E. (1962) "Subjective organization in free-recall of "unrelated" words." *Psychological Review,* 69:344–354.

Tulving, E. (1966) "Subjective organization and effects of repetition in multi-trial free-recall learning." *Journal of Verbal Learning and Verbal Behavior,* 5:193–197.

Tulving, E. (1974) "Recall and recognition of semantically encoded words." *Journal of Experimental Psychology,* 102:778–787.

Tulving, E., and Osler, S. (1968) "Effectiveness of retrieval cues in memory for words." *Journal of Experimental Psychology,* 77:593–601.

Tulving, E., and Patkau, J. E. (1962) "Concurrent effects of contextual constraint and word frequency on immediate recall and learning of verbal material." *Canadian Journal of Psychology,* 16:83–95.

Tulving, E., and Pearlstone, Z. (1966) "Availability versus accessibility of information in memory for words." *Journal of Verbal Learning and Verbal Behavior,* 5:381–391.

Tulving, E., and Thomson, D. M. (1973) "Encoding specificity and retrieval processes in episodic memory." *Psychological Review,* 80:352–373.

Tulving, E., and Watkins, M. J. (1975) "Structure of memory traces." *Psychological Review,* 82:261–275.

Turnbull, C. (1973) *The Mountain People.* London: Cape.

Turner, E. A., and Rommetveit, R. (1968) "The effects of focus of attention on storing and retrieving of active and passive voice sentences." *Journal of Verbal Learning and Verbal Behavior,* 7:543–548.

Turnure, J., Buium, N., and Thurlow, M. (1976) "The effectiveness of interrogatives for promoting verbal elaboration productivity in young children." *Child Development,* 74:851–855.

Ullman, L. P., and Krasner, L. (1965) *Case Studies in Behavior Modification.* New York: Holt, Rinehart and Winston.

Underwood, B. J., Ekstrand, B. R., and Keppel, G. (1965) "An analysis of intralist similarity in verbal learning with experiments on conceptual similarity." *Journal of Verbal Learning and Verbal Behavior,* 4:447–462.

Underwood, B. J. and Schulz, R. W. (1960) *Meaningfulness and Verbal Learning.* Philadelphia: Lippincott.

Vincent-Smith, L., Bricker, D., and Bricker, W. (1974) "Acquisition of receptive vocabulary in the toddler-age child." *Child Development,* 45:189–193.

Von Frisch, K. (1927) *The Dancing Bee.* London: Methuen.

Von Wright, J. N. (1957) *An Experimental Study of Human Serial Learning.* Societas Scientiarum Fennica. Commentationes Humanarum Litterarum, 23, No. 1.

Vygotskii, L. S. (1962) *Thought and Language.* Cambridge, Massachusetts: M. I. T. Press.

Warren, H. C. A. (1921) *A History of the Association Psychology.* New York: Scribner.

Washburn, S. L. (1978) "Human behavior and the behavior of other animals." *American Psychologist,* 33:405–418.

Waters, H. S., and Waters, E. (1976) "Semantic processing in children's free recall: evidence for the importance of attentional factors and encoding variability." *Journal of Experimental Psychology: Human Learning and Memory,* 2:370–380.

Watson, J. B., and Rayner, R. (1920) "Conditioned emotional reactions." *Journal of Experimental Psychology,* 3:1–14.

Watts, G. H., and Anderson, R. C. (1971) "Effects of three types of inserted questions on learning from prose." *Journal of Educational Psychology,* 62:387–394.

Weener, P. (1974) "Note-taking and student verbalization as instrumental learning activities." *Instructional Science,* 3:51–74.

Weisberg, P. (1963) "Social and nonsocial conditioning of infant vocalizations." *Child Development,* 34:377–388.

Welford, A. T. (1976) *Skilled Performance: Perceptual and Motor Skills.* Glenview, Illinois: Scott, Foresman.

Wellman, H. M. (1977) "The early development of intentional memory behavior." *Human Development,* 20:86–101.

West, L. J. (1967) "Vision and kinesthesis in the acquisition of typewriting skill." *Journal of Applied Psychology,* 51:161–166.

Wheeler, A. J., and Sulzer, B. (1970) "Operant training and generalization of a verbal response form in a speech-deficient child." *Journal of Applied Behavior Analysis,* 3:139–147.

White, B. L. (1971) *Human Infants: Experience and Psychological Development.* Englewood Cliffs, New Jersey: Prentice-Hall.

Whorf, B. L. (1956) *Language.* New York: Wiley.

Wickelgren, W. A. (1964) "Size of rehearsal group and short-term memory." *Journal of Experimental Psychology,* 68:413–419.

Wickelgren, W. A. (1965) "Acoustic similarity and retroactive interference in short-term memory." *Journal of Verbal Behavior,* 4:53–61.

Wilcoxon, H. C. (1969) "Historical introduction to the problem of reinforcement." In J. Tapp (ed.), *Reinforcement and Behavior.* New York: Academic Press.

Williams, C. D. (1959) "The elimination of tantrum behavior by extinction procedures." *Journal of Abnormal and Social Psychology,* 59:269.

Winograd, T. (1972) *Understanding Natural Language.* Edinburgh University Press.

Wolpe, J. (1958) *Psychotherapy by Reciprocal Inhibition.* Stanford University Press.

Wood, G. and Clark, D. (1969) "Instruction, ordering and previous practice in free-recall learning." *Psychonomic Science,* 14:187–188.

Worden, P. E. (1976) "The effects of classification structure on organized free recall in children." *Journal of Experimental Child Psychology,* 22:519–529.

Zaporozhets, A. V. (1965) "The development of perception in the preschool child." In P. H. Mussen (ed.), *European Research in Cognitive Development.* Monographs of the Society for Research in Child Development, Vol. 30.

Zeaman, D., and House, B. J. (1967) "The relation of IQ and learning." In R. M. Gagné (ed.), *Learning and Individual Differences.* Columbus, Ohio: Merrill.

Zimmerman, B. J. and Rosenthal, T. L. (1974) "Observational learning of rule governed behavior by children." *Psychological Bulletin,* 81:29–42.

Zunich, M. A. (1961) "A study of relationships between child-rearing attitudes and maternal behavior." *Journal of Experimental Education,* 30:231–241.

Author Index

Furth, H., 117
Fusella, V., 283
Fygetalis, L., 238

Gagné, R. M., 101–102, 106–108
Galanter, E., 62
Galton, F., 33, 366
Garcia, J., 112–113
Gardner, B. T., 245–247
Gardner, R. A., 245–247
Gates, A. I., 353
Gay, J., 392, 394–395, 398
Geis, M. F., 321
Geiselman, R. E., 314
Gerst, M. S., 137
Gesell, A., 29
Gewirtz, J. L., 82, 89, 124, 127–128,
   149, 152
Gibson, E. J., 89, 205–207
Gibson, J. J., 206–207
Glaze, J. A., 251–254
Glick, J. A., 392, 394–395, 398
Glick, M. J., 285
Godfrey, J., 358
Gottlieb, G., 95
Gower, E. C., 204
Grant, S., 282
Gray, B. B., 238
Greene, J., 227, 244
Groninger, L. D., 273
Gruneberg, M. M., 270
Grusec, J. E., 137
Guess, D., 133–134, 236–237
Guthrie, E. R., 32

Haber, R. B., 283–284
Haber, R. N., 283–284
Hagen, J. W., 326
Haith, M. M., 95, 115
Hall, D., 321
Hall, J. F., 253–254
Hall, R. V., 173
Halliday, M. S., 47, 80, 83
Hallstein, J. R., 195–196
Hamlyn, D. W., 83
Hargrave, S., 326
Harris, F. R., 180
Harris, M. B., 237–238, 358
Harrison, R. J., 123
Harter, N., 217
Hartley, D., 32–33
Hartley, J., 358
Hassemer, W. G., 238

Hayden, S. D., 284
Hein, A., 204
Heise, G. A., 333
Held, R., 204
Herbart, J. F., 57
Hermelin, B., 381
Herrnstein, R. J., 234
Hess, E. H., 383–384, 386
Hess, R. D., 389
Hirsch, J., 367
Hobbes, T., 31
Hogan, J. A., 333
Hogan, R. T., 147
Holding, D. H., 222
House, B. J., 207, 379
Howe, M. J. A., 123, 158, 279, 293,
   295, 316–317, 319–323, 325, 330,
   347–349, 352, 360–368, 362,
   393–394
Hull, A. J., 299
Hull, C. L., 51–52, 58–59
Hume, D., 32
Hunt, E., 366–367, 370–374, 376, 398
Hunter, I. M. L., 270
Huttenlocher, J., 326

Inhelder, B., 231–232
Irion, A. L., 59

Jack, O., 333
Jackson, D., 173
Jaffe, J., 142
Jahnke, J. C., 295
James, W., 55, 57, 100, 330–331
Jarman, R. F., 372
Jenkins, J. J., 114, 255, 305–306
Jensen, A. R., 261–262, 266, 388, 405
Johnson, M. K., 342–344
Johnston, W. A., 333
Jones, P., 264
Jorm, A. F., 277

Kant, E., 29
Karlin, J. E., 333
Kausler, D. H., 287
Kay, H., 16, 205, 215, 218, 346–347
Kaye, H., 70–71
Kaye, K., 143
Kazdin, A. E., 200
Keele, S. W., 279, 372
Kelly, E., 100
Keppel, G., 255
Kessen, W., 89, 95

Subject Index

80 81 82 83 9 8 7 6 5 4 3 2 1